With the co... **W9-AWL-210**

Bee-Yan Aw

National Bureau of Economic Research
1050 Massachusetts Avenue
Cambridge, Massachusetts 02138

Empirical Studies of Commercial Policy

A National Bureau
of Economic Research
Conference Report

Empirical Studies of Commercial Policy

Edited by   Robert E. Baldwin

 The University of Chicago Press

Chicago and London

ROBERT E. BALDWIN is the Hilldale Professor of Economics at the University of Wisconsin at Madison and a research associate of the National Bureau of Economic Research.

The University of Chicago Press, Chicago 60637
The University of Chicago Press, Ltd., London
© 1991 by the National Bureau of Economic Research
All rights reserved. Published 1991
Printed in the United States of America
00 99 98 97 96 95 94 93 92 91   5 4 3 2 1

Library of Congress Cataloging-in-Publication Data

Empirical studies of commercial policy / edited by Robert E. Baldwin.
        p. cm.—(A National Bureau of Economic Research conference report)
    "The result of a conference held by the National Bureau of Economic Research in Cambridge, Massachusetts, on 16–17 March 1990"—P. iv
    Includes bibliographical references (p.   ) and index.
    ISBN 0-226-03569-7
    1. Commercial policy—Econometric models—Congresses.
    2. Competition, International—Econometric models—Congresses.
    3. United States—Commercial policy—Econometric models—Congresses.
    I. Baldwin, Robert E.   II. (National Bureau of Economic Research)
    HF1410.5.E47   1991
    382.3—dc20   91-27053
                                                                            CIP

♾The paper used in this publication meets the minimum requirements of the American National Standard for Information Sciences—Permanence of Paper for Printed Library Materials, ANSI Z39.48-1984.

National Bureau of Economic Research

Officers

George T. Conklin, Jr., *chairman*
Paul W. McCracken, *vice chairman*
Martin Feldstein, *president and chief
executive officer*

Geoffrey Carliner, *executive director*
Charles A. Walworth, *treasurer*
Sam Parker, *director of finance and
administration*

Directors at Large

John H. Biggs
Andrew Brimmer
Carl F. Christ
George T. Conklin, Jr.
Kathleen B. Cooper
Jean A. Crockett
George C. Eads
Morton Ehrlich

Martin Feldstein
George Hatsopoulos
Lawrence R. Klein
Franklin A. Lindsay
Paul W. McCracken
Leo Melamed
Michael H. Moskow
James J. O'Leary

Robert T. Parry
Peter G. Peterson
Robert V. Roosa
Richard N. Rosett
Bert Seidman
Eli Shapiro
Donald S. Wasserman

Directors by University Appointment

Jagdish Bhagwati, *Columbia*
William C. Brainard, *Yale*
Glen G. Cain, *Wisconsin*
Franklin Fisher, *Massachusetts Institute of
Technology*
Jonathan Hughes, *Northwestern*
Saul H. Hymans, *Michigan*
Marjorie B. McElroy, *Duke*

James L. Pierce, *California, Berkeley*
Andrew Postlewaite, *Pennsylvania*
Nathan Rosenberg, *Stanford*
Harold T. Shapiro, *Princeton*
Craig Swan, *Minnesota*
Michael Yoshino, *Harvard*
Arnold Zellner, *Chicago*

Directors by Appointment of Other Organizations

Rueben C. Buse, *American Agricultural
Economics Association*
Richard A. Easterlin, *Economic History
Association*
Gail Fosler, *The Conference Board*
A. Ronald Gallant, *American Statistical
Association*
Robert S. Hamada, *American Finance
Association*
David Kendrick, *American Economic
Association*

Ben E. Laden, *National Association of
Business Economists*
Rudolph A. Oswald, *American Federation of
Labor and Congress of Industrial
Organizations*
Dean P. Phypers, *Committee for Economic
Development*
Douglas D. Purvis, *Canadian Economics
Association*
Charles A. Walworth, *American Institute of
Certified Public Accountants*

Directors Emeriti

Moses Abramovitz
Emilio G. Collado
Frank W. Fetter

Thomas D. Flynn
Gottfried Haberler
Geoffrey H. Moore

George B. Roberts
Willard L. Thorp
William S. Vickrey

Since this volume is a record of conference proceedings, it has been exempted from the rules governing critical review of manuscripts by the Board of Directors of the National Bureau (resolution adopted 8 June 1948, as revised 21 November 1949 and 20 April 1968).

Contents

Acknowledgments

This volume is the result of a conference held by the National Bureau of Economic Research in Cambridge, Massachusetts, on 16–17 March 1990. The conference was part of the Bureau's Trade Relations Project. I would like to thank Kirsten Foss Davis and Ilana Hardesty of the NBER for the efficient manner in which they handled the conference arrangements and Jane Konkel of the NBER for ensuring that the papers and comments were in the appropriate form for submission to the University of Chicago Press. The editorial staff of the University of Chicago Press, particularly Julie McCarthy, has been very helpful in facilitating the publication of this volume.

Funding for the Trade Relations Project has been provided by the Ford Foundation. All involved with the conference are especially thankful for the encouragement and guidance provided by Tom Trebat of the Ford Foundation.

Introduction

Robert E. Baldwin

New Empirical Approaches

Important changes in the nature of research on trade policy issues are taking place. Traditionally, papers in this area have been mainly concerned with estimating the welfare losses of such trade-distorting policies as tariffs and export subsidies or the welfare gains of eliminating such measures. The usual procedure has been to model behavior in the sectors of interest and then, using estimates of such parameters as import demand and export supply elasticities made by other investigators (or perhaps estimated by the author), to simulate the price, trade volume, and welfare effects of various trade policies. Generally these studies have focused on particular industries and used partial equilibrium analysis in making their estimates. However, computable general equilibrium (CGE) models have also been constructed with which to analyze the effects on a country or group of countries of broad trade policy changes such as the elimination of all tariffs or the tariff cuts in the Kennedy and Tokyo Rounds of GATT-sponsored multilateral trade negotiations.

There is no doubt that this approach has improved our understanding of the possible effects of the various types of trade policies and continues to provide insights about the consequences of major policy changes that have significant general equilibrium implications. However, the results of simulation exercises are highly sensitive to the nature of the underlying model, the level of sectoral detail, and the magnitudes of the key parameters. There are also doubts about the appropriateness of utilizing parameters estimated for models quite different from the one being used for simulation purposes or that may not be relevant for the policy change being simulated.

As a consequence of these difficulties with simulation methodology, trade

Robert E. Baldwin is the Hilldale Professor of Economics at the University of Wisconsin–Madison and a research associate of the National Bureau of Economic Research.

policy researchers are increasingly using rigorous econometric methods and relevant empirical data to test the hypotheses derived from their models. Moreover, stimulated by the new interest in analyzing trade policies under imperfectly competitive market conditions and within a political economy framework, investigators are exploring topics more diverse than just the welfare implications of various policies.

An objective of this conference volume is to facilitate this shift in research strategy. Two of the ten papers utilize simulation methodology, since this is still the most useful approach to understanding the implications of certain broad trade policy changes. But authors were encouraged to model policy behavior of interest to policymakers and to test derived hypotheses using actual data and econometric methodology. Besides being asked to include nontechnical discussions of their models and econometric techniques, they were also urged to describe the political and institutional conditions relevant for better understanding their analyses.

Analyses Within a Political Economy Perspective

A common feature of the first four papers in the volume is their use of a broad political economy perspective in empirically analyzing the effects of trade policies. In the first paper Robert W. Staiger and Guido Tabellini investigate whether the degree of government discretion influences the nature of trade policy. They assume that the government uses tariff policy to redistribute income after a decline in the price of the good produced in the import-competing sector. In one of the two sets of circumstances they analyze theoretically, the government irrevocably commits to a particular tariff, and then workers in the injured industry, after observing this policy, decide whether to move to another industry. In the other, the government has the discretion of choosing a tariff after the workers in the injured sector have decided whether to move.

Their analysis of these two scenarios indicates not only that the tariff will be higher in the discretion case but also that the government will take account of the distortionary effects of its policies on both consumption and production decisions in the commitment case but only on consumption decisions in the discretionary situation, since in this latter case labor allocations and thus production decisions have already been made when the government sets the tariff level. An implication of this is that the optimal tariff under commitment will lie farther below its discretionary level the larger the output share of consumption and the wage share of output. In the discretion case these variables should not be significantly related to the tariff level.

The authors empirically test this hypothesis by contrasting U.S. tariff changes across industries under escape-clause (section 201) cases and in the implementation of the negotiated tariff-cutting formula, including exceptions to the rule, in the Tokyo Round. Since injury must proceed an affirmative finding in the escape-clause cases, many of the allocative decisions by the private sector have already been made when the president determines the appropriate tariff response. Consequently, one would not expect the ratio of the wage bill to consumption (the combined form of the output share of consumption and wage share of output) to be a significant variable in the decision-making process. In contrast, most allocational decisions by the private sector probably were made after the government made its Tokyo Round tariff-cutting decisions.

Staiger and Tabellini do find some support in their empirical work for these hypotheses. A common set of political variables tend to be significant in explaining tariff responses in both situations, but in the escape-clause analysis the ratio of the wage bill to consumption is never significantly negative, whereas this variable does have the expected sign in some specifications of the analysis of the Tokyo Round cuts.

In the second paper in this group, Thomas J. Prusa investigates why such a large proportion of antidumping cases are withdrawn by the petitioners during the period in which the Commerce Department is determining whether dumping is occurring and the International Trade Commission (ITC) is determining whether the industry is materially injured as a result of the dumping. He notes that roughly 25 percent of U.S. cases filed are subsequently withdrawn and that most of these cases involve some type of agreement between domestic and foreign producers.

Prusa explores two hypotheses to explain the withdrawal of cases: self-selection and political pressure. Under the first hypothesis, he reasons that firms withdraw only if the profits from withdrawing are greater than the expected profits from the official ITC decision. In contrast, under the political-pressure hypothesis, cases are withdrawn because it is in the political interests of the United States to arrange a negotiated settlement in order to avoid retaliatory actions by foreign countries.

In testing these hypotheses, Prusa models the dumping determination process as a two-stage decision problem. In the first stage the government decides whether to arrange for a withdrawal of the case by negotiating some type of price agreement, taking account of the ITC's expected final decision. In the second stage the ITC makes a binary decision whether to find injury, conditional on the case not having been withdrawn. He reasons that under the self-selection process the parties will seek a settlement if economic conditions in the industry indicate a likely injury determination. However, if conditions indicate no injury, then the case will be withdrawn without a settlement. In contrast, under the political-pressure hypothesis, cases are withdrawn not because of the inevitability of the outcome but because it is in the interest of the government to arrange a settlement.

Using a nested-logit econometric model and economic-political data for the four-digit SIC industries in which the cases can be assigned, Prusa analyzes the determinants of the withdrawal decision and then the determinants of the injury decision. His finding that the most significant variables in determining the withdrawal decision are the employment size of an industry and the number of countries against whom the antidumping case is filed rather than such economic factors as the change in employment or the change in capacity utilization suggests to Prusa that the withdrawal decision is chiefly influenced by political pressure. Furthermore, unlike some other studies, he does not find economic factors to be significant in the second-stage decision by the ITC. He believes his finding that the withdrawal decision is based on political pressure rather than a self-selection process indicates that industries can strategically manipulate the law to gain protection where none is warranted.

Stefanie Ann Lenway and Douglas A. Schuler open up a new area of political economy research in their paper on the steel industry. Instead of focusing on the industry as the unit exerting political pressure for protection and inquiring why certain industries are more successful than others in gaining protection, the authors examine the political pressures brought by the various firms within an industry. In particular, they ask whether the firms investing the most resources to influence trade policy in the steel industry are also the firms that gain the most from the imposition of trade restraints.

The authors combine three types of lobbying activities in constructing a political involvement variable for firms in the steel industry: their campaign contributions to members of the House Ways and Means Committee and Senate Finance Committee, the number of appearances by a firm's top management before congressional committees considering trade policy matters, and the number of escape-clause, antidumping, and countervailing duty actions initiated by the firms. The change in the stock price of individual steel firms after the announcement of protection is their measure of the benefits of protection to individual firms.

They find no consistent relationship between the level of a firm's political involvement in efforts to gain protection and the benefits the firm receives as reflected in the market's evaluation of its future earning potential. As Lenway and Schuler point out, this finding challenges the basic conclusion of collective action theory, namely, that there is a positive relationship between expected and actual returns to the provision of a collective good such as the lobbying activity in an industry.

The paper by Elias Dinopoulos and Mordechai E. Kreinin asks two questions about the voluntary export restraints (VERs) introduced on machine tools from Japan and Taiwan in 1987. What were the political and economic factors that enabled this industry to gain protection and what were the trade volume and price effects of the export restraints?

Not only is the machine tool industry composed of many small firms, unlike the steel or automotive industries, but it is also a relatively small industry (78,000 employees), unlike the textile/apparel industry, for example. Both characteristics suggest that such an industry will have a difficult time in gaining protection. The relative ease with which displaced workers obtain jobs in other sectors and their high level of wages also indicate that granting protection on adjustment-assistance or equity grounds are also not convincing arguments. The authors conclude that the main factors persuading the president to grant protection were the rise in the import penetration ratio in this sector from about 25 percent in 1980 to over 50 percent in 1987 and the importance of the machine tools for national security purposes.

Dinopoulos and Kreinin estimate the increase of U.S. prices of machine tools in 1988 as a result of the VERs to be 17 percent and the rent transfer to Japan and Taiwan to be $100 million. Surprisingly, both of these effects seemed to disappear by 1988, possibly due, they suggest, to increased production by Japanese firms located in the United States. They also do not find any clear-cut evidence of quality upgrading as a result of the restrictions.

The Effects of Trade Policy under Imperfectly Competitive Market Conditions

The next three papers focus on the effects of trade policy under imperfectly competitive market conditions. K. C. Fung investigates whether the existence of industrial groups in Japan (Japanese *keiretsu*), which involve close manufacturer-supplier, banking-industry, and distribution linkages among member firms, influence U.S.-Japanese industry trade balances. As he points out, U.S. trade negotiators maintain that the existence of these Japanese conglomerates, by supporting each other's activities, reduce trading opportunities for foreign firms and thus weaken the import-increasing effects in Japan of reductions in Japanese tariffs and conventional nontariff barriers.

Fung analyzes the possible effects of the special relationships among Japanese by modeling an oligopolistic situation in which a U.S. and a Japanese firm, each producing its output with labor and a purchased intermediate input, compete in the Japanese market. However, unlike the American producer of the intermediate good, the Japanese intermediate producer is a member of the same industrial group as the Japanese producer of the final good and, therefore, includes the profits of this producer in its own profit function. As would be expected, one of the factors negatively affecting the net exports of the American firm is the degree of group affiliation between the Japanese firms.

This hypothesis is tested by analyzing econometrically the net exports of twenty-two U.S. industries to Japan in 1980. Besides measures of U.S. and Japanese unit labor costs and U.S. and Japanese tariffs and quotas, Fung's regressions of U.S. trade balances with Japan by industry include the degree of group affiliation in Japan as proxied by either the sales of group-affiliated companies as a percentage of total industry sales or the share of employment accounted for the group-affiliated corporations in an industry. He finds under a variety of equations generated by his theoretical model that the higher the degree of affiliation within an industry the lower are U.S. net exports in an industry.

Mark J. Roberts and James R. Tybout test for another important relationship that one would expect to hold in imperfectly competitive markets, namely, an increase in efficiency as trade liberalization in an industry occurs and small inefficient plants are eliminated and the remaining firms operate at lower cost levels. Following other authors, they first develop a simple model of imperfect competition in which unit costs of firms decline as output increases due to the existence of fixed costs and in which there is marginal cost heterogeneity among firms. As they show, in such a model an inward shift in demand due to trade liberalization is likely to bring about efficiency gains, but this is not a necessary outcome. Consequently, they conclude that it is an empirical question whether trade liberalization leads to increases in the average scale of production, in the share of the market controlled by large producers, and in productivity.

The authors utilize annual census data covering all manufacturing plants with at least ten workers in both Columbia and Chile over a period of five to ten years to study the effects on these variables of the degree of exposure of an industry to international trade. Perhaps the most surprising relationship revealed by their regression analysis is that increased import competition in these countries reduces the average size of both large and small plants in the short run and long run but especially in the latter. In addition, there is no clear evidence that the degree of trade exposure affects industry productivity.

In the last of the three papers examining how imperfectly competitive market structures affect international trade, Bee-Yan Aw investigates whether the existence of VERs by Taiwan and Korea on footwear shipments to the United States led to or enhanced noncompetitive pricing actions by domestic or foreign producers of nonrubber footwear. As she notes, a familiar argument in the literature on imperfect competition is that protection of a domestic industry may allow domestic producers to increase their markups at the expense of domestic consumers.

To test this hypothesis, Aw formulates an econometric model of the U.S. footwear industry in an imperfectly competitive setting that includes a variable representing the degree of competitiveness in pricing behavior. The data set with which the industry's demand and supply relations can be estimated simultaneously consists of observations of prices and quantities on several categories of domestic footwear from 1974 to 1985, a period that overlaps the VER period of 1977–81.

Aw's empirical analysis indicates that domestic footwear producers priced competitively during both the non-VER and VER periods. However, the reduction in foreign supply did raise the price of U.S. domestic footwear by about 5 percent. She also reports that another of her studies of this industry finds no evidence of noncompetitive pricing by Taiwanese exporters during the constrained or unconstrained periods. However, the restraints did create a 22 percent scarcity premium for Taiwanese exporters.

A New Measure of Trade Restrictiveness and Estimates of Trade Policy Effects with CGE Models

James E. Anderson also analyzes the effects of quantitative restrictions in a particular industry, namely, the U.S. cheese industry. However, his main motivation is to contrast these effects as measured by a new index of trade restrictiveness, which he has developed together with Peter Neary,[1] and by the conventional method of calculating trade-weighted tariff-equivalents. The Anderson-Neary index of trade distortion, which they call "the coefficient of trade utilization," is equal to 1 plus the percentage weighted average quota expansion required to reach free trade (or any reform position). This measure is also the ratio of the shadow value of the new quota bundle to the shadow value of the quota bundle needed to maintain the initial level of welfare. The coefficient of trade utilization, which resembles the Hicksian compensating variations in income, is clearly a more meaningful indicator of the degree of restrictiveness of quantitative restriction than the ad valorem equivalent of these restrictions.

In his empirical analysis, Anderson finds that changes in the degree of restrictiveness of cheese import quotas for 1965–79 as measured by the annual rate of change in average tariff equivalents differs considerably from the annual rate of change of the coefficient of trade utilization. Indeed, in only eight of the fifteen years was the direction of the annual changes in the two measures the same. Since the coefficient of trade utilization is no more difficult to calculate with quantitative restrictions than the ad valorem equivalents of these restrictions, Anderson urges other researchers to adopt this index in analyzing the restrictive effects of quantitative measures. With this measure he finds that the tightening of cheese import quotas over the period 1965–79 effectively cut cheese imports in half every seven years.

As noted in the beginning of this introduction, the effects of certain trade policies are best explored by using computable general equilibrium models to simulate the policies. The introduction of a general import surcharge, a step that has been recommended on numerous occasions as a means of reducing the U.S. trade deficit, is one such policy. Barry Eichengreen and Lawrence H. Goulder undertake this task in their paper. Since we are interested in the trade balance effects of an import surcharge over time, their dynamic model is especially suitable for analyzing the effects of this policy.

As they point out, a temporary tax on all imports raises the prices of current goods relative to future goods, thereby shifting absorption toward the future and improving the current trade balance. But, by reducing current absorption,

---

1. James E. Anderson and J. Peter Neary, "A New Approach to Evaluating Trade Reform" (Department of Economics, Boston College, 1989); idem, "The Coefficient of Trade Utilization: Back to the Baldwin Envelope," in *The Political Economy of International Trade: Essays in Honor of Robert Baldwin*, ed. R. Jones and A. Krueger (Cambridge, England: Basil Blackwell, 1990).

temporary tariffs depress world interest rates and encourage households to shift spending back to the present. The net effect of these two forces could be to improve or worsen the trade balance. To demonstrate this in detail, they develop a simple two-period model which captures the incentives for both intersectoral and intertemporal substitution produced by temporary and permanent tariffs.

The authors then utilize their CGE model to represent the U.S. economy and the effects of an import surcharge more realistically. Among their findings are that both a temporary surcharge and a permanent import surcharge improve the trade balance in the short run but produce larger deficits (or smaller surpluses) in the longer term. Under certain assumptions about the source of the trade deficit, both policies delay the date by which the initial deficits are finally eliminated.

Another fruitful use of CGE models has been to analyze the welfare effects of general trade liberalization under conditions of increasing returns to scale. However, as Jaime de Melo and David Roland-Holst point out in their paper, analyses of this nature have been confined mainly to developed countries. Their contribution is to investigate the implications for a developing country, namely, Korea, of liberalization under conditions of increasing returns. Korea is an especially appropriate country to study within this framework, since its liberalization in the 1980s followed a period in the 1970s where the country's development efforts focused on heavy and chemical industries. These efforts produced a domestic industrial structure that was highly concentrated and highly protected.

Three of the seven sectors in their model—consumer goods, producers goods, and heavy industry—are calibrated with either a medium or high degree of scale economies. Behavior in these sectors is modeled alternatively as a contestable markets situation and as a conjectural variations case. Outcomes with and without entry are explored in the conjectural variations case. A variant of the model in which protection allows for supernormal profits because of entry barriers is also explored. The welfare effects of removing protection under these various conditions are compared with the situation of constant returns to scale in all industries.

The authors estimate liberalization under constant returns to yield a 1.1 percent increase in national income. Under the various increasing returns scenarios, the welfare gains amount to as much as 5 percent when there are no excess profits and up to 10 percent when excess profits can be earned.

I Analyses with a Political Economy Perspective

1 Rules versus Discretion in Trade Policy: An Empirical Analysis

Robert W. Staiger and Guido Tabellini

1.1 Introduction

An important determinant of the optimal setting of any (second-best) tariff policy is the degree to which the supply side of the economy can respond to the imposition of the tariff. This follows from the fact that a tariff is both a subsidy to producers and a tax on consumers of the import good, and therefore distorts two decisions. Thus, for instance, if a tariff is used to address an existing production distortion, the optimal tariff setting will come closer to free trade the less are resources able to respond to the tariff (the smaller the marginal impact of the tariff on the existing production distortion). Alternatively, if a tariff is imposed to address an existing consumption distortion, its optimal setting will come closer to completely eliminating the consumption distortion the less are resources able to respond to the tariff (the smaller the production distortion it induces on the margin). In the presence of a trade distortion (the case of a large country), the optimal tariff will be higher the less are resources able to respond to the tariff (the lower the foreign import demand elasticity). And if a tariff is used to redistribute income, not only the costs of distorted production but, as is well known from Stolper-Samuelson and specific factors results, the redistributional impacts of the tariff as well may depend crucially on the ability of productive resources to respond.

Robert W. Staiger is an associate professor of economics at Stanford University and a research associate of the National Bureau of Economic Research. Guido Tabellini is an associate professor of economics at the University of California at Los Angeles and a faculty research fellow of the National Bureau of Economic Research.

The authors are greatly indebted to John Alfaro, Robert Baldwin, Drusilla Brown, Kishore Gawande, Howard Gruenspecht, William Hart, Edward Leamer, Terry Obrien, and Daniel Trefler for help with various aspects of the data, and to Robert Baldwin, Richard Clarida, Michael Moore, and seminar participants at the University of California at Santa Cruz and at the NBER Conference on Empirical Studies of Commercial Policy for helpful comments. Phil Levy provided outstanding research assistance. This research is funded by the National Science Foundation under grant SES89-11188.

All this suggests that governments may behave very differently when setting tariff levels depending on the degree to which the supply side of the economy is in a position to respond to the actual policy choice. An important determinant of the magnitude of this response is the timing of the government decisions relative to those of the private sector or, to put it differently, the freedom with which the government can reoptimize once private decisions are made. In particular, resources that can move after observing the government policy action can condition their sectoral location decision on the observed tariff choice. On the other hand, resources that move simultaneously with or before the government tariff choice must base their decisions on the expected (rather than actual) policy; the sectoral allocation of these resources is then taken as given by the government when it chooses a tariff level. The greater the government's opportunities to reoptimize, the greater is its degree of policy discretion relative to the private sector, and the greater is the proportion of factors that base their decisions on the expected government action, lowering the government's overall assessment of supply responsiveness when making its tariff decision.

Of course, in a repeated setting those factors of production that move prior to or simultaneously with the government tend to base their allocation decisions on expected tariff actions that turn out in equilibrium to be correct: hence, the government does not in fact find it possible to exploit the timing of its decisions to surprise the private sector. On the contrary, unless the government can credibly bind itself to a tariff policy which is not ex post optimal, its timing "advantage" will turn into a liability: the government loses control of the private sector's expectations and remains trapped in a suboptimal time-consistent tariff equilibrium.

It is this logic that underlies much of the recent literature on the efficacy of rules versus discretion in trade policy. For example, Staiger and Tabellini (1987) have analyzed the costs of policy discretion when a government attempts to use tariffs as a redistributive tool. Lapan (1988) has characterized the equilibrium when a large country attempts to impose its optimal tariff in a discretionary policy regime. And Staiger and Tabellini (1989) argue that, because of the second-best nature of most trade policy intervention, the issue of credibility is likely to be an important determinant of the extent as well as the efficacy of trade policy in most environments.

In addition to the small body of theoretical literature on credibility and trade policy, there is a large amount of work on rules versus discretion in macroeconomic policy, generated by the seminal paper of Kydland and Prescott (1977). However, as is true of all the work on rules versus discretion, this literature is almost exclusively theoretical.[1] This is a serious omission, given the very sharp normative implications of this debate for actual policymaking. It is perhaps this omission that explains why some economists have suspended their

---

1. Recent exceptions are Judd (1989) in public finance, Romer (1989) for monetary policy, and Edwards and Tabellini (1990) for monetary and fiscal policy.

judgment on the relevance of these issues, or have de facto ignored them in their research on economic policy.

In this paper we test empirically for evidence that trade policy depends on the degree of government discretion. We do this by studying government tariff choices in two distinct environments. One environment is that of tariffs set under the escape clause (section 201 of the U.S. Trade Act of 1974). We argue that these decisions afford the government with ample opportunity to reoptimize and with correspondingly little ability to commit. The other environment is the Tokyo Round of GATT negotiations and the determination of the set of exclusions from the general formula cuts. We argue that these decisions provided the government with a much diminished opportunity to reoptimize and with a correspondingly greater ability to commit. Comparing decisions made in these two environments allows us to ask whether different degrees of policy discretion have a measurable impact on trade policy decisions.

While we explore the effects of discretion in trade policy within the context of the escape clause, we feel that the issue is of much broader interest, especially in light of the recent literature on trade policy in the presence of imperfect markets. While much of this literature is concerned with various conditions under which activist trade policies are warranted, taken together the results of the literature suggest a second, more subtle, implication: The new activist trade policy, if it is to be pursued at all, must be pursued with discretion, judging each situation on a case by case basis.[2] As such, the current debate over the appropriate degree of activism in trade policy is unavoidably a debate over the appropriate degree of policy discretion as well. The results of our empirical analysis should thus be relevant to this broader debate.

The next two sections set out in some detail the theoretical framework discussed informally above. Section 1.4 motivates our empirical approach. Section 1.5, which describes the escape clause and Tokyo Round tariff-setting environments, argues that a crucial difference between the two is the degree of government discretion. We discuss the data and present our empirical findings in section 1.6 and present our conclusions in section 1.7. Data sources are described in the appendix.

1.2 Credibility and Trade Policy

1.2.1 The General Framework

In this section we formalize the argument that the timing of tariff-setting decisions relative to private sector decisions matters. We begin by abstracting

---

2. For instance, Dixit (1987) concludes: "The current median view of the profession in this matter can be fairly characterized as (i) a recognition that the existence of imperfect competition does modify or overturn some conventional beliefs about trade policy, and (ii) an awareness that the design of policy to fit each situation requires close attention to its specific details. This suggests that research should be directed toward improving our understanding of the realities of some industries that are likely candidates for strategic trade policies."

from distributional issues and consider a one-consumer economy within the general framework laid out by Dixit (1985). Our purpose here is to illustrate that the potential for credibility problems in trade policy is widespread. The next section focuses in detail on trade policy motivated by redistributive goals and derives the main testable implications of our theory.

Consider first a small open (one-consumer) economy that faces a given vector of world prices, r, and has exogenous domestic consumption and production distortions. The role of trade policy is to offset these distortions. Let the consumption and production distortions be summarized by the vectors α and β, respectively, and let τ be a vector of specific tariffs. Then, the relationship between domestic prices, world prices, distortions, and tariffs can be written as

$$(1) \qquad p = r + \tau + \alpha,$$

$$(2) \qquad q = r + \tau + \beta,$$

where p and q denote consumers' and producers' prices (in terms of a numeraire commodity). Let $E(1,p,u)$ be the expenditure function, with the numeraire good labeled by zero and its price normalized to unity, and with u the consumer's utility level. We assume for simplicity that all goods are traded. Define $\pi(1,q)$ as the profit function with the same convention about the numeraire. Profits are assumed to be taxed at 100 percent so that consumer and producer prices can be independently normalized. All tax and tariff revenues are returned to the consumer lump sum. Using standard properties of the expenditure and profit functions, the equilibrium balanced trade condition can be written as

$$(3) \qquad E_0 - \pi_0 + r \cdot (E_p - \pi_q) = 0$$

where subscripts denote derivatives.

Our timing assumptions are as follows. First sector i chooses a supply response to the vector of expected tariff choices of the government τ^e. Next, or simultaneously with sector i's choice, the government commits to its vector of tariffs τ. Then, after observing τ, sector i is permitted a dampened supply response to the difference between actual and expected tariffs, with the elasticity of sector i's ex post (after τ is observed) supply curve being $(1 - \psi_i)$ $\epsilon[0,1]$ of its ex ante (before τ is observed) elasticity. All consumption decisions are made after the government tariffs are in place. Thus, ψ_i parameterizes the inflexibility of sector i's supply decisions relative to the policy decisions of the government. If $\psi_i = 0$, all supply decisions are made after observing the governmental choice. In this case, the government can enter into binding policy commitments and there is no credibility problem. In the opposite extreme case, $\psi_i = 1$, all supply decisions are made before observing the policy, and the ex post supply response is zero. More generally, $1 > \psi_i > 0$, in which case the ex ante and ex post supply responses differ. Accordingly, the ex ante and ex post optimal policies also differ.

Naturally, in equilibrium the expected tariff τ^e coincides with the ex post optimal policy, and the government fulfills those expectations. In the literature on rules versus discretion, this equilibrium policy has been called the "time-consistent" policy, or the "discretionary" policy. Throughout this section we will simply call it the equilibrium policy, to emphasize that it is the optimal government response under a particular assumption about the timing of moves.

Differentiating (3) and using (1) and (2) provides the key relationship from which the equilibrium tariff is determined.:

$$(4) \qquad (E_{0u} + r \cdot E_{pu})du = (\alpha + \tau)'E_{pp}d\tau$$
$$- (\beta + \tau)'[\pi_{qq}d\tau^e + (I - \psi)\pi_{qq}(d\tau - d\tau^e)],$$

where for simplicity ψ is taken to be a square diagonal matrix with ith diagonal element ψ_i, and I is the identity matrix of the same dimension. Throughout, primes will be used to denote transposes.

Under these timing assumptions, the government takes the expected tariff as given ($d\tau^e = 0$) when it sets policy: The expected tariff only matters for those production decisions that have already been made (and hence can no longer be altered) when the actual policy is determined. Moreover, in equilibrium policy surprises are ruled out ($\tau = \tau^e$). Thus, the equilibrium (ex-post optimal) policy is determined by

$$(5) \qquad (E_{0u} + r \cdot E_{pu})du = (\alpha + \tau)'E_{pp}d\tau - (\beta + \tau)'(I - \psi)\pi_{qq}d\tau.$$

The coefficient on the left-hand side of (5) is the income effect on all commodities, and it can be shown to be positive. Hence, the change in utility as tariffs are changed has the same sign as the right-hand side of (5). The terms $E_{pp}\, d\tau$ and $\pi_{qq}\, d\tau$ on the right-hand side denote the consumption and production substitution effects, respectively. Hence, the two terms on the right-hand side reflect the welfare effect of moving consumption and production when there are distortions or tariffs.

According to equation (5), the equilibrium policy depends on the matrix ψ that parameterizes the degree of government discretion relative to that of private producers. The traditional case considered in the literature on optimal trade policy is a special case of (5): it corresponds to $\psi = 0$, in which case the ex ante and ex post optimal policies coincide (i.e., the government can precommit in advance of *all* productive decisions). We now turn to a characterization of the equilibrium tariff response to production and consumption distortions when ψ_i is allowed to vary between 0 and 1 for all i.

1.2.2 Production Distortions

Consider first the use of tariffs to address a production distortion ($\beta \neq 0$, $\alpha = 0$). The equilibrium tariff $\hat{\tau}$ is given, using (5), by the solution to

$$(6) \qquad \frac{du}{d\tau} = 0 = [E_{0u} + r \cdot E_{pu}]^{-1}[\hat{\tau}'E_{pp} - (\beta + \hat{\tau})'(I - \psi)\pi_{qq}]$$

or

(7) $$\hat{\tau}' = \beta'(I - \psi)\pi_{qq}[E_{pp} - (I - \psi)\pi_{qq}]^{-1}.$$

Thus, the equilibrium tariff policy is affected by the timing of the government move. In particular, if $\psi = 0$ so that no supply-side decisions need be committed until after the government tariff choice is observed, then (7) coincides with the traditional expression for the optimal tariff in the presence of a production distortion (e.g., see Dixit 1985). At the other extreme, if $\psi = I$ so that all supply-side decisions must be made prior to or simultaneously with the government, the actual tariff set by the government will have no impact on the production distortion once expectations are given, and the equilibrium has $\hat{\tau} = 0$: the tariff will be completely ineffective as a policy tool to correct production distortions.

1.2.3   Consumption Distortions

Consider next the existence of consumption distortions. This corresponds to the case where $\alpha \neq 0$ and $\beta = 0$. The equilibrium tariff $\hat{\tau}$ is given, using (5), as the solution to

(8) $$\frac{du}{d\tau} = 0 = [E_{0u} + r \cdot E_{pu}]^{-1}[(\alpha + \hat{\tau})'E_{pp} - \hat{\tau}'(I - \psi)\pi_{qq}]$$

or

(9) $$\hat{\tau}' = -\alpha'E_{pp}[E_{pp} - (I - \psi)\pi_{qq}]^{-1}.$$

Again, the equilibrium tariff is affected by the timing of the government decision. If the government has no opportunity to surprise the supply side of the economy ($\psi = 0$), the equilibrium tariff coincides with that prescribed by the theory of optimal taxation (see again Dixit 1985). At the other extreme, if the government moves after all supply-side decisions have been made ($\psi = I$), then all production distortions introduced by the tariff will be ignored by the government in equilibrium, and $\hat{\tau}' = -\alpha'$: The equilibrium tariff completely eliminates the consumption distortions.

1.2.4   Terms of Trade

Finally, consider the case of a large country wishing to exploit its monopoly power in trade and unconcerned about the possibility of retaliation. For simplicity we assume that the matrix ψ applies both domestically and in the rest of the world. The large country analogue to equation (4) is

(10) $$\begin{aligned}(E_{0u} + r \cdot E_{pu})du = {}& (\tau + \alpha)'E_{pp}[dr + d\tau] \\ & - (\tau + \beta)'[\pi_{qq}(dr^e + d\tau^e) + (I - \psi)\pi_{qq}((dr + d\tau) \\ & - (dr^e + d\tau^e))] - m \cdot dr,\end{aligned}$$

where m is the vector of net imports from the rest of the world, and where the world price vector r is determined by

$$(11) \qquad E_p - \pi_q = \pi_r^{\text{row}} - E_r^{\text{row}},$$

with π^{row} and E^{row} the profit and expenditure functions, respectively, for the rest of the world. The large country analogue for (5) is then

$$(12) \qquad \begin{aligned} (E_{0u} + r \cdot E_{pu})du &= (\alpha + \tau)'E_{pp}(dr + d\tau) \\ &- (\beta + \tau)'(I - \psi)\pi_{qq}(dr + d\tau) - m \cdot dr \end{aligned}$$

with

$$dr = [(E_{pp} + E_{rr}^{\text{row}}) - (I - \psi)(\pi_{qq} + \pi_{rr}^{\text{row}})]^{-1}\{[(I - \psi)\pi_{qq} - E_{pp}]d\tau - [E_{pu} + E_{rr}^{\text{row}}]du\}.$$

A trade distortion is represented by the condition $dr \neq 0$, $\alpha = 0$, and $\beta = 0$. The equilibrium tariff is given using (12) by the solution to

$$(13) \qquad \frac{du}{d\tau} = 0,$$

which after manipulation yields

$$(14) \qquad \hat{\tau}' = m'[(I - \psi)\pi_{rr}^{\text{row}} - E_{rr}^{\text{row}}]^{-1}.$$

As before, the equilibrium tariff vector for a large country is affected by the timing of government moves, and will in general be higher the greater is the proportion of resources that must allocate prior to or simultaneously with the government tariff decision (the closer ψ is to I) (see also Lapan 1988).

1.2.5 Discussion

These three instances of equilibrium trade policy lead to the same broad conclusion. In equilibrium, the degree of discretion in government decisions relative to that of the private sector has a profound impact on the chosen tariff policies. In particular, the greater the government's degree of discretion relative to the private sector, and therefore the greater the fraction of resources that move prior to, or simultaneously with, it (the closer ψ is to I), the smaller will be the assessment of factor supply responsiveness ($[I - \psi]\pi_{qq}$) implicit in the government's tariff choice. Naturally, the allocation of productive resources fully reflects the government policy even if the government moves after some productive decisions have been made. In other words, both the expected and the actual policy matter. However, in equilibrium the government does not take into account the effects of expected policies, but only those of actual policies. This discrepancy, between what the government takes into account and the overall effects of the (actual and expected) policy, increases with the extent of government discretion (i.e., with ψ). Hence, the welfare properties of the equilibrium depend on the extent of government discretion: the larger is the degree of discretion, the less the government takes into account the full effects of the policy and, ceteris paribus, the lower is social welfare. For this reason, policy discretion can be counterproductive.

1.3   Credible Trade Policy and Income Distribution

We now study trade policy motivated by redistributive goals. As argued in the next section, the observed policy interventions that we exploit in our empirical test largely reflect this motivation. The model of this section generalizes Staiger and Tabellini (1987), to which we refer the reader for a more detailed investigation of credible trade policy in this framework.

1.3.1   The Model

Consider a small open economy with two traded goods and two inputs to production, labor, and capital. Capital is immobile across sectors, and technology is homogeneous of degree 1 in both inputs. To simplify notation, we assume that both sectors share the same production function, and that each sector is endowed with one unit of capital. The production technologies are given by

$$(15) \qquad i = f(N^i), \quad i = x,y, \quad f'(\cdot) > 0, \quad f''(\cdot) < 0,$$

where $N^i \equiv$ labor employed in sector i; $x \equiv$ exported good; and $y \equiv$ imported good.

In each sector, firms combine labor with their fixed stock of capital, up to the point where the value of labor's marginal product is equated to the nominal wage measured in terms of any numeraire, W^i:

$$(16) \qquad P^x f'(N^x) = W^x; \quad P^y (1 + t) f'(N^y) = W^y$$

where P^x is the world price of the exported good, t is the ad valorem tariff on imports, and P^y is the world price of imports. Wages are assumed to be perfectly flexible so that equation (16) yields the nominal wage that clears the labor market in each sector.

Throughout this section, we consider the reaction of private agents and of the government to a shock that lowers the world price of good y. To simplify notation, let $P^x = 1$ and let P^y be the post-shock realization of the price of good y.

The aggregate supply of labor in the economy as a whole is assumed fixed and equal to $\bar{N}$. Labor is mobile between sectors and reallocates in response to the shock on the basis of the expected intersectoral wage differential. We contrast equilibrium trade policy under two opposite timing assumptions. Under *discretion,* the government sets policy after all the workers in sector y have chosen whether or not to reallocate to the other sector based on the expected wage differential. By (16), the expected wage differential subsequent to the shock but prior to the policy action is

(17)
$$\frac{W^{ye}}{W^{xe}} = \frac{P^y\,(1\,+\,t^e)f'[N^y\,(t^e)]}{f'[N^x(t^e)]}.$$

Under *commitment,* the timing is reversed: first the government irrevocably commits to a tariff. And then all the workers, having observed the policy, choose whether or not to reallocate from y to x based on the actual wage differential. In this case the actual wage differential is defined as in (17) with t replacing t^e. Consumption decisions are always made after the government policy is in place.

A crucial assumption of the model is that labor's intersectoral mobility comes only at a cost. Specifically, we assume that, whenever one unit of labor moves from one sector to the other, its marginal product falls by the fraction $(1\,-\,\lambda)$, $1 > \lambda > 0$. These moving costs differ across individuals: the parameter λ is distributed uniformly on the unit interval across workers.

Consider the regime with discretion. Here, workers must make their sectoral allocation decision *before* observing the government action. Any worker for which $\lambda > W^{ye}/W^{xe}$ finds it optimal to reallocate from y to x. Let $\tilde{\lambda}^e \equiv W^{ye}/W^{xe}$ be the marginal worker, who is just ex ante indifferent between reallocating or not. It can be shown that $\tilde{\lambda}^e$ is an increasing function of the *expected* tariff, t^e. Intuitively, a higher expected tariff reduces the relative wage differential in sector x. Hence only the low moving-cost (high λ) workers find it optimal to reallocate. Similarly, consider the regime with commitment, and let $\tilde{\lambda} \equiv W^y/W^x$ be the marginal worker who is ex post indifferent between relocating or not (i.e., after the tariff is in place). It can be shown that $\tilde{\lambda}$ is an increasing function of the *actual* tariff, t. The intuition is the same as above. Under either regime, equilibrium requires that $t = t^e$, and hence $\tilde{\lambda} = \tilde{\lambda}^e$.

Based on this notation, and the assumption that λ is uniformly distributed in the population, we can write the fraction of workers who remain in sector y as $\tilde{\lambda}$ under commitment and $\tilde{\lambda}^e$ under discretion, respectively. To simplify the analysis, we express labor in efficiency units. Thus, the effective quantity of labor employed in each sector once the adjustment to the shock is completed is given by

(18)
$$N^y = \tilde{\lambda}N^y_0,$$

(19)
$$N^x = N^x_0 + N^y_0 \int_{\tilde{\lambda}}^{1} \lambda d\lambda = N^x_0 + (1\,-\,\tilde{\lambda}^2)/2.$$

where N^i_0 is the initial employment in sector i.

The remainder of the model is straightforward and is identical to that in Staiger and Tabellini (1987). Specifically, let I be national disposable income valued at domestic prices. Imposing the condition of balanced trade at world prices, abstracting from domestic taxes, and assuming that the tariff is nonprohibitive, it follows that, subsequent to the shock,

(20) $$I = f(N^x) + P^y (1 + t)f(N^y) + T,$$

where the tariff revenue T is defined by

(21) $$T = t[C^y - f(N^y)]P^y,$$

C^y being aggregate demand for the imported good y. Substituting (21) into (20), national income valued at domestic prices is given by

(22) $$I = f(N^x) + P^y [f(N^y) + tC^y].$$

To focus on the redistributive consequences of tariffs for the labor allocation decision, we assume that the distribution of income is determined solely on the basis of the wage differential between the two sectors. Thus, income from capital and tariff revenues is distributed to each worker in proportion to the share of his labor income in the economywide wage bill. Define the income share variable, φ, as

(23) $$\varphi^i \equiv \frac{I^i}{I} = W^i/W \quad i = x,y,y\lambda,$$

where W is the average wage rate, I^i is total disposable income of a worker of the ith type (valued at domestic prices), and the superscripts x, y, and $y\lambda$ denote workers originally in sector x who remain there, workers originally in sector y who remain there, and workers of type λ originally in sector y who move to sector x, respectively. Using the previous notation, and recalling that $W^{y\lambda} = \lambda W^x$, the average wage rate W under commitment is

(24) $$W = \frac{N_0^x W^x + N_0^y W^y [\bar{\lambda} + (1 - \bar{\lambda}^2)/2]}{\bar{N}}.$$

Under discretion, the average wage rate is defined as in (24) with $\bar{\lambda}^e$ replacing $\bar{\lambda}$.

Each worker consumes a bundle of x and y, chosen to maximize an identical homothetic utility function, subject to a standard budget constraint. The indirect utility function of a representative consumer of the ith type can be written in terms of the previous notation as

(25) $$V^i = V(P^x,P^y,I^i), \quad i = x,y,y\lambda.$$

Letting V_p^i and V_I^i denote the partial derivatives of (25) with respect to P^y and I^i, respectively, the consumption of y on the part of consumers of the ith type can be expressed, using Roy's identity, as

(26) $$C_i^y = - \frac{V_p^i}{V_I^i} = \varphi^i C^y, \quad i = x,y,y\lambda.$$

The second equality follows from the assumption that the common utility function is homothetic.

Finally, the government is assumed to care about the three types of workers in proportion to their frequency in the population. However, we allow the relative weights in the government objective function to be affected by political considerations, which we represent by the parameter α^y. Thus, under commitment the government maximizes:

$$\tilde{J} \equiv (1 - \alpha^y)N_0^x V^x + \alpha^y N_0^y \tilde{\lambda} V^y + \alpha^y N_0^y \int_{\tilde{\lambda}}^1 V^{y\lambda} d\lambda$$

or, with normalization,

$$(27) \qquad\qquad J \equiv \gamma V^x + \tilde{\lambda} V^y + \int_{\tilde{\lambda}}^1 V^{y\lambda} d\lambda,$$

where $\gamma \equiv [(1 - \alpha^y)/\alpha^y] \, N_0^x/N_0^y$. Under discretion the government maximizes a function analogous to (27), except that $\tilde{\lambda}$ is replaced by $\tilde{\lambda}^e$. Note that a value of $\alpha^y = \frac{1}{2}$ would correspond to a utilitarian social welfare function, while $\alpha^y > \frac{1}{2}$ ($\alpha^y < \frac{1}{2}$) implies that workers in sector y receive relatively greater (lower) weight in the government decision. The determinants of α^y will be discussed in the following sections.

We assume the absence of any market mechanisms for reallocating the risk associated with the terms-of-trade shock. If such private insurance markets existed and worked perfectly, there would be no role for government intervention in the form of protection in our model.[3]

1.3.2 Equilibrium under Commitment

This subsection derives the equilibrium trade policy when the government can commit. Since the results here and in the next subsection form the basis for our empirical work, we impose the simplifying assumption of logarithmic utility to ensure a reasonably simple form for the equilibrium tariff. The first-order conditions for a government optimum are

$$(28) \qquad \frac{dJ}{dt} = (V^y - V^{y\tilde{\lambda}})\frac{d\tilde{\lambda}}{dt} + \gamma\frac{dV^x}{dt} + \tilde{\lambda}\frac{dV^y}{dt} + \int_{\tilde{\lambda}}^1 \frac{dV^{y\lambda}}{dt} \, d\lambda = 0,$$

where we have

$$(29) \qquad \frac{dV^i}{dt} = P^y V_p^i + V_I^i[I\frac{d\varphi^i}{dt} + \varphi^i\frac{dI}{dt}] = V_I^i[I\frac{d\varphi^i}{dt} + \varphi^i(\frac{dI}{dt} - P^y C^y)].$$

The second equality in (29) follows from (26). The first term on the right-hand side of (29) captures the direct redistributive effect of the tariff on the ith individual. The remaining terms capture the effect on the ith individual's welfare due to the consumption and production distortions of the tariff.

---

3. See Eaton and Grossman (1985) for a defense of this assumption and Dixit (1989) for a criticism of it.

After some simple algebra, we have[4]

(30) $$\frac{dI}{dt} - P^y C^y = \frac{P^y t}{1 + t}[C^y + y\eta^y],$$

where η^y is the elasticity of output supply in sector y. By the assumption that the workers' utility function is logarithmic,

(31) $$V_I^i = \frac{1}{I^i} = \frac{1}{\varphi^i I}.$$

Combining (29), (30) and (31), we obtain

(32) $$\frac{dV^i}{dt} = \frac{1}{\varphi^i} \frac{d\varphi^i}{dt} - \frac{P^y t}{(1 + t)I}[C^y + y\eta^y].$$

Moreover, in equilibrium $V^y = V^{y\hat{\lambda}}$ by definition of $\hat{\lambda}$. Hence, combining (32) and (31), we can rewrite the government first-order conditions as

(33) $$\gamma \frac{1}{\varphi^x} \frac{d\varphi^x}{dt} + \hat{\lambda} \frac{1}{\varphi^y} \frac{d\varphi^y}{dt} + \int_{\hat{\lambda}}^1 \frac{1}{\varphi^{y\hat{\lambda}}} \frac{d\varphi^{y\lambda}}{dt} d\lambda$$
$$= \frac{t}{1 + t} (1 + \gamma)P^y [C^y + y\eta^y] \frac{1}{I}.$$

The left-hand side of (33) is the marginal benefit of protection, taking the form of redistribution from high- to low-income workers. The right-hand side is the marginal cost of the tariff, net of tariff revenues, due to production and consumption distortions. At the optimum, the marginal benefit and the marginal cost of the tariff must be equal.

To complete the description of the equilibrium, it remains to discuss the effect of the tariff on the distribution of income. By (23) and (29), after some simplifications,

(34) $$\frac{d\varphi^x}{dt} = - \frac{\varphi^y \varphi^x}{1 + h} \frac{d\hat{\lambda}}{dt} < 0; \quad \frac{d\varphi^y}{dt} = (1 - \frac{\hat{\lambda}\varphi^y}{1 + h}) \varphi^x \frac{d\hat{\lambda}}{dt} > 0;$$
$$\frac{d\varphi^{y\hat{\lambda}}}{dt} = - \frac{\lambda\varphi^y \varphi^x}{1 + h} \frac{d\hat{\lambda}}{dt} < 0,$$

where $h \equiv N_0^x/N_0^y$ and the signs follow from $d\hat{\lambda}/dt > 0$. Thus, a tariff redistributes in favor of those who remain in the injured sector. Intuitively, if workers were to reallocate from y to x based on the expectation of no protection subsequent to the shock, then a surprise tariff would leave this labor allocation unaffected and would raise the value of labor's marginal product in sector y directly by raising the domestic price of y; this, in turn, would increase W^y relative to W^x. However, in equilibrium, workers are not surprised by the gov-

---

4. Equation (30) has been derived from equations (22), (19), and (18) and by exploiting the definition of $\hat{\lambda}$ and the assumption of a logarithmic utility function.

ernment action, so that this redistributive effect is partially offset by the fact that fewer workers will leave the injured sector y subsequent to the shock, knowing that protection is forthcoming. Nevertheless, since moving costs $(1 - \lambda)$ differ across individuals by assumption, and since workers choose to leave the injured sector y in ascending order of moving costs (descending order of λ), the fact that fewer workers leave sector y as a result of the tariff implies that the marginal worker who is just indifferent between staying in y and moving to x corresponds to a higher value of λ as a result of the government's tariff response (formally, $d\tilde{\lambda}/dt > 0$). Hence in equilibrium the tariff succeeds in raising W^y/W^x, (which equals $\tilde{\lambda}$) despite the induced effect on the allocation of labor.[5]

Combining (33) and (34) and simplifying, we obtain the equilibrium tariff under commitment:

$$(35) \qquad \frac{t^c}{1 + t^c} = \frac{(N^y/\bar{N})(1 - \delta\varphi^y)\eta^w}{(P^yM^y/I)\eta^{My}},$$

where $\delta \equiv [(1 + h(1 - \alpha^y)/\alpha^y)/(1 + h)]$ is a weight that reflects the government distributive goals, η^w is the elasticity of the equilibrium wage differential with respect to the tariff, M^y is imports of y, and η^{My} is import demand elasticity taken positively. It can be shown that $\eta^w \leq 1$: as noted above, the redistributive effects of protection are partially offset by the induced smaller reallocation of labor. The greater is labor mobility, the smaller is $d\tilde{\lambda}/dt$, and as a result the smaller is the elasticity η^w. Note also that a government maximizing a utilitarian social welfare function ($\alpha = \frac{1}{2}$) would correspond to $\delta = 1$, so that income equality (preserving the status quo) is the government's goal. However, if $\alpha^y > \frac{1}{2}$ ($\alpha^y < \frac{1}{2}$), then $\delta < 1$ ($\delta > 1$) and the government prefers income to be distributed unequally in favor of sector y (the rest of the economy).

Equation (35) conforms with intuition. The numerator refers to the marginal benefits of protection, in the form of income redistribution, which enhance government welfare. The marginal benefits of protection are higher the larger is the fraction of employment in the injured sector, $N^y/\bar{N}$, the greater is α^y, the weight placed on the utility of an injured-sector worker, the greater is the extent of injury (the lower is φ^y), and the greater is the elasticity of the wage differential with respect to the tariff η^w (because the greater is the redistributive impact of trade protection). The denominator refers to the marginal production and consumption distortions of the tariff, captured by the elasticity of import demand, η^{My}, weighted by the import share of national income. The greater these distortions, the smaller is the equilibrium tariff. Finally, for con-

---

5. In this respect, the model differs from that of Staiger and Tabellini (1987), who assume a single value of λ for all workers and hence conclude that under commitment trade policy cannot affect the wage differential across sectors; in that model, the direct effects of the tariff are exactly offset by the induced smaller reallocation of labor from y to x.

venience in comparing the optimal tariff under commitment to that under discretion, we note that the assumption of logarithmic utility allows the denominator of the right-hand side of (35) to be written equivalently as $(P^yM^y/I)\eta^{My}$ $= (P^yC^y/I)(1 + \sigma^y\eta^y)$ where σ^y is the ratio of output to consumption in sector y. With this, we rewrite (35) as

$$(36) \qquad \frac{t^c}{1 + t^c} = [\frac{(N^y/\bar{N})(1 - \delta\varphi^y)}{(P^yC^y/I)}][\frac{\eta^w}{1 + \sigma^y\eta^y}].$$

1.3.3 Equilibrium under Discretion

We next derive the trade policy implemented when the government cannot commit. In this case, labor allocates based on the expectation of the tariff, and prior to observing the actual policy. Hence, when the policy is chosen, the government is forced to treat the labor allocation as given. In terms of the previous notation, $d\bar{\lambda}^e/dt = 0$. This has two effects on the government optimality conditions. On the one hand, the government neglects the production distortions induced by trade policy. Repeating the previous steps under the additional constraint $d\bar{\lambda}^e/dt = 0$, we can rewrite the government optimality condition as in (33), except that $y\eta^y$ disappears from the right-hand side (intuitively, the ex post output elasticity is zero, since all production decisions have been made once the tariff is implemented). On the other hand, the redistributive effects of trade policy now appear greater, since the direct effects of the tariff on P^y are not partially offset by the smaller reallocation of labor from y to x. Specifically, by (23) and (24), we can rewrite (34) as

$$(37) \qquad \frac{d\varphi^x}{dt} = \frac{(\varphi^y)^2}{(1 + t)(1 + h)} < 0; \quad \frac{d\varphi^y}{dt} = \frac{\varphi^y[(1 + h) - \bar{\lambda}\varphi^y]}{(1 + t)(1 + h)} > 0;$$
$$\frac{d\varphi^{y\lambda}}{dt} = \frac{-\lambda(\varphi^y)^2}{(1 + t)(1 + h)} > 0.$$

The signs of (37) and (34) are the same. But the expressions in (37) can be shown to be larger in absolute value than those in (34).

Combining (37) with the analogue of (33) for the regime with discretion, we obtain the equilibrium tariff when the government cannot commit:

$$(38) \qquad \frac{t^d}{1 + t^d} = \frac{(N^y/\bar{N})(1 - \delta\varphi^y)}{(P^yC^y/I)},$$

which has the same intuitive interpretation as (36).

1.3.4 Commitment versus Discretion

We now compare the equilibrium under discretion to that under commitment. By (38) and (36), there are only two differences. They both are due to the fact that the ex post elasticities that are relevant under discretion differ from the ex ante elasticities that matter when the government can commit. First, the ex post elasticity of the wage differential is equal to unity. Hence, $\eta^w = 1$ in (38) but not in (36). This is because if the government cannot commit, it sets policy after the labor reallocation is completed. Hence, the redistributive effects of the tariff are not offset by a smaller reallocation of labor away from the injured sector, and the wage differential moves in the same proportion as the tariff. Second, the ex post elasticity of output supply is zero. Hence, $\eta^y = 0$ in (38) but not in (36). Again, this is because under discretion the government sets policy after production decisions have been made.

Since under commitment $\eta^w < 1$ and $\eta^y > 0$, equations (38) and (36) imply that $t^d > t^c$: The government provides more protection under discretion than under commitment. In equilibrium, however, the private sector correctly anticipates the trade policy decisions, so that any hope of actually using policy discretion to surprise the private sector is futile. Hence, the government welfare is higher with commitments than under discretion, since the latter equilibrium involves an excessive amount of protection. This and other normative issues are further addressed in Staiger and Tabellini (1987).

1.4   Empirical Methodology

In this section we discuss the framework within which our assessment of the empirical importance of discretion in the determination of trade policy will be carried out. To motivate our empirical methodology, we employ the distributional assumption on λ to rewrite the expression for the optimal tariff under commitment in (36) as

$$(39) \qquad \frac{t^c}{1 + t^c} = \left[\frac{(N^y/\bar{N})(1 - \delta\varphi^y)}{(P^yC^y/I)}\right]\left[\frac{1}{1/\eta^w + \sigma^y\theta^y}\right],$$

where θ^y is the wage bill divided by the value of output in sector y. Comparing (39) with (38), the optimal tariff under commitment will lie further below its discretionary level the smaller is the ex ante redistributive effect of the tariff (η^w) and the larger the output share of consumption (σ^y) and the wage bill share of output (θ^y). These last two effects can be understood by recalling that under commitment the government takes into account the distortionary effect of its policies not only on consumption decisions but on labor allocation decisions as well, and through these on production decisions, while under discretion the government only takes into account the distortionary impact of its policies on consumption decisions; hence, the greater is the importance of labor in output (θ^y) and the greater is output relative to consumption (σ^y), the greater is the impact of this difference on tariff choices in the two environments. Finally, under the assumption that $f''(\cdot)$ is sufficiently close to zero, η^w

takes on a value of approximately one.[6] With this last simplifying assumption, and taking logs of (38) and (39), the optimal tariff under discretion is given by

$$(40) \qquad \ell n\!\left(\frac{t^d}{1 + t^d}\right) = \ell n(N^y/\bar{N}) + \ell n(1 - \delta\varphi^y) - \ell n(P^yC^y/I)$$

and under commitment given by

$$(41) \qquad \ell n\!\left(\frac{t^c}{1 + t^c}\right) \doteq \ell n(N^y/\bar{N}) + \ell n(1 - \delta\varphi^y) - \ell n(P^yC^y/I) - \sigma^y\theta^y.$$

Thus, (40) and (41) suggest a simple test for whether the degree of policy discretion matters; namely, to check whether the last term on the right-hand side of (41), $\sigma^y\theta^y$, enters as a significant explanatory variable in the tariff choices. According to our theory, it should have a negative and significant coefficient only if the government can enter binding commitments. The next two sections describe how we carry out this test.

1.5   Tariff Setting under Section 201 and the Tokyo Round

In this section we argue that tariff decisions made under the escape clause and exclusions granted from formula cuts under the Tokyo Round correspond roughly to the model outlined in section 1.3, with the former decisions reflecting a high degree of government discretion relative to the latter. Our approach is to analyze decisions made in these two environments within the framework provided by (40) and (41) and to test for evidence that the degree of discretion matters in the determination of tariff policy.

In one sense, the determination of escape-clause tariffs and the determination of exclusions from the Tokyo Round tariff-cutting rules represent the same conceptual experiment. In each case, an initial drop in the domestic price level for a particular sector had occurred (or was expected to occur), and the government was faced with a decision as to how to respond to this event. In the case of an escape-clause decision, the initial drop in the domestic price level would not typically have been policy-induced (the 1974 act dropped the requirement existing in the Trade Act of 1962 that trade concessions be the major cause of increased imports). In the case of determining Tokyo Round exclusions, the (expected) price drop was a direct result of the agreed-upon (Swiss) tariff-cutting rule. In both cases, given the initial sectoral injury (or

---

6. Explicit calculation yields the following expression for η^w:

$$\eta^w = 1/[1 - N^x\left(\frac{f''(N^y)}{f'(N^y)} + \bar{x}\frac{f''(N^x)}{f'(N^x)}\right)],$$

with η^w approaching one from below as $f''(\cdot)$ approaches zero. Thus, with $f''(\cdot)$ close to zero, the difference between the optimal tariff under commitment and that under discretion is due primarily to the perceived difference in distortions (rather than redistributive effects) brought about by the tariff.

expected injury), the government was then faced with the decision of choosing a tariff response: in the case of escape-clause action the tariff response would be set directly, while in the case of the Tokyo Round exclusions the tariff response would be chosen indirectly by setting an exclusion from the agreed-upon tariff reductions. In both cases, the government could anticipate that any action it took would be met by reciprocal responses from foreign trading partners: Article XIX of the GATT provides for this explicitly in the context of escape-clause actions (see Richardson 1988), while the give and take between governments in arriving at exclusions from the Tokyo Round tariff cuts is well documented (see Baldwin and Clarke 1987).

There are, however, three potentially important differences between these decision-making environments. The first concerns differences in the *constraints* under which the government operated. The second concerns possible differences in the perception of the degree of *permanence* of the government decision in each case. And the third concerns the degree of government *discretion* in each case and the timing of government decisions relative to those of the private sector.

As to the first, in escape-clause decisions the government was constrained not to lower tariffs below their current level. This constraint was absent when exclusions were determined to the Tokyo Round tariff-cutting rule. In fact, Baldwin and Clarke (1987) note that during the determination process the United States did offer "negative exclusions" (i.e., tariff cuts which were of greater magnitude than the tariff-cutting rule) on a range of low-tariff products. We will attempt to control for this difference in the empirical work to follow by restricting our attention when considering the Tokyo Round exclusions to sectors in which pre-Tokyo round tariffs exceeded 5 percent.[7] A related point concerns the possibility that the government could set exclusions from the Tokyo Round reductions with a more general equilibrium view in mind than would be possible in the context of the sector-by-sector decisions under escape clause actions. However, as Baldwin and Clarke (1987, 259, n. 1) note, "The procedure for determining what items would not be subject to the tariff-cutting rule and what withdrawals would be made in response to the other countries' exceptions was similar to traditional item-by-item negotiation." This suggests that general equilibrium considerations were not an important element in the determination of exclusions from the negotiated tariff reductions of the Tokyo Round.

As to the second difference, the Tokyo Round exclusions, once set, were in principle not explicitly meant to be temporary, while an escape-clause action is in principle an explicitly temporary measure, with its termination or decline contemplated from year to year. However, in practice, the differences in the duration of tariff responses under the two regimes is less pronounced. The mean duration of episodes of escape-clause protection initiated since 1975 is

7. Baldwin (1985) adopts a similar procedure.

approximately five years. The conclusion of the Tokyo Round negotiations in 1979 marked the seventh round of multilateral trade-barrier reductions that have been negotiated under GATT auspices since 1947, implying that the mean length of time between GATT rounds is between five and six years. Hence, in practice, the permanence of the government decisions which we consider under the two regimes is roughly equivalent.

This brings us to the third difference in the decision-making environment, that of the degree of government discretion with respect to the private sector. It is this difference that we attempt to exploit as the basis for our empirical work. In particular, the negotiated tariff reductions of the Tokyo Round, including exclusions from those reductions, were completed in 1979, and were implemented beginning in 1980 over a period of up to eight years. Thus, the determination of the exclusion from the general tariff-cutting rule was commonly known by the private sector well in advance of its actual implementation. Moreover, any government reconsideration of these decisions prior to the period of "open season" renegotiation which occurred three years after the conclusion of the Tokyo Round required the impacted industry to file an escape-clause petition. Since the initial filing of a section 201 petition involves substantial cost on the part of petitioners, the government's opportunity for reoptimization is quite limited in this setting. This in turn implies that, when determining the exclusions, the government would be making its tariff decision *before* the great bulk of resources affected by the decision would respond and would have limited opportunity to reoptimize once private sector decisions were made.

The procedure for setting escape-clause tariffs, on the other hand, offers the government ample opportunity to reoptimize once private sector decisions have been made. Because some degree of injury must precede the filing of a section 201 petition that has any hope of getting to the president, many of the allocational decisions of the private sector are likely to be made by the time the president determines the tariff response.[8] Moreover, escape clause tariffs are automatically subject to annual review, providing additional opportunities for the government to reoptimize conditional on private sector decisions. Even a presidential decision that protection is not in the national economic interest does not rule out a later opportunity to reoptimize; the law states that an industry may refile the *same* petition with the ITC provided that one year has elapsed since the ITC's previous report to the president concerning this petition.[9] Thus, the petitioner's cost of refiling is small, and the opportunity for reoptimization on the part of the government is accordingly large.

8. For example, in establishing the threat of serious injury, the law instructs the ITC to consider evidence of "a decline in sales, a higher and growing inventory, and a downward trend in profits, wages, or employment (or increasing underemployment) in the domestic industry concerned" (Public Law 93-617, 2 January 1975).

9. The requirement that one year elapse since the petition was last filed can also be waived when the ITC determines that "good cause" exists.

Note that this argument has nothing to do with whether escape-clause actions have "surprised" the private sector more or less than the tariff exclusions under the Tokyo Round. In fact, in our theoretical work the equilibrium policy involves no surprise. The question is whether, in determining the policy, the supply responses were taken into account by the government equally under these two institutional environments.

This discussion leads us to conclude that the most significant difference between the environments within which Tokyo Round exclusions and escape-clause tariffs were chosen appears to be the degree of discretion enjoyed by the government relative to the private sector. Hence, an analysis of the different tariff decisions made under the two regimes may provide evidence on the degree to which discretion matters in determining the character of trade policy. We turn next to the data and our empirical results.

1.6   Empirical Results

Our empirical strategy can now be easily described. We wish to estimate a version of equation (41) for tariff decisions made by the president under the escape clause and for exclusions granted from the formula cuts under the Tokyo Round. Our theory implies that the last variable in the right-hand side of (41), $\sigma^y \theta^y$, should enter negatively and significantly only in the Tokyo Round exclusions and not in the escape-clause decisions. Rejecting this implication would mean that the government has found a way to cope with the credibility problems of policy discretion, through reputation or otherwise. A failure to reject this implication, on the other hand, would suggest that reputation is not a good substitute for commitment and that policy discretion imposes a binding credibility constraint on trade policy.

However, in implementing this strategy we face a difficulty: We are not really committed to the assumptions about functional forms that are implicit in (41). Moreover, the theoretical model of section 1.3 treats as a "black box" the many political economy considerations which enter into our model through the parameter α^y and which are likely to be important in the actual determination of trade policy. We deal with this problem by checking whether our results are robust across several alternative specifications. In particular, we consider a number of variations on the simple linear equation

$$(42) \qquad t = \beta_1 + \beta_2(N^y/\bar{N}) + \beta_3(P^y C^y/I) + \beta_4(\sigma^y \theta^y) + \beta_5 \Gamma + \varepsilon,$$

where Γ denotes a column vector of variables that proxy for the term $(1 - \varphi^y \delta)$ in the theoretical model of equation (41), β_5 is the corresponding row vector of coefficients, and ε is a classical disturbance term.

As explained in section 1.4, the term $(1 - \varphi^y \delta)$ reflects the government distributive goals. As a proxy we use the extent of injury (that is, how far relative income in the injured sector has fallen from its status quo) and a number of different political variables suggested by the existing literature on the political economy of trade policy.

According to our theory, the tariff response should be larger the greater the fraction of the labor force employed in the injured sector and the smaller is consumption of the injured sector good as a fraction of total expenditure, irrespective of whether the government can or cannot make policy commitments. Thus, we would expect β_2 to be positive, and β_3 to be negative, regardless of the government's ability to commit. Moreover, and also irrespective of the ability to commit, we expect the tariff response to be positively related to the extent of injury. However, since only under commitment does the government take into account the distortionary effects of its policies on labor allocation decisions and through these on production, the tariff response should be lower the greater is the importance of the wage bill in output and the greater is output relative to consumption *only if the government can commit to its tariff choices*. We thus expect β_4 to be negative under the Tokyo Round and zero under the escape-clause procedure.

A complete listing of data sources is provided in the Appendix. While it is possible to obtain measures of ad valorem exclusions from the formula cuts negotiated under the Tokyo Round by four-digit SIC manufacturing industry, presidential responses under the escape clause often take the form of quantitative restrictions. Rather than employing various elasticity measures to convert these to tariff equivalents, we choose simply to treat the president's escape-clause decision as a 0/1 variable, and estimate equation (42) as a Probit model for escape-clause decisions. Of the forty presidential escape-clause decisions in our sample, fifteen cases ended in some form of presidential action (other than expedited adjustment assistance reviews, which were counted as no action).

An important issue of sample selection is raised by the fact that the forty observations of presidential escape-clause decisions in our sample were not generated randomly but were instead determined by the joint requirement that (*a*) the industry chose to file an escape-clause petition and that (*b*) the ITC found the industry to be facing serious injury or a threat thereof. If the random factors influencing the decisions at either of the first two stages are correlated with the error term in the tariff equation (42), as they would be, for example, if an unobserved industry characteristic influenced decisions at all three stages, then simple probit estimators of the coefficients of (42) will be biased and inconsistent. In fact, in a study of ITC injury determination decisions relating to escape-clause, antidumping, and countervailing-duty investigations, Hansen (1990) produced evidence of self-selection among industries filing for protection; the likelihood of a positive ITC ruling was found to be a determinant of the industry decision of whether to apply. Nevertheless, it seems unlikely that sample-selection issues pose a serious problem at the presidential decision stage, since self-selection in the filing decision is presumably more reflective of the likelihood of getting past the initial screening of the ITC than of a favorable presidential finding, while the ITC injury determination is itself logically separable from the presidential decision of whether protection is in the national interest, and determinants of the ITC and presidential decisions are as a consequence likely to be distinct. Thus, we proceed to estimate (42) as a simple Probit model, and postpone a more rigorous treatment of sample selection issues to future research.

The explanatory variables by sector suggested by our theory include the ratio of production worker employment to total manufacturing production-worker employment, the ratio of consumption to national income, and a measure of the sectoral shock, as well as the ratio of the production-worker wage bill to consumption.[10] As a measure of the shock for the escape-clause equation, we try the change in the import penetration ratio and the change in the wage in the period leading into the presidential decision; for the Tokyo Round exclusion equation we use the formula tariff reduction. In addition to the explanatory variables suggested by our theory, we consider a host of political variables discussed by Baldwin (1985). These include a measure of establishment size, four-firm concentration ratio, value-added share of output, employment, import penetration ratio, and average wage, as well as a number of dummies constructed to control for political differences (e.g., presidential party, proximity of the decision to an election date) and cyclical differences (e.g., aggregate trade balance as a fraction of GNP) across escape-clause decisions.

In estimating equation (42) for the four-digit SIC Tokyo Round exclusions, 1978 values at the four-digit SIC level were used for all explanatory variables, on the grounds that this was the most recent year of data that could enter into decisions completed in 1979. Also since as noted in the previous section, low-tariff products often received negative exclusions as a way of maintaining deep average cuts in the face of exclusions in other sectors, we restrict our sample for the Tokyo Round exclusion equation to four-digit sectors with ad valorem pre–Tokyo Round tariffs greater than 5 percent. For the escape-clause equation, measures of explanatory variables were taken from the relevant four-digit SIC sector in which the petitioning industry belonged for the year prior to the year in which the presidential decision was made.[11]

We begin with estimates of equation (42) in the context of presidential escape-clause decisions. Table 1.1 presents probit results under a variety of

10. Note that consumption here includes intermediate products, since it is constructed as sales minus exports plus imports.

11. In particular, we do not have data tailored to the particular set of industries represented by each section 201 petition. While in principle such data could be collected from the published case reports themselves, in practice the data published in these reports are irregular and incomplete. Moreover, it is not uncommon for the reports to provide four-digit SIC data when more detailed data are unavailable. While we plan to construct a more detailed data set in future work, it seems unlikely that the error introduced by using four-digit SIC data (as opposed to the specific set of industries within the four-digit grouping that were covered by the petition) could account for our results.

Table 1.1   **Presidential Escape Clause Decisions[a] (Probit)**

Variable[b]	Eq. (1)	Eq. (2)	Eq. (3)	Eq. (4)
Constant	−8.78	4.74	6.91	−7.29
	(−1.74)	(0.73)	(0.76)	(−0.66)
COMMIT	191.64	6.32	24.57	43.45
	(2.39)	(1.74)	(1.47)	(1.34)
PREMP	703.13	−0.39	0.77	0.67
	(0.60)	(−0.26)	(0.71)	(0.53)
CONS	2.49	2.80	0.42	1.53
	(1.37)	(1.51)	(0.45)	(0.97)
SHOCK	29.93	10.37	3.01	7.66
	(1.73)	(1.22)	(0.46)	(1.02)
REP201	9.56	3.13	1.31	2.63
	(2.32)	(2.11)	(1.97)	(1.80)
VALOUT	−65.88	−8.32	−13.67	−6.93
	(−2.40)	(−2.03)	(−2.09)	(−2.09)
IMPEN	28.00	2.32	4.71	2.01
	(2.47)	(1.98)	(1.84)	(1.53)
ESTSIZE	−28.40	−1.81	−1.44	−1.58
	(−2.06)	(−2.07)	(−0.62)	(−1.80)
CONCEN	0.04	−0.69	−0.02	−0.41
	(1.03)	(−0.76)	(−0.80)	(−0.48)
No. of observations	40	40	40	40

Note: Specifications: Eq. (1): all variables in levels; eq. (2): all variables in logs, except SHOCK and REP201; eq. (3): PREMP, CONS in logs, all other variables in levels; and eq. (4): COMMIT, SHOCK, REP201 in levels, all other variables in logs.

[a]Dependent variable: 1 if president imposed protection, 0 otherwise.

[b]See text for variable descriptions and differences among equations; *t*-statistics in parentheses.

specifications. Of the list of political variables described above, five were at least occasionally significant, and are included in each specification listed in the table. These include the import penetration ratio (IMPEN), the ratio of value added to output (VALOUT), average employment per establishment as a measure of establishment size (ESTSIZE), the four-firm concentration ratio for 1976 (CONCEN), and a dummy variable that takes a value of 1 if the industry has previously filed a section 201 petition (REP201). As Baldwin (1985) notes, industries with low import penetration ratios are unlikely to be viewed by government officials as attractive candidates for protection, implying that the expected sign of the coefficient on the political variable IMPEN is positive. Inclusion of the variable VALOUT is motivated by the "pressure group" model of tariff determination (Olson 1965); the smaller an industry's value added share of output, the larger will be the percentage change in factor rewards associated with a given tariff change, and thus the greater the industry's incentive to fight for protection. Thus, the expected sign of the coefficient on the political variable VALOUT is negative. Also, according to the pressure group model, variables such as ESTSIZE and CONCEN that are related to the ability of an industry to internalize free-rider problems should be important determinants of industry protection. According to this argument, the coefficients on ESTSIZE and CONCEN are expected to be positive. However, under the "adding-machine" model as put forth by Caves (1976), governments are more concerned with protecting industries composed of a large number of small firms than industries which are highly concentrated, suggesting that the coefficients on ESTSIZE and CONCEN should be negative. Thus, we have no strong prior beliefs on the signs of these coefficients. Finally, REP201 is included to control for any repetition effect that may be present.

The specifications presented in table 1.1 include (42) estimated in levels (eq. [1]), in logs (eq. [2]), and in the form which most closely mirrors (41)— $\sigma^y \theta^y$ in levels and the remaining economic variables in logs—with political variables in levels (eq. [3]) or logs (eq. [4]). The variable SHOCK is measured as the change in import penetration ratio going into the year in which the escape-clause petition was considered. The coefficient on SHOCK is always of the expected sign but never significant at the 5 percent level, although it is occasionally significant at the 10 percent level (this is also true when SHOCK is measured as the change in wage). The coefficients on the political variables VALOUT and IMPEN are always of the expected sign and typically significant. The coefficients on the political variables ESTSIZE and CONCEN are typically negative and occasionally significant, lending some support to the adding machine model. The coefficient on the political dummy variable REP201 is always positive and typically significant, implying that industries that have previously filed a section 201 petition have a better chance of receiving escape clause protection. The coefficients on CONS (consumption as a fraction of GNP) and PREMP (production-worker employment as a fraction of total manufacturing production-worker employment) are often of the wrong sign but never significant, while the coefficient on COMMIT ($\sigma^y \theta^y$, which reduces to the ratio of production-worker wage bill to consumption) is always of the wrong sign and occasionally significant.

The first two columns of table 1.2 present the results of estimation when COMMIT is dropped from the equation, as is appropriate if escape-clause decisions are characterized by a high degree of policy discretion. The first column (eq. [1]) presents the equation in levels while the second column (eq. [2]) presents the equation in logs. Now, all coefficients take their theoretically expected signs. In particular, the coefficients on each of the economic variables PREEMP, CONS, and SHOCK take their expected signs, although only the coefficient on PREEMP is significant. The apparent unimportance of the cost of protection to consumers in the escape-clause decision (the insignificant coefficient on CONS) is consistent with the empirical findings of other studies of tariff determination and reflects perhaps a greater concern with producer as opposed to consumer interests in setting escape-clause tariffs. The uniformly poor performance of our SHOCK measures in the escape-clause equations is not

Table 1.2   **Presidential Escape Clause Decisions[a] (Probit)**

Variable[b]	Eq. (1)	Eq. (2)	Eq. (3)
Constant	2.37	8.73	2.68
	(0.98)	(1.91)	(0.73)
COMMIT	. . .	. . .	. . .
WAGE	. . .	. . .	−1.22
			(−0.11)
PREMP	1178.96	2.11	1174.72
	(2.23)	(2.33)	(2.23)
CONS	−0.70	−0.50	−0.68
	(−1.55)	(−0.80)	(−1.43)
SHOCK	15.44	5.10	15.51
	(1.58)	(0.70)	(1.56)
REP201	2.21	1.52	2.26
	(2.18)	(2.05)	(2.01)
VALOUT	−12.95	−4.73	−13.24
	(−2.12)	(−2.19)	(−1.98)
IMPEN	2.37	0.69	2.18
	(1.25)	(1.62)	(0.89)
ESTSIZE	−8.46	−0.78	−8.72
	(−1.44)	(−1.51)	(−1.37)
CONCEN	0.01	−0.29	0.01
	(0.25)	(−0.39)	(0.27)
No. of observations	40	40	40

Note: Specifications: Eq. (1): all variables in levels; eq. (2): all variables in logs, except SHOCK and REP201; and eq. (3): all variables in levels.

[a]Dependent variable: 1 if president imposed protection, 0 otherwise.

[b]See text for variable descriptions and differences among equations; *t*-statistics in parentheses.

entirely surprising either; this may in part reflect the fact that, as discussed above, the ITC sends to the president only those petitions associated with industries facing serious injury or an established threat thereof. Finally, the negative and significant coefficient on VALOUT and the generally negative but insignificant coefficients on ESTSIZE and CONCEN lend some support to both the pressure group and adding machine political economy models of tariff determination.

In summary, under no specification do we find the coefficient on COMMIT to be significantly less than zero, while dropping this variable leaves us with an equation that conforms reasonably well to theoretical predictions.[12] We conclude that presidential escape-clause decisions appear to conform to the predictions of a model in which tariffs are set without the ability to commit.

We turn next to analogous estimates for the exclusions to the formula cuts

12. We also experimented with dropping variables other than COMMIT from the estimating equation. In all specifications, the coefficient on COMMIT was never found to be significant and of the right sign.

negotiated in the Tokyo Round. Here we have ad valorem exclusion measures for 369 four-digit SIC sectors, and can thus estimate equation (42) by OLS rather than Probit. The Swiss formula for determining post–Tokyo Round tariffs was $z = (14x)/(14 + x)$, where x is the pre–Tokyo Round ad valorem tariff and z is the post–Tokyo Round tariff. Thus, for instance, a sector whose pre–Tokyo Round ad valorem tariff was 14 percent would, according to the Swiss rule, receive a seven percentage-point reduction in its ad valorem tariff as a result of the Tokyo Round. If, after exclusions, the actual tariff change emerging from the Tokyo Round for that sector was, say, a three percentage-point reduction in the pre–Tokyo Round ad valorem tariff, then the ad valorem exclusion from the (Swiss) formula cut for that sector would be four percentage points. It is this ad valorem exclusion—the difference between the post–Tokyo Round tariff and the tariff that would have resulted under the Swiss rule—that we use as our dependent variable.

As mentioned above, we restrict our sample to sectors with a pre–Tokyo Round tariff larger than 5 percent, leaving a total sample size of 201 sectors. In addition to eliminating from our sample those low-tariff sectors whose negative exclusions were used to balance the positive exclusions of other sectors, this also serves to provide a "minimum injury" standard associated with the Swiss formula cuts; all sectors in the sample faced formula tariff cuts of no less than 1.3 percentage points.[13] Finally, while the most natural measure for SHOCK would be the Swiss formula reductions themselves, these are likely to be endogenous, since the formula was designed to cut high tariffs by more than low tariffs (to achieve some degree of "harmonization"), and since the same characteristics that lead industries to enjoy high pre–Tokyo Round tariffs are likely also to enter into their ability to secure exclusions from the formula cuts. To avoid this problem of endogeneity and still make some attempt to control for the size of the shock, we have constructed the exclusion measure as a percentage of the formula reduction for that sector. As it turns out, our results are the same whether this measure or simply the ad valorem exclusion is used as the dependent variable in equation (42). Since the latter specification conforms more closely to earlier empirical work along these lines (see, e.g., Baldwin 1985), we present our results in the form of ad valorem exclusions.

The first four columns of table 1.3 present the results. As before, (42) is estimated in levels (eq. [1]), in logs (eq. [2]), and in the form which most closely mirrors (41) with political variables in levels (eq. [3]) or logs (eq. [4]). The political variables that were at least occasionally significant are the same as in the escape-clause estimation, except that REP201 no longer applies.

The coefficients on the political variables VALOUT and IMPEN are always of the expected sign and often significant. While the coefficient on CONCEN is never significant, the positive and sometimes significant coefficient on

---

13. While we do not present results on the full sample, they are roughly equivalent.

Table 1.3   Tokyo Round Exclusions from Swiss Formula Cuts[a] (OLS)

Variable[b]	Eq. (1)	Eq. (2)	Eq. (3)	Eq. (4)	Eq. (5)
Constant	0.013	−0.027	0.013	0.016	0.027
	(1.64)	(−1.13)	(0.91)	(0.75)	(2.71)
COMMIT	0.008	−0.021	−0.049	−0.050	. . .
	(0.19)	(−2.34)	(−0.85)	(−0.93)	
WAGE	. . .	. . .	. . .	. . .	−0.002
					(−2.21)
PREMP	0.567	0.016	0.008	0.007	−0.197
	(0.48)	(2.39)	(1.43)	(1.27)	(−0.17)
CONS	−1.205	−0.018	−0.008	−0.009	0.397
	(−0.74)	(−2.86)	(−1.58)	(−1.80)	(0.23)
VALOUT	−0.033	−0.013	−0.033	−0.020	−0.028
	(−1.80)	(−1.53)	(−1.75)	(−2.37)	(−1.90)
IMPEN	0.025	0.002	0.019	0.003	0.014
	(1.85)	(2.08)	(1.39)	(2.52)	(1.03)
ESTSIZE	0.015	0.008	0.015	0.007	0.018
	(1.42)	(3.26)	(1.44)	(2.81)	(1.76)
CONCEN	0.001	−0.005	0.001	−0.004	0.001
	(0.43)	(−1.17)	(0.63)	(−0.88)	(0.80)
R^2	.05	.15	.06	.13	.08
No. of observations	201	199	201	199	201

Note: Specifications: Eq. (1): all variables in levels; eq. (2): all variables in logs; eq. (3): PREMP, CONS in logs, all other variables in levels; and eq. (4): COMMIT in levels, all other variables in logs; and eq. (5): all variables in levels.

[a]Dependent variable: ad valorem exclusion from Swiss formula cut.

[b]See text for variable descriptions and differences among equations; *t*-statistics in parentheses.

ESTSIZE tends to support the pressure group model. When entered as levels, none of the coefficients on COMMIT, PREMP, or CONS are significant. However, when entered as logs, the coefficients on COMMIT, PREMP, and CONS are all significant and of the expected sign. The finding of a negative and significant coefficient on COMMIT in the (logs) exclusion equation, and the absence of such a finding for any of the escape-clause equations, suggests that the different degree of policy commitment across the two decision-making environments may indeed have a measurable impact on the determination of trade policy. Clearly, however, this conclusion is sensitive to the specification of our estimating equation.

To get a better sense of what the data is telling us, we return to equations (40) and (41) and note that an additional implication of the model of section 1.3 is that the wage level should enter negatively in the determination of the tariff response under commitment (through the wage bill W^yN^y) but should be absent under discretion (except possibly through the shock measure). Intuitively, all else equal, a higher wage reflects a higher marginal product of labor, and thus a higher elasticity of output with respect to employment, which reduces the tariff response under commitment but not in its absence. In fact, a comparison of (40) and (41) confirms that the wage level is the only additional information entering into the determination of the equilibrium tariff under commitment which is not present under discretion. Moreover, replacing the variable COMMIT with the wage level should have little effect on coefficient estimates in the escape-clause equation but should make of indeterminant sign the coefficients on PREMP and CONS in the exclusion equation, since by (41) the total effect of a change in N^y on t (both directly and indirectly through θ^y) is composed of two effects of opposite sign, and similarly for P^yC^y. In summary, denoting as WAGE the production-worker wage, (40) and (41) imply

$$t^d = t^d \overset{(0)}{(\text{WAGE,}} \overset{(+)}{\text{PREMP,}} \overset{(-)}{\text{CONS,.)}},$$

$$t^c = t^c \overset{(-)}{(\text{WAGE,}} \overset{(?)}{\text{PREMP,}} \overset{(?)}{\text{CONS,.)}}.$$

Thus, estimating an equation of the form

(43) $t = \beta_1 + \beta_2(N^y/\bar{N}) + \beta_3(P^yC^y/I) + \beta_4(W^y) + \beta_5\Gamma + \varepsilon,$

we expect to find the coefficient on WAGE insignificantly different from zero and little change in the other coefficients for the escape-clause equation, and a significantly negative coefficient on WAGE for the exclusion equation, with the coefficients on PREMP and CONS of indeterminant sign. Note also that the hypothesized relationship between the wage level and the tariff response is distinct from that which comes out of the "social change" model of tariff determination (Ball 1967), since this political model would imply that WAGE should be negatively related to tariff responses in both the escape-clause and Tokyo Round exclusion equations (reflecting the hypothesized desire to bring about a more egalitarian income distribution rather than simply aiming to preserve the status quo), while our model suggests that it should only appear negatively in the latter.

The last columns of tables 1.2 and 1.3 present the results of estimation of equation (43) for the escape-clause and the Tokyo Round exclusions. For each equation, only the results under a level specification are reported, since the log specification contains no additional information over the regression of table 1.3 (when all variables are measured in logs, eq. [43] is just a rearrangement of eq. [42]). The results conform to the model's predictions, and reinforce the tentative conclusions drawn from the previous regressions. The coefficient on WAGE in the escape-clause equation is never significant, and leaves the performance of the equation largely unaffected. In contrast, the coefficient on WAGE in the Tokyo Round exclusion equation is always significant and of the expected sign and, as expected, the coefficients on PREMP and CONS become insignificantly different from zero. Combined with the results presented in the previous regressions, we view these results as generally pointing to the empirical importance of the degree of government discretion in the determination of trade policy.

1.7 Conclusions

The debate on rules versus discretion has received a great deal of attention in the theory of economic policy, in macroeconomics, public finance, and trade policy. But the existing literature has focused almost exclusively on theoretical aspects of this debate. To date there has been little empirical study of how relevant the distinction between rules and discretion is in the real world and no study within the context of trade policy.

Trade policy lends itself particularly well to an empirical investigation of these issues, for two reasons. First, as developed in section 1.3, the theory yields very sharp predictions of how trade policy chosen under discretion differs from that chosen under rules. Second, and perhaps more important, trade policy in the United States is implemented under a variety of institutional arrangements. A major difference between some of these arrangements is the commitment technologies that they provide. Hence, by comparing the policies implemented within these different environments, one can examine whether or not the capacity to undertake binding policy commitments matters.

We have attempted to do just that by comparing trade policy actions taken in the highly discretionary environment of escape-clause decisions with those taken under less discretion within the context of the Tokyo Round. While our empirical results are far from conclusive, they are at least suggestive that the degree of discretion matters in trade policy decisions. Perhaps more importantly, our results signal the need for further empirical work before one can conclude with confidence that the degree of discretion does—or that it does not—matter in the determination of trade policy.

Data Appendix

This appendix defines the variables and describes the data sources underlying our reported empirical results. We do not include sources for those variables (e.g., certain political variables) which we experimented with but did not report. All the independent variables were constructed from data contained in the National Bureau of Economic Research (NBER) Trade and Immigration Data Set. This is an annual data set covering four-digit SIC manufacturing industries from 1958 through 1985.

All independent variables in the Tokyo Round regressions were constructed using 1978 values, except for the four-firm concentration ratio which was available only for 1976. All independent variables for the escape clause regressions were taken from the four-digit industry (or industries) associated with the petition, with the year being that associated with the month fifteen months prior to the ITC ruling date. Where a single petition spanned several four-digit SIC industries, we treated each four-digit industry as a separate presidential decision on the grounds that the president did often distinguish among industries or products of a given petition in the final escape-clause determination (e.g., Color TV [TA-201-19] and Non-Electric Cookware [TA-201–39]). The rule for choosing the year associated with each escape clause petition reflects our attempt to generate preshock variables and leads to independent variables that are measured generally one to two years prior to the year of the ITC ruling. We experimented with other rules, with no change in the results. The one exception to this rule was the four-firm concentration ratio which, as noted, was only available for 1976.

The dependent variables for the Tokyo Round regressions were constructed from World Bank data supplied to us by Kishore Gawande and Daniel Trefler. The exclusions from the Swiss rule cuts were constructed by beginning with line-item changes and aggregating up to the four-digit SIC level using 1980 U.S. trade weights. The dependent variable for the escape-clause regressions was constructed by assigning a zero to presidential decisions which ended in no action or expedited adjustment assistance procedures, and a one otherwise.

The variable definitions and their data sources are:

COMMIT:	ratio of production worker payroll to consumption (CONS)
WAGE:	average production worker wage, deflated by CPI
PREMP:	ratio of production worker employment to total production worker employment in U.S. manufacturing sector
CONS:	ratio of shipments minus net exports to GNP
VALOUT:	ratio of value added to shipments
IMPEN:	ratio of imports to consumption (CONS)
ESTSIZE:	average employment per establishment
CONCEN:	four-firm concentration ratio for 1976
SHOCK:	annual percentage change in IMPEN or WAGE
REP201:	dummy variable that takes a value of one if a president has considered an escape-clause petition from the industry before, and zero otherwise

References

Baldwin, R. E. 1985. *The political economy of U.S. import policy.* Cambridge, Mass.: MIT Press.

Baldwin, R. E., and R. N. Clarke. 1987. Game-modeling multinational trade negotiations. *Journal of Policy Modeling* 9.

Ball, D. S. 1967. United States effective tariffs and labor's share. *Journal of Political Economy* 75.

Buckler, M., and C. Almon. 1972. Imports and exports in an input-output model. *American Statistical Association,* Proceedings of the Business and Economic Statistics Section.

Caves, R. E. 1976. Economic models of political choice: Canada's tariff structure. *Canadian Journal of Economics* 9.

Dixit, A. 1985. Tax policy in open economies. In *Handbook of Public Economics,* ed. A. J. Auerbach and M. Feldstein. Amsterdam: North-Holland.

———. 1987. Strategic aspects of trade policy. In *Advances in Economic Theory: Fifth World Congress,* ed. T. F. Bewley. New York: Cambridge University Press.

———. 1989. Trade and insurance with imperfectly observed outcomes. *Quarterly Journal of Economics* 104.

Eaton, J., and G. M. Grossman. 1985. Tariffs as insurance: Optimal commercial policy when domestic markets are incomplete. *Canadian Journal of Economics* 18.

Edwards, S., and G. Tabellini. 1990. Explaining fiscal deficits and inflation in developing countries. *Journal of International Money and Finance.*

Hansen, W. L. 1990. The International Trade Commission and the politics of protectionism. *American Political Science Review* 84.

Judd, K. 1989. Optimal taxation in dynamic stochastic economies: Theory and evidence. Manuscript.

Kydland, F. and E. Prescott. 1977. Rules rather than discretion: the inconsistency of optimal plans. *Journal of Political Economy* 85.

Lapan, H. E. 1988. The optimal tariff, production lags and time consistency. *American Economic Review* 78.

Olson, Mancur. 1965. *The logic of collective action: Public goods and the theory of groups.* Cambridge, Mass.: Harvard University Press.

Richardson, J. David. 1988. Safeguards issues in the Uruguay Round and beyond. In *Issues in the Uruguay Round,* ed. Robert E. Baldwin and J. David Richardson. NBER Conference Report. Cambridge, Mass.: National Bureau of Economic Research.

Romer, D. 1989. Does the absence of precommitment in monetary policy matter? A simple test. Manuscript.

Staiger, R. W., and G. Tabellini. 1987. Discretionary trade policy and excessive protection. *American Economic Review* 77.

———. 1989. Rules and discretion in trade policy. *European Economic Review* 33.

White, H. 1980. A heteroskedasticity-consistent covariance matrix estimator and a direct test for heteroskedasticity. *Econometrica* 48.

Comment   Richard H. Clarida

I enjoyed and learned from this paper, even though I think the best parts are too short and some nice implications are left out. The authors are to be commended for their empirical strategy; I think they make exactly the right choice by employing exclusion restrictions to test their theory. The authors are also to be congratulated for explicitly incorporating distribution effects into their 1987 model. Before I comment in more detail on these two main parts of the paper, let me first discuss the role of discretionary trade policy in an economy in which ex post supply elasticities differ from ex ante supply elasticities, and in which tariffs are the only instrument available to the policymaker.

Richard H. Clarida is assistant professor of economics at Columbia University and a research associate at the National Bureau of Economic Research.

As outlined in section 1.2 of the paper, because under discretion the government moves after supply has responded to any expected tariff, the optimal discretionary policy ignores the ex ante supply elasticity to the expected tariffs. When there are only production distortions, the optimal equilibrium—time-consistent—tariff is increasing in the ex post supply elasticity: if the technology is putty-clay, the equilibrium tariff is zero, while if the technology is putty-putty, the equilibrium tariff is positive and equates the marginal benefit of reducing the production distortion with the marginal cost of distorting consumption. When there are consumption distortions, the optimal tariff is decreasing in the ex post supply elasticity. If the technology is putty-clay, the optimal time-consistent tariff ignores the induced distortion in production and is set to eliminate the consumption distortion. If the technology is putty-putty, the optimal time-consistent tariff is lower because the marginal benefit of reducing the consumption distortion must be equated to the marginal cost of the induced distortion in production. Note that there is no presumption that tariffs set under discretion—a putty-clay world in which firms "move first"—will be higher than under commitment—a putty-putty world in which firms can fully adjust factor proportions after the policymaker's "move."

I now turn to the authors' two-sector model of trade policy as a tool of income redistribution. In this model—which is a generalization of the authors' 1987 paper—the cost of changing sectors differs among workers in the import-competing sector. A fall in the price of imports redistributes income away from workers who are stuck in the import sector to workers in the export sector. Because workers differ in their cost of changing sectors, trade policy can influence the wage differential between sectors. The policymaker selects the tariff to maximize a social welfare function that weighs the utility of workers by their population share. There are three types of workers: workers in the export sector who stay there; workers in the import sector who shift to the export sector; and high-adjustment-cost workers who are stuck in import sector.

The optimal tariff—and thus income redistribution—depends of course on whether the policymaker has discretion in setting the tariff. If the tariff is set after workers have chosen their sector of employment, the optimal tariff is increasing in the share of employment in the import sector, increasing in the magnitude of the terms of trade shock, and decreasing in the share of expenditure that falls on the import competing good. Under discretion, the tariff is not influenced by the induced production distortion as measured by the share of wages in the total output of the import competing good. By contrast, under commitment, the larger the share of wages in total output, the larger is the production distortion induced by redistribution and, thus, the smaller is the tariff. Indeed, strictly speaking, the theory predicts that given the share of employment in the import sector, the magnitude of the terms of trade shock, and the share of expenditure that falls on the import competing good, the difference between the optimal tariff under discretion and commitment depends entirely on the magnitude of the production distortion as measured by the share of wages in the total output of the import competing good. Thus, because the policymaker's objective is to redistribute income to injured workers, the optimal tariff is larger under discretion than under commitment, because the induced production distortions are ignored under the former regime.

This result provides a key restriction that is sufficient to distinguish between a tariff set under commitment from a tariff set with discretion. Under commitment, the magnitude of the production distortion induced by a tariff should be negatively correlated with the level of the tariff once the influence of the share of employment in the import sector, the magnitude of the terms of trade shock, and the share of expenditure that falls on the import competing good are taken into account. By contrast, the level of a tariff set with discretion should be uncorrelated with the magnitude of the induced production distortion once employment, the size of the shock, and the induced consumption distortion are taken into account. This exclusion restriction provides the basis for the authors' empirical work. In my view, this is a real contribution of the paper because it allows for a simple test of the proposition that discretion matters in the setting of trade policy. In a regime such as the Tokyo Round of the GATT in which tariffs—and their exclusions—are negotiated over a number of years in advance of their implementation, and largely in advance of any private sector resource flows that occur as a result, an optimal tariff should incorporate the production distortion that will be induced. By contrast, the granting of escape clause (section 201) relief occurs only after a finding of injury to an import competing sector has been established by the ITC and thus, so it is postulated, after the bulk of factor supply decisions have been made. In such a regime, the "optimal" granting of escape-clause relief should not take into account the magnitude of the production distortion that has been induced by the expectation of the granting of the relief!

I must say that, while I applauded the elegance of this test, before reading section 1.6 of the paper I was skeptical that the outcome of such an empirical exercise would support the restriction that the share of wages in output does not enter significantly in the granting of section 201 relief, and that the wage share enters *negatively* in an equation predicting size of Tokyo Round exclusions. The empirical work has changed these priors, at least to some extent. As reported in table 1.2, when the share of wages is excluded from probit equations for predicting escape-clause decisions, the employment and consumption variables enter with the expected signs—positive and negative, respectively—are usually significant. When the wage share is included in the equations, nothing except the political dummy variables is significant. The results for the Tokyo Round exclusion equations are somewhat more supportive of the theory. To my surprise, the wage variable enters negatively in three of the four specifications, and is even statistically significant in one. In all equations the employment and consumption variables enter with the "correct" signs, and all three variables are statistically significant in one of the specifications (eq. [2] in table 1.3).

To sum up, this is a good paper. It develops an interesting theoretical model that is used to devise an elegant test of the role of discretion in the granting of protection. It applies this test to data sets that, certainly based on my priors, could have been expected to reject the predictions of the theory. I was surprised that a variable that acts as a proxy for the magnitude of the consumption distortion generally enters with a negative coefficient, since the conventional wisdom is that those who grant protection usually ignore the "hidden" costs that such protection imposes on consumers. My one particular complaint with the empirical work is that I would have liked to see all of the equations run *sans* the political dummy variables. If the results depend on any particular choice of dummies, this should be reported specifically. I will close with the following observation. It is often argued—sometimes by me—that presidential discretion in the granting of protection is valuable because a president is much less subject to the rent seeking of firms and workers from one particular state or industry than are the congressional committee chairmen who would be expected to draft the "rules of the game" in any regime in which the president's discretion is diminished. This argument overlooks the fact, documented nicely in this paper, that there is a cost to discretion, in that social welfare can be enhanced if policymakers can make binding commitments. Thus, it is not at all clear that costly discretion dominates a rules regime in which the rules are subject to rent seeking.

Comment   Michael O. Moore

Robert W. Staiger and Guido Tabellini attempt in this paper to evaluate empirically the role of discretion in trade policy outcomes. The project is based on a generalization of theoretical work they have developed elsewhere.[1] The generalization, like the earlier research, is insightful. Their attempts to test the theory empirically are more problematic, however.

The theoretical construct is offered as an alternative to political economy models to explain the existence of suboptimal tariff rates. The critical result is that a benevolent government with discretion will impose higher (and nonoptimal) tariffs than those in a regime of precommitment because of time-consistency problems. This prediction is also consistent with lobbying models in the political economy tradition; the more discretion vote-seeking politicians

Michael O. Moore is assistant professor of economics at the George Washington University.
1. R. W. Staiger and G. Tabellini, "Discretionary Trade Policy and Excessive Protection," *American Economic Review* 77 (1987): 823–37.

have, the more likely they might be influenced by lobbying efforts. In this sense, the *general* predictions of this model and lobbying models may not be empirically distinguishable from one another. This makes estimation based explicitly on a theoretical model all the more useful. Fortunately, the authors' model has an implication that a particular form of supply response will influence tariffs in a regime of commitment. There is no equivalent prediction from lobbying models of which I am aware. Consequently, testing for such supply responses has significant potential, not only in determining whether commitment matters in general but also whether this particular type, rather than political commitment, explains trade policy.

The authors go on to argue that a benevolent redistributionist government would prefer commitment because it yields lower tariffs and higher social welfare but is unable to do so because this policy is time-inconsistent. This seems at odds (at least on a casual basis) with many recent trade policy "reforms." Congress has moved to remove discretion from the hands of the president and the U.S. Trade Representative, most notably in the "Super 301" provisions of the 1988 Omnibus Trade Act. This change may have been instituted to force the government to precommit to lower tariffs but I have my doubts. Rather, it seems to be either a "backdoor" means of obtaining protection or perhaps a way to force market access through a commitment to retaliatory import restrictions.

This brings up a more general issue. The degree of discretion and commitment available to the government is not entirely exogenous. In the United States, Congress can choose how much trade policy authority to delegate and, moreover, how much it should tie its own hands. Naturally, one can argue that a unilateral announcement by Congress that trade policy will be nondiscretionary may not be credible in a final equilibrium. However, until the laws are changed, the government may have very little leeway in making decisions. Important examples of this include U.S. antidumping and countervailing-duty procedures. A more general theory (though clearly not the intent of this paper) might help explain why the "government" chooses to precommit in some policy areas but retain discretion in others. A related issue is why would some industries pursue protection through the escape clause and others through GATT-round exclusions. If firms can choose between them, why would any industry ever seek protection through a process where there is commitment, since, according to Staiger and Tabellini's model, they would receive lower tariffs.[2]

In the empirical section, Staiger and Tabellini use the results of their model along with assumptions about specific functional forms to derive estimable equations. They then estimate parameters for two policy outcomes, distin-

2. Insight into this issue may be found in M. Moore and S. Suranovic, "Lobbying vs. Administered Protection: Endogenous Industry Choice and National Welfare," *Journal of International Economics* (forthcoming, 1992).

guished primarily, they argue, by the degree of commitment. While this attempt is welcome (few political economy models have yielded specific equations to be estimated), the implementation has certain difficulties.

For example, the models derived from the theory involve the natural logs of both $t/(1 + t)$ and the explanatory variables. Since the major advantage of theory-based econometrics involves the derivation of specific relationships, the use of the *level* of t as the dependent variable is troubling.

The focus of the study is on the predictive power of supply-side responses in explaining tariff rates. The variable derived from theory, $1/\eta^w + \sigma^y\omega^y$, was unavailable because of data problems with η^w. Two alternative measures were proposed: $\sigma^y\omega^y = w^yN^y/P^yC^y$ and w^y. Some difficulties clearly arise in how to interpret the estimates associated with these "instrumental" variables. Discussion about the nature of the resulting bias would be useful.

The optimal tariff for both discretion and commitment depends positively on $(1 - \sigma^y) = (w - w^y)/w$, where w is the average wage rate. For industries with low wages, the optimal tariff is positive. Thus, this model provides an alternative to equity-concern models for why low-wage workers receive high tariffs.[3] This formulation also means that higher-than-average industry wage rates should lead to a *negative* optimal tariff. Given that some of the U.S.'s most protected industries have high wages (the auto and steel industries, for example), some interpretation of this result would be appropriate.

Perhaps the most problematic aspect of the empirical work involves the data used in the escape clause analysis. The authors choose to use four-digit level SIC data for explaining these outcomes. This seems inappropriate given that the industries must offer the International Trade Commission (ITC) much more disaggregated data in support of their petition. Use of this publicly available data might be much more helpful in prediction.

The authors have chosen two processes characterized by differing levels of precommitment. However, there are many other differences in these two procedures, involving different institutions and decision-makers. Consequently, one should be careful in assigning all differences in the empirical results to precommitment. One way to avoid this would be to analyze an alternative pair of trade policy outcomes, in particular the ITC decisions in antidumping/countervailing duty cases and ITC escape clause decisions. In the former, considerable precommitment is apparent. If the ITC rules affirmatively (assuming a positive dumping or subsidy margin), the result is either a duty, a price-undertaking, or a VER-type arrangement. An industry with a "good" case may feel confident that some protection will be forthcoming. With the escape clause decision, the ITC makes a serious injury ruling but does not commit

3. For the traditional reasoning, see N. Fielke, "The Tariff Structure for Manufacturing Industries in the United States: A Test of Some Traditional Explanations," *Columbia Journal of World Business* 11, no. 4 (Winter 1976): 98–104; and R. E. Baldwin, *The Political Economy of U.S. Import Policy* (Cambridge, Mass.: MIT Press, 1985).

the government to any action; the president makes the final decision. This pair of decisions has three advantages: (a) the same dependent variable would be used, (b) the same institution is making the decision (the only difference then would be the level of commitment), and (c) similar explanatory variables would be available.

Staiger and Tabellini have made a useful contribution in this paper, most importantly by deriving equations from theory to test for the importance of discretion. The particular implementation strategy has problems, in large part because of data availability. The final results would be more persuasive if they took advantage of available ITC data sets. Finally, other pairs of policies might be more appropriate for resolving whether commitment plays an important role in trade outcomes.

2   The Selection of Antidumping Cases for ITC Determination

Thomas J. Prusa

2.1   Introduction

One of the most remarkable changes in international trade during the past two decades has been the emergence of nontariff barriers (NTBs) as the new form of protectionism (Bhagwati 1988; Page 1987). Voluntary export restraints, orderly marketing arrangements, countervailing duty complaints, and antidumping actions are the most commonly used weapons of the new protectionism. Of specific interest for this paper is the widespread popularity of antidumping actions. While it is generally agreed that countervailing duty and antidumping laws have a legitimate role in maintaining "free and fair" trade, there is growing fear that such laws have been used to unfairly impede trade and harass rival foreign suppliers.

Bhagwati (1988) argues that the design and implementation of antidumping law have encouraged its strategic use. For instance, the Commerce Department's procedures for calculating dumping margins can lead to positive margins even though the average sales price across countries is the same. Domestic industries are not penalized for filing "frivolous" cases, and therefore are more likely to file with the intent to harass their rivals. Most importantly, since many actions are settled (i.e., involve some type of price or quantity agreement), merely analyzing the incidence of antidumping duties greatly understates the true trade distortion. Messerlin (1988, 1989) and Prusa (1988) have shown that on average withdrawn cases are at least as restrictive as cases that actually result in duties. This is an important result, implying that in practice

Thomas J. Prusa is assistant professor of economics at State University of New York at Stony Brook.

The author is grateful to John Caputo for excellent research assistance. He would like to thank Bob Baldwin, Jim Brown, Wendy Hansen, Audrey Light, Tracy Murray, and Bob Stern for their advice and comments. Gary Horlick also provided valuable assistance. The American Council of Learned Societies provided financial assistance. All remaining errors are the author's.

antidumping law is far more protective than is typically measured. As we will discuss further in section 2.2, there are many reasons why a petition could be withdrawn, some of which do not have any implication on the firms' pricing practices. But many others imply that prices for the goods involved will increase.

While economists are beginning to understand the implications of such petition withdrawals (Prusa 1988; Staiger and Wolak 1988, 1991), there has not been a systematic analysis of what determines whether a case will be withdrawn or whether the International Trade Commission (ITC) will make the final decision. The purpose of this paper is to perform such an analysis. Since many (but not all) of the petition withdrawals have involved the steel industry, the simple answer is that cases involving the steel industry are withdrawn but others proceed through to the ITC's injury-determination process. Given that the steel industry has apparently entered a period of "managed" trade, we might expect the settlement issue to fade away. However, a closer look at the data suggests there are certain characteristics that seem to predict quite strongly how a case will ultimately be resolved. Therefore, I believe it is better to think of the steel industry as a special case of a more general phenomenon. The analysis also reveals that the way in which an industry uses antidumping law (i.e., filing patterns, countries involved, etc.) strongly influences the outcome. Since many other industries also feature the same characteristics that apparently lead to settled outcomes, it is likely that we will continue to observe a large number of antidumping cases being withdrawn.

In particular, an antidumping investigation is best thought of as a two-stage decision problem. At the first stage the industry (or the U.S. Trade Representative) decides whether to settle the case. If the case is settled, the ITC never has to make its final injury decision. However, if the case is not settled, the ITC will make its final decision. One advantage of this model is that we can partially capture the dynamics of the first-stage decision problem. In particular, if we find that the characteristics (e.g., high unemployment, low capacity utilization) which influence the ITC's final decision also lead to settlements (suggesting the foreign industry settles because it realizes it will inevitably lose its case), then the welfare implications of such settlements may not be particularly adverse. If on the other hand, we find that political pressure plays the major role in determining whether a case is settled (independent of the injury criteria), then the welfare implications of such agreements are much more unfavorable.

The paper proceeds as follows. Section 2.2 discusses the institutional background of U.S. antidumping law and provides a broad description of its use during the past decade. Section 2.3 discusses the political pressures and economic criteria that may affect how a case is resolved and examines the relationship between political and economic variables and case outcomes. Section 2.4 tests more formally these relationships, using a nested logit model to analyze the decision problem. Section 2.5 provides concluding comments and discussion.

2.2   Antidumping Law: The Statute and Recent Trends

The purpose of this brief summary of antidumping law is to highlight the relevant aspects for this study. For a more in depth presentation, Jackson and Vermulst (1989) provide an excellent and up-to-date discussion, especially for those concerned with legal issues. Note also that since the Trade Agreement Act of 1979 made significant changes to U.S. antidumping law, this discussion will focus only on actions during the 1980s.

Simply put, "dumping" describes the sale of products for export at a price less than the price for which those products are sold in the home market (the "normal" price). While such a simple definition is adequate for this paper, one should be aware that as applied, the concept of dumping is extremely complicated. For instance, there are adjustments if there are too few home market sales, adjustments if the country is a nonmarket economy, and adjustments if sales are made below cost. For many studies these various complications are important considerations, but for the approach taken in this paper it is convenient if we think of dumping in its simplest terms.

Typically an industry, or some group representing an industry (e.g., a trade association or union), simultaneously files a petition with the Commerce Department's International Trade Administration (ITA) and with the ITC. In order for duties to be levied against the foreign industry, the ITA must determine that goods have been sold at less than fair value (LTFV) and the ITC must determine that the domestic industry has been or is threatened with material injury by reason of dumped imports. It is noteworthy that each petition is filed against a single country. However, if the domestic industry believes that several countries have sold at LTFV, it will simultaneously file a petition against each country. A multiple petition filing increases the likelihood of an affirmative injury decision because the ITC follows the "cumulation principle" when determining injury. The cumulation principle allows the ITC to consider the total volume of allegedly dumped imports from all involved countries. For example, if the domestic industry files antidumping complaints against three countries, each of which has 5 percent of the U.S. market, the ITC will base its injury determination on the injurious effect of a 15 percent market share, even if the dumping margins differ by large amounts. The more countries involved in the investigation, the greater is the volume of trade, and therefore the greater is the likelihood of an affirmative injury determination. Since 1980, approximately 70 percent of antidumping petitions have been part of a multiple petition filing.

Once the petition has been filed, the ITA and ITC each make a series of decisions. Within 45 days the ITC makes a preliminary injury decision. If this decision is negative, the case is terminated. Review of ITC cases suggests that the material injury standard is lower at the preliminary stage than at the final decision, and therefore cases terminated at the preliminary injury stage do not appear to have merit (see Moore 1988 for statistical evidence). The purpose of the preliminary determination is to filter out these "frivolous" petitions. If the ITC's preliminary decision is affirmative, the ITA makes a preliminary LTFV decision within 160 days and then a final LTFV decision within 75 days of its preliminary decision. A final LTFV determination is made regardless of the preliminary decision (i.e., the ITA's preliminary decision does not terminate the investigation). The chief purpose of the preliminary LTFV decision is to set a temporary bond rate that is in effect until the case is officially resolved. The bond grants the domestic industry temporary protection for the course of the investigation. If the foreign industry is found to have dumped, it forfeits the bond. If the ITA's final decision is affirmative, the ITC must make its final injury decision no longer than 75 days after the ITA's final determination. If the ITC's final decision is affirmative, duties are collected for a period of no less than two years. If the ITC's final decision is negative, the case is terminated and any bond paid during the course of the investigation is refunded.

At any time during the investigation, the party that filed the petition can withdraw its petition. There are several reasons why this may happen. First, a disadvantageous decision or a piece of unfortunate evidence might be revealed which leads the party to withdraw its petition. For instance, the ITA may decide to calculate dumping margins using a different set of adjustment procedures than was proposed in the petition. Rather than proceed with a hopeless petition, the petition may be withdrawn. Second, the U.S. government may arrange a quantity or price agreement with the foreign government/industry that eliminates the injury. Once an agreement is achieved, the U.S. government pressures the domestic industry to withdraw its petition. The 1982 and 1984 steel arrangements are examples of this type of withdrawal. Third, the case can be suspended if the foreign industry agrees to eliminate LTFV sales to the U.S. market. The 1985 semiconductor agreement is an example of this type of withdrawal. Fourth, the party may withdraw its petition on its own accord, without any clear reason why it is doing so. It is possible that such withdrawals are based on some type of private agreement between the foreign and domestic parties. Prusa (1988) argues that such agreements are provided antitrust immunity by the *Noerr-Pennington* Doctrine.

As this discussion indicates, there are a number of ways a settlement can be reached, and one should not infer that a withdrawal is an indication of an unsuccessful petition. In fact, a review of the cases confirms that at least 80–90 percent of withdrawn cases involve some type of agreement. Unfortunately, given the way the U.S. government reports antidumping outcomes, it is sometimes impossible to know with certainty whether or not a withdrawal involves a settlement. To keep the analysis as simple as possible, we will treat all withdrawn cases as if they involved some type of settlement agreement, and hence we use the terms interchangeably. Further, the analysis in the following sections only depends on the assumption that petition withdrawals maximize firm profits.

A look at recent trends in antidumping actions reveals that a surprisingly large number of cases (25 percent) are withdrawn. Table 2.1 presents a summary of antidumping actions by product description and year for the 1980–88 period. The broadly defined metals and metal products (MMP) industry has clearly been the heaviest user of antidumping law during the 1980s, accounting for nearly two-thirds of the 395 cases. Despite its heavy use of the law, the MMP industry has only had moderate success in (officially) winning its cases, obtaining duties in approximately one-third of its cases. However, this is a bit deceptive since the MMP industry has accounted for over 90 percent of the withdrawn cases, obtaining some type of relief in about ninety additional cases. All in all, no other industry has had as much success with antidumping law as the MMP industry. The chemicals industry is the second largest user of antidumping law, while the agricultural products industry is third. However, neither of these industries display the same propensity for settlements as the MMP industry.

Table 2.2 breaks down cases by year. It is somewhat surprising that during the entire time period only twenty-four cases were terminated by a negative LTFV determination. This is consistent with the belief that the rules governing the ITA's calculation procedures are biased against foreign producers. In contrast, showing material injury has proven to be more difficult. The ITC has rejected sixty-five cases at the preliminary stage, despite the fact that (*i*) the foreign industry's has extremely limited time for defense preparation and (*ii*) that the preliminary injury standard is less exacting than the final injury standard. This suggests that many frivolous cases are indeed filed. The ITC has also terminated an additional fifty-six cases at the final injury determination. Although there have been petition withdrawals nearly every year, approximately 60 percent occurred in either 1982 or 1984, the years of the steel arrangements.

Table 2.3 provides a regional tabulation of cases. All told, more than fifty countries have been charged with dumping, with seven countries accounting for nearly 50 percent of the cases.[1] Japan has been the country most often alleged to have dumped, although the EC (as a region) has been involved in far more cases. The incidence of duties levied is probably the most striking difference between Japan and the EC: more than 50 percent of cases against Japanese firms have resulted in duties, while the corresponding rate for EC firms is only 18 percent. However, when one adjusts for the number of cases withdrawn, the incidence of successful cases against the EC and Japan is not terribly different. The fact that Japan is less inclined to settle antidumping

---

1. Japan, West Germany, Taiwan, Italy, Canada, Brazil, and South Korea are the countries most often involved (in descending order).

Table 2.1   Antidumping Case Summary, 1980–1988, by TSUSA Code

TSUSA Code and Product Description	Dumping Order	No Injury (Preliminary)	No Injury (Final)	No LTFV Sales	Withdrawal/ Agreement	Petition Dismissed	Total
100 Animal and vegetable products	12	6	3	3	0	1	25
200 Wood and paper, printed matter	2	1	1	1	0	0	5
300 Textile fibers and textile products	6	4	2	1	2	0	15
400 Chemicals	23	10	6	6	5	0	50
500 Nonmetallic metals	0	11	11	0	0	0	22
600 Metals and metal products	87	33	25	8	100	6	259
601–629 Metals	47	22	16	2	85	6	178
630–659 Metal products	17	4	3	2	7	0	33
660–679 Machinery	4	0	1	2	1	0	8
680–689 Electric machinery	17	3	4	1	5	0	30
690–699 Transportation equipment	2	4	1	1	2	0	10
700 Miscellaneous products	5	0	8	5	1	0	19
No. of cases	135	65	56	24	108	7	395

Note: See appendix for data sources. Excludes 16 cases that have not been resolved.

Table 2.2   **Antidumping Case Summary, 1980–1988, by Year Initiated**

Year	Dumping Order	No Injury (Preliminary)	No Injury (Final)	No LTVF Sales	Withdrawal/ Agreement	Petition Dismissed	Total
1978	1	0	0	0	0	0	1
1979	4	0	3	1	0	0	8
1980	4	13	1	1	10	0	29
1981	5	2	1	1	4	2	15
1982	13	18	5	3	23	3	65
1983	19	7	10	5	3	2	46
1984	8	2	10	6	44	0	70
1985	27	12	7	2	15	0	63
1986	44	8	9	3	7	0	71
1987	8	2	3	0	2	0	15
1988	2	1	7	2	0	0	12
No. of cases	135	65	56	24	108	7	395

Note: See appendix for data sources. Excludes 16 cases that have not been resolved. Nine of the antidumping cases initiated during 1978 and 1979 were not resolved until after the 1979 Trade Agreement Act took effect.

cases in a politically agreeable fashion is somewhat surprising, given its propensity for managed trade agreements; in addition, the heightened publicity surrounding official ITC decisions probably contributes to the feelings that Japan competes unfairly.

2.3 Political Pressure vs. Economic Criteria

The overview presented in the previous section showed that antidumping law has been used by a wide variety of industries and against a large number of countries. It also revealed that a striking number of cases are withdrawn. Figure 2.1 depicts the hypothesized decision process. At the first stage the domestic complainant and foreign respondent decide whether to settle. If the case is not settled/withdrawn, the ITC will proceed with its determination. For simplicity we will assume that frivolous cases have been eliminated at the ITC's preliminary determination and that the ITA has found dumping. Given the data presented in section 2.2, these are reasonable assumptions.

What factors influence whether a case is withdrawn? This paper will explore two hypotheses: self-selection and political pressure. The self-selection hypothesis argues that cases are settled to avoid the inevitable ITC outcome. Specifically, if the domestic industry files its antidumping petition (and the foreign industry defends itself) in order to increase profits, the petition will be withdrawn only if the profits from withdrawing are greater than the expected profits from an official ITC decision. Letting Π_w (Π_w^*) denote the domestic (foreign) industry's profits from withdrawing, Π_D (Π_D^*) denote the domestic (foreign) industry's profits if the ITC levies duties, Π_N (Π_N^*) denote the domestic (foreign) industry's profits if the ITC rejects the petition, and C (C^*) denote

Table 2.3   **Antidumping Case Summary, 1980–1988, by Region**

Region/Country	Dumping Order	No Injury (Preliminary)	No Injury (Final)	No LTFV Sales	Withdrawal/ Agreement	Petition Dismissed	Total
European Community	23	36	13	6	43	5	126
NICs	26	5	12	6	5	0	54
Latin America	19	6	7	4	16	1	53
Japan	25	6	8	2	8	0	49
Nonmarket economies	18	1	4	3	21	1	48
Canada	9	6	5	0	2	0	22
Other Europe	4	4	3	1	6	0	18
Asia	4	0	0	1	0	0	5
Other	7	1	4	1	7	0	20
No. of cases	135	65	56	24	108	7	395

Note: See table 2.1.

the domestic (foreign) industry's *additional* legal expenses if the case proceeds through the injury decision, the petition will be withdrawn if

$$(1) \qquad \Pi_W \geq \rho\Pi_D + (1 - \rho)\Pi_N - C,$$
$$\Pi_W^* \geq \rho^*\Pi_D^* + (1 - \rho^*)\Pi_N^* - C^*,$$

where ρ (ρ^*) denotes the domestic (foreign) industry's subjective probability of an affirmative injury decision. Clearly, $\Pi_D > \Pi_N$ and $\Pi_D^* > \Pi_N^*$. That is, the domestic industry benefits and the foreign firm loses when duties are levied. Further, we will assume $\Pi_D \geq \Pi_W \geq \Pi_N$ and $\Pi_D^* \leq \Pi_W^* \leq \Pi_N^*$. That is, the payoff or value of a withdrawn case falls somewhere between the payoffs under the other two alternatives.[2]

As the ITC's investigation proceeds, both parties will estimate ρ (ρ^*). The ITC typically cites changes in capacity utilization, employment, and import market share, etc., in its reports, and thus these variables will be used to estimate ρ (ρ^*). If the economic criteria indicate injury, then the parties will attempt to reach some agreement (i.e., ρ and ρ^* close to 1). Under these circumstances, withdrawn cases are self-selected based on their likely outcome. If self-selection describes the withdrawal process, then settlements have roughly the same welfare consequences (for consumers) as duties. In particular, domestic consumers will pay higher prices for the foreign goods because there has been a violation of fair trade principles.

In contrast, under the political pressure hypothesis, cases are withdrawn not

2. Prusa (1988) has shown that this ranking of payoffs need not always hold. For the present analysis, however, it is convenient to assume that the domestic industry's payoff from withdrawal is less than the payoff when duties are levied.

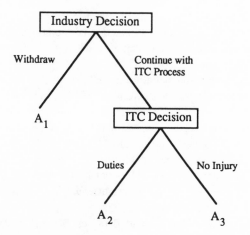

Fig. 2.1   Estimated decision tree

because the inevitability of the outcome but rather because it is in the political interest of the United States to arrange a negotiated settlement. An antidumping action might become a political issue if the filing involves multiple countries. The *threat* of duties being levied against a large number of countries elevates the issue into a major international dispute. In 1984, for instance, in response to the wave of antidumping petitions filed against EC steel producers, the EC threatened retaliation against paper, beef, and fertilizers (Howell et al. 1988). Obviously neither the United States nor the EC wanted a trade war, so they negotiated a settlement. In other words, the way in which an industry files its petitions can increase its chances for "negotiated" protection. Under this political pressure hypothesis, equation (1) need not be satisfied for a settlement agreement to be achieved. For example, suppose both parties know that it is very likely the case will be rejected if it proceeds through the ITC's final decision (i.e., $\rho = \rho^* \approx 0$). The domestic firm will agree to virtually any settlement since $\Pi_W \geq \Pi_N - C$; however, the foreign firm will only commit to a price undertaking if $\Pi_W^* \geq \Pi_N^* - C^*$. If C^* is small, the foreign firm will not be willing to offer a price undertaking (since $\Pi_W^* \leq \Pi_N^*$) and thus it is not likely that case will be settled.[3]

However, under the political pressure hypothesis, the foreign industry may be forced (by its own government) to offer a price undertaking even if it has not injured the domestic industry. By filing multiple petitions the domestic industry can force the U.S. and foreign governments to deal with a sectoral

---

3. If $\rho = 0$, the domestic industry may prefer to withdraw its petition (without any undertaking) to avoid spending C.

problem in the broader context of overall U.S. foreign relations; the mere investigation and threat of duties threatens trade relations and can lead to the imposition of a price/quota agreement even when it is unlikely that duties will be levied.[4]

The theory of "congressional dominance" provides another justification for the political pressure hypothesis (Weingast 1981; 1984; Weingast and Moran 1983). Under this theory Congress controls agency decisions via oversight committees and budget decisions. Members of Congress favor agencies who "serve their constituencies" and penalize those who do not. Baldwin (1985) argues that the structure of the ITC insulates the commissioners from undue congressional pressure;[5] however, Moore (1988) argues that because Congress has complete control (no OMB oversight) over the ITC's budget, Baldwin underestimates Congress's leverage.

Using different methodology and data sets, Moore (1988) and Hansen (1990) have both found that oversight committees exert significant influence on ITC decisions. One advantage of Moore's approach is that he uses data reported in the official ITC reports. However, this also severely limits the type and quantity of data he can use, since only cases with ITC injury determinations enter his analysis. In addition, confidentiality prevents data from being published for those cases involving a small number of firms. Because much of the data he uses is unavailable for many cases, his data set coverage is much more limited than mine. Moreover, since the cases that do not enter Moore's analysis all have a similar industry structure, his results must be carefully interpreted. Hansen takes a different approach, estimating the ITC's decision function for antidumping, countervailing duty, and escape clause cases for the 1975–84 period. Her data set is much broader than mine, but since the injury criteria for an escape clause determination is quite different from antidumping and countervailing duty determinations, her injury estimation does not have a natural interpretation. Furthermore, and most relevant for this analysis, neither Hansen nor Moore consider the (firm's) first-stage decision in their analysis, and therefore they ignore a sizable number of cases. The chief advantage of the approach taken in this paper is that by also measuring the influence exerted at the withdrawal stage, it permits a more precise characterization of the (potential) political pressure. For instance, congressional oversight committees could influence the likelihood of a settled case by (i) pressuring the U.S. Trade Representative (USTR) to negotiate a settlement and/or (ii) by raising the likelihood of an affirmative decision via pressure of the ITC. Further, there are a couple reasons why Congress would prefer protection granted

4. Howell et al. (1988) argue that steel quotas have been agreed to when it appeared that there would be a "no injury" finding.

5. Commissioners cannot be reappointed, they are nominated by the executive branch but approved by the legislative branch, and no more than three commissioners can be from the same party.

via petition withdraws rather than via ITC decisions. First, if members of Congress are risk averse, they would prefer the certainty of a settled outcome to the uncertain ITC outcome. Second, settled cases do not enter the official measures of protectionism. Thus, in the context of trade negotiations, Congress may prefer protection granted via unofficial settlements since it provides a veil for trade restrictions.

Before proceeding to the formal econometric test, one can gain quite a bit of insight into the data by simply examining simple cross-tabulation relationships among variables. For instance, to examine political pressure, I partitioned the data set into those cases with and without production facilities in states (districts) which had a representative on the Senate International trade Subcommittee or House Trade Subcommittee (table 2.4), the subcommittees that have direct oversight responsibilities for the ITC. Note that in this table (and all of the following) I focus only on those cases that were withdrawn or were subject to a final ITC decision. Also due to data limitations I was forced to drop eighteen cases, most of which involved agricultural products. A more detailed discussion of the methods used to construct the data series used in this paper can be found in the appendix.

If the null hypothesis is that these subcommittees influence decisions, then we would expect industries with oversight representation to gain protection more often than those industries without representation. Looking first at the top panel (Senate), it is clear that congressional representation has a strong affect on the withdrawal decision. Of the 106 withdrawals, 104 were represented by at least two senators, while 99 were represented by at least five senators. Virtually the identical pattern is found when we look at the House oversight subcommittee. Since withdrawals typically involve some type of protection, these numbers suggest that industries with strong oversight representation are more likely to be protected. However, in contrast with the Moore (1988) and Hansen (1990) studies, this table suggests the oversight committees do not exert undue influence on the ITC's injury decision. Overall, of the 175 cases that proceeded to the ITC, 126 (72 percent) resulted in duties. When we control for congressional representation, we find rather surprisingly that cases *without* congressional representation have a higher probability of obtaining protection than those with representation. Although the differences in conditional probabilities are not as dramatic as those for the first stage, they do suggest that if Congress does influence antidumping outcomes, the major effect is on the settlement process.

The data in table 2.1 revealed that the majority of withdrawn cases involved metal products and thus it is natural to explore this relationship further. In table 2.5, I partition the cases by whether they involve steel products and find (as expected) most of the withdrawn cases (87 percent) involve steel; however, the second-stage decision appears to be independent of whether the steel industry is involved. This is a bit surprising since a number of steel analysts

Table 2.4   **Congressional Oversight**

	Petition Withdrawn/ Agreement	Dumping Order	No Injury (Final)	Total
	Senate International Trade Subcommittee			
Senators with production facilities in their state:				
Cases with < 2 members	2	17 (81%)	4 (19%)	23
Cases with ≥ 2 members	104	109 (71%)	45 (29%)	258
Cases with < 5 members	7	62 (77%)	19 (23%)	88
Cases with ≥ 5 members	99	64 (68%)	30 (32%)	193
Overall	106	126 (72%)	49 (28%)	281
	House of Representatives Trade Subcommittee			
Members of Congress with production facilities in their state:				
Cases with < 2 members	5	27 (75%)	9 (25%)	41
Cases with ≥ 2 members	101	99 (71%)	40 (29%)	240
Cases with < 4 members	10	53 (67%)	26 (33%)	89
Cases with ≥ 4 members	96	73 (76%)	23 (24%)	192
Overall	106	126 (72%)	49 (28%)	281

Note: Numbers in parentheses are conditional probabilities (i.e., probability of affirmative [negative] ITC decision, given that case proceeds to final decision). See appendix for data sources.

Table 2.5   **Steel Industry Effect**

	Petition Withdrawn/ Agreement	Dumping Order	No Injury (Final)	Total
Cases not involving steel products	14	59 (69%)	26 (31%)	99
Cases involving steel products	92	67 (74%)	23 (26%)	182
Overall	106	126 (72%)	49 (28%)	281

Note: See table 2.4

have argued quite strongly that foreign dumping has greatly injured the U.S. steel industry.[6] However, if cases are being withdrawn because of self-selection, we would expect this result. For instance, if it was known that the steel industry received preferential treatment from the ITC, rational parties would take this into account when forming their expectations of ρ (ρ^*). Since the withdrawal decision will adjust for the industry-specific preferential treatment at the ITC, the steel cases that proceed to the ITC will have the same chance of obtaining protection as nonsteel cases, even though on their objective merits, steel cases could be weaker than nonsteel cases. Therefore, the

6. See Howell et al. (1988) for numerous references.

Table 2.6   **Number of Countries Involved in Filing**

	Petition Withdrawn/ Agreement	Dumping Order	No Injury (Final)	Total
Filings with 1 Country	15	51 (74%)	18 (26%)	84
Filings with > 1 Country	91	75 (71%)	31 (29%)	197
Filings with ≥ 2 Countries	22	75 (74%)	26 (26%)	123
Filings with > 2 Countries	84	51 (69%)	23 (31%)	158
Filings with ≤ 4 Countries	43	112 (76%)	35 (24%)	190
Filings with > 4 Countries	63	14 (50%)	14 (50%)	91
Overall	106	126 (72%)	49 (28%)	281

Note: See table 2.4.

independence of the second-stage decision from known variables (may) merely reflect that agents are acting optimally at the first stage.[7]

It was argued above that the practice of filing multiple petitions has become quite standard. Filing multiple petitions raises the international visibility of the dumping allegations, increasing the likelihood of a settlement. Table 2.6 verifies this. Over 80 percent of the withdrawn cases involved at least three countries. It is also argued that filing multiple petitions increases the probability of injury via the "cumulation principle." However, the conditional probability of an affirmative ITC decision does not appear to be affected by the number of countries involved. This suggests either that cumulation is not as "protective" as originally thought or that cumulation affects the outcome via the self-selection process.

We also expect that the economic criteria that the ITC uses to determine injury to influence both the first- and second-stage decisions. Tables 2.7 and 2.8 present data on employment, capacity utilization, and concentration ratios; a review of ITC case reports suggests that these variables play an important role in ITC decisions. A dramatic fall in employment or capacity utilization may reflect injury.[8] The concentration ratio serves as a proxy for the appropriability of the benefits of protection. Industries with high concentration ratios will not suffer from the free-rider problem that might plague more competitive industries and thus might be able to more effectively lobby for protection. Note, however, that other criteria such as import market share, exports, and inventory are also sometimes cited as important factors; unfortunately the unavailability of data prevented these variables from being used in this study. More will be said on this subject in section 2.5.

---

7. Priest and Klein (1984) formally develop this selection argument for litigation cases.

8. The ITC actually determines injury after controlling for changes due to cyclical changes in the overall economy. Therefore, one would actually like to examine the relationship between the changes in employment and capacity utilization after purging these variables of cyclical components. If the time series existed as monthly data then one could regress capacity utilization on GNP to remove the cyclical component. Because I only have annual data, I do not detrend the variables.

Table 2.7   **Economic Criteria—Distributions**

	Petition Withdrawn/ Agreement	Dumping Order	No Injury (Final)	Overall
	Mean			
Capacity Utilization (year t_0)	59.5	66.7	66.4	64.5
%Δ capacity utilization (between year t_0 and t_{-1})	−11.0%	2.0%	2.4%	−2.9%
%Δ capacity utilization (between year t_{-1} and t_{-2})	16.0%	−0.9%	5.8%	4.4%
Employment (thousands)	234.5	108.3	115.2	148.4
%Δ employment (between year t_0 and t_{-1})	−8.1%	−5.6%	−4.0%	−6.4%
%Δ employment (between year t_{-1} and t_{-2})	−7.1%	−4.0%	−5.4%	−5.2%
Final ITA Duty Margin	. . .	28.98%	30.32%	. . .
	Median			
Capacity Utilization (year t_0)	59	66	66	66
%Δ capacity utilization (between year t_0 and t_{-1})	−10.6%	−2.6%	0%	−5.6%
%Δ capacity utilization (between year t_{-1} and t_{-2})	0%	−3.6%	0%	−3.6%
Employment (thousands)	247.3	73.3	43.7	90.6
%Δ employment (between year t_0 and t_{-1})	−2.6%	−5.2%	−2.6%	−4.3%
%Δ employment (between year t_{-1} and t_{-2})	−3.3%	−3.1%	−1.2%	−3.1%
Final ITA Duty Margin	. . .	14.71%	17.58%	. . .

Table 2.7 presents the mean and median of these criteria, conditional on outcome. A number of insights emerge from this table. First, withdrawn cases have the lowest capacity utilization; however, if the case proceeds to the ITC, capacity utilization does not appear to be an important predictor of the final outcome. This pattern is consistent with the self-selection hypothesis. Withdrawn cases have also had the greatest fall in capacity utilization (during the year prior to the petition), which also suggests that cases are being self-selected on the basis of injury criteria. Second, withdrawn cases tend to be from "large" industries, having employment about twice as great as those cases that proceed to the ITC. This is consistent with the adding-machine model of Caves (1976) and suggests that industries with many employees are more effective lobbyers. However, employment does not appear to have any significant affect on the ITC's decision, which is consistent with Baldwin's conjecture that the ITC is insulated from lobbying pressure. It is also consistent with the argument that any measurable employment effects are eliminated

Table 2.8   **Economic Criteria Influence**

Cases with	Petition Withdrawn/ Agreement	Dumping Order	No Injury (Final)	Total
Capacity utilization < 66	33	84 (74%)	29 (26%)	146
Capacity utilization ≥ 66	73	42 (68%)	20 (32%)	135
Employment < 137	18	91 (75%)	31 (25%)	140
Employment ≥ 137	88	35 (66%)	18 (34%)	141
Concentration < 42	17	79 (77%)	24 (23%)	120
Concentration ≥ 42	89	47 (65%)	25 (35%)	161
Overall	106	126 (72%)	49 (28%)	281

Note: Numbers in parentheses are conditional probabilities (i.e., probability of affirmative [negative] ITC decision, given that case proceeds to final decision). See appendix for data sources. The partitioning cutoffs are the distribution medians. Employment is in thousands.

via self-selection. Withdrawn cases also have had the greatest fall in employment (during the year prior to the petition). Finally, the results in Table 2.7 suggest that the ITC ignores the dumping margin when determining injury since average duties are higher for "no injury" decisions than for injury decisions.

Table 2.8 partitions the data set into those cases that fall above and below the median value of capacity utilization, employment, and concentration ratio. The capacity utilization results continue to be quite consistent with the self-selection hypothesis. The employment and concentration results suggest that large concentrated industries are more able to negotiate a withdrawal than small competitive industries. However, as has been the case for all the other "predictors," none of these variables appear to be a significant predictor of the ITC's final decision.

2.4   Estimating the Decision Tree

The hypothesized two-stage decision problem lends itself naturally to nested-logit analysis. In the first stage the industry (or USTR) makes a binary decision whether to settle/withdraw (choice A_1), taking into account the expected ITC decision. In the second stage the ITC makes a binary choice whether the domestic industry has been injured (choice A_2) or not (choice A_3), conditional on the case not having been withdrawn. Since the econometric theory is well established my presentation of the model will be brief. McFadden (1978) and Hausman and McFadden (1984) are the seminal presentations of the theory; my presentation most closely follows that of Maddala (1983).

At the first stage, we will assume that the ith case's withdrawal decision is given by

(2)
$$y_i^* = X_i\beta + \mu_{1i},$$

where y_i^* is a latent continuous measure of the likelihood that the petition is withdrawn. However, we do not observe y_i^* but rather an indicator function y_i defined by

(3)
$$y_i = \begin{cases} 1, & \text{if } y_i^* > 0, \\ 0, & \text{otherwise.} \end{cases}$$

Equations (2) and (3) imply that the probability of observing choice A_1 can be written as

(4)
$$\begin{aligned} P(y_i = 1) &= P(y_i^* > 0 \mid X_i) \\ &= P(\mu_{1i} > -X_i\beta) \\ &= 1 - F(-X_i\beta), \end{aligned}$$

where $F(\cdot)$ is the cumulative distribution function of μ_{1i}.

Similarly, at the second stage, we will assume the ith case's final decision is given by

(5)
$$v_i^* = Z_i\gamma + \mu_{2i},$$

where v_i^* is a latent continuous measure of the likelihood that duties are levied. Once again, we do not observe v_i^* but rather an indicator function v_i defined by

(6)
$$v_i = \begin{cases} 1, & \text{if } v_i^* > 0, \\ 0, & \text{otherwise.} \end{cases}$$

Equations (5) and (6) imply that the probability of observing choice A_2 can be written as

(7)
$$\begin{aligned} P(v_i = 1) &= P(v_i^* > 0 \mid Z_i) \\ &= P(\mu_{2i} > -Z_i\gamma) \\ &= 1 - G(-Z_i\gamma), \end{aligned}$$

where $G(\cdot)$ is the cumulative distribution function of μ_{2i}.

X is a vector of exogenous variables that determine the withdrawal decision while Z is a vector of exogenous variables that determine the final decision. The μ_{1i} and μ_{2i} are residuals that capture unmeasured variables, case idiosyncrasies, etc. In this case, the observed values of y_i and v_i are just realizations of a binomial process given by equations (4) and (7), varying from case to case (i.e., depending on X_i and Z_i). If we assume that μ_{1i} and μ_{2i} are independently distributed we can write the likelihood function as

(8)
$$L = \prod_{y_i=1} [1 - F(-X_i\beta)] \prod_{y_i=0} F(-X_i\beta) \times$$
$$\left[\prod_{v_i=1} [1 - G(-Z_i\gamma)] \prod_{v_i=0} G(-Z_i\gamma) \right].$$

The functional forms for $F(\cdot)$ and $G(\cdot)$ in equation (8) will depend on the assumptions made about μ_{1i} and μ_{2i} in equations (2) and (5), respectively. Assuming that μ_{1i} and μ_{2i} are i.i.d. with the generalized extreme-value distribution allows us to write the discrete choice probabilities as[9]

$$P(A_1 \mid Z, X; \beta, \gamma) = p_1 = \frac{e^{X\beta}}{e^{X\beta} + e^{Z\gamma} + 1},$$

$$P(A_2 \mid Z, X; \beta, \gamma) = p_2 = (1 - p_1)\frac{e^{Z\gamma}}{e^{Z\gamma} + 1},$$

$$P(A_3 \mid Z, X; \beta, \gamma) = p_3 = (1 - p_1)\frac{1}{e^{Z\gamma} + 1}.$$

Given these probabilities, the log likelihood can be written as

$$(9) \qquad LOGL(\beta, \gamma) = \sum_{n=1}^{N} \sum_{j=1}^{3} D_{jn} \log P(A_j \mid Z, X; \beta, \gamma),$$

where $D_{jn} = 1$ if the nth case is resolved via outcome A_j and zero otherwise.

In many applications the choice of X and Z is restricted by economic theory. In the current application model specification is more open-ended. For this paper we will use the economic and political pressure variables discussed in section 2.3. Further discussion of this issue is found in section 2.5.

Given our model, the first-stage decision will be influenced by the expectation of the second-stage decision and possibly more directly by other political and economic factors. To distinguish whether a variable affects the withdrawal decision directly or indirectly via its affect on the injury decision, I will first present a variety of specifications of the withdrawal decision without altering the second-stage specification. Then, after the withdrawal decision has been adequately characterized, I will present a variety of specifications of the injury decision without altering the first-stage specification. Thus, in a sense the econometric analysis proceeds in two steps, since we first analyze the determinants of the withdrawal decision and then analyze the determinants of the injury decision. It is important to stress that each model specification involves reestimating the entire decision tree (i.e., both stages). Table 2.9 presents a variety of specifications that help clarify the decision process. The first set of regressions (models 1–6) concentrates on the first-stage decision, while the second set of regressions (models 7–11) focuses on the second-stage decision.

The analysis of the first-stage withdrawal decision reveals that the level of employment and the number of countries involved in the filing are the key characteristics of a case that predict whether a petition will be withdrawn.

---

9. In McFadden's (1978) original formulation of the nested-logit model, he estimates an inclusive value that weights the second-stage decision. In this application, since the Z vector is chooser-specific, the inclusive value is not identified. In this case, the nested logit is equivalent to a conditional logit model.

Table 2.9 Nested Logit Estimates

	Model 1	Model 2	Model 3	Model 4	Model 5	Model 6
First stage:						
Constant	-0.696	-1.702	-1.763	-1.401	-2.136	-1.710
	(-2.195)	(-4.534)	(-4.622)	(-1.774)	(-2.838)	(-4.395)
Steel dummy ($=1$ if steel)	1.005		0.180			
	(2.342)		(0.383)			
No. countries in Filing ($=1$ if >2)	1.104	1.333	1.281	1.387	1.336	1.240
	(2.851)	(3.930)	(3.126)	(4.315)	(3.926)	(3.277)
Employment		0.009	0.009		0.009	0.009
		(6.317)	(5.670)		(6.000)	(5.448)
Senate oversight ($=1$ if ≥2)				1.338	0.482	
				(1.712)	(0.638)	
%Δ capacity util. (t_0 and t_{-1})						-2.879
						(-1.929)
%Δ capacity util. (t_{-1} and t_{-2})						0.301
						(0.262)
%Δ employment (t_0 and t_{-1})						-0.378
						(-0.111)
%Δ employment (t_{-1} and t_{-2})						-0.237
						(-0.088)
Second stage:						
Constant	0.825	0.744	0.731	0.904	0.739	0.714
	(3.425)	(3.058)	(3.006)	(3.755)	(3.026)	(2.756)
%Δ capacity util. (t_0 and t_{-1})	2.037	1.466	1.482	1.884	1.456	-0.135
	(2.349)	(1.673)	(1.682)	(2.127)	(1.635)	(-0.126)
%Δ capacity util. (t_{-1} and t_{-2})	-1.458	-1.763	-1.726	-1.578	-1.715	-1.587
	(-1.679)	(-1.952)	(-1.857)	(-1.866)	(-1.888)	(-1.634)

		Model 7	Model 8	Model 9	Model 10	Model 11
%Δ employment (t_0 and t_{-1})	−0.241	−1.778	−1.904	0.683	−1.759	−2.031
	(−0.138)	(−0.997)	(−1.059)	(0.399)	(−0.985)	(−0.946)
%Δ employment (t_{-1} and t_{-2})	4.366	3.734	3.626	4.892	3.662	3.480
	(2.219)	(1.825)	(1.726)	(2.535)	(1.769)	(1.318)
Final ITA duty margin	0.019	0.016	0.015	0.021	0.016	0.015
	(4.093)	(3.258)	(3.224)	(4.343)	(3.253)	(3.009)
Log likelihood	−243.257	−224.034	−223.941	−245.162	−223.849	−220.195
% correct predictions						
First stage	80.43%	85.41%	85.41%	78.65%	85.41%	82.21%
Second stage	72.57%	73.14%	73.14%	73.14%	73.14%	73.71%

	Model 7	Model 8	Model 9	Model 10	Model 11
First stage:					
Constant	−1.683	−1.608	−1.740	−1.677	−1.683
	(−4.397)	(−4.040)	(−4.493)	(−4.372)	(−4.122)
No. countries in filing ($=1$ if >2)	1.263	1.081	1.341	1.263	1.282
	(3.643)	(2.672)	(3.692)	(3.637)	(3.671)
Employment	0.009	0.009	0.009	0.009	0.009
	(5.993)	(6.041)	(6.137)	(5.897)	(4.660)
%Δ capacity util. (t_0 and t_{-1})	−3.021	−3.152	−3.059	−3.008	−2.995
	(−2.474)	(−2.582)	(−2.464)	(−2.435)	(−2.441)
Second stage:					
Constant	0.737	0.845	0.558	1.001	0.215
	(2.980)	(2.979)	(1.916)	(1.947)	(0.174)
%Δ capacity util. (t_0 and t_{-1})	−0.204	−0.260	−0.336	−0.214	−0.540
	(−0.206)	(−0.260)	(−0.332)	(−0.217)	(−0.485)
%Δ capacity util. (t_{-1} and t_{-2})	−1.740	−1.637	−2.018	−1.699	−1.831
	(−1.920)	(−1.760)	(−2.240)	(−1.863)	(−1.957)

(*continued*)

Table 2.9   Nested Logit Estimates (*continued*)

	Model 7	Model 8	Model 9	Model 10	Model 11
%Δ employment (t_0 and t_{-1})	-2.014	-2.462	-1.139	-1.967	-2.753
	(-1.111)	(-1.329)	(-0.632)	(-1.082)	(-1.301)
%Δ employment (t_{-1} and t_{-2})	3.654	3.817	4.136	3.542	2.808
	(1.799)	(1.883)	(2.000)	(1.743)	(1.303)
Final ITA duty margin	0.015	0.015	0.016	0.015	0.015
	(3.093)	(3.130)	(3.237)	(3.037)	(3.020)
No. countries in filing (=1 if >2)		-0.291			
		(-0.830)			
Steel dummy (=1 if steel)			0.434		
			(1.296)		
Senate oversight dummy (=1 if ≥2)				-0.294	
				(-0.557)	
Employment					0.000
					(0.250)
Concentration ratio					-0.011
					(-1.090)
Capacity utilization					0.012
					(0.682)
Log likelihood	-220.256	-219.945	-219.404	-220.095	-219.617
% correct predictions					
First stage	82.21%	82.21%	82.21%	82.21%	82.21%
Second stage	73.71%	73.71%	73.71%	74.29%	73.71%

Note: t-statistics in parentheses. First-stage estimates Pr(Withdrawal); second-stage estimates Pr(Duties | No Withdrawal).

When regressed without employment, the steel industry dummy and senate oversight dummy are positive and significant (see model 1 and model 4, respectively).[10] A positive coefficient implies that the steel industry and senate oversight dummies increase the likelihood of a withdrawal. However, when employment is added to the specification both variables lose their significance, being dominated by the employment effect (models 3 and 5, respectively). Moreover, when employment is regressed without either the steel or oversight dummies, the results are virtually the same as the specifications with the dummies included (model 2). This may reflect collinearity between employment and the steel dummy, but it also suggests that although the steel industry has accounted for most of the withdrawals, the more general attribute that influences the withdrawal decision is an industry's size. Also, in all specifications the number of countries involved has a positive and significant influence on the withdrawal decision, which suggests that the "multiple petition" strategy can significantly increase the likelihood the industry will receive some type of protection (in the form of some price/quantity agreement). I interpret this as implying that the tension created by a multiple petition filing pressures the countries into arranging a settlement. Finally, in model 6 the economic criteria (which are known to the parties at the first stage) are tested for their influence on the withdrawal decision. The only significant variable is the percentage change in capacity utilization during the year immediately prior to the petition filing. The estimated coefficient implies that a fall in capacity utilization increases the chances of the petition being withdrawn. The coefficient on this variable at the second stage, although insignificant, is also negative, providing only weak evidence that cases are withdrawn because of self-selection.[11]

The second set of regressions (models 7–11) concentrate on the second stage decision, controlling for the first stage decision using the number of countries dummy, employment, and percentage change in capacity utilization during the prior year. The analysis of the second-stage decision reveals that (1) the economic criteria do relatively poorly predicting the decision, (2) the Senate oversight effect is not significant, and (3) the ITA's final duty margin is an important predictor of the injury decision.

Consider first the set of economic criteria. In all the specifications the percentage change in employment and capacity utilization perform poorly. Most of the coefficients are insignificant. This is consistent with both the Hansen (1990) and Moore (1988) studies, suggesting that although the commissioners state that these economic criteria are important, it is difficult to measure their importance. In contrast, in all the specifications the final dumping margin has

10. I also tested for the significance of the House oversight committee dummy. Results were virtually identical to the Senate dummy and are available on request.

11. I also ran other specifications to test for the importance of the other economic criteria (the level of capacity utilization and the concentration ratio), but they were not significant. Results are available on request.

a positive and significant effect on the outcome. This is a bit surprising since the simple cross-tabulation results (table 2.7) suggested that there should be little effect. Note further that the final dumping margin is the one key variable not known during most of the investigatory period. In model 8 the number of countries involved in the filing is included in the specification. It is negative but insignificant. A negative coefficient implies that, conditional on the case not being withdrawn, multiple petitions decrease the chance of protection. Model 9 estimates the steel industry's effect, while model 10 estimates the Senate oversight effect; neither are significant. In contrast with the Hansen (1990) and Moore (1988) studies, I do not find that the Senate oversight committee exerts influence on the ITC's final decision. This result, along with the results of models 4 and 5, suggests that political pressure is most significant at the first stage. This is consistent with Baldwin's (1985) conjecture that the ITC's structure insulates it from political pressure. Finally, in model 11 I find that the levels of capacity utilization, employment, and concentration ratio do not affect the outcome.

2.5   Concluding Comments and Interpretation of Results

In this paper I have argued that the history of U.S. antidumping usage requires we model the process as a two-stage problem. Given that approximately 25 percent of petitions are withdrawn (usually with some type of protection), a true understanding demands that we analyze the first-stage withdrawal decision. Because protection granted via a price/quota agreement appears to be so desirable, we must analyze whether the failure to arrange an agreement is a signal of the eventual ITC decision.

The key insight gained from the analysis in section 2.4 is that industry size and the number of petitions filed are the key determinants of the first-stage decision. Although the simple cross-tabulations (section 2.3) suggested that economic criteria influence the withdrawal decision, I found very little econometric evidence that the economic criteria influence the withdrawal decision. This suggests that the withdrawal decision is chiefly influenced by political pressure. Moreover, (1) the steel industry dummy, (2) number of countries involved in the petition, and (3) industry employment are all significant determinants of the withdrawal decision but are not significant determinants of the injury decision. This, too, is consistent with the political pressure hypothesis but runs counter to the self-selection hypothesis.

Furthermore, the analysis in section 2.4 also suggests that the economic criteria are not significant predictors of the injury decision. Although this result is a bit paradoxical, especially in light of the arguments and discussion found in the ITC's case reports, it is consistent with both Moore's (1988) and Hansen's (1990) findings, which suggests that it is difficult to measure the economic criteria (if any) that are truly related to injury. As discussed earlier, there are most likely other variables such as import market share, exports, and inventory that are used by the ITC in determining injury. The unavailability of these variables precluded their inclusion in the analysis. Future analysis would surely benefit if these variables could be constructed. The unavailability of these variables also makes the results a bit more difficult to interpret. If these "missing" economic criteria are well proxied by the "known" economic criteria, then this result, that economic criteria have little predictive power, will not be altered by the inclusion of these additional economic variables. However, if the excluded variables are not related to the economic criteria already used, then this result may not be robust.

The fact that I find no congressional oversight influence on the injury decision is an important and interesting difference between this work and that of Moore (1988) and Hansen (1990). This is most likely due to the differences in the data sets—Moore's analysis includes only a subset of all antidumping cases while Hansen's analysis combines countervailing duty and escape clause actions with antidumping cases—which suggests that it is too early for any general insights about the influence of congressional oversight committees.

If cases are withdrawn because of political pressure rather than self-selection, then the welfare implications of such withdrawals are disturbing. Antidumping law was conceived as a protective measure to eliminate the potential threat of predatory pricing. However, it appears that industries of substantial size can strategically manipulate the law (by filing multiple petitions) to gain protection when none may be warranted. The requirement that injury must be shown can be circumvented if the potential political fall-out is significant.

This analysis, along with the earlier findings of Messerlin (1988, 1989) and Prusa (1988), suggests that the filing of an antidumping petition may often be as strategically motivated as it is economically motivated. Hopefully these findings will encourage others to further study the reasons for, and the effects of, such behavior.

Data Appendix

1. Basic case information such as the outcome, date of initiation, subject, country, and the number (and type) of petitioners was found in the *Fed-Track Guide to Antidumping Findings and Orders*. Products are identified by their seven-digit TSUSA code. TSUSA codes can be found in the *Federal Register* notices that accompany each petition. The four-digit SIC code corresponding to the TSUSA code can be found in *U.S. Foreign Trade Statistics, Schedule 6*. Gary Horlick also provided assistance in determining which withdrawn petitions involved officially sanctioned agreements.

2. Capacity utilization (practical rate) at the four-digit SIC level by year

was obtained from U.S. Bureau of the Census *Current Industrial Reports, Survey of Plant Capacity.*

3. Total employment at the four-digit SIC level by year was obtained from U.S. Bureau of the Census, *Census of Manufactures, Subject Series.*

4. Four-firm concentration ratios at the four-digit SIC level was obtained from U.S. Bureau of the Census, *Census of Manufactures, Industry Series.*

5. Congressional influence was measured by matching (four-digit SIC) industry location with congressional districts. Typically, each product (identified by SIC code) is produced in a number of regions in the country. If a product is produced in a district whose congressional representative (House of Representatives or Senate) is a member of the Trade Subcommittee of the House Ways and Means Committee or the International Trade Subcommittee of the Senate Finance Committee, then I considered there to be a potential political pressure from that congressman. The *Almanac of American Politics* was used to determine subcommittee membership. Data for industry location by district and year at the four-digit SIC level were obtained from the *Census of Manufactures, Geographic Area Series.* An industry had to employ at least a thousand people in a district to be considered as potentially exerting political influence.

References

Almanac of American Politics. 1988. *Almanac of American politics.* Crawfordsville, Ind.: National Journal, Inc.

Baldwin, R. E. 1985. *The political economy of U.S. import policy.* Cambridge, Mass.: MIT Press.

Bhagwati, J. 1988. *Protectionism.* Cambridge, Mass.: MIT Press.

Caves, R. A. 1976. Economic models of political choice: Canada's tariff structure. *Canadian Journal of Economics* 9(2): 278–300.

Fed-Track. 1988. *Fed-Track guide to antidumping findings and orders.* Washington, D.C.: Fed-Track.

Hansen, W. L. 1990. The International Trade Commission and the politics of protectionism. *American Political Science Review* 84(1): 21–46.

Hausman, J., and D. McFadden. 1984. Specification tests for the multinomial logit model. *Econometrica* 52:1219–40.

Howell, T. R., W. A. Noellert, J. G. Kreier, and A. W. Wolff. 1988. *Steel and the state.* Boulder, Colo.: Westview Press.

Jackson, J. H., and E. A. Vermulst. 1989. *Antidumping law and practice.* Ann Arbor: University of Michigan Press.

McFadden, D. 1978. Modelling the choice of residential location. In *Spatial interaction theory and residential location,* ed. A. Karlquist, 75–96. Amsterdam: North-Holland.

Maddala, G. S. 1983. *Limited-dependent and qualitative variables in econometrics.* Cambridge: Cambridge University Press.

Messerlin, P. A. 1988. The EC antidumping regulations: A first economic appraisal: 1980–85. World Bank, Washington, D.C. Typescript.

———— 1989. *GATT-inconsistent outcomes of GATT-consistent laws: The long-term evolution of the EC antidumping laws.* World Bank, Washington, D.C. Typescript.

Moore, M. 1988. Rules or politics? An empirical analysis of ITC antidumping decisions. Department of Economics, George Washington University. Typescript.

Page, S. 1987. The rise in protection since 1974. *Oxford Review of Economic Policy,* 3(1): 37–51.

Priest, G. L., and B. Klein. 1984. The selection of disputes for litigation. *Journal of Legal Studies* 13:1–55.

Prusa, T. J. 1988. Why are so many antidumping petitions withdrawn? Department of Economics, State University of New York, Stony Brook. Typescript.

Staiger, R. W., and F. A. Wolak. 1988. Antidumping law as enforcement of tacit international collusion. Typescript.

———— 1991. The strategic effects of domestic antidumping law in the presence of tacit foreign collusion. *Journal of International Economics.*

U.S. Bureau of the Census. 1980. *U.S. foreign trade statistics.* Washington, D.C.: U.S. Department of Commerce.

U.S. Bureau of the Census. 1983. *Current industrial reports.* Washington, D.C.: U.S. Department of Commerce.

U.S. Bureau of the Census. 1987. *Census of manufactures.* Washington, D.C.: U.S. Department of Commerce.

U.S. International Trade Commission. various issues. *Annual Report.* Washington, D.C.: U.S. International Trade Commission.

Weingast, B. R. 1981. Regulation, reregulation, and deregulation: The political foundations of agency clientele relations. *Law and Contemporary Problems* 44:147–77.

———— 1984. The congressional-bureaucratic system: A principal-agent perspective with applications to the SEC. *Public Choice* 41:147–92.

Weingast, B. R., and M. J. Moran. 1983. Bureaucratic discretion or congressional control? Regulatory policymaking by the Federal Trade Commission. *Journal of Political Economy* 91:765–800.

Comment   Robert M. Stern

Let me begin by saying that I liked this paper very much. It is dealing with an especially important aspect of U.S. trade policies. Prusa sets up his analysis clearly, organizes the data well, and interprets his empirical results in a sensible manner.

Most of my remarks are designed to elaborate further some of the analytical and policy issues involved in antidumping (AD) actions, but I will also raise some questions about Prusa's modeling decisions, selection of variables, and interpretation of results.

In order to set Prusa's paper in context, it is worth noting that AD actions constitute by far the most intensively used of the available instruments of trade

Robert M. Stern is professor of economics and public policy in the Department of Economics and Institute of Public Policy Studies at the University of Michigan.

policy that are designed ostensibly to deal with "unfair" trade practices and import disruption. For example, according to Hoekman and Leidy,[1] there were 1,277 AD investigations initiated and 541 AD actions actually carried out during the period 1980–85. The chief countries/blocs involved were Australia (416; 138); Canada (230; 152), European Community (280; 122), Japan (1; 0) and the United States (350, 129). This compares to a total of 450 countervailing duty (CVD) actions initiated and 110 actually implemented, 23 escape clause actions implemented, and 120 voluntary export restraints (VERs) implemented during this same period.

These data provide some indication of the prevalence of AD actions in the major trading countries/blocs, and they also demonstrate as well the comparatively small use that is made of escape clause actions. It thus seems reasonably clear, as Hoekman and Leidy argue, that one can interpret the intensive use of AD actions as well as the related proliferation of VERs as an indication of the ineffectiveness of present arrangements governing the use of safeguards. This further implies that the resort to AD actions may have less to do with alleged dumping per se and more to do with market disruption more generally due to increased imports. If AD actions are observed to have important detrimental effects on resource allocation and welfare, the question then becomes one of how to reduce reliance on these and other measures such as VERs. This means finding ways to limit the resort to AD actions and/or to strengthen the use of safeguards agreements in the GATT.

Turning now to Prusa's analytical discussion, he notes that, for his purpose, it is adequate to use a simple definition of dumping, which is based on selling abroad at a lower price than at home. While this may be acceptable in a broad sense, there may in fact be important administrative differences involved in AD cases that are based on price differences as compared to those in which selling below cost may be the basis for an allegation of dumping. In particular, there would appear to be much more administrative discretion involved in selecting cost criteria and then calculating dumping margins based on these criteria. What I am wondering therefore is if it might be possible to distinguish the AD actions initiated according to whether they are price or cost based, and if it makes a difference as to whether or not there will be a settlement.

Prusa notes that there are numerous "frivolous" AD actions initiated that are subsequently dismissed by the ITC. He chooses to exclude these actions from his analysis. There is a difficulty here, however, since the very existence of the AD legal mechanism and the filing of actions may affect the behavior of foreign and domestic firms in ways that correspond to the effects of AD actions that make their way farther through the administrative process. A more careful look at the characteristics of the so-called frivolous actions might therefore be worthwhile.

1. Bernard M. Hoekman and Michael P. Leidy, "Dumping, Antidumping, and Emergency Protection," *Journal of World Trade* 23 (October 1989): 29.

Prusa puts forth two hypotheses—self-selection and political pressure—relating to the withdrawal of AD actions. He notes that multiple filings of AD complaints against several countries may be indicative of the exercise of political pressure. But there is a related interpretation of multiple filings, which involves the recognition by the complainants that it is in their interest to broaden their complaints as much as possible since it is known that more selective AD actions will work less effectively. Thus, the more countries that can be targeted in an AD filing, the greater the likelihood of success that the complainants may achieve in protecting their economic interests.

In selecting the economic variables to be included in his analysis, Prusa identifies especially changes in capacity utilization and changes in employment as indicators that are apparently used by the ITC. What he does not make clear, however, is whether these are the only important variables. For example, does the ITC pay attention to such matters as changes in industry or firm profitability, changes in sales, and the degree of import penetration? Are the variables that Prusa has chosen really the important ones? If so, do they serve as adequate proxies for other excluded variables? If not, is he missing some important variables? This latter question is pertinent since his empirical results suggest that economic factors are not of great importance in explaining ITC decisions.

In reporting his nested logit results for models 1–6 in Table 2.9, Prusa notes that the inclusion of the employment variable dominates the steel dummy. He then concludes that the results reflect industry size but not the special characteristics of the steel industry, which was a major AD complainant especially in 1982 and 1984. In view of the finding that the steel dummy is statistically significant by itself but not in combination with employment, isn't this suggestive of multicollinearity? And, if so, is it correct to say that the results do not reflect the unusual importance of the steel industry, which also happens to be a rather large industry in terms of employment?

The inclusion of the final dumping margin comes through as a statistically significant variable. Prusa does not have a ready answer as to why this is the case, since he mentions that the size of this margin is not precisely known until the final decision has been made. But isn't it possible that those involved have some notion of how large this margin might be in specific circumstances? The question, then, is that if the final dumping margin is found to be significant, is it acting as a proxy for some other determining variable?

A further question that I have about the results concerns whether it is possible to say anything about the goodness of fit of the nested logit model. In particular, can anything be said about how to interpret the residuals of the estimating equations? Along the lines discussed above in choosing variables, are there some important omitted variables that should have been taken into account?

It is interesting in conclusion to mention some implications of Prusa's paper that might be worth pursuing in further research. As noted above, the use of

AD actions is concentrated especially in Australia, Canada, the European Community, and the United States. It would be interesting in this light to consider whether Prusa could adapt his framework to investigate the determinants of AD complaints and actions in other political environments and to determine the similarities and differences as compared to U.S. experience. The same thing might apply in investigating the factors governing the use of AD and CVD actions and the relation of both types of actions to the introduction of VERs.

I interpret Prusa's main finding to be that AD actions are dominated primarily by political rather than strictly economic considerations. The data cited earlier suggest that AD actions have become increasingly prevalent because of the ineffectiveness of safeguards procedures. The issue, then, is that AD actions are being justified on grounds of alleged dumping, whereas the more fundamental problem is how domestic firms should respond to disruption from imports. In a setting in which there are structural changes in comparative advantage often combined with swings in real exchange rates, it is not surprising that domestic firms will find themselves under considerable pressure at given points in time. The challenge for policy thus ought to be the design and implementation of more effective safeguards measures and, at the same time, a movement to phase out AD measures or, as Hoekman and Leidy suggest,[2] to introduce more elements of safeguards into the AD measures.

2. Ibid., 41–42.

3 The Determinants of Corporate Political Involvement in Trade Protection: The Case of the Steel Industry

Stefanie Ann Lenway and Douglas A. Schuler

3.1 Introduction

In this paper we analyze the relationship between the magnitude of resources that a firm invests in trade protection and the changes in a firm's market value that result from the imposition of trade restraints. The study focuses specifically on trade protection in the U.S. steel industry between 1977 and 1984. The analysis is grounded in collective action theory, which assumes that firms will only invest in the political process if the expected benefits of their influence over the public policy process are greater than the costs of political activity (Olson 1971). Firms in an industry seek trade protection because the higher domestic prices resulting from the restriction of imports bring income gains in the short run when capital is relatively immobile among industries (Baldwin 1985, 11). Our concern is with the relationship between firm political activity and the change in market value of the firm within a single industry, not with the ability of the steel industry to overcome the free-rider problem.

Several previous studies of the steel industry have estimated the impact of trade restraints on the industry as a whole. Crandall (1981, 46) develops an econometric model of the impact of the trigger price mechanism (TPM) on U.S. import prices, U.S. domestic prices, and the import share of steel in the U.S. market. In this analysis he is specifically concerned with the responsiveness of U.S. steel prices to world market conditions and to pressures from imports. He found that the TPM raised imported steel prices by about 5 percent a year or 10 percent by 1979 and that aggregate domestic steel prices averaged 2.7 percent more than they would have without the TPM. Assuming

Stefanie Ann Lenway is an associate professor of strategic management at the Carlson School of Management at the University of Minnesota. Douglas A. Schuler is a doctoral student in the department of Strategic Management and Organization in the Carlson School of Management at the University of Minnesota.

that imports constitute 15 percent of the U.S. market, he found that the price increase of U.S.-produced steel that could be attributed to the TPM was about 1.1 percent (p. 111). He further found that the decline in the value of the dollar and inflation did more to explain the reduction in the market share of imports than the TPM. Crandall concludes that the TPM affected import prices much more than domestic prices.

Hufbauer, Berliner, and Elliott (1986) also estimate the effect of import restraint programs on the domestic price of steel. For the period 1979–81, they estimate that the TPM resulted in a 6.4 percent increase in the cost of domestic steel and about a 15.9 percent increase in foreign steel prices. They further estimate that by 1981, the gains from the restraints to US producers amounted to $2.77 billion.

Tarr and Morkre (1984) and Hickock (1985), using Crandall's (1981) estimates of price elasticities, have estimated the cost of an 18.5 percent import quota on total U.S. steel imports. Tarr and Morkre calculated the discounted present value of the losses to the U.S. economy over a four-year period to be $2.83 billion. The discounted present value of the gains to U.S. producers were estimated to be $1.52 billion while the quota rents to foreigners discounted over the four-year period were about $2.02 billion. Hickock concludes that the cost to consumers of reducing imports to 18.5 percent of the U.S. market would be about $2 billion annually. This is based on her findings that the restrictions will result in a 5 percent price increase on imported steel and a 4 percent price increase on domestically produced steel.

Tarr (1989) states that the proliferation of voluntary restraint agreements (VRAs) on steel imports costs the U.S. $600 million a year in 1984 dollars. This analysis does attempt to estimate the amount that goes to U.S. steel producers. Instead he argues that the U.S. could achieve the same level of import protection at 15 percent of the cost if exporters were not allowed to keep the quota rents.

A 1984 study by the Congressional Budget Office (CBO) analyzes the potential economic effects of a 15 percent quota on steel imports, predicting that from 1985 to 1989, $12.5 billion (1982 dollars) would be transferred to domestic producers. This amount reflects the increase in revenues to firms able to sell their pre-quota amounts of steel at the higher post-quota prices. By 1989, according to the study, domestic producers would be able to charge $51 a ton above the no-quota price (1984, 43).

All the above studies suggest that the potential financial gains to the steel industry as a whole are great enough to motivate individual firms to persuade the government to restrict imports. In contrast, we measure the benefits of trade protection to individual firms, using event study methodology from finance and accounting. The central question we address is whether firms that invest the most resources in attempting to influence trade policy are the biggest beneficiaries from the imposition of trade restraints. More specifically, the objective of the empirical analysis is to determine whether firms that devote the most resources to the political pursuit of trade protection receive the greatest returns, as evaluated by their shareholders, from the reduction of imports.

To provide some context for the empirical analysis, we briefly review the restrictive trade programs for steel put in place between 1977 and 1984. We next discuss the theory of collective action that is used to structure our empirical analysis. This is followed by a description of (1) the empirical model we test; (2) the specific measures used in the analysis; and (3) the regression results. We conclude by discussing the implication of our results for collective action theory and more generally for trade policy.

3.2   The Political Activity of Steel Firms

3.2.1   1977: Trigger Price Mechanism

A sharp downturn in world steel demand in 1975 seriously affected the steel industry worldwide. The ensuing scramble for market shares sent prices downward and eroded profit margins, which especially hurt the relatively inefficient producers in the United States and the European Community. The November 1975 voluntary export restraint (VER) between the EC and Japan provided incentives to both Japanese and European steelmakers to seek expanded export markets, predominantly the U.S. (Jones 1986, 113). Import share of the U.S. market rose from 13.4 percent in 1974 to 17.8 percent by the beginning of 1977 (Hufbauer et al. 1986, 156, 165). (Table 3.1 documents the increase in foreign import penetration in the U.S. steel market.)

U.S. steel producers responded defensively to increased import penetration. Gilmore Steel petitioned against Japanese producers for selling steel plate in West Coast markets below the cost of production. Steel industry lobbyists also descended on Washington, prompting their allies in Capitol Hill's Steel Caucus to propose several pieces of protectionist legislation. Congres-

Table 3.1   Imported Steel Shares in the U.S. Market

| Period | Share of U.S. Market Held by | | | | |
	EC	Japan	Canada	Others	Total
1969–73	6.5	5.9	1.0	1.4	14.8
1974–78	5.2	6.5	1.4	2.4	15.5
1980	4.1	6.3	2.5	3.4	16.3
1982	7.3	6.8	2.4	5.3	21.8
1984	6.3	6.6	3.2	10.1	26.2

Source: U.S. International Trade Commission, "Carbon and Certain Alloy Products," U.S. International Trade Commission Publication 1553, vol. 1 (Washington, D.C.: GPO, July 1984), a-139; Standard & Poor's Industry Surveys, "Steel and Heavy Machinery," Basic Analysis, 7 July 1988, sec. 2, 27.

sional steel sympathizer Rep. Charles Vanik (D.–Ohio), criticized the slow administrative process of antidumping investigations: "By the time you do something with this (dumping) process," he lamented, "industry won't be around in your community anymore" (*Purchasing* 1977b, 9). The industry used the media to tell the American public that imported steel was the cause of massive layoffs and the domestic industry's competitive demise.

Japanese and European steel-producing interests, sensing the protectionist sentiment in the United States, offered to continue voluntary restraint agreements, which were originally implemented in 1969. To avoid violating GATT rules, the Carter administration adopted the trigger price mechanism (TPM), a solution based on referent prices, in December 1977 (effective 1 January 1978). The TPM established a floor price of steel based on Japanese production costs (deemed to be the lowest in the world) plus a margin for transport and profit markups. Any sales of imports below the this price would trigger an immediate antidumping investigation by the U.S. Treasury Department. In exchange for this program aimed at reducing imports from 20 percent to 12–14 percent of the U.S. market (*Purchasing* 1978, 21), U.S. steel firms agreed to abandon their unfair trading petitions against foreign producers.

3.2.2   1980: Trigger Price Mechanism Reinstated

In 1979 steel producers were optimistic about the strength of U.S. steel sales. On 1 January 1979 the trigger price was raised 7 percent, which was expected to cut imports by 20 percent to sixteen million tons annually (*Business Week* 1979a, 64). Steel producers argued that import restrictions contributed to the government's anti-inflation efforts because their costs per ton were lowest when they ran at 90 percent capacity.

Although the implementation of the TPM in January 1978 was initially followed by a reduction in imports (especially from Japan), imports gained shares in mid-1979 and 1980. Several factors contributed to the ineffectiveness of the TPM, including inadequate enforcement; evasion of violations of trigger prices by exporters through various discount and customs adjustments; a policy of import controls among members of the EC which gave European producers a strong incentive to search for export markets; and a strong U.S. dollar. The TPM-initiated antidumping suits filed by the Treasury Department concentrated on small suppliers to the United States (Taiwan, Poland, Spain) while ignoring significantly more disruptive sources of imports from the EC and Japan (Jones 1986, 136). Domestic producers were increasingly vocal in advocating tighter restrictions on imports, evidenced by U.S. Steel's filing of antidumping complaints against seven EC producers in early 1980. In response to this filing, the Carter administration rescinded the TPM.

A summer of poor operating results and layoffs and heated election-year politics forced President Carter to develop a new plan for steel imports. His administration reinstated the TPM in October of 1980, with 12 percent higher trigger prices and updated monitoring and auditing procedures. In return U.S. Steel withdrew its dumping and subsidy complaints against the European steelmakers.

3.2.3   1982: Voluntary Restraint Agreements with the European Community

Despite a profitable 1981 for most of the large U.S. steel companies, the firms were dissatisfied with the fortified TPM shortly after its reinstatement. High levels of import penetration and sluggish demand weakened the competitive position of U.S. steelmakers in 1981 and early 1982. Furthermore, EC producers, facing their own domestic pressures, disregarded the trigger prices and increased deliveries into the U.S. market in late 1981. Imports in 1981 were six to eight million tons higher than forecasted at the beginning of the year and caused a sharp decrease in domestic shipments (*Industry Week* 1981a, 110). The unprecedented 25 percent import penetration reached during the summer of 1981 prompted U.S. Steel's CEO David Roderick to comment, "Anyone who would say—after the August totals—that the TPM is working . . . well, you have to question his sanity" (*Industry Week* 1981b, 32).

Under pressure from U.S. steel companies, the Commerce Department initiated unfair trade investigations against five countries (Belgium, France, Romania, Brazil, and South Africa) in November 1981. In early 1982, seven U.S. steel firms filed over a hundred antidumping and subsidy suits against several countries, mostly directed against EC producers (Hufbauer et al. 1986, 170). After the filings, the Commerce Department suspended the TPM and its own subsidy investigations (*Industry Week* 1982a, 22).

The Europeans, although upset at U.S. actions, were under economic and political pressures to reach a negotiated resolution rather than risk the possibility that the United States would impose antidumping and countervailing duties. Talks continued with the United States throughout 1982. Meanwhile, the USITC made a preliminary ruling in February 1982 that found injury in thirty-nine of ninety-two cases. U.S. firms, concerned that a broader range of products was not covered, pressured the Commerce Department to find large dumping margins which could be used to bring the EC to negotiate quotas or market-sharing arrangements (Jones 1986, 141).

In a preliminary determination, the Commerce Department did find high margins and required American importers to post cash bonds equivalent to the estimated subsidy and dumping margins (Jones 1986, 141). When the Europeans threatened retaliation, negotiations became tense. The EC and the United States reached an initial agreement in August 1982, but it was rejected by U.S. steel producers.

On 21 October 1982, the EC and the United States finally reached a settlement which limited EC exports to 5.5 percent of the U.S. market on ten steel products, with a separate arrangement for pipes and tubes. The VRA agreement took effect on 1 November 1982, and was to run until 31 December 1985. In exchange for the agreement, forty-five charges of unfair trade practices by eight U.S. producers against European producers were dropped.

3.2.4   1984: Voluntary Restraint Agreement Expanded

The 1982 VRA with the EC managed to stem the tide of imports in the eleven types of carbon steel products from one source. An International Trade Commission analysis of the economic effects of this agreement, however, found only a 1.63 percent decline in imports of total steel mill products (U.S. International Trade Commission 1985, 22). Steel imports continued to come into the U.S. market in relatively high quantities from other countries.

U.S. producers continued to pursue actions against non-EC exporters of carbon steel products. These actions included suits filed against steel pipe and tube producers from South Korea and Taiwan in April 1983; antidumping petitions filed against Mexico, Brazil, and Argentina in November 1983; and an escape clause petition filed by the Bethlehem Steel Corporation and the United Steelworkers of America (USWA) in January 1984. By May, there were 121 cases at the USITC regarding steel products.

Along with the unfair trade and escape clause petitions, a Fair Trade in Steel Act of 1984 (S. 2380, H.R. 5081), pushed by U.S. Steel Corporation and the American Iron and Steel Institute, was introduced in Congress in April 1984. This bill, which died in committee, would have limited imports of all steel products (including specialty steel) to 15 percent of U.S. consumption for a five-year period (Hufbauer et al. 1986, 171).

The USITC found injury on five major products (out of nine) in the Bethlehem-USWA 201 petition. With strong protectionist sentiment in Congress and uneasy American trading partners, President Reagan announced a new set of VRAs aimed at limiting the U.S. market to 20.5 percent of imports. These VRAs were to be negotiated with steel exporters having over 0.3 percent of the U.S. market (in 1983), including Japan, EC, South Korea, Brazil, Mexico, Spain, South Africa, Australia, Argentina, Finland, and Canada. The five-year plan covered all steel products, continuous use of unfair trade laws (per sec. 301) by the Department of Commerce, possible termination of existing unfair trade cases, and negotiations with trading partners over unfair trading practices (Jones 1986, 148–49). By November 1985, the USTR had negotiated fifteen VRAs covering 80 percent of the U.S. imports (Hufbauer et al. 1986, 173).

3.3   Political Investments: A Theory of Costs and Benefits

Olson (1971) offers a model to explain the participation of individual economic actors in the provision of a public good. The decision to allocate corporate resources to political activity is treated like any other investment decision in which the magnitude of the resources allocated to attempting to obtain the decision is carefully weighed against the expected benefits to the firm. This rational model of political investment has been used primarily to explain the variation in political activity on the part of firms with an economic interest in the provision of a public good.

In Olson's model, size is the key variable that distinguishes participants from nonparticipants and reflects the intensity of a firm's commitment to politics. A critical assumption underlying this model is that there is a positive relationship between the size of the firm and the amount that the firm benefits from the public good. Relatively large firms, which have the most to gain from the provision of a public good, engage in political activity because their expected benefits exceed their political investment. This activity results in free goods for smaller firms. As a result of receiving a large benefit from the public good for free, Olson (1971) argues smaller firms have little or no incentive to contribute to the provision of a public good.

Yoffie (1987, 45), like Olson, believes that economic self-interest is the key motivation for firms to participate in politics. He questions, however, whether firm size explains the degree of a firm's involvement in the provision of a public good. In an effort to explain collective action in terms of behavioral models of corporate decision making, Yoffie raises two objections to Olson's model.

The first involves resource constraints. In contrast to Olson, Yoffie does not assume that every firm that stands to benefit from a public good will have enough resources to invest in political activity. Only the more profitable firms can afford to engage in politics.

Second, Yoffie argues that a firm's strategic choices affect the level of its political involvement. Specifically, he suggests that Olson's model does not take the impact of diversification into account. A firm that derives significant revenues from several divisions may perceive that it gains less from trade protection than a firm that depends heavily on sales of the threatened products. Thus a highly diversified firm is likely to be less active in politics even though the public good would benefit one of its strategic business units.

Yoffie further suggests that a firm's competitive strategy—low cost or differentiation—may affect the nature and extent of the benefits that it expects to receive from the public good. This in turn may have an impact on the intensity of its political involvement.

3.4   The Model

We model first the level of political investment as a function of variables that explain why managers seek trade protection. We then use the same set of independent variables in a regression analysis in which the dependent variable is the increase (or decrease) in the market value of the firm that results from the announcement of trade protection. To determine whether there is a relationship between the level of a firm's political investment and the change in the value of the firm that results from the announcement of trade restraints, we compare the signs and the significance levels of the coefficients. We cannot use the change in the market value of the firm to explain the level of firm involvement in politics because the actual returns of the investment are unknown and, as such, do not influence the decision to invest a priori.

This model is based on the assumption that managers expect the discounted present value of an investment to be positive, whether resources are allocated to political activity, such as the preparation of antidumping and countervailing-duty petitions, or to a new production technology. Yet there is a critical difference between these two investment decisions because the returns of the investment in the new production technology can usually be captured entirely by the firm making the investment, whereas the returns of a successful antidumping or countervailing-duty petition accrue to some or all of the firms in the industry. We further assume that the benefits to an individual firm are capitalized when a specific trade policy is announced, not when a specific political action is taken.

Our sample includes all firms in the U.S. steel industry between 1976 and 1984 as compiled by the American Iron and Steel Institute and published yearly in *Iron Age* as well as steel firms listed in the *Value Line Investment Survey*. All the firms in the sample have daily return data available from the University of Chicago's Center for Research in Security Prices (CRSP). Our sample size decreases from twenty-two firms in 1977 to eighteen firms in 1984 because of mergers and bankruptcies.

3.5   The Dependent Variables

3.5.1   Dependent Variable I: An Estimate of Firm Political Involvement

To estimate the level of resources that firms devote to the provision of a public good, we develop measures reflecting the level of a firm's political involvement in influencing specific policy initiatives taken by the U.S. government to protect the steel industry. Our objective is not to determine a precise dollar estimate of the cost of a firm's political activities (firms do not report many of the expenses involved). Instead, using publicly available information, we have constructed a measure of political involvement that reflects the differences in the relative magnitude of the political involvement of the firms in our sample.

This measure of political involvement has three components, two of which involve firm political activity toward the Congress. Although the Congress does not typically play a direct role in the resolution of trade disputes, in the case of steel trade, Congress's threat to restrict imports unilaterally puts pressure on the president to adopt restrictive measures. Implicit in our construction of this variable is the assumption that firms which are the most politically active in ways we can observe will also be the most active in ways we cannot observe.[1]

The first component of this measure is political action committee (PAC) campaign contributions. We assume that PAC contributions to congressional candidates are dispersed to increase the ability of firms to influence congressional actions. In defining this variable, we adopt the model of the Congress (Shepsle and Weingast 1987) in which oversight committees, because of their agenda-setting power, are the most influential in determining the actions that Congress might take on a specific issue. Thus, in measuring the level of political involvement of firms, we include only contributions to members of the House Ways and Means Committee and the Senate Finance Committee, the two major oversight committees on trade policy.

The second measure that we use to capture the intensity of a firm's political involvement is the number of appearances by members of a firm's top management team before congressional committees on issues involving trade policy. We assume that these appearances are costly to the firm in terms of top management time, the resources involved in the preparation of testimony, and the reputation of the firm that results from taking a public position on a political issue. To confirm that the testimony of the firm's representative was in support of trade restrictions, we reviewed the text of each testimony. The only CEO to testify in opposition to trade restraints during the period analyzed was Kenneth Iverson of the Nucor Steel Company, who testified at the 1984 hearing of the House Ways and Means Subcommittee on Trade:

> We fall in an unusual category, we are a profitable steel company and we are opposed to trade restrictions on steel products. We believe that tariff or nontariff trade barriers will delay modernization of our steel industry, will cost the consumer billions of dollars, and could seriously injure both our economy and smaller steel producers. (U.S. Congress, House Ways and Means Committee Subcommittee on Trade 1984, 286).

The third measure of the level of a firm's political involvement in efforts to obtain trade protection is the number of escape-clause, antidumping, or countervailing-duty petitions filed by the firm individually or together with other firms. We include this measure because steel companies devoted considerable resources to obtaining trade protection through affirmative findings by the Treasury Department, the International Trade Administration of the Commerce Department, and the International Trade Commission. Although the majority of import restraints on steel were not the direct result of these peti-

---

1. We realize that unobservable political activity may also play an important role in determining public policy and may not be consistent with what can be observed. In this analysis, however, since the intent of firms to gain financially through import protection is considered legitimate by the majority of the public, there seems to be no reason to expect that firms would support import protection in public but oppose it in private.

tions, the sheer number of the petitions filed put pressure on the executive branch to devise a more efficient mechanism to limit steel imports.

To determine the level of a firm's political investment in each of these separate trade actions, we include the activities undertaken by the firms prior to the announcement of a trade restraint program. Thus, for the 1977 TPM, we include the political activities of firms from 1976 to October 1977. The political investments that led to the 1980 reimposition of the TPM include those made in 1978, 1979, and 1980. We consider that the political investments made by firms in 1981 and 1982 resulted in the 1982 VRA, while the payoff for those made in 1983 and 1984 was the announcement of the program to negotiate more VRAs in 1984.

Political involvement encompasses several activities: PAC contributions, congressional testimony, and administrative petitions, each capturing one aspect of political involvement. Simply choosing one as the dependent variable and analyzing it separately would lead to biased estimators due to measurement error.

One way to relate these three observed activities to the understanding of political involvement is through factor analysis. In this case, we would expect that the three observed variables would be defined by single latent factor, political involvement. In this analysis, the three political activities were factor analyzed, and the results for the factor analysis were used to estimate a factor score for each firm's political activity. The factor scores were then used in a regression analysis to establish the relationship between the independent variables and political involvement. Estimating factor scores can help to reduce measurement error (Bollen 1989). Therefore, use of factor scores is useful in improving the consistency of estimates.

Factor analysis was conducted for each of the time periods, 1977, 1980, 1982, and 1984. The results are in appendix B. These results were then used to calculate the factors scores. The factor scores were created using the "regression" option in SPSS's factor analysis program. The factor loadings are generally quite high (above .70), indicating that the observed variables are highly related to the latent variable, political involvement. The communalities indicate how much of the variance in the observed variables is explained by the latent factor. The variances are all generally quite high. The Cronbach's alpha for the factor scores varies between .63 and .87, indicating that the observed variables are reliable measures of political involvement.

3.5.2 Dependent Variable II: An Estimate of the Change in Firm Market Value

The dependent variable used in the second regression equation is based on the impact of the announcement of trade protection on the stock price of individual steel firms. As Schwert (1981, 121–22) suggests, given the efficient-markets/rational expectations hypothesis which "posits that security prices reflect all available information," the change in a security price that results from the announcement of an unanticipated government policy is "an unbiased estimate of the value of the change in future cash flows to the firm." These "event returns" can vary among firms because of differences in the product mix and the competitiveness of each firm.

We use the estimates of these event returns to calculate the investors' expectations of the change in the value of individual steel firms in response to government announcements of trade restrictions. Schwert (1981) argues that stock price data could be used to measure the effects of economic regulation. While several studies have investigated the impact of regulatory announcements on stock prices,[2] two previous studies have used event study methodology to estimate the value to shareholders of an increase in trade protection. Using a seemingly unrelated regression analysis, Lenway, Rehbein, and Starks (1990) find that the steel industry as a whole gains significantly from trade protection in 1977 and 1982. In a cross-sectional analysis, the results indicated that the primary beneficiaries for these two events were the smaller integrated steel firms. Hartigan, Perry, and Kamma (1986) analyzed the returns to firms in industries for which escape clause petitions were filed from 1975 to 1980. Using weekly returns for a period extending from two weeks before the petition was filed through four weeks after the ITC decision, they found that the cumulative average return was significantly positive for only two of the nineteen industries. One of the industries received trade protection, and the other did not.

Grossman and Levinsohn (1989, 1065), in a different application of this methodology, measured the responsiveness of the returns to capital investment in several U.S. industries to changes in the import prices. They found in five of six industries that an unanticipated change in the import price of a good resulted in substantial gains or losses for shareholders in the industry.

We use the following equation to estimate the change in the market value for each firm in the sample in response to the government's announcement of the trade restraint programs:

$$(1) \qquad r_{it} = a_i + a_i d_j + b_i r_{mt} + b_i r_{mt} d_j + \sum_{t=-10}^{t=+1} w_{ijt} e_{jt} + u_t,$$

where

r_{it} = the return on the stock price of firm i at time t ($t = -250$ to $+250$, where $t = 0$ is the announcement date);

d_j = a dummy variable, equal to one for every day after the announcement period until the last observation in the sample and zero otherwise;

b_i = the covariance ($r_i r_m$) divided by the variance (r_m);

2. See Shipper and Thompson (1983), Binder (1985), Rose (1985), Smith, Bradley, and Farrell (1986), Hughes, Magat, and Ricks (1986), and Prager (1989).

r_{mt} = the return on a market proxy portfolio, in this case the return on the CRSP value-weighted index, at time t;

e_{jt} = a dummy variable for each date during a given event period, equal to 1 if event j occurs during t and equal to 0 otherwise;

t = day relative to the announcement;

and

u_t = a random error term with expected value of zero,

where

$E(u_{it})$ =
$E(u^2_{it})$ = δ_i^2
$E(u_{it}u_{is})$ = 0 (for a specific firm, no serial correlation).

Here time t runs from -250 to $+250$ ($t = 0$ is the announcement date of the trade restraints). See appendix A for the exact announcement date used for each event. The window that we use to estimate the event period returns is $t = -10$ to $t = +1$. We chose this window because information about the trade programs may have been leaked prior to the official announcement. In searching the *Wall Street Journal* around the event dates, we found that the discussion of the specific measures taken in a new trade program was within ten days prior to the announcement date.

The inclusion of the CAPM beta allows us to isolate the change in the stock price of a steel firm that is associated with the changes in the overall market from those that result from the announcement of trade protection. The dummy variables, the d_j, allow the intercept and slope terms to shift when the market's expectation of the effects of trade protection changes. Seemingly unrelated regression analysis is used to allow for across-equation correlation of error terms to generate more efficient estimates, since our event time equals calendar time for all firms in the industry.

The coefficients on the e_{jt} (the w_{ijt}) lend themselves to a natural interpretation. They are equivalent to the event return to firm i for each date. Thus, they allow us to interpret the sign, magnitude, and significance of the return to a specific firm in response to the announcement of a new restrictive trade policy. The sign reflects the market's evaluation of whether the firm will gain or lose from increased trade protection. The magnitude of the coefficient indicates the percentage change in the firm's stock price that results from the introduction of the new trade policy. These coefficients are not consistently significant because our tests may not be strong enough to detect the impact of the trade policy upon the firm's stock price. In some cases the trade policy announcement may not significantly affect the stock price of the firm.

Table 3.2 reports the average event period returns, the t-statistics, and the change in the firm's market value for each of the individual steel firms included in our analysis by announcement date. In appendix C, we report the coefficients for each of the variables in equation (1). To calculate the change

Table 3.2   **Event Period Results**

$$(1) \qquad r_{it} = a_i + a_i d_j + b_i r_{mt} + b_i r_{mt} d_j + \sum_{t=-10}^{t=+1} w_{ijt} e_{jt} + u_t$$

	1977			1980		
Firm	Change in Market Value ($)	W_{ijt}	t-statistic	Change in Market Value ($)	W_{ijt}	t-statistic
ARMCO	77,113,416	0.005	1.539	−47,437,215	−0.002	−0.489
ATHLONE	2,387,412	0.004	0.890	−2,679,395	−0.004	−0.797
BETHLEHEM	10,464,036	0.001	0.206	−47,062,822	−0.004	−0.751
CARPENTER TECHNOLOGY	1,951,800	0.001	0.186	43,055,472	0.010	1.783*
COPPERWELD	−1,531,752	−0.001	−0.222	−18,392,495	−0.009	−1.589
CYCLOPS	7,107,180	0.008	1.563	−6,009,132	−0.006	−0.957
FLORIDA STEEL	−8,638,284	−0.007	−1.361	−15,758,859	−0.006	−0.957
INLAND STEEL	17,937,840	0.002	0.713	−8,812,368	−0.001	−0.341
INTERLAKE	7,726,332	0.003	0.945	−12,364,459	−0.006	−1.064
KAISER	N.A.	N.A.	N.A.	−14,756,202	−0.004	−0.399
KEYSTONE	1,307,004	0.005	0.942	−264,045	−0.001	−0.153
LTV	6,029,964	0.005	0.614	4,260,054	0.001	0.073
LUKENS	−343,872	0.000	−0.044	−340,229	0.000	−0.063
MCLOUTH	2,660,244	0.004	0.588	−1,991,010	−0.004	−0.471
NATIONAL	20,034,732	0.003	0.903	−16,733,668	−0.003	−0.650
NORTHWESTERN	5,596,272	0.002	0.617	2,983,697	0.001	0.302
NUCOR	−2,921,276	−0.003	−0.582	21,054,549	0.002	0.401
PHOENIX	371,076	0.002	0.147	N.A.	N.A.	N.A.
REPUBLIC	7,836,096	0.002	0.504	−2,308,894	−0.001	−0.115
SHARON STEEL	24,480	0.002	0.343	141	0.000	0.002
TIMKEN	−58,764	−0.004	−1.140	67,461	0.004	0.991
U.S. STEEL	102,379,308	0.003	0.867	−135,315,729	−0.006	−1.058
WASHINGTON	−475,080	−0.001	−0.213	N.A.	N.A.	N.A.
WHEELING-PITTSBURGH	2,946,840	0.006	1.047	6,139,528	0.007	0.874
	1982			1984		
ARMCO	45,617,652	0.004	0.634	−33,020,676	−0.002	−0.307
ATHLONE	86,568	0.000	0.030	4,084,536	0.007	1.292
BETHLEHEM	77,610,120	0.008	1.552	−73,378,212	−0.007	−1.441
CARPENTER TECHNOLOGY	49,312,788	0.014	2.676**	1,171,644	0.000	0.063
COPPERWELD	2,459,424	0.001	.216	−23,448,264	−0.013	−1.987*
CYCLOPS	7,516,296	0.009	1.662*	4,215,984	0.003	0.664
FLORIDA STEEL	26,634,348	0.023	3.002**	−4,653,060	−0.005	−0.805
INLAND STEEL	86,097,984	0.013	2.503*	46,983,456	0.006	1.343
INTERLAKE	−200,064	0.000	−0.023	613,656	0.000	0.055
KAISER	−28,261,800	−0.017	−1.691*	N.A.	N.A.	N.A.
LTV	47,558,700	0.007	1.005	−31,880,136	−0.003	−0.532
LUKENS	7,528,680	0.011	1.596	1,224,480	0.001	0.253

(continued)

Table 3.2   (continued)

		1982			1984	
Firm	Change in Market Value ($)	W_{ijt}	t-statistic	Change in Market Value ($)	W_{ijt}	t-statistic
NATIONAL	147,816,288	0.009	1.425	−45,628,740	−0.006	−1.078
NORTHWESTERN	19,042,572	0.008	1.828*	−3,756,432	−0.003	−0.400
NUCOR	−5,365,320	−0.006	−1.069	−22,062,384	−0.004	−0.709
TIMKEN	224,652	0.012	2.717**	−29,112	−0.002	−0.516
U.S. STEEL	313,756,056	0.010	1.703*	−46,925,760	−0.001	−0.387
WHEELING- PITTSBURGH	49,671,876	0.015	1.645	313,008	.000	0.028

*Significant at the .1 level.
**Significant at the .01 level.

in firm market value, the event return is multiplied by the value of the firm's common stock at $t = 0$. This is an estimate of the dollar gain (or loss) to an individual firm that results from the increase in trade protection.

3.6 The Independent Variables

3.6.1 Factors Underlying Cross-sectional Differences Among Steel Firms

Our choice of independent variables reflects two distinct explanations for the positive relationship between the level of a firm's political investment and event return from the announcement of trade protection. In the first explanation, based on Olson's (1971) model of collective action, high expectations of gain evoke a high level of political involvement. The second based on Yoffie's extension (1987) of Olson includes factors that reflect resource constraints and strategic choices made by firms.[3]

We use the firm's market share to measure the benefits that the firm expects to receive from the imposition of increased trade restraints. Olson argues that a firms' return from the provision of a public good is positively related to its market share because its expected benefits exceed the amount of its political investment. Thus, we expect that firms with high market share will be more politically involved and also benefit more from trade restraints than will firms with low market share.

To test Yoffie's rational model of corporate political behavior, we measure whether a firm has adequate resources by taking its average return on equity in the years leading up to the introduction of a new trade program. We measure the strategic salience of increased trade restrictions on steel imports to

3. We had originally planned to include a measure of firm-level labor costs but dropped it when we found it to be highly correlated with the other independent variables, especially market share.

the individual firms by the percentage of steel sales to their total sales. Because of the assumption in this model that firm political behavior is based on economic self-interest, we expect a high average return on equity and a high dependence of a firm on its steel sales will lead to high political involvement and high returns from trade protection.

To obtain an adequate sample size, we have included firms that are "minimills" as well as integrated steel producers. These firms tend to have very different competitive strategies than integrated steel firms. Minimills have been more competitive with imports because of their cost structure. Barnett and Crandall (1986, 27) find that "minimills pay less than integrated firms for labor, metallic inputs, and energy, but they are also more efficient in the use of these inputs." Because minimills are more competitive, we expect them to be less involved in the politics of trade protection. With respect to event returns, we have no prediction on the sign for this variable because although trade restraints allow minimills to charge higher prices, they also may have resulted in the delaying the retirement of USX and Bethlehem's relatively inefficient plants which produce products similar to those produced by the minimills (Barnett and Crandall 1986, 111). To allow for the possibility that minimills may have distinct political strategies or benefit differently from the imposition of trade restraints, we include a dummy variable to indicate whether a firm is a minimill.

We use OLS regression to test the following hypotheses:

(2) $\text{PINV} = a + b_1\text{SHARE} + b_2\text{ROE} + b_3\text{STSALES} + b_4\text{MINMILL} + u$

and

(3) $\text{CHAV} = a + b_1\text{SHARE} + b_2\text{ROE} + b_3\text{STSALES} + b_4\text{MINMILL} + u,$

where PINV is level of political investment, CHAV is change in firm market value, SHARE is market share, ROE is average return on equity, STSALES is steel sales as percentage of total sales, MINMILL is whether a firm is a minimill ($1 = \text{minimill}$), and u is an error term. The hypotheses relating these factors to both political investment and the change in firm market value are summarized below.

	Political Investment	Change in Firm Market Value
1. SHARE	Positive	Positive
2. ROE	Positive	Positive
3. STSALES	Positive	Positive
4. MINMILL	Negative	?

By comparing the results of the two regression equations, we test the hypothesis that the level of firm political involvement accounts for the change in the firm's market value resulting from the announcement of trade protection.

3.7 Results

The cross-sectional results for political investment are reported in table 3.3. For each of the events, the F-statistics indicate that the model fits the data very well. In all four periods, however, market share is the only significant variable that explains corporate political investment in trade protection. These results suggest that firms with the highest market share and thus the highest expectations of financial benefits from trade restraints expend the most effort in attempting to influence U.S. trade policy.

The average return on equity for the years leading up to the introduction of the four restrictive programs has the expected sign for 1977, 1982, and 1984, and the coefficient for each event approaches significance at the .1 level. For 1980, however, average ROE is negative and insignificant in explaining corporate political investment. These results offer only tentative support that relatively profitable firms are likely to involve themselves in politics because of their access to resources.

The sign for the variable reflecting the extent to which firms have diversified out of steel is negative but not significant for all four periods. The high level of political activity on the part of major integrated firms diversifying out of steel might account for the unexpected negative signs for this variable.

Finally, we find that the sign for the dummy variable indicating whether a firm is a minimill is positive in for all four events, although again the coefficient is not significant. Our lack of results could be attributed to multicollinearity between minimills and market share because minimills tend to be con-

Table 3.3   Determinants of Firm Political Involvement

Variable	1977	1980	1982	1984
SHARE	18.40422	.16464	.21702	.20920
	(5.517)***	(4.347)**	(6.957)***	(5.646)***
ROE	4.28242	−.62597	.90593	1.90807
	(1.631)	(−.215)	(1.588)	(1.493)
STSALES	−.19686	−1.20935	−.36009	−.67443
	(−.252)	(−1.379)	(−.703)	(−1.075)
MINMIL	.05915	.35805	.46764	.38361
	(.149)	(.801)	(1.472)	(1.128)
Constant	−.81298	.31246	−.62376	−.23131
	(−1.181)	(.469)	(−1.522)	(−.439)
F-statistic	8.46822	6.60455	13.47536	10.73158
Signif F	.0009	.0025	.0001	.0005
Adjusted R^2	.61124	.52850	.71388	.69603
No. of observations	20	21	21	18

Note: t-statistic in parentheses.
**Significant at the .01 level.
***Significant at the .001 level.

sistently smaller than integrated steel firms. An analysis of the raw data indicates that none of the minimills were politically active in 1977, 1980, and 1984. Only Keystone, a relatively old minimill, whose stock price declined by more than 80 percent between 1976 and 1985 (Barnett and Crandall 1986, 15) was involved in two countervailing-duty and one dumping petition that led to the 1982 VRA with the EC.

To determine whether there is a relationship between the level of political involvement and the capital market's assessment of the change in the market value of the firm that results from the announcement of a restrictive trade program, we used the same set of independent variables as in the political investment equation. Table 3.4 reports these results.

In contrast to the previous results, market share is only positive and significant in 1982. Market share is positive and insignificant in 1977 and negative and significant in 1982 and 1984. This variable, which most consistently explains why firms are politically involved, does not appear to be as useful in explaining the distribution of benefits from trade protection. The negative relationship between market share and the change in the market value of the firm indicates that for two of the four events, firms expecting to gain the most from trade protection may actually have been hurt.

Average return on equity is positive for each of the four events but only significant in 1982 at the .05 level. These results suggest that relatively profitable steel firms gain more from trade restraints than the less profitable firms. The positive sign for three of the four events in the previous analysis of political involvement taken together with these results offers tentative evidence

Table 3.4   **Determinants of Change in Firm Market Value**

Variable	1977	1980	1982	1984
SHARE	.26133	−.9041	1.09045	−.58159
	(.8040)	(−7.4260)***	(6.5660)***	(−2.0830)*
ROE	.12875	.08649	.39775	.08476
	.4210	(.7450)	(2.5230)*	(.2740)
STSALES	−.04233	.38153	.08157	.25846
	(−.1520)	(3.1340)**	(.6210)	(.9660)
MINMIL	−.25001	−.31789	−.02519	−.02987
	(−.0840)	(−2.3990)*	(−.1890)	(−.9040)
Constant	.5390	−1.880	−.8010	−.7850
F-statistic	.57735	15.50718	13.63553	1.61185
Signif F	.6846	.0000	.0001	.2346
R^2	.16139	.79495	.80753	.34950
No. of observations	23	20	18	17

Note: t-statistic in parentheses.
*Significant at the .1 level.
**Significant at the .01 level.
***Significant at the .001 level.

that for the more profitable firms, there may be a relationship between political involvement and the gains to the firm from the imposition of trade protection.

The sign for steel sales as a percentage of total sales is positive in 1980, 1982, and 1984 but only significant in 1980. The coefficient is negative but not significant in 1977. These results, together with those from the previous equation (in which the sign for this variable was consistently negative), suggest that the highest returns need not go to the most politically active firms.

The variable indicating whether a firm is a minimill is consistently negative for all four events although only significant in 1980 at the .05 level. These relationships suggest that minimills may not have gained from the restrictions on steel imports.

In general, these results do not provide consistent support for the hypothesis that the most politically active firms gain the most from trade protection. For two of the four variables analyzed, we find that the most politically active firms may have been made worse off from the imposition of trade restraints. While we find that the announcement of trade protection may have made the minimills worse off, we cannot draw any inferences about the relationship between the political activity of these firms and gains (or losses) from trade protection.

3.8 Discussion and Conclusion

Our finding that market share helps to explain the level of a firm's political involvement supports Olson's (1971) hypothesis that the firms expecting to gain the most are the most politically active. Yet we do not find that market share helps to explain the distribution of the benefits once a new program to restrict steel imports is announced.

We find mixed support for the alternative hypothesis suggested by Yoffie (1987). Except in 1980, the relationship between a firm's average ROE and level of political involvement was positive, although the coefficients are not significant. The relationship between ROE and the wealth increase to the steel firms is also consistently positive. At best, this offers extremely tentative support for the hypotheses derived from Yoffie's model that the more profitable firms will engage in politics and that firm profitability helps explain which firms will benefit from trade protection.

The negative, but statistically insignificant, relationship between firm diversification and political involvement does not support Yoffie's proposition that political activity is related to the perceived impact of a specific policy on a firm. It is possible that even though certain firms have diversified, top management remains more committed to steel than to their other businesses. Yet the positive and significant relationship between steel sales as a percentage of total sales and the change in the market value of the firm in 1980 and the positive but insignificant relationship in 1982 and 1984 indicate that diversified firms, although the most politically active, did not gain from trade protection. The consistently negative sign for minimills in the analysis of the change in firm value suggests that the stock market did not react as if trade restraints were expected to help these firms.

These results suggest that there is no consistent relationship between the level of a firm's political involvement in attempts to obtain trade protection and the benefits that they receive as reflected in the market's reevaluation of their future earning potential.[4] In other words, the primary beneficiaries from trade protection do not appear to be the firms that devote the most resources to congressional lobbying and the preparation of petitions filed at the International Trade Commission and the Commerce Department. This finding challenges one of the basic assumptions of rational models of corporate political behavior, namely, that there is a positive relationship between expected and actual returns to the provision of a public good. In fact, this relationship may be much more complex than originally assumed.[5]

One possible alternative explanation is that managers face an extremely high degree of uncertainty in assessing the degree to which their firm will benefit from trade protection relative to others in the industry. Unlike the estate owner in Olson's world, who has considerable certainty that if taxes are reduced, she will benefit more than will the owners of a modest cottage, the management of a politically active steel firm may not know how the reduction of imports will benefit their firm relative to their domestic competitors. Journalistic accounts indicate that steel firms typically respond to the imposition of trade restraints by raising prices, but this does not reveal much about the competitive dynamics among U.S. steel producers, which ultimately affects the distribution of benefits from trade protection. Another possible explanation is that the firms with the largest market share are absorbing some of the costs of political activity as part of their responsibilities as the industry's political leaders, even though they do not expect to benefit in the short run.

4. We also ran a simple regression analyzing the change in the market value of the firm in terms of a firm's political involvement. Given the high correlation between market share and political involvement, it was not possible to include market share as an independent variable in this analysis. We found that political involvement explained the increase in the value of the firm at almost the .05 level of significance in 1977 and at the .01 level in 1982. In 1980 and 1984 the results were negative and significant at the .05 level. One inference that could be drawn from these results is that there is no consistent relationship between the gains (or losses) that a firm experiences as a result of increased import protection and its level of political investment. The negative relationship in 1980 and 1984 could also indicate that the stock market had anticipated more stringent restraints than were implemented by the government.

5. Because we are performing these tests on individual securities, the changes that result from the announcement of the imposition of trade restraints are very small. In addition, because many uncertain factors affect stock returns, it is possible that the impact of the announcement of trade protection will be insignificant. Since we may not capture fully the complete wealth effect of the change in the level of trade protection, we also ran eq. (2) using as the dependent variable the firm's standardized abnormal return to weigh more heavily the event returns of the firms whose returns are significant as well as to correct for heteroscedasticity (Schwert 1981, 138). The results, both in term of signs and significance levels, lend themselves to the same interpretation as above.

Further research is needed to determine what factors explain the distribution of benefits resulting from trade protection to individual steel firms. This would involve using measures that reflect both the product mix of the companies and the product coverage of the steel trade programs as well as macroeconomic variables to control for the level of aggregate economic demand. Comparing the factors that affect the distribution of benefits from trade protection with those that affect the level of a firm's political involvement may lead to a better understanding of why managers do not appear to act in their shareholders' interests in their pursuit of trade protection.

Our investigation may have an impact on trade policy if it is possible to develop a systematic explanation of why the most important proponents of trade protection are not the biggest beneficiaries. Legislators and policymakers have determined that trade restraints help the industry and assume that they will help those firms that claim import competition is unfair. This study provides tentative evidence that these policies may not be helping the firms making the claims and may put the most efficient of U.S. steel firms, the minimills, at a competitive disadvantage.

Appendix A
Summary of the Event Dates

5 December 1977	The trigger price mechanism was imposed by the Carter administration.
1 October 1980	The trigger price mechanism was strengthened and reinstated.
21 October 1982	The United States announced a program to negotiate a series of voluntary restraint agreements with members of the European Community.
14 September 1984	The United States announced a program to negotiate voluntary restraint agreements with countries not covered by the previous arrangement, including Korea, Spain, Brazil, Mexico, South Africa, and Australia. Japanese imports were also limited to 5.8 percent of the U.S. market.

Appendix B
Factor Analysis of Political Involvement Variables

PAC = Firm political action committee contributions
CONG = Congressional testimony by corporate executives
TOTADM = Number of escape-clause, countervailing-duty, and antidumping
        petitions filed by firms

1977

Factor matrix:

	Political Involvement
PAC	.87853
TOTADM	.70752
CONG	.88749

Final statistics:

Variable	*Communality*	*Factor*	*Eigenvalue*	*% of Var*	*Cum %*
PAC	.77181	1	2.06004	68.7	68.7
TOTADM	.50059				
CONG	.78765				

Cronbach's alpha for factor scores = .77

1980

Factor matrix:

	Political Involvement
PAC	.64855
CONG	.83672
TOTADM	.76422

Final statistics:

Variable	*Communality*	*Factor*	*Eigenvalue*	*% of Var*	*Cum %*
PAC	.42062	1	1.70474	56.8	56.8
CONG	.70010				
TOTADM	.58403				

Cronbach's alpha for factor scores = .63

1982

Factor matrix:

	Political Involvement
PAC	.87843
CONG	.79926
TOTADM	.85110

Final statistics:

Variable	Communality	Factor	Eigenvalue	% of Var	Cum %
PAC	.77164	1	2.13483	71.2	71.2
CONG	.63881				
TOTADM	.72437				

Cronbach's alpha for factor scores = .77

1984

Factor matrix:

	Political Involvement
PAC	.93974
CONG	.83559
TOTADM	.93620

Final statistics:

Variable	Communality	Factor	Eigenvalue	% of Var	Cum %
PAC	.88311	1	2.45779	81.9	81.9
CONG	.69820				
TOTADM	.87648				

Cronbach's alpha for factor scores = .87

Appendix C
Event Period Results

(1)

$$r_{it} = a_i + a_i d_j + b r_{mt} + b r_{mt} d_j + \sum_{t=-10}^{t=+1} w_{ijt} e_{jt} + u_t$$

Firm	Parameter				
	a_i	$a_i d_j$	b_i	$b_i d_j$	w_{ijt}
	All Variables for the Period Ending 1977				
ARMCO	−0.0002	0.00002	0.93976	0.07532	0.00537
	(.265)	(.018)	(6.722)***	(.437)	(1.539)
ATHLONE	0.00054	0.00025	0.79911	0.04813	0.00387
	(.563)	(.185)	(4.589)***	(.224)	(.890)
BETHLEHEM	−0.00203	0.00132	1.78841	−0.18968	0.00095
	(−2.007)*	(.926)	(9.684)***	(−.833)	(.206)
CARPENTER TECHNOLOGY	0.00111	0.00005	1.11283	−0.29178	0.00092
	(1.026)	(.036)	(5.633)***	(−1.198)	(.186)
COPPERWELD	−0.00044	0.00047	0.31184	−0.05414	−0.00084
	(−.538)	(.406)	(2.064)*	(−.291)	(−.222)
CYCLOPS	0.00009	0.00027	0.86756	0.35519	0.00822
	(.080)	(.177)	(4.121)***	(1.368)	(1.563)
FLORIDA STEEL	0.00033	0.00037	0.23805	0.16486	−0.00651
	(.313)	(.253)	(1.244)	(.699)	(−1.361)
INLAND	−0.00078	0.00047	0.72333	0.11432	0.00202
	(−1.259)	(.538)	(6.372)***	(.817)	(.713)
INTERLAKE	−0.00067	0.00029	0.91974	−0.5621	0.00329
	(−.878)	(.267)	(6.579)***	(−3.261)**	(.945)
KEYSTONE	−0.00208	0.00213	0.39711	0.24356	0.0052
	(−1.725)*	(1.250)	(1.796)*	(.984)	(.942)

(*continued*)

Appendix C (*continued*)

Firm	Parameter				
	a_i	$a_i d_j$	b_i	$b_i d_j$	w_{ij}
LTV	-0.00237	0.00265	1.65455	0.28109	0.00524
	(-1.269)	(1.006)	(4.845)***	(.668)	(.614)
LUKENS	0.00071	-0.00029	1.0442	-0.59216	-0.0002
	(.715)	(-.206)	(5.726)***	(-2.634)**	(-.044)
MCLOUTH	-0.00226	0.00141	0.55077	0.49219	0.00374
	(-1.627)	(.720)	(2.165)*	(1.569)	(.588)
NATIONAL	-0.00095	0.00031	0.79996	-0.17546	0.00268
	(-1.468)	(.334)	(6.743)***	(-1.200)	(.903)
NORTHWESTERN	-0.00042	0.00065	0.28959	0.08368	0.00239
	(-.500)	(.547)	(1.867)*	(.438)	(.617)
NUCOR	0.00161	0.00012	0.95272	-0.04802	-0.00315
	(1.359)	(.073)	(4.401)***	(-.180)	(-.582)
PHOENIX	0.00013	0.00252	-0.32448	1.427	0.00203
	(.043)	(.592)	(-.589)	(2.099)*	(.147)
REPUBLIC	-0.00085	0.00077	1.14477	-0.24751	0.00174
	(-1.125)	(.719)	(8.267)***	(-1.450)	(.504)
SHARON STEEL	0.00006	0.00166	0.23515	0.14377	0.00201
	(.047)	(.918)	(1.004)	(.498)	(.343)
TIMKEN	0.00033	-0.00026	0.66119	-0.18522	-0.00366
	(.468)	(-.261)	(5.151)***	(-1.170)	(-1.140)
U.S. STEEL	-0.00168	0.00025	1.42047	-0.15497	0.00336
	(-1.977)*	(.209)	(9.151)***	(-.810)	(.867)

WASHINGTON	0.00151 (1.282)	−0.00083 (−.498)	0.39035 (1.812)*	−0.29454 (−1.109)	−0.00115 (−.213)
WHEELING-PITTSBURGH	−0.00233 (−1.748)*	0.00159 (.844)	0.77023 (3.153)**	0.57338 (1.904)*	0.00639 (1.047)

All Variables for the Period Ending 1980

ARMCO	−0.00039 (.381)	−0.00028 (−.201)	0.97334 (9.656)***	−0.09929 (−.670)	−0.00225 (−.489)
ATHLONE	0.00032 (.307)	0.00046 (.318)	0.8592 (8.329)***	−0.51493 (−3.398)**	−0.00376 (−.797)
BETHLEHEM	−0.00007 (−.067)	0.00006 (.036)	0.93619 (8.631)***	−0.05243 (−.329)	−0.00372 (−.751)
CARPENTER TECHNOLOGY	−0.0007 (−.554)	0.00158 (.899)	0.74865 (5.989)***	−0.38343 (−2.088)	0.01018 (1.783)*
COPPERWELD	0.00019 (.148)	0.0029 (1.632)	0.48189 (3.810)**	0.17243 (.928)	−0.00918 (−1.589)
CYCLOPS	−0.00029 (−.215)	0.00137 (.707)	1.26067 (9.181)***	−0.40571 (−2.011)*	−0.006 (−.957)
FLORIDA STEEL	0.002214 (1.410)	−0.00014 (−.066)	0.56273 (3.820)**	0.29829 (1.308)	−0.00678 (−.957)
INLAND	−0.00087 (−1.090)	0.00079 (.704)	0.54689 (6.897)***	−0.06501 (−.558)	−0.00123 (−.341)
INTERLAKE	−0.00012 (−.104)	0.00176 (1.083)	0.76879 (6.635)***	−0.1636 (−.961)	−0.00564 (−1.064)
KAISER	0.00075 (.332)	−0.00048 (−.155)	1.09386 (4.923)***	−0.09506 (−.291)	−0.00405 (−.399)

(*continued*)

Appendix C (*continued*)

Firm	a_i	a_id_j	b_i	b_id_j	w_{ijt}
			Parameter		
KEYSTONE	-0.00161	0.0043	0.44899	0.51708	-0.00125
	(-.894)	(1.717)*	(2.520)**	(1.975)*	(-.153)
LTV	0.00051	0.0009	1.97311	-0.10412	0.00061
	(.276)	(.349)	(10.707)***	(-.385)	(.073)
LUKENS	-0.00002	0.00007	0.38659	0.14968	-0.00039
	(-.014)	(.038)	(2.841)**	(.749)	(-.063)
MCLOUTH	-0.00125	0.00067	0.81859	0.10235	-0.00406
	(-.654)	(.251)	(4.345)***	(.370)	(-.471)
NATIONAL	-0.00075	0.00046	0.53292	-0.13611	-0.00272
	(-.812)	(.354)	(5.811)***	(-1.010)	(-.650)
NORTHWESTERN	-0.00058	0.0012	0.29499	-0.23263	0.00139
	(-.570)	(.846)	(2.916)**	(-1.565)	(.302)
NUCOR	0.00121	-0.00123	1.35078	-0.04689	0.00212
	(1.032)	(-.756)	(11.653)***	(-2.753)**	(.401)
REPUBLIC	-0.00089	0.00159	0.7202	-0.06318	-0.0005
	(-.926)	(1.180)	(7.502)***	(-.448)	(-.115)
SHARON STEEL	0.002889	-0.00416	1.24344	-0.2816	0.00002
	(1.029)	(-1.067)	(4.484)***	(-.691)	(.002)
TIMKEN	-0.00045	0.00034	0.58325	-0.25669	0.00361
	(-.562)	(.305)	(7.319)***	(-2.192)*	(.991)
U.S. STEEL	-0.00026	0.00165	0.95721	-0.05251	-0.00591
	(-.213)	(.958)	(7.824)***	(-.292)	(-1.058)
WHEELING-PITTSBURGH	-0.00091	0.00231	1.24554	-0.13171	0.00669
	(-.535)	(.980)	(7.430)***	(-.535)	(.874)

All Variables for the Period Ending 1982

ARMCO	−0.001923	0.00171	0.75748	0.18646	0.00362
	(−1.558)	(.983)	(6.005)***	(1.030)	(.634)
ATHLONE	−0.0013	0.00225	0.31803	0.02892	0.00017
	(−1.042)	(1.279)	(2.492)*	(.158)	(.030)
BETHLEHEM	−0.00126	0.00172	1.12747	−.06286	0.00811
	−(1.119)	(1.084)	(9.786)***	(−.380)	(1.552)
CARPENTER TECHNOLOGY	−0.00161	0.002378	0.37379	0.26218	0.01369
	(−1.461)	(1.529)	(3.315)**	(1.620)	(2.676)**
COPPRWELD	−0.00159	0.00183	0.3001	0.27824	0.00139
	(−1.158)	(.939)	(2.126)*	(1.374)	(.216)
CYCLOPS	−0.00197	0.00367	0.58492	−0.25087	0.00927
	(−1.634)	(2.159)*	(4.756)***	(−1.421)	(1.662)*
FLORIDA STEEL	−0.00185	0.00286	0.77114	0.022775	0.02294
	(−1.121)	(1.231)	(4.577)***	(.094)	(3.002)**
INLAND	−0.00031	0.00023	0.51574	0.63475	0.01345
	(−.270)	(.141)	(4.354)***	(3.734)**	(2.503)*
INTERLAKE	−0.00088	0.00276	0.25671	−0.03504	−0.00009
	(−1.099)	(2.448)*	(3.138)**	(−.298)	(−.023)
KAISER	−0.00206	0.00493	0.78754	−0.041359	−0.01662
	(−.972)	(1.648)	(3.634)**	(−1.330)	(−1.691)*
LTV	−0.00272	0.00291	1.58289	0.16294	0.00747
	(−1.698)*	(1.287)	(9.658)***	(.693)	(1.005)
LUKENS	−0.00183	0.00238	0.65548	0.26829	−0.01137
	(−1.192)	(1.096)	(4.172)***	(1.190)	(1.596)
NATIONAL	−0.00179	0.00246	0.87714	0.81681	0.00879
	(−1.348)	(1.311)	(6.447)***	(4.131)***	(1.425)
NORTHWESTERN	−0.0094	0.00099	0.18846	0.18498	0.008456
	(−.944)	(.704)	(1.848)*	(1.264)	(1.828)*

(continued)

Appendix C (*continued*)

Firm	Parameter				
	a_i	$a_i d_j$	b_i	$b_i d_j$	w_{ijt}
NUCOR	-0.00077	0.00223	1.10819	-0.58302	-0.00639
	(-.597)	(1.230)	(8.410)***	(-3.083)**	(-1.069)
TIMKEN	-0.00088	0.00088	0.44024	0.13877	0.01192
	(-.934)	(.662)	(4.550)***	(.999)	(2.717)**
U.S. STEEL	-0.00193	0.00267	0.97134	0.00405	0.01024
	(-1.488)	(1.457)	(7.324)***	(.021)	(1.703)*
WHEELING-PITTSBURGH	-0.00281	0.00382	0.67238	0.13814	0.01383
	(-1.547)	(1.493)	(3.627)**	(.519)	(1.645)
All Variables for the Period Ending 1984					
ARMCO	-0.00213	0.00069	1.35427	0.17361	-0.00174
	(-1.529)	(.356)	(7.148)***	(.576)	(-.307)
ATHLONE	-0.00026	-0.000212	0.34617	0.28539	0.0066
	(-.228)	(-.134)	(2.264)*	(1.173)	(1.292)
BETHLEHEM	-0.00088	0.00004	1.7705	-0.26936	-0.00711
	(-.807)	(.028)	(11.973)***	(-1.145)	(-1.441)
CARPENTER TECHNOLOGY	-0.00011	-0.00045	0.56889	0.06193	0.00025
	(-.124)	(-.362)	(4.694)***	(.321)	(.063)
COPPRWELD	0.00015	-0.00245	0.69291	-0.11139	-0.01327
	(.100)	(-1.190)	(3.466)**	(-.350)	(-1.987)
CYCLOPS	0.00047	0.00034	0.51834	-0.25264	0.00253
	(.565)	(.293)	(4.538)***	(-1.390)	(.664)

FLORIDA STEEL	−0.00197	0.00249	0.97232	−0.1953	−0.00473
	(−1.529)	(1.381)	(5.530)***	(−.0698)	(−.805)
INLAND	−0.00128	0.00031	1.2249	−0.18134	0.00638
	(−1.227)	(.707)	(8.612)***	(−.801)	(1.343)
INTERLAKE	0.00044	−0.00048	0.32398	0.18171	0.00016
	(.702)	(−.546)	(3.788)**	(1.335)	(.055)
LTV	−0.00143	−0.00079	1.55517	0.12886	−0.00333
	(1.039)	(−.410)	(8.297)***	(.432)	(−.532)
LUKENS	−0.00051	0.00099	0.93481	−0.25399	0.00166
	(−.354)	(.488)	(4.743)***	(−.810)	(.253)
NATIONAL	0.00007	−0.00039	1.5034	−1.04645	−0.00586
	(.059)	(−.238)	(9.227)***	(−4.035)***	(−1.078)
NORTHWESTERN	−0.00159	−0.00035	0.19919	0.35722	−0.00276
	(−1.046)	(−.165)	(.965)	(1.087)	(−.400)
NUCOR	−0.00055	0.00144	0.89299	0.04713	−0.00386
	(−.455)	(.861)	(5.480)***	(.182)	(−.709)
TIMKEN	−0.00025	−0.00005	0.43959	−0.09224	−0.00159
	(−.367)	(−.051)	(4.759)***	(−.627)	(−.516)
U.S. STEEL	−0.00048	0.00095	1.19715	−0.14619	−0.00146
	(−.585)	(.820)	(10.616)***	(−.814)	(−.387)
WHEELING-PITTSBURGH	−0.0004	−0.00364	1.05016	0.06664	0.00023
	(−.223)	(−1.450)	(4.295)***	(.171)	(.028)

*Significant at the .10 level.
**Significant at the .01 level.
***Significant at the .001 level.

References

Baldwin, Robert. 1985. *The political economy of U.S. import policy.* Cambridge, Mass.: MIT Press.

Barnett, Donald F., and Robert W. Crandall. 1986. *Up from the ashes: The rise of the steel minimill in the United States.* Washington, D.C.: Brookings Institution.

Binder, John. 1985. Measuring the effects of regulations with stock price data. *Rand Journal of Economics* 16: 167–83.

Bollen, Kenneth A. (1989). *Structural equations with latent variables.* New York: Wiley-Interscience.

Business Week. 1978. Steelmen move closer to another price rise. 5 June, 54–55.

———. 1979a. Steel: Washington triggers a buoyant mood. 8 January, 63–68.

———. 1979b. Small steelmakers open fire on imports. 15 January, 37.

Congressional Budget Office. 1984. *The effects of import quotas on the steel industry.* Washington, D.C.: GPO, July.

Crandall, Robert W. 1981. *The U.S. steel industry in recurrent crises: Policy options in a competitive world.* Washington, D.C.: Brookings Institution.

Fama, Eugene F. 1976. *The foundations of finance.* New York: Basic Books.

Grossman, Gene M., and James A. Levinsohn. 1989. Import competition and the stock market return to capital. *American Economic Review* 79: 1065–87.

Hartigan, James, Philip Perry, and Sreenivas Kamma. 1986. The value of administered protection: A capital market approach. *Review of Economics and Statistics* 4: 610–17.

Hickock, Susan. 1985. The consumer cost of U.S. trade restraints. *Federal Reserve Bank of New York Quarterly Report* 10, no. 2 (Summer): 1–12.

Hufbauer, Gary C., Diane T. Berliner, and Kimberly A. Elliot. 1986. *Trade protection in the United States: 31 case studies.* Washington, D.C.: Institute for International Economics.

Hughes, John, Wesley Magat, and William Ricks. 1986. OSHA cotton dust standards: an analysis of stock price behavior. *Journal of Law and Economics* 29: 29–59.

Industry Week. 1981a. Roderick braces for a showdown in court. 19 October, 111–12.

———. 1981b. Quotas their goal? TPM is no solution, steelmakers insist. 2 November, 31–32.

———. 1982a. Trade-law violations charged: U.S. steelmakers go for the jugular. 25 January, 22.

———. 1982b. $1 billion worth? More red ink awaits steelmakers. 20 September, 82–83.

Jones, Kent. 1986. *Politics vs. economics in world steel trade.* London: Allen & Unwin.

Kim, Jae-On, and Charles W. Mueller. 1978. *Factor analysis: Statistical methods and practical issues.* Beverly Hills, Cal.: Sage University Press.

Lenway, Stefanie Ann, Kathy Rehbein, and Laura Starks. 1990. The impact of protectionism on firm wealth: The experience of the steel industry. *Southern Economic Journal* 56: 1079–93.

Olson, Mancur. 1971. *The logic of collective action.* Cambridge: Harvard University Press.

Prager, R. 1989. Using stock price data to measure the effects of regulation: The Interstate Commerce Act and the railroad industry. *Rand Journal of Economics* 20: 280–88.

Purchasing. 1977a. Steel buyers expect prices to jump 5%. 24 May, 13.

———. 1977b. Dumping ruling: First break in steel's import impasse. 8 November, 8–9.

————. 1978. Trigger price system may cost $1 billion. 8 February, 21.

Rose, Nancy L. 1985. The incidence of regulatory rents in the motor carrier industry. *Rand Journal of Economics* 16: 300–318.

Schwert, G. William. 1981. Using financial data to measure the effects of regulation. *Journal of Law and Economics* 15: 121–59.

Shepsle, Kenneth A., and Barry R. Weingast. 1987. The institutional foundations of committee power. *American Political Science Review* 81: 85–104.

Shipper, Katherine, and Rex Thompson. 1983. The impact of merger-related regulations on the shareholders of acquiring firms. *Journal of Accounting Research* 21: 184–221.

Smith, R., M. Bradley, and G. Farrell. 1986. Studying firm-specific effects of regulation with stock price data: An application to oil price regulation. *Rand Journal of Economics* 17: 467–89.

Tarr, David G. 1989. *A general equilibrium analysis of the welfare and employment effects of U.S. quotas in textiles, autos and steel.* Bureau of Economics Staff Report, Federal Trade Commission. Washington, D.C.

Tarr, David G., and Morris E. Morkre. 1984. *Aggregate costs to the United States of tariffs and quotas on imports: General tariff cuts and removal of quotas on automobiles, steel, sugar, and textiles.* Bureau of Economics Staff Report, Federal Trade Commission. Washington, D.C.

U.S. Congress, House Ways and Means Committee Subcommittee on Trade. 1984. *Problems of the U.S. steel industry.* Washington, D.C.: GPO, 26 April, 2 and 8 May, 20 June, 3 August. Government Printing Office.

U.S. International Trade Commission (USITC). 1985. *The effects of restraining U.S. steel imports on the exports of selected steel-consuming industries.* USITC Publication 1788 (December). Washington, D.C.

————. 1988. *U.S. global competitiveness: Steel sheet and strip industry.* USITC Publication 2050 (January). Washington, D.C.

Yoffie, David. 1987. Corporate political strategies for political action: A rational model. In *Business Strategy and Public Policy,* ed. Alfred Marcus et al. Westport, Conn.: Quorum Books.

Comment   Timothy J. McKeown

Stimulated in large measure by federal campaign finance legislation in the mid-1970s and the wealth of newly available data generated as a result of that legislation's reporting requirements, a number of political scientists, sociologists, and economists recently have developed models of corporate political effort. The paper by Lenway and Schuler is broadly similar to existing work but offers a number of potentially fruitful innovations. First, this is one of the first attempts to relate above-normal returns to prior political activity. Second, it acknowledges that corporate political activity is a multidimensional phenomenon, and it displays some awareness of the possibility that the determi-

Timothy J. McKeown is visiting associate professor, Fuqua School of Business and Department of Political Science, Duke University, and associate professor of political science, University of North Carolina, Chapel Hill.

nants of visible activity may not be the same as the determinants of unobservable activity. Third, it offers a detailed examination of individual firms within a sector rather than of a sample drawn from all manufacturing (the more common procedure). Because the work is exploratory both theoretically and empirically, I will focus on three broad areas: the proposed model and alternative specifications, the interpretation of findings, and possibilities for additional research.

The Proposed Model

The Yoffie model by way of Lenway and Schuler argues that political activity is an increasing function of rate of return. Zardkoohi has also suggested such a relationship, based not on the necessity of relying on internal resources but instead simply on a conventional assumption about the income elasticity of political activity.[1] There are, however, other arguments. Salamon and Siegfried argue that firms which visibly pursue political objectives while earning high profits invite unfriendly attention and counter-mobilization.[2] A behavioral theory of the firm[3] suggests that when financial performance falls below aspirations, then search and innovation and presumably political effort will be intensified. A variant of this theory argues that performance that significantly exceeds aspirations will also lead to more search and innovation, as various organizational subunits seize slack resources and use them for their own pet projects.[4] These hypotheses imply an nonlinear relationship between financial performance and political activity; thus the specification offered in this paper hardly exhausts the theoretical possibilities.

The unusual feature of the paper is the way in which return on equity is conceptualized. Rather than being treated as a factor affecting the motivation to act politically, it is used to indicate the capability to act. Of course, the rate of return indicates this only when one already knows the size of the capital stock on which the returns are being reaped. It would seem more direct to use corporate income in dollars to model this capability. If one were interested in modeling the level of corporate PAC expenditures, it would be appropriate to use the number of white-collar employees and their average salary, since these are the people who decide to contribute, at least in a juridical sense.

The authors argue that diversification tends to undercut the motivation to engage in political action in any sector. This is based on the notion that top

1. Asghar Zardkoohi, "On the Political Participation of the Firm in the Electoral Process," *Economic Journal* 51(1985): 804–17.

2. Lester M. Salamon and John J. Siegfried, "Economic Power and Political Influence: The Impact of Industry Structure on Public Policy," *American Political Science Review* 71 (3) (1977): 1026–43.

3. Richard M. Cyert and James G. March, *A Behavioral Theory of the Firm* (Englewood Cliffs, N.J.: Prentice-Hall, 1963).

4. James G. March, "Footnotes to Organizational Change," *Administrative Science Quarterly* 26 (4) (1981): 563–77.

managers are only boundedly rational, that their attention is limited, and that only the most salient political opportunities and threats are perceived by these managers. However, political action can to some extent be decentralized in multidivisional firms, as, for example, when a steel firm like USX establishes different political action committees for different divisions of the firm. In addition, management of the firm's political environment may be a heavy responsibility for top management, so that they shed other responsibilities before they give up supervision of the firm's political strategy. One simple reason why multidivisional firms may be less politically active on a given issue than single-product counterparts is that different divisions may have conflicting interests in protection of steel. This would follow if the multidivision enterprise is both a producer and a consumer of steel.

Interpreting the Empirical Results

The findings on political involvement show that market share is consistently positively related to level of activity. This is not inconsistent with Olson's standard argument, but a curvilinear rather than a linear relationship would seem to be implied by a free-riding argument. The main puzzle that the authors set for themselves is the disparity between the results on political involvement and those on abnormal returns. Why are the results dissimilar? One reason is the very explanation that the authors reject. If small firms derive the same advantages from protection as large firms, but free ride, or at least make proportionately no greater political efforts than the large firms, then market share would have no relationship to abnormal returns, but it would be positively related to level of political effort. That is exactly what their findings show.

The minimills, other things being equal, are as (in)active as the integrated producers. This is so in the face of results on the abnormal returns equations that suggest a weak tendency for minimills to lose wealth from the trade restraints secured by the integrated producers. One way to make sense of these results is to consider the possibility of strategic interaction between the integrated producers and the minimills. The minimills may have refrained from political action not because they were free riding on the integrated producers but rather because of a rational calculation that enhanced political activity could easily be matched by greater efforts by the integrated producers, thus producing no change in political outcomes but a greater expenditure of resources for all concerned.

Extensions of the Research

Lenway and Schuler suggest that considering the specific product mix of firms compared to the products covered by protective measures would likely improve the performance of the abnormal returns equation. I agree, and also suggest that they consider the geographic region where the firm's sales take place and relate that to the countries that are the target of the protective measures. For example, West Coast producers will benefit more from protection imposed on East Asian producers, East Coast producers will be relatively more concerned about protection levied against European producers.

A number of alternative strategies for modeling political activity are implicit in my previous comments. In addition, the following measures could be taken:

1. Model the individual elements of a vector of political activities rather than using factor analysis to create a single summary statistic. This would be particularly helpful if one were attempting to evaluate the ways in which different mixes of political activity are chosen by different firms, or if one were interested in the degree of substitutability of different political activities.

2. Explicitly model the level of political activity by firms opposed to proposed policy changes. This is another possible source of a disparity between protectionist political effort and protectionist political results.

3. Model the nature of the political situation in which political activity is occurring. The degree of success may be affected by the thinness of the governing coalition's majority, the time left until the next election, and the level of demands being placed on the government by other groups, including foreigners.

Comment   Wendy E. Takacs

I found the Lenway and Schuler paper very interesting. The results of the hypothesis testing were enlightening, but in addition I found some of the intermediate results to be equally intriguing, perhaps because they provide evidence for some hypotheses of my own about what determines attempts to obtain protection and the importance of the form of protection granted.

My comments begin with some observations on the results and conjectures as to why those results were obtained, add some miscellaneous observations, and end with some suggestions for extensions.

The main thrust of the paper is to provide empirical evidence on a number of questions pertaining to the involvement of individual firms in attempts to gain protection:

1. What factors determine a firm's degree of political involvement in attempts to obtain protection where the political activity is measured by political contributions, testimony before Congress, and the number of cases launched in the three established procedures for petitioning for protection: antidump-

Wendy E. Takacs is associate professor of economics at the University of Maryland Baltimore County.

ing-duty investigations, countervailing-duty investigations, and escape-clause actions?

2. Do these *same* factors determine the benefits of protection, measured by abnormally high stock prices during a period of time surrounding the announcement of the protection?

3. Are the more politically involved firms the ones that receive the greatest benefits from protection?

The clearest result is that market share is the most significant determinant of the amount of resources firms devote to the activity of attempting to get protection. The authors conclude, "firms with higher expectations of financial benefits from trade restraints expend the most effort in attempting to influence U.S. trade policy." It is useful to note that the expectation of financial benefits from trade restraints has two components: (1) the expectation of a positive result, that is, the expectation of being able to influence policymaking in the desired direction, and (2) the size of the gain if protection is obtained.

Larger firms probably have a higher expectation of being able to influence policy by their individual actions than do smaller firms *and* probably have more to gain than smaller firms. Larger firms have more employees and therefore more votes; larger firms are more likely to be multiple plant operations and therefore be constituents to more politicians. Particularly in an industry like steel, they are probably accustomed to being able to influence their product market, so why not the political market for protection as well? They may perceive themselves as having a higher probability of influencing the political process. On the second point, firms with larger market share have more output, and so if prices increase due to protection, they stand to receive larger rent transfers.

I also found it noteworthy that firms with a higher return on equity in years leading up to the protectionist episode appeared to devote more resources to attempts to obtain protection. This relationship did not quite reach a level of statistical significance at conventional levels. But it still contradicts the image of hard-pressed import competing firms with their backs to the wall seeking protection as a last resort out of desperation. The results indicate that firms devote resources to further improving their profitability when they are relatively better off. This result, albeit tentative because of the lack of statistical significance, has important implications for the duration of protection. Obtaining protection will encourage firms to devote yet more resources to the campaign to maintain the protection because it increases their expectations of being able to influence the political process and increases their profitability, giving them more resources to devote to the campaign to maintain the protectionist measures.

At first it struck me as perplexing that the factors that explain firms' degree of political involvement did not appear to explain the benefits they receive from the protection, and that there was no apparent direct relationship between the magnitude of firms' political activities and the benefits they receive, at least as measured by increases in share prices. Let me offer some conjectures as to why this result was obtained.

The first has to do with the role of expectations and the method that the authors use to measure the benefits of protection. The authors use two windows of abnormal returns, one starting ten days before and ending ten days after the announcement of protection, and the other starting ten days before and ending one day after the announcement. Both of these periods may be too short, in that share prices may already reflect the expected benefits of the government's expected action well before this. In that case, the windows used would reflect abnormally high returns only if the protection received was greater than had been expected, and abnormally low returns only if the announced protection was *less* restrictive than anticipated.

To make a comparison with some similar work, Hartigan, Perry, and Kamma used a similar methodology to test for the impact of escape clause actions on share prices.[1] Their study used weekly data, and a window starting two weeks before an escape-clause petition was filed and ending four weeks after the final decision, a period that averaged about forty weeks. Lenway and Schuler might be able to better measure the expected benefits of protection by expanding the window backward, but it is not clear that doing so will dramatically alter the results, because even with the longer window Hartigan and his colleagues found that only two of nineteen industries had significantly positive abnormal returns. Their work does provide some support for the notion that protectionist measures more or less restrictive than those anticipated will affect stock prices. They analyzed the behavior of stock prices around the key dates of the USITC and presidential decisions, and found one case with a significantly negative reaction of stock prices to a presidential decision to protect the petitioning industry. In that case, however, the ITC had recommended import quotas, but the president decided to negotiate a VER, which may have been viewed as less restrictive than anticipated, causing stock prices to fall when that decision was announced.

My second conjecture as to the lack of perceived profitability of the announced protection is that the costs of the attempts to obtain protection eat into the increased profits from it, leaving little net gain. The behavior of stock prices may reflect a correct assessment of the benefits of protection, coupled with recognition of the magnitude of the costs involved in lobbying, and the lawyers' and consultants' fees required to initiate and carry through with an antidumping, countervailing-duty, or escape-clause petition. The results in the paper thus could be interpreted as evidence of the wastefulness of rent-seeking behavior, which leaves little net gain even for the firms most actively involved.

1. James C. Hartigan, Philip R. Perry, and Sreenivas Kamma, "The Value of Administered Protection: A Capital Market Approach," *Review of Economics and Statistics* 68 (1986): 610–17.

In addition to commenting on the results, I would like to say something about the data reported by the authors. I found the data on abnormal returns for the four protective episodes examined particularly intriguing because of the positive and highly significant abnormal returns when the OMA was negotiated with the EC in 1982, as compared with the trigger price mechanism in 1977, its reinstitution in 1980, and the extension of the OMA in 1984. This information provides some empirical support for the notion that in relatively concentrated industries, quantitative restrictions provide greater possibilities for increased prices and profits than price-oriented measures. Given my point above about expectations, this would have to be interpreted as unanticipated use of quotas rather than price-oriented measures. This interpretation seems reasonable in that in 1982 the steel companies filed countervailing duty and antidumping duty petitions, which normally would have been expected to result in extra duties, but instead the administration reacted by negotiating the OMA.

With respect to extensions, I agree with the authors that it would be useful to include a variable to capture the effect of the particular firm's product mix. Political involvement might be found to depend on the degree of import penetration in the firm's major products, and abnormal returns might be found to depend on the firms' product mix relative to the restrictiveness of the protective measure for various products.

A variable to capture the effects of geography might also help to capture the relative benefits of protection across firms. It is my understanding that firms near the coasts, particularly the West and Gulf coasts, were under more competitive pressure from imports than firms in the center of the country. Perhaps this dimension could be captured by a variable based on the distance of the firm's plants from the nearest deepwater port or some measure of import penetration by region relative to the location of the firm's plants.

Lastly, it is also interesting to contemplate the extension of this methodology to other industries. What if any modifications or additional variables would be necessary to capture differences among firms in those industries? Two other industries that have campaigned to obtain protection are footwear and automobiles. In those industries a very important factor, which does not appear in the steel case, is the degree to which the firm is involved in importing for domestic sale as well as selling domestically produced output. It is not surprising that the auto escape-clause petition in 1980 was filed by Ford Motor Company and the United Auto Workers, without direct participation by General Motors or Chrysler, who were more deeply engaged in the activity of selling imported small cars and trucks, the so-called captive imports.

When firms in an industry differ in the degree to which they import as well as produce at home, attempts to gain protection may be an attempt by domestic firms to gain an advantage relative not only to foreign firms but also to other domestic firms. This idea is consistent with Lenway and Schuler's report that at least one domestic steel firm testified against imposing import restrictions and the result that abnormal returns were significantly lower for minimills when protection was announced in 1977. The possible use of protectionist measures as strategic maneuvering vis-à-vis other domestic firms deserves more attention and investigation.

4   The U.S. VER on Machine Tools: Causes and Effects

Elias Dinopoulos and Mordechai E. Kreinin

4.1   The Machine-Tools VER

In March 1983 the Association for Manufacturing Technology (NMTBA) (the U.S. trade association of machine-tool producers) petitioned the Secretary of Commerce to limit imports of machine tools on national security grounds. A restriction was requested for eighteen types of machine tools, with the objective of limiting imports to 18 percent of domestic consumption. In May 1986, following several years of pressure, President Reagan decided to seek voluntary export restraint (VER) agreements with Japan, Taiwan, Germany, and Switzerland, on several categories that make up half of total machine-tool imports into the United States. In November 1986 he secured a formal five-year agreement (beginning 1 January 1987) with Japan and Taiwan, covering: machining centers, milling machines, lathes (NC [numerically controlled] and non-NC), punching and shearing machines (NC and non-NC). The VER limits were imposed as a fixed percentage of estimated U.S. consumption per category. Although West Germany and Switzerland refused to accept VERs, there was an informal understanding that these countries would not take advantage of the vacuum created by the VERs with the two Far Eastern countries. Table 4.1 indicates the limits on the exports of Japan and Taiwan expressed as a percentage of projected U.S. apparent consumption (in units). As can be seen, the limits vary greatly among categories.

Figure 4.1 displays total machine-tool imports into the U.S. as a percentage of consumption. Imports began growing rapidly around the mid-1970s (coin-

Elias Dinopoulos is associate professor of economics, University of Florida. Mordechai E. Kreinin is professor of economics, Michigan State University.

The authors wish to thank Robert Baldwin, Kala Krishna, Larry Kenny, Steven Matusz and an anonymous reviewer for useful comments; Prakash Loungani for statistical assistance; and Seith Kaplan and Hugh Arce of the U.S. International Trade Commission for supplying data and other information.

Table 4.1   Limitations on U.S. Machine Tool Imports as a Percentage of U.S.
                   Consumption Under the VER

Type of Machine	VER as a Percentage of U.S. Consumption		U.S. Apparent Consumption (Units)	
	Japan	Taiwan	1987	1988
NC (numerically controlled) lathes (horizontal & vertical)	57.47%	3.23%	5,897	6,175
Non-NC lathes (horizontal & vertical)	4.81	14.70	4,521	4,827
Machining centers	51.54	4.66	3,806	4,095
Milling machines	3.15	19.29	11,275	11,664
NC punching & shearing	19.25	—	770	704
Non-NC punching & shearing	9.14	—	3,780	4,072

Source: VER Agreement between the U.S. and Japan and between the U.S. and Taiwan.

ciding with the introduction of new computer technologies), but growth ended with the VERs in 1987.

Administration of the VERs was placed in the hands of the two exporting countries. Each year the U.S. government forecasts apparent consumption for the following year and allocates the respective quotas to Japan and Taiwan on this basis. In turn, the government of each of the two countries distributes export licenses to its respective producers. The U.S. customs insists that a certificate endorsed by the Japanese or Taiwanese governments accompany each shipment into the United States.

In the next section we explore the reason why VER protection was given to the machine-tool industry.

4.2   Causes of the VER: The Political Economy of Protection

In recent years there has been a burgeoning professional literature attempting to explain the existence and level of protection in terms of certain features of the protected industry (endogenizing protection). In this section, we explore the awarding of a VER to the machine-tool industry by examining in succession each of the characteristics commonly used in this strand of the literature.[1]

1. *The pressure group model* (associated with Olson (1965) and Pincus (1975)), which states that a small number of firms or high degree of concentration is necessary for an industry to organize itself and lobby for protection, can hardly explain the machine-tool case. The industry consists of nearly thirteen hundred firms, two-thirds of which have fewer than twenty employees

---

1. The characteristics are those listed in Baldwin (1984, 1989), and Hamilton (1989). For a description of these models see Kreinin (1991, 384–86, and the literature cited in note 5).

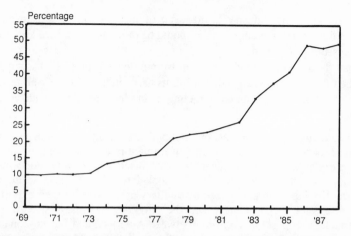

Fig. 4.1   U.S. machine tool imports as a percentage of U.S. machine-tool consumption
Sources: The Economic Handbook of the Machine Tool Industry 1989/90 (Arlington, Va.: National Machine Tool Builders Association, 1990), 127

Table 4.2   **Structure of the U.S. Machine-Tool Industry, 1982**

	No. of Firms	No. of Employees
A. No. of employees:		
1–49	1,132	12,100
50–499	214	29,200
500–2,500	46	36,300
Total	1,392	77,600
B. Region:[a]		
New England	166	14,590
Middle Atlantic	178	12,100
North Central	669	46,010
South	71	1,630
West	165	2,910

Note: Includes both restricted and unrestricted categories of machine tools.
Source: National Machine Tool Builders Association 1990.
[a]The regional data includes states with 150 employees or more.

each. At the other end of the spectrum, fifteen companies have over a thousand employees; and only one has more than twenty-five hundred employees. The size distribution of firms is shown in table 4.2, A. Not only does the industry consist of many small firms, but American machine-tool builders are known to be fiercely independent (Harvard Business School 1988). And although there is a measure of geographical concentration in the north-central states, the industry is widely scattered throughout the country (table 4.2, B).

In sum, since the industry is made up of many small establishments and spread throughout the continent, it should be difficult to organize according to the pressure group model.

That the industry found it difficult to mobilize for protection is supported by the following quotation concerning its early attempts to seek protection in light of Japanese government targeting of the industry for subsidized development:[2]

Historically, American machine tool builders were fiercely independent entrepreneurs who sought to avoid government intervention in their business. One of the first cracks in this tradition occurred in 1977 when concerns over rising imports led the NMTBA to look into alleged Japanese dumping. After the Japanese announced a voluntary price floor for their exports, the U.S. Justice Department seized the NMTBA records. Justice was concerned about possible collusion between American and Japanese manufacturers to fix prices. This effectively stalled any further action by the NMTBA until 1980 when the case was dropped.

The next effort to seek government intervention came from Houdaille Industries, one of the makers of NC machining centers bearing the brunt of the Japanese invasion. Fearing the permanent loss of market share and its own demise, Houdaille petitioned the federal government for relief from imported machine tools, claiming unfair competition from a government-subsidized Japanese cartel. Desiring a quick response, Houdaille avoided the better-known legal avenues toward import relief which mandated studies or hearings and routed the petition through slow, deliberative bodies, such as the International Trade Commission (ITC). Rather, Houdaille called upon Section 103 of the Internal Revenue Act of 1971 to deny investment tax credits for purchases of imported machine tools, submitting the brief in June 1982. Fees for the 714-page brief alone cost Houdaille half a million dollars and Houdaille's president, Philip A. O'Reilly, devoted considerable personal effort stumping for the cause.

Section 103 had never before been used. It allowed that the president could exclude foreign goods from eligibility for the investment tax credit if the foreign government had engaged in discriminatory acts. Houdaille argued that the Japanese practice of "industry targeting" constituted due discrimination. Houdaille chose to use Section 103 because, unlike more commonly used remedies in U.S. trade law, it left enforcement entirely up to the discretion of the executive which meant, theoretically, that the president could act on it immediately. Unfortunately for Houdaille, President Reagan decided to defer action indefinitely. Observers speculated that by early 1983 Reagan had decided to reject the Houdaille petition and was simply waiting for the most opportune moment to do so publicly.

The expected failure of the Houdaille petition put the responsibility for a trade initiative back into the hands of the NMTBA. There was considerable debate among the members about whether the industry should request trade restrictions at all; if they did, what kind of trade barriers would be most

2. For an account of MITI's treatment of the industry see Sarathy (1989).

beneficial to the industry; and which administrative routes offered the most promising prospects for success. (Harvard Business School 1988)

2. *The adding machine model,* proposed by Caves (1976), stresses the importance of an industry's size in employment terms in achieving protection. With a grand total of 77,600 employees and value added of $3.3 billions, the industry does not appear to represent sufficient voting strength to secure protection. Machine tools constitute 0.1 percent of GDP in the U.S., 0.6 percent in Germany, and 0.3 percent in Japan.

3. *The adjustment assistance model* was developed by Cheh (1974). According to this model, protection tends to be given to those industries in which it is difficult for workers to move to new jobs with comparable pay. One way to infer the sector specificity of the industry's labor force is to examine the existence and persistence of unemployment in the face of changing employment conditions in the industry. Although there are no hard data, the impression of well-informed observers is (*a*) that there is no persistent unemployment in the industry as workers who lose their jobs find employment elsewhere, and (*b*) that the skills of machine-tool builders translate well into machinist requirements in other industries. Thus there appears no need for adjustment-assistance-triggered protection.

4. *The equity concern model* states that industries with low wages are more likely to obtain protection. Although the average hourly compensation of production workers in the machine-tool industry is lower than that in the heavily unionized industries (such as autos and steel), it is 9 percent above the average for the manufacturing sector. It is also higher than in other countries (if values are converted to other currencies by the 1986 exchange rate). Most important, as column (1) of table 4.3 demonstrates, the ratio of compensation in the machine-tool industry to that in all manufacturing is higher in the United States than in any other major country except Japan. It is difficult to justify protection, and the implied income redistribution toward the industry, on grounds of equity.

Table 4.3   **Average Hourly Compensation, 1986**

Country	All Manufacturing (1)	Non-electrical Machinery (2)	Ratios (2)/(1)
United States	$13.21	$14.38	109%
Canada	11.04	11.43	103
France	10.27	10.69	104
Germany	13.35	13.93	104
Italy	10.01	10.57	105
Japan	9.47	10.82	114
Sweden	12.43	12.13	98
United Kingdom	7.50	7.67	102

Source: National Machine Tool Builders Association 1990.

5. *The international bargaining model,* which was proposed by Helleiner (1977), suggests that in its trade policy the government attempts to influence the policy of other governments. Although the United States has bargained intensely to induce Japan to open up its markets, the sequence of events leading to the machine-tools VER does not point to this model as a motivating factor.

6. *Comparative cost model:* According to this model, industries that lose comparative advantage and face increased import competition are more likely to be given protection (e.g., Bhagwati 1982). Between 1973 and 1987 U.S. unit labor cost (ULC) in metal-working machinery (the industry that includes machine tools) increased by 9.1 percent annually, while that of Japan rose by 6.2 percent. This annual difference of 2.7 percent is higher than in other capital-good industries, including motor vehicles (Yamamoto 1989–90, table 3). It is consistent with the deterioration in the industry's competitive position, which was sharper than that of many other industries (ibid., table 1). The deterioration is also indicated by the decline in U.S. net exports (exports minus imports); the rise in the import penetration ratio (ratio of import to apparent consumption as shown in fig. 4.1); and the decline in the U.S. share of global output and exports (fig. 4.2). This evidence suggests that loss of comparative advantage could constitute a cause for protectionist action.

On the other hand the machine-tool industry produces highly differentiated products that give rise to considerable intra-industry trade. Most industrial countries import as well as export machine tools (table 4.4). Evidently, certain segments of the U.S. industry compete well in international markets, and that factor would lessen somewhat the strength of the comparative cost model as an explanation of protection.

7. *The status quo model,* associated with Lavergne (1983), asserts that protection obtained in the past is positively correlated with present and future protection. Because the industry does not have a history of protection, this model can be rejected as an explanation of the VER accorded to machine tools.

8. *Summary.* With the exception of the comparative cost model, none of the conventional political economy explanations of protectionism fits the machine-tool industry. What is left to consider is the national security argument.

9. *National defense:* As early as the 1940s the U.S. government considered machine tools essential for national defense:

Machine tools underpin the entire industrial economy by providing tools to make tools. The first item embargoed for sale to Japan by the U.S. in 1940 was machine tools. In 1948, Congress passed legislation to establish a national reserve of machine tools to be used in cases of national emergency, with national defense and security very much in mind. When the Korean War found the U.S. short of critical machine tools, Congress passed a res-

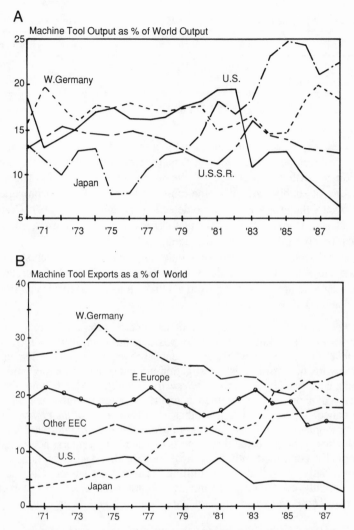

Fig. 4.2   Shares of the U.S. in world output and exports of machine tools
Source: The Economic Handbook of the Machine Tool Industry 1988/89, and 1989/90
(Arlington, Va.: National Machine Tool Builders Association, 1989, 1990).

olution indicating that the U.S. should not be dependent on foreign sources for critical machine tools. (Sarathy 1989, 139)

The original request for protection by the industry and the U.S. government's reason for granting it were explicitly based on national defense arguments. There appears to be little doubt that the industry is important to na-

Table 4.4   Exports and Imports of Machine Tools, 1983 ($ millions)

	U.S.	Germany	Japan	U.K.	France	Switzerland
Exports	355	1,440	1,178	263	242	603
Imports	799	348	105	224	330	102

Source: National Machine Tool Builders Association 1990.

tional security. Indeed, the numerically controlled machine-tool technology was first developed under Defense Department sponsored research. And the relation is further highlighted by the well-publicized Toshiba sale to the U.S.S.R. of sophisticated machine tools used for milling quiet propellers to aid Soviet submarines in avoiding detection (Sarathy 1989, 139). Certainly sophisticated machine tools are critical for the aerospacè industry, where demands for close tolerance and precision must be met.

National security was used as the determining criterion at each step of the decision to select the particular product lines eligible for VER protection. Following is a direct quotation from a White House press release on the subject, dated 20 May 1986:

> In February 1984, the Secretary of Commerce submitted a report to the President concluding that *imports posed a national security threat in a number of product lines.* The President subsequently asked the Secretary to review his findings in this investigation in light of new planning guidelines being developed by *the National Security Council.* In March 1986, the Secretary of Commerce submitted a report incorporating the new planning guidance. The report concluded that *imports of seven of the eighteen product categories under consideration pose a threat to the national security.* Specifically, he indicated that imports of machining centers, horizontal numerically controlled lathes, vertical numerically controlled lathes, nonnumerically controlled lathes, milling machines and numerically and nonnumerically controlled punching and shearing machines *pose a security threat. These categories account for about half of U.S. machine tool imports.*
>
> The President has determined that we must take steps to *maintain a viable machine tool industry for national security purposes.* He also believes that the industry needs time to make adjustments to improve its competitive position. These adjustments cannot be made with the current level of imports. The President has decided to seek up to a five year program of voluntary import restraint. We anticipate that our trading partners will be willing to cooperate with us to help *maintain a critical element of the U.S. defense base.* (emphasis added)

Note the involvement of the National Security Council in all stages of the deliberations, and that the selection of seven of the eighteen product categories requested by the industry was made on national security grounds.

Thus the comparative cost model in conjunction with the national defense argument offers the most credible explanation of the machine-tool VER. Although the NMTBA was not formed for the purpose of seeking import protection, its existence facilitated the pressure on the government to negotiate the VERs. Other countries, such as Japan, have similar trade associations. The U.S. recession in the early 1980s resulted in accelerating the deterioration in the industry's competitive position. Output and profits dropped sharply[3] and the import penetration ratio increased rapidly (see fig. 4.1). Between 1981 and 1983 total employment in the industry decreased by 35 percent. These conditions induced the industry to increase its pressure for protection. The NMTBA initiated its petition for the imposition of a VER in March 1983. Consequently, the comparative cost model and the U.S. recession in the early 1980s determined the timing of protection, whereas the industry was perceived to be important on national defense grounds since the early 1940s.

It should be emphasized that the VER was part and parcel of a comprehensive program by the Departments of Defense and Commerce to revive the U.S. machine-tool industry. The program included an undertaking by the Defense Department to integrate the U.S. industry into the defense procurement process by providing advance information of defense needs; research and other subsidies to modernize the industry; and the possibility of antitrust exemption for cooperative research and development effort in the industry.

4.3 Effects of the VERs

4.3.1 Trade Volume

Table 4.5 shows imports into the United States (in units) of machine-tool categories restricted by VERs from the restricted countries (Japan, Taiwan), the threatened countries (Germany, Switzerland), two other major suppliers (the United Kingdom, France), and the world as a whole.

That machine-tool imports are highly cyclical is illustrated by the sharp drop during the recession of the early 1980s, and the recovery after 1983. But the decline in both 1987 *and* 1988 occurred only in the restricted and threatened source countries as well as France. It did not occur in 1988 in the United Kingdom or the world as a whole. At least some of the decline can be attributed to the VER: It reduced the exports to the United States from the restricted and threatened countries, and in 1988 it appears to have caused substitution from the United Kingdom and the rest of the world. U.S. output of machine tools rose from 41,992 in 1987 to 48,668 in 1988. The resulting decline in the U.S. import to consumption ratio of five restricted machine-tool categories is shown in figure 4.3.

---

3. See National Machine Tool Builders Association (1990, 42, 262), for data on machine-tool shipments and profits.

Table 4.5   VER-restricted Machine Tool Imports Into the U.S. (units)

	Source Country						
Year	Japan	Taiwan	Germany	Switzerland	U.K.	France	World
1980	6,089	11,442	1,118	314	2,683	381	31,133
1981	7,676	9,000	1,123	325	2,331	313	29,884
1982	5,550	5,624	915	336	1,563	159	20,723
1983	4,523	3,572	459	233	1,214	113	13,680
1984	6,995	5,733	756	420	1,455	144	20,423
1985	9,190	7,118	1,235	349	1,778	112	26,270
1986	8,927	6,614	1,179	286	1,994	214	25,158
1987	6,209	4,190	648	268	1,689	199	17,706
1988	5,408	3,788	651	115	2,660	58	18,682

Source: Tabulations supplied by the International Trade Commission.

4.3.2   Unit Value

To assess the price effect of reduced imports into the United States, we used the following procedure. We estimated a price function for the years 1971–86 where the unit value (P) was a function of unit labor cost in manufacturing (ULC) (worker's compensation divided by productivity). Both variables were measured in dollars and transformed into logarithms. The resulting regression is

$$(1) \qquad \log{(P)} = -4.78 + 1.77 \log{(ULC)} \qquad R^2 = .94$$
$$\qquad\qquad\qquad (0.12) \qquad\qquad\qquad DW = 1.43,$$

where the number in parenthesis represents the standard error.[4] This equation was used to estimate a predicted price for 1987 and 1988. The excess of the actual over the predicted price is considered the effect of the VER on the price of machine tools produced by U.S. firms.[5] In 1987 that excess was $11,000, which is 17 percent of the actual price ($64,980). For 1988 there was no significant difference between the two prices. We conclude that the VER produced a substantial boost in the U.S. price but only in the first year of its existence.

How is the price hike reflected in corresponding changes in the export prices of Japan and Germany? Table 4.6 presents export unit values for these two countries. Column (1) includes only the *VER-restricted categories* of machine tools and shows their *export price (in thousands) to the United States* as

4. The prices were calculated from National Machine Tool Builders Association (1990, 93) and from U.S. Department of Commerce series MQ-35W. Unit labor costs were obtained from the U.S. Department of Labor, Bureau of Labor Statistics tabulations.

5. A similar methodology was used in Crandall (1985) and in Dinopoulos and Kreinin (1988). The latter study employed both hedonic regression analysis and time series analysis to calculate the price impact of the auto VER. Both analytical approaches resulted in very similar estimated price increases due to the VER.

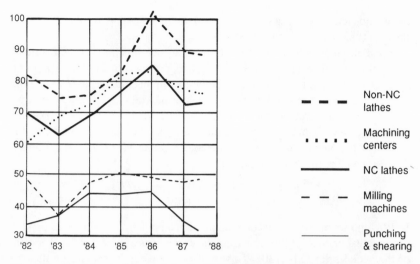

Fig. 4.3   Machine-tool imports in the United States, consumption import market share (percentage)
Source: E. E. Sprow, "Machine-Tool VRA's: Too Little too Late?" *Tooling and Production* (March 1989):64–70.
Note: Unit import share can exceed 100 percent because of reexporting.

well as an index number form (1980 = 100). Columns (2)–(5), presented for purposes of comparison, are in index numbers form and represent exports *to the world as a whole*. Column (2) shows the price index of metal working machinery, a category that contains machine tools. But the effect of the VER is diluted (relative to col. [1]) in two ways: first, column (2) includes many nonrestricted items; and second, column (2) shows export prices to the world as a whole rather than just to the United States. The price increases in all columns since 1985 reflect largely the depreciation of the dollar. It is the *differential percentage change between columns* that may reveal a VER effect (see fig. 4.4).

Between 1986 and 1987 Japan's dollar price of the restricted machine tools exported to the United States, rose by 19 percent,[6] that of metal-working machinery (which contains restricted machine tools) to the world rose by 16 percent, while the prices shown in columns (3)–(5) rose by 11 percent. The eight (19–11) percentage point differential suggests a significant price effect of the VER in the first year that corresponds to the rise in U.S. prices discussed earlier. Similarly for Germany the increase between 1986 and 1987 in column (1) was 43 percent, in column (2), 25 percent, and in the remaining columns 23 percent. Again this suggests a price effect of the VER threat. Thus both

6. Figure 4.5 displays Japanese domestic prices of machine tools in terms of yen, showing a temporary effect of price cutting in the restricted categories relative to overall machine tools. The general price reduction probably reflects a response to the depreciation of the dollar.

Japan and Germany appeared to have restricted their export volume and raised the export price to the United States.

As an alternative approach we estimated a price function for the restricted categories over the years 1971–86 for each exporting country. The export unit value (P) is made a function of unit labor cost in manufacturing (ULC). Both variables are measured in dollars and transformed into logarithms.[7] The estimated coefficients were used to predict the price for 1987 and 1988. The difference between actual[8] and predicted values is considered the effect of the VER. But the only country for which credible results were obtained is Taiwan. The estimated regression for that country is

$$
(2) \qquad \log (P) = -5.01 + 1.32 \log (ULC) \qquad R^2 = 0.92
$$
$$
(0.20) \qquad\qquad DW = 1.22.
$$

In 1987 the actual price exceeded the predicted price by $2,540, or 25 percent of the actual price ($9,980). For 1988 the excess was $980 which is 10 percent of the actual price ($10,130). This reinforces the earlier conclusion that the VER caused an export price increase in the exporting countries, resulting in a transfer of economic rents from the United States. A similar phenomenon was observed in the case of the auto VER, and indeed it is what economic theory leads us to expect.

One possible reason for the disappearance of the price effect in 1988 (in the U.S. regression) is the increase in Japanese production capacity in the U.S. that circumvents the VER. In the late 1980s Japanese investment accelerated. Added Japanese capacity in 1986–88 amounted to twenty-one plants and created three thousand new jobs, which represent about 5 percent of the industry's total employment. In other words, the Japanese investment share of total domestic employment increased from 2.2 percent in 1985 to 7 percent in 1987 (see *Wall Street Journal*, 8 January 1990, A9B). And the trend continued in 1989. There is reason to believe that a substantial portion of this investment activity was stimulated by the VER.[9]

Another reason for the relatively small price effect of the VER and its temporary nature could be the difference in market structure between machine-tool buyers and sellers. Buyers of machine tools in the auto and other industries are oligopsonists, and the U.S. machine-tool builders are competitive firms. This relative market structure may affect the pricing outcome. The Jap-

---

7. The unit labor costs were obtained from the U.S. Department of Labor tabulations; the export unit value for 1980–88 from the International Trade Commission and for 1971–79 was calculated from the U.S. Census tabulations of import statistics (*U.S. Import for Consumption* FT246).

8. From the actual prices one can glean an idea of quality and product mix and hence a measure of substitutability between sources of supply. The average export unit values of the restricted categories in 1987, all expressed in thousands of dollars, were Japan, 87; Taiwan, 10; U.K., 17; Germany, 123; France, 45; Italy, 35. In the U.S. the average domestic unit value of all machine tools was $65,000.

9. See, for example, a quotation attributed to Hitachi in Sprow (1989, 67).

Table 4.6   **Export Unit-Value Indexes for Japan and Germany (dollar basis)**

Year	Machine Tools Exported to U.S. (1)	Metal-Working Machinery (2)	Exported to World Special Machinery (3)	Electrical Machinery (4)	All Manufacture (5)
			Japan		
1980	58 (100)	100	100	100	100
1981	72 (124)	107	104	102	105
1982	75 (129)	107	102	94	98
1983	64 (110)	108	98	90	97
1984	68 (117)	107	103	89	97
1985	69 (119)	110	107	86	97
1986	73 (126)	144	121	106	123
1987	87 (150)	167	131	118	137
1988	90 (155)	—	—	—	—
			Germany		
1980	60 (100)	100	100	100	100
1981	53 (88)	85	84	84	85
1982	61 (102)	89	82	82	83
1983	62 (103)	82	80	80	81
1984	85 (142)	76	74	73	75
1985	60 (100)	77	74	73	75
1986	86 (143)	108	103	100	104
1987	123 (205)	135	127	123	127
1988	92 (153)	—	—	—	—

Notes: Col. (1) includes only the VER-restricted categories of machine tools and gives actual prices, in $ thousands, *of exports to the U.S. by Japan and Germany,* followed by an index (1980 = 100) (information obtained from International Trade Commission). All other columns show unit-value indexes of exports to the world as a whole (from U.S. *Monthly Bulletin of Statistics,* Novermber 1989). Col. (2), "Metal-Working Machinery," includes machine tools. But the impact of the VERs is diluted in two ways. The category is far more inclusive than just the restricted items, and the column shows, relative to col. (1), export prices to the world as a whole rather than just to the United States.

anese machine-tool industry is also competitive (Sarathy 1989, 141, 142), facing an oligopsonist U.S. industry. And that would affect the distribution of *VER rents* between the two countries.

The Congressional Budget Office[10] estimated in early 1987 that the annual quota rents accruing to Japan and Taiwan were $100 million for 1987, 1988, and 1989, assuming a 23 percent increase in export prices due to the VER.

10. See Parker (1987). This study assumes that the VERs were designed to reduce the import value of machine tools to the 1981 share of domestic consumption. Assuming an import demand price elasticity of −1, the study arrives at an estimated 23 percent average quota rent per unit which is used to calculate the VER rent transfer.

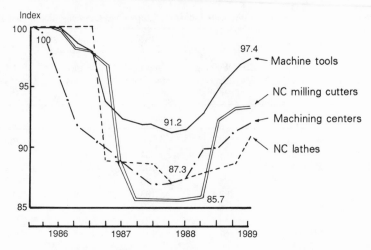

Fig. 4.4   Price changes in Japan expressed in yen
Source: Nikko Monthly Bulletin, June 1989.
Note: Compiled with data from Bank of Japan, "Monthly Report of Price Indices."

Our analysis suggests that the machine tool VER had virtually no effect on export prices beyond 1987 (that is, in 1988). An estimate of VER rents for 1987 is about $110 million for Japan and $10 million for Taiwan, assuming a 20 percent maximum increase in export prices.

4.3.3   Quality Upgrading

Because the VER restriction is applied separately to each of seven categories, quality upgrading can occur only within each category. But data on characteristics necessary to run hedonic regressions (as in the case of automobiles) are not available. So the possible existence of upgrading can be examined only superficially.

Each of the restricted categories contains several seven-digit tariff-line items, and these vary greatly in price. To check for the possible existence of upgrading, we examined the percentage distribution of U.S. imports from Japan within each category to see whether there has been a shift toward the more highly priced items. Examples of two categories are presented in table 4.7. In the first case the results are mixed, while in the second case there has been a noticeable shift toward the higher-priced items. In the other five categories the results are mixed, and no clear-cut picture of upgrading emerges.

But the question of upgrading in the case of capital goods is complicated by the activity-specific nature of the machine, which limits the extent of interitem substitution and hence of upgrading. For example, hardly any substitution is possible between vertical NC lathes and horizontal NC lathes. There is also much information available to the buyers about the specifications of alterna-

Table 4.7   **Percentage Distribution of Quantities of U.S. Imports from Japan within Each Restricted Category**

TSUSA Category	1987 Unit Value	Percentage Distribution of Quantity		
		1984	1986	1987
Machining centers:				
6743404	$88,000	66	61	58
6743406	105,000	3	9	5
6743409	164,000	23	17	25
6743411	82,000	8	13	12
		100	100	100
Milling machines:				
6743464	$128,000	28	53	63
6743467	18,000	29	2	4
6743468	45,000	12	15	3
6743469	52,000	31	30	30
		100	100	100

Source: U.S. Bureau of the Census, *Import for Consumption*, Publication FT246.

tive machines.[11] We conclude that if any upgrading took place, it was limited in scope.

4.4 Conclusions

This paper investigates the causes and effect of the U.S. VER on machine tools negotiated with Japan and Taiwan in 1986 and the VER threat against Germany and Switzerland. The research is less tractable than a similar study of the auto VER (see Dinopoulos and Kreinin 1988) for several reasons. Less information exists for machine tools; the VER was negotiated only for a segment of the industry, for which the data is even scarcer and less well defined than for the entire industry; and the small size of the industry makes the VER effect difficult to capture. Finally, post-VER data are available for only two years, 1987 and 1988.

In terms of the political economy of protection, we show that a plausible explanation of the awarding of protection to a relatively small and geographically scattered industry is the erosion of its competitive position coupled with its perceived importance to national security. All other widely held hypotheses are not applicable to the machine-tools case.

We have shown that the VER resulted in a decline in the import share in the U.S. apparent consumption. The decline was concentrated in the restricted sources, and there was some substitution from nonrestricted sources such as the United Kingdom. During the first year of the VER, U.S. prices of machine

11. Corporate machine buyers often must compare three to seven competitive bids before they make a purchase decision. See Kreinin (1989).

tools rose, as did the prices of exports to the United States by Japanese, German, and Taiwanese supplies. Presumably there was some redistribution from buyers to sellers within the United States as well as a transfer of economic rents from the United States to the exporting countries. Because of scarcity of data, it is difficult to assess the extent of these transfers. But $100 million in 1987 and zero in 1988 is a reasonable estimate. Finally, there is no clear-cut evidence of quality upgrading because of the VER.

References

Baldwin, R. E. 1984. Trade policies in developed countries. In *Handbook of international economics,* eds. Ronald W. Jones and Peter B. Kenen, vol. 1, 572–82. Amsterdam: North Holland.
———. 1989. The political economy of trade policy. *Journal of Economic Perspectives* 3(4): 119–36.
Bhagwati, J. N. 1982. Shifting comparative advantage, protectionist demands, and policy response. In *Import competition and response,* ed. J. N. Bhagwati. Chicago: University of Chicago Press.
Caves, R. E. 1976. Economic models of political choice: Canada's tariff structure. *Canadian Journal of Economics* 9:278–300.
Cheh, J. H. 1974. United States concessions in the Kennedy Round and short-run labor adjustment costs. *Journal of International Economics* 4:323–40.
Crandall, R. 1985. Assessing the impact of the automobile voluntary export restraints upon U.S. automobile prices. Washington, D.C.: Brookings Institution. Typescript.
Dinopoulos, E., and M. E. Kreinin. 1988. Effects of the U.S.-Japan auto VER on European prices and on U.S. welfare. *Review of Economics and Statistics* 70, no. 3 (August): 484–91.
Feenstra, R. C. 1984. Voluntary export restraint in U.S. autos 1980–81: Quality, employment, and welfare effects. In *The Structure and Evolution of Recent U.S. Trade Policy,* ed. R. Baldwin and A. Krueger. Chicago: University of Chicago Press.
Hamilton, C. 1989. The political economy of transient new protectionism. *Weltwirtschaftliches Archiv,* no. 3.
Harvard Business School. 1988. Searching for trade remedies: The U.S. machine tool industry, 1983. Case Study No 9-388-071. Cambridge, Mass.
Helleiner, G. K. 1977. The political economy of Canada's tariff structure: An alternative model. *Canadian Journal of Economics* 4:317–26.
Kreinin, M. E. 1989. How open is Japan's market? additional evidence. *World Economy,* 529–42.
———. 1991. *International economics: A policy approach.* 6th ed. New York: Harcourt Brace Jovanovich.
Lavergne, R. P. 1983. *The political economy of U.S. tariffs: An empirical analysis.* New York: Academic Press.
National Machine Tool Builders Association. 1990. *The economic handbook of the machine tool industry, 1989–90.* Arlington, Va.: National Machine Tool Builders Association.
Olson, M. 1965. *The logic of collective action: Public goods and the theory of groups.* Cambridge: Harvard University Press.

Parker, S. 1987. Revenue estimate for auctioning existing import quota. Congressional Budget Office Memorandum, 27 February.

Pincus, J. 1975. Pressure groups and the pattern of tariffs. *Journal of Political Economy* 83:757–78.

Sarathy, R. 1989. The interplay of industrial policy and international strategy: Japan's machine tool industry. *California Management Review* 31, no. 3 (Spring): 132–60.

Sprow, E. E. 1989. Machine-tool VRAs: Too little too late? *Tooling and Production* (March): 64–70.

Yamamoto, S. 1989/90. Japan's trade lead: Blame profit-hungry American firms. *Brookings Review* 8(1): 14–19.

Comment   Kala Krishna

This paper has two goals: First, to use a number of standard models of the political economy of protection in order to say something about why the machine-tool industry might have been successful in obtaining protection. Dinopolous and Kreinin conclude that the erosion of the competitive position of U.S. producers, and the perceived importance of the industry for national security reasons appear to be the reasons for the protection. Second, they seek to say something about the restrictiveness of the quota and the extent of implicit quota rents. Here they point out, as does the Congressional Budget Office study to which they refer, that the size of quota rents depends on demand and supply conditions as well as the form and level of the VER.

Dinopoulos and Kreinin are relatively successful in attaining their first goal but less so in attaining their second one. I shall direct my comments to their second goal, as this best complements Tom Bayard's discussion. I have four broad sets of comments to make on their approach.

First, they model machine tools as being perfect substitutes. This assumption does need some justification, as machine tools are almost certainly differentiated. Each firm typically chooses a niche in the spectrum of products possible. Thus, even the existence of a large number of producers need not guarantee zero profits. A monopolistic competition model or a model of monopolistic competition with a competitive fringe may be more appropriate. Some idea from industry sources on the price-cost margins typical for the industry, as well as the extent of product differentiation, would help in choosing the model.

Second, they argue that as the VER is in terms of market share, it does not bind when demand shifts out *if* the supply curve of the restricted suppliers is steeper than that at home. The argument seems plausible since in this case a price increase leads to a small response from foreign suppliers but a large one

Kala Krishna is associate professor of economics at Harvard University and a faculty research fellow at the National Bureau of Economic Research.

from domestic suppliers, the combination of which would make the VER non-binding. In an appendix to their paper, they use a linear supply-and-demand model of homogeneous products to try to show this. They show that if b and b^* are the slopes of domestic and foreign inverse supply, and a and a^* are the intercepts, and inverse demand has an intercept of M and slope of $-K$, and

$$(1) \qquad b^* > \frac{(1 - R)b}{R},$$

then for any given R, where R is the market share to which foreigners are restricted, the VER would not bind if demand increases. Unfortunately, their argument is not complete. This is most easily seen in a counterexample given in figure 4C.1. Depicted in this figure are domestic demand (D), domestic supply (S), residual domestic demand $(RD = D - S)$, and foreign supply (S^*).

The intersection of S^* and RD gives the free trade price and quantity, P^F and Q^F. The line $\theta^F S^F$ emanating from the intercept of S and through the intersection of S^* and RD gives the free trade market share of imports. If this is to the right of foreign supply at a given price, foreign supply is not restricted by the VER at that price. If it is to the left of it, foreign supply is restricted. In figure 4C.1, domestic supply is flatter than foreign supply, yet a VER at the free trade level only constrains foreign supply for prices above P^F. Thus, an outward shift in demand, and hence in residual demand, makes the VER bind.

Diagrams such as figure 4C.1 show that when the price (y-axis) intercepts are the same, the VER always binds if $R < R^F$, independent of their relative slopes, and does not ever strictly bind if $R \geq R^F$, even when demand shifts outward. If the U.S. supply has a higher intercept, then outward shifts in demand do not make a VER at the free-trade level bind. If the opposite is true, as depicted in figure 4C.1, outward shifts in demand do make the VER bind. This suggests that the result that an outward shift in demand makes the quota bind depends on the relative intercepts of the supply curve and is *independent* of their relative slopes.

The argument given by the authors in the appendix is that, when *starting* from the free trade equilibrium, the VER is ineffective when demand shifts outward. This gives them the result in equation (1). However, as this expression is only valid *at* the free trade equilibrium, it is only valid if R is set *at* the trade level. Using their linear model, it can be shown that at free trade

$$(2) \qquad \frac{1 - R}{R} = \frac{b^*(m - a) - K(a - a^*)}{b(m - a^*) + K(a - a^*)}$$

From this it is easy to show that for $R \in (0,1)$ equation (1) holds if $a > a^*$.

This odd result, even for the linear case (homogeneous goods) and competition, suggests that with market share restrictions, the whole shape of the

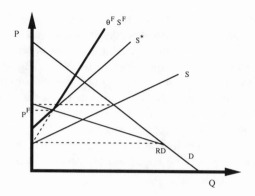

Fig. 4C.1

domestic and foreign supply curves is likely to be relevant and points out the need for care in the analysis.

The third, and most serious, reservation I have about the paper has to do with the econometric specification used. What is the regression of price on a constant and unit labor costs for each country meant to capture? It is *not* a supply curve assuming that marginal costs are upward sloping as quantity supplied does not enter. If it is assumed that marginal costs are constant and equal to price, and products are homogeneous, then only the lowest cost country would be producing, so this interpretation also fails.

A possible interpretation might be that it is the reduced form of the simultaneous equation system. It is clear that a simultaneous equation model is needed here, as a simple supply function cannot be estimated. This is because exchange rate changes affect the foreign supply curve, shifting it around, while at the same time demand shocks shift demand around so that equilibrium prices and quantities trace out neither demand nor supply.

As this regression is run for each country separately, a differentiated product model seems to be what is being used. In such a model the marginal cost (i.e., the inverse supply) from each country would depend on factor prices in the supplying country converted into dollars, as well as the *total* amount supplied by the country. Demand for each country would depend on all prices charged and on the aggregate demand conditions in the U.S. Thus, a reduced form equation system would involve not only unit industry labor cost of the supplying country and the bilateral exchange rate but also the unit costs of all other countries, their bilateral exchange rates, and aggregate demand in the United States at the very least. It would be worthwhile specifying such a system carefully and implementing it to cover the kinds of questions their paper addresses. Since their specification lacks a number of elements, it is hard to take their results on implicit quota rents very seriously.

Fourth, other pieces of evidence they look at are worth mentioning. They suggest that there was a decline in import share in 1985–87. This could be due to the high yen, so that Japanese supply shifted inward rather than because of the VER. The evidence presented in table 4.7 of the paper is also interesting and suggests that there *were* some effects of the VER. This kind of analysis, given the limited data available to the authors, is very worthwhile. Also, if data is really so limited, it might be worthwhile to use the structure imposed by calibration models in addition to the econometric models that are, of course, to be preferred in ideal circumstances.

To conclude, the authors look at interesting policy relevant issues. For this reason, if no other, it is to be hoped that this study will be improved on in subsequent work.

Comment   Thomas O. Bayard

This is an excellent and valuable study. The case of machine tools is fascinating because it is one of only two industries (the other is oil) where imports have been found to "threaten to impair national security" under the terms of section 232 of the Trade Expansion Act of 1962. This study is the first rigorous, independent empirical analysis of the impact of the VER that was negotiated to reduce the threat to national security. It will be valuable to policymakers because they are likely to face industry demands to renew the VER when it expires in late 1991. The authors' methodology is the best available, given data limitations, and their results can be readily updated if the question of renewing the VER arises.

As valuable as the paper is, I was disappointed that it did not address two central policy questions: (1) Did machine-tool imports really pose a significant threat to national security? (2) If so, was the VER the best policy instrument to reduce the security threat? I am not an expert on this case and cannot answer these questions definitively, but I would like to provide some factual information and sketch an approach that will help answer these questions.

Did Imports Pose a Threat to National Security?

Richard Hooley has written an invaluable case study of the government's decision to seek a VER for machine tools.[1] Based on his description, it appears to me that there was a valid national security concern in this case.

In planning for war, the Department of Defense (DOD) seeks assurance that

Thomas O. Bayard is deputy director and a research fellow at the Institute for International Economics.

1. R. Hooley, "Protection for the machine tool industry: Domestic and international negotiations for voluntary restraint agreements," Graduate School of Public and International Affairs, University of Pittsburgh, Case Studies in International Negotiation no. 13 (1987).

it can acquire the additional equipment it needs, when it needs it. This ability to acquire military goods quickly is called surge capacity. The usual military planning scenario assumes two simultaneous conflicts—for example, a major war in Europe and a smaller conflict in the Middle East. DOD runs its production requirements through a detailed input-output matrix to find input needs, which are compared with existing input supplies and productive capacity.

DOD planners did this exercise for machine tools and found that the domestic industry did not have adequate surge capacity. They then calculated how much consumption could be supplied by imports from Europe, Taiwan, and Japan. Much of the debate over whether to assist the industry revolved around the reliability of import supply during wartime. In the end, it was the joint chiefs of staff who swung the decision in favor of assisting the machine-tool industry on the grounds that the military could not guarantee adequate import supplies during war.

Based on the available information, there appears to be a reasonable national security argument for somehow maintaining domestic capacity. The next issue to be considered is the selection of the best policy instruments to achieve this objective.

How Is the National Security Goal Best Achieved?

The optimal form of policy intervention to achieve a desired surge capacity will probably depend on specific characteristics of the industry. In general, however, we know from studies by Bhagwati and Srinivasan that the most efficient way to achieve the policy objective is to select policies that affect the goal most directly.[2] In what follows, I pose a series of questions that seek to identify the appropriate policy objective and hence optimal policy.

First, what is the binding constraint on surge capacity? In the machine-tool case, for example, was the constraint the availability of tools for production of military goods, or was it the availability of skilled machinists to produce machine tools?

If the binding constraint was the availability of machine tools, a second-level question needs to be answered. How much substitutability is there between machine tools used to produce civilian and military goods? If there is substantial civilian-military substitutability, optimal policy would be an investment subsidy, perhaps a special investment tax credit, for imported and domestically produced machine tools used in the United States. Apparently, direct investment subsidies were not considered, but the president did provide technical assistance and modest ($5 million per year) support for research and development in the machine-tool industry. If, however, there is little dual use

2. See J. N. Bhagwati and T. N. Srinivasan, "Optimal intervention to achieve non-economic objectives," *Review of Economic Studies* 36 (1969): 27–38, and T. N. Srinivasan, "The national defense argument for government intervention in foreign trade," in *U.S. Trade Policies in a Changing World Economy,* ed. R. M. Stern (Cambridge, Mass.: MIT Press, 1987).

of machine tools, optimal policy would be to stockpile tools for military production. Stockpiling of machine tools has occurred in the past, but apparently was not considered an option in this case. It takes several years to train a skilled machinist. If the constraint on surge capacity is the availability of skilled labor, optimal policy would be a wage subsidy for machine-tool operators.

On the surface, at least, the VER appears to be a very costly way to maintain surge capacity, since it taxed industrial users of machine tools and thus raised production costs throughout the economy. There are several possible reasons the VER was chosen. First, while subsidies and stockpiling are more cost effective than export restraints, their costs would be included in the military budget. VERs, by contrast, are "off budget" since their costs are borne by consumers. The military and the industry would undoubtedly prefer to keep the costs off budget and less visible to taxpayers, albeit at higher social cost.

A second possible explanation for the VER is suggested by the authors' remark that the export restraint may have ceased to be binding by the second year due to increased foreign direct investment (FDI) in the machine-tool industry. It is possible that the decision to employ a VER was intended to encourage FDI in the industry. As Graham and Krugman point out, protection does not necessarily induce FDI.[3] But, to the extent that it biases the economy toward the production of goods in which foreign firms have a competitive advantage, it may encourage foreign investment. American policymakers had the experience of VER-induced foreign investment in the television and auto industries and may have hoped for the same result in the machine-tool industry. In any event, the VER may well have been a reasonably cost-effective way to increase surge capacity, since it encouraged efficient and innovative foreign producers to quickly invest in the United States. Moreover, as in the case of autos, the presence of foreign-owned machine-tool producers in the United States may provide a valuable demonstration effect for U.S.-owned firms on how to become more efficient.

Although national security cases have been rare in the past, there may be more in the future, despite the reduction in East-West military competition. The most likely future cases are in the high technology area, particularly in super computers and high definition television. If so, the Dinopoulos/Kreinin study will be a valuable model of how national security policy toward imports can be subjected to rigorous economic analysis.

3. E. M. Graham and P. R. Krugman, *Foreign Direct Investment in the United States*, (Washington, D.C.: Institute for International Economics, 1989).

II   Trade Policy Effects Under Imperfectly Competitive Market Conditions

5 Characteristics of Japanese Industrial Groups and Their Potential Impact on U.S.-Japanese Trade

K. C. Fung

5.1 Introduction

Given the economic importance of the two nations, the economic relationship between the United States and Japan is perhaps the most significant bilateral economic linkage in the world economy today. Unfortunately, the dominant feature of the relationship in recent years has been disputes about trade. The core of the problem is undoubtedly the persistent trade imbalance between the two nations.

The magnitude of the trade imbalance remains large. The United States ran a merchandise trade deficit of over $118.5 billion in 1988, and $109 billion in 1989. Japan had a global trade surplus of $78.3 billion in 1988 and $65 billion in 1989. On a bilateral level, the trade imbalance between the United States and Japan was $51.8 billion in 1988 and $49 billions in 1989.

U.S.-Japanese bilateral trade disputes have several important facets. The first element is the set of overall macroeconomic factors. Many economists have pointed out that the large U.S. government budget deficit, the low U.S. savings rate, and the high value of the dollar in the early 1980s provide the fundamental environment that sustains the trade deficit. In 1985, the high U.S. exchange rate began to reverse itself. But the rise of the Japanese yen failed to affect the U.S. trade balance significantly.[1]

K. C. Fung is assistant professor at the University of California–Santa Cruz and a visiting scholar at Stanford University.

The author is very grateful to Bob Baldwin for his detailed comments and continuous encouragement throughout this project. Satya Das, Elias Dinopoulos, and Jim Tybout gave the author suggestions. He would also like to thank Peter Petri and Ed Ray for supplying him with the necessary data. Nancy Fung-Justin and Leilei Xu provided him with valuable computer assistance. Financial support from the University of California Pacific Rim Research Grant is appreciated.

1. This has created some new puzzles and has stimulated further research on the relationship between changes in the exchange rates and the trade balance. For important studies, see Krugman and Baldwin (1987) and Dixit (1989).

A second important dimension of the U.S.-Japan trade problem centers on alleged policies carried out by the Japanese government to promote Japan's industries. Johnson (1982) and Scott and Lodge (1985) highlight how Japanese trade and industrial policies have contributed to the success of Japan's exports in the world market. However, Krugman (1984) and Saxonhouse (1983a, 1983b) dispute the effectiveness of such industrial targeting. The alleged government policies include subsidies, tax incentives for investment, subsidized loans, government-sponsored cooperative research and development projects, and protection of infant industries.

The third important aspect of the U.S.-Japan trade problem is the structure of industry in Japan and how its unique organization can affect the trade balance, the so-called structural impediments to trade. The areas of scrutiny involve banking-industry relationships, the manufacturer-supplier relationships, the alliances between various business concerns, and the behavior of the distributors. It is often alleged that the cooperative Japanese *keiretsu* (industrial groups) and the complex and inefficient Japanese distribution network constitute invisible barriers to trade. For example, it has been pointed out that firms belonging to the same group often purchase from one another rather than from foreign sources.[2] Foreign producers also complain that they cannot find appropriate distributors to carry their products in Japan.

As long as the U.S.-Japan trade imbalances continue to be significant, these elements will be widely discussed. Recent events have focused attention on the last facet—the structure of Japanese industries. In May 1989, the U.S. government, invoking a provision of the 1988 Omnibus Trade Act (the Super 301) singled out Japan and two other countries for maintaining a pattern of unfair trade barriers that are harmful to U.S. exports. Negotiations are being conducted to improve U.S. trade balance with Japan. In April 1990, the United States and Japan reached accords to expand sales of American wood products, satellites, and supercomputers to Japanese markets. Since these agreements, no new formal trade complaints have been launched against Japan. Nevertheless, broad-scale talks are continuing that are aimed at modifying the economic structures of Japan, talks meant to remove Japan's "major structural barriers to imports." One such major area of discussion is the phenomenon and conduct of Japanese industrial groupings.

In this paper I present an analysis of the relationship between the Japanese *keiretsu* and U.S.-Japanese industry trade balances. Although there is a consensus that the aggregate trade deficit is best explained by macroeconomic factors, it is often alleged that the Japanese *keiretsu* interfere with trade at an industry level because of their extensive intragroup dealings. In the next section, I present some summary statistics and institutional background concerning Japan's corporate groups. In section 5.4 I construct an oligopolistic model of how Japan's *keiretsu* can affect both U.S. and Japanese exports. Based on

2. For an interesting case study, see Kreinin (1988).

this model, I conduct some simple empirical tests of whether Japan's *keiretsu* is a factor in U.S.-Japan trade. Some concluding remarks are given in the last section.

5.2 The Japanese *Keiretsu*

5.2.1 Classification of Industrial Groups

A Japanese industrial group consists of a group of firms that are related economically. Group members are interconnected in a variety of ways, including cross-holding of shares; intragroup financing by nucleus banks; existence of general trading firms (*sogo shosha*) as trading arms and as organizers of various projects; formation of clubs (*shacho-kai*) where presidents of member companies meet and exchange information; mutual appointment of directors, officers and other key personnel; and joint investment by group members in new industries.[3]

There are three types of industrial groups.[4] One is the descendant of the prewar *zaibatsu* (giant business combines), a second is the bank group (consisting of firms that center on major banks), while the third group is composed of one or more large independent industrial manufacturers, their subsidiaries, affiliates, and suppliers. Unlike the first two groups, which deal with a wide range of products, this last group tends to concentrate in particular industries.

In this paper we will focus on the leading sixteen industrial groups.[5] Three of these groups—Mitsubishi, Matsui, and Sumitomo—are of *zaibatsu* origin. The prewar *zaibatsu* were groups of companies partly owned and controlled by a family holding company. Each family *zaibatsu* included a bank, a trust company, an insurance company, and a trading company to buy and sell goods on behalf of the member firms. Until World War II, the Japanese economy was heavily influenced by ten major *zaibatsu*, which accounted for approximately 35 percent of the aggregate paid-up capital of all Japanese companies in 1946. After the war, all the major *zaibatsu* were dissolved. However, gradually some splinter companies reestablished their former associations, exchanging shares with other firms bearing the common *zaibatsu* name and doing business with one another through the trading companies. They exchanged directors and set up clubs where company presidents could meet. In this way there was a revival between 1952 and 1965 of the industrial groups with prewar connections. Mitsubishi Shôji (currently Mitsubishi Corporation), which was split into 140 companies, was reestablished in 1954. Through a merger of three split companies Mitsubishi Heavy Industries was revived in 1964. It should

---

3. Not all groups engage in all these joint activities.

4. In some classifications, the last type (prime manufacturer-supplier) is subsumed under the previous two.

5. Again, under other classification schemes, the focus is on six groups rather than sixteen. The six are Mitsubishi, Mitsui, Sumitomo, Fuyo, DKB, and Sanwa.

be noted, however, that the postwar *zaibatsu* groups are much more loosely connected than their prewar counterparts, which involved a vertical hierarchy in which the family holding company held majority or near majority shares of all group companies and exercised vertical control. However, holding companies were outlawed in postwar Japan under the antimonopoly law and the shares of companies of a *zaibatsu* group were distributed among the member companies.

The second type of industrial group centers on a principal bank. Examples of this type include Fuyo, DKB, Sanwa, Takai, and IBJ. For most of Japan's modern history (until perhaps the late 1970s), capital and foreign exchange have been in relatively short supply. The formation of these financial keiretsu during the 1950s and 1960s probably came in response to the banks' ability to finance firm operation and investment. The various members, though typically all indebted to the group bank, need not be particularly closely associated with one another. Transactions among group companies are never exclusive, and affiliated firms often engage in transactions with outsiders. As table 5.1 shows, in 1985 bank financing of affiliated companies ranged from 12.1 percent to 27.7 percent of all financing. The remaining finance came from sources that were not members of the same group. The bank groups are expected to be less and less cohesive over time, since other sources of financing, including the domestic stock market, issuance of bonds, and borrowing from foreign banks, are becoming relatively more important.[6]

The last type of industrial group is formed around a prime manufacturing company (*motouke*). This type includes, among others, the Toyota and Nissan groups in the auto industry, the Nippon Steel group in the iron and steel industry, the Hitachi, Matsushita, and Toshiba-IHI groups in the electrical and electronic industry. It is made up of a cluster of subsidiaries, affiliates, supplies, and subcontractors, with the major manufacturer at the apex.

There will be dozens and even hundreds of smaller suppliers and sales companies around the major company and its important affiliates. One or more of the group companies or affiliates will hold shares of the smaller members. Member companies will be engaged in a range of interrelated activities. This type of group resembles a vertical hierarchy with large and stable leaders at the top and firms of decreasing size and skill level beneath them. Besides shareholding, the linkages are maintained by extension of credit and subcontracting. These manufacturing groups are formed by a combination of two processes. One is the consolidation into groups of small firms that for various reasons come to depend on large group members for customers, while the second process is the spinning off of specialized divisions from main manufacturers.

As an example of the manufacturer-supplier relationship, according to a

---

6. Note, however, that many main banks are involved as underwriters in the issuance of bonds abroad.

Table 5.1   **Intragroup Financing**

	Six Major Groups	Share of Total Financing
	Mitsui	21.2%
	Mitsubishi	22.4
	Sumitomo	27.7
	Sanwa	20.3
	Fuyo	18.4
	DKB	12.1

Source: Oriental Economist (Kigyu Keiretsu Soran) 1987.

survey conducted in 1977 (Japanese Agency for Small and Medium-sized Enterprises 1977), an unnamed Japanese auto manufacturer (believed to be Toyota) had direct relations with 122 first-tier suppliers and indirect relationships with 5,437 second-tier suppliers and 41,703 third-tier subcontractors. Between 1973 and 1984 only 3 firms exited from the association of first-tier Toyota suppliers while 21 firms entered. This example shows that typically the main manufacturer is at the top of a pyramid of a large number of stratified smaller firms.

Unlike the bank *keiretsu,* the manufacturer-subcontractor grouping seems to be increasing in importance. Large firms rely more and more on subcontracting to perform a variety of activities. According to the survey just mentioned, the proportion of subcontractors in the manufacturing sector has increased from 53.1 percent in 1966 to 65.5 percent in 1981. For the electric and electronics industry, the figure is even higher. In 1981, 85.3 percent of the small and medium-sized firms in that industry were subcontractors to larger firms.

5.2.2   The Importance of Industrial Groups

In this section, we provide some summary statistics concerning the importance of the industrial groups in Japan. Among the sixteen groups that this paper highlights, Mitsubishi, Mitsui, Sumitomo, Fuyo, DKB, and Sanwa are the most important and are sometimes categorized separately in the following tables. The number of companies, number of employees, annual sales, and net profit as a percentage of all nonfinancial Japanese companies for each group in 1980 are given in table 5.2. In 1980, the sixteen industrial groups accounted for 920 companies, 2.8 million employees, 194,401 billion yen in sales and their net profits were 2,176 billion yen.

As a percentage of all nonfinancial Japanese companies, about 0.06 percent of Japanese firms and 9.9 percent of Japanese employees are members of industrial groups. In terms of sales and net profits, the sixteen groups accounted for 23.7 percent and 23.6 percent, respectively, of the totals for nonfinancial companies.

How do these Japanese groups compare with corporations abroad? In terms

Table 5.2   **Importance of Industrial Groups**

Industrial Group	No. of Companies	Sales as Share of Total Sales of Nonfinancial Companies	Employment as Share of Total Employment of Nonfinancial Companies	Profits as Share of Total Profits of Nonfinancial Companies
Six major groups:				
Mitsubishi	139	3.9	1.4 (0.69)	3.2 (3.07)
Mitsui	108	2.9	0.7 (0.69)	1.5 (5.07)
Sumitomo	117	3.0	1.2 (0.38)	3.4 (1.42)
Fuyo	110	2.7	0.9 (0.96)	2.5 (3.59)
DKB	64	2.9	0.8 (1.92)	1.1 (3.03)
Sanwa	84	2.4	0.8 (1.16)	1.1 (3.03)
Other ten industrial Groups:				
Tokai	25	0.6	0.1	0.3
IBJ	23	0.3	0.1	0.2
Nippon Steel	40	0.9	0.5	1.3
Hitachi	38	0.6	0.5	1.4
Nissan	27	0.7	0.5	1.3
Toyota	38	1.4	0.7	2.8
Matsushita	25	0.7	0.4	1.8
Toshiba-IHI	40	0.4	0.5	0.7
Tokyu	19	0.2	0.2	0.2
Seibu	22	0.2	0.2	0.1
Total	919	23.7	9.9	23.6

Note: The percentages in parentheses are for the year 1985. However, they do not come from the same source as the data for 1980.

Source: Dodwell Marketing Consultants *Industrial Groupings in Japan*, rev. 1982–83, *Oriental Economist (Kigyo Keiretsu Soran)*, 1987; *Japan Economic Journal (Nihon Keizai Shimbun)*, 1 January 1980.

of annual sales, each of the six leading industrial groups is larger than most major multinationals. The Mitsubishi Group, the largest industrial group in Japan, is about twice as large as Royal Dutch/Shell. The DKB group, the Mitsui group and the Fuyo group are each almost equivalent to Exxon, the largest company in the world in 1980. In table 5.3, we compare the sales of six major Japanese groups with those of other leading multinationals.

5.2.3   Linkages Between Group Members

One important linkage among affiliated companies is through share cross-holding. In table 5.4 I present some statistics of the extent of intragroup cross shareholding by the major groups. The cross-holding ratio is defined as the total value of members' shares held by all group members as a percentage of the total value of all paid-up capital of the entire group companies listed on the stock exchange.

Another important linkage among group members is their relationships

Table 5.3   **Comparison of Six Major Japanese Groups with Multinationals**

	Country	1980 sales (US $ million)	Index (Mitsubishi Group = 100)
Mitsubishi Group	Japan	144,900	100
Sumitomo	Japan	111,300	77
DKB	Japan	107,800	74
Mitsui	Japan	106,600	74
Fuyo	Japan	100,800	70
Sanwa	Japan	90,400	62
Exxon	USA	103,100	71
Royal Dutch/Shell	Neth/UK	77,100	53
GM	USA	57,700	40
Ford Motor	USA	37,100	26
IBM	USA	26,200	18
Fiat	Italy	25,200	17
GE	USA	25,000	17
US Steel	USA	12,500	9
Procter & Gamble	USA	10,800	7

Source: Dodwell Marketing Consultants, *Industrial Groupings in Japan,* rev. ed. (1982–83).

Table 5.4   **Crossholding of Shares in Six Major Groups**

	1971	1974	1980	1985
Mitsubishi	27.6	30.6	20.7	25.2
Mitsui	14.3	17.4	17.7	17.9
Sumitomo	24.7	27.9	21.4	25.0
Fuyo	20.5	17.4	16.4	15.8
DKB	18.6	21.2	14.1	13.3
Sanwa	14.1	16.0	13.6	16.8

Sources: Japanese Fair Trade Commission, *Second Report on the Operations of the General Trading Companies,* 1975; Dodwell Marketing Consultants, *Industrial Groupings in Japan* (1982–83). rev. ed. (1990), *Oriental Economist (Kigyo Keiretsu Soran), 1987.*

with general trading companies. General trading companies (*Sogo shosha*) are important trading arms of seven major industrial groups: Mitsubishi, Mitsui, Sumitomo, Fuyo, DKB, Sanwa, and Tokai. The activities of these companies are quite diverse. They trade in more than twenty thousand different commodities on a commission basis, invest in domestic and overseas markets, and extend credit to affiliated companies and customers. They also coordinate the setting up of joint ventures overseas. Their functions include marketing/distribution, financing, project organizing, and information gathering. The nine leading general trading companies and their affiliations are listed in table 5.5.

The existence of group-affiliated general trading companies is important in our context because of their significant involvement in international trade. In 1980, the value of exports handled by the nine Sogo shosha amounted to $66

Table 5.5   Affiliations of Leading General Trading Companies

General Trading Companies	Industrial Group
Mitsubishi Corp.	Mitsubishi
Mitsui & Co.	Mitsui
Sumitomo Corp.	Sumitomo
Maruberi Corp.	Fuyo
C. Itoh & Co.	DKB[a]
Nissho-Iwai	Sanwa
Toyo Menka	Tokai[a]
Karematsu-Gosho	DKB
Nichimen Corp.	Sanwa

Sources: Dodwell Marketing Consultants, *Industrial Groupings in Japan,* rev. ed (1982–83). M. Y. Yoshino and T. Lifson, *The Invisible Link: Japan's Sogo Shosha and the Organization of Trade* (Cambridge, Mass.: MIT Press, 1988).

[a]These are primary affiliations. C. Itoh & Co. is also related to Sumitomo and Toyo Menka is related also to Mitsui.

billion and the value of imports was $80 billion. These amounts accounted for roughly half of Japan's export and import activities (table 5.6).

The major exports of the general trading companies are machinery and iron and steel. Their main imports are fuels, foodstuffs, and ferrous and nonferrous metals. The general trading companies are also active in extending financial assistance in the form of business credits, loans, and payment guarantees to their affiliated group members.

These statistics indicate that the Japanese *keiretsu* constitute a fairly significant portion of the Japanese economy. The extent of interconnectedness varies from group to group, as do the forms of linkages. Group affiliations, however, almost never translate into exclusive dealings. For example, group companies borrow from nonmember banks and affiliated suppliers supply to nonmember consuming corporations. With the liberalization of the Japanese economy, it is expected that Japanese groups will diminish in importance. Nonetheless, existing group behavior may still have an impact on U.S.-Japanese trade.

5.2.4   Comparison of Japanese Groups with U.S. Institutions

When we compare the features of Japanese groups with U.S. industry characteristics and institutions, the picture becomes more complex and there are both differences and similarities.[7]

The existence of long-term manufacturer-supplier relationships is not unique to Japan. For example, Cole and Yakushiji (1984) estimated that in 1983 General Motors purchased 40 percent of its parts, components, and materials from its suppliers; for Ford and Chrysler, the respective figures were 50

7. Intercorporate ties are also found in West Germany, with banks and some holding companies playing a key role. See Scherer and Ross (1990, chap. 3).

Table 5.6 **Trade of Nine General Trading Companies**

	Exports		Imports	
	Nine General Trading Companies (Billion Yen)	Share of Total Exports	Nine General Trading Companies (Billion Yen)	Share of Total Imports
1977	10,860	49.8%	9,204	49.7%
1978	9,604	48.1	8,730	51.2
1979	11,798	48.2	15,055	54.5
1980	14,640	48.2	17,624	56.0

Note: Exports are in FOB value, while imports are in CIF.

Source: Dodwell Marketing Consultants, *Industrial Groupings in Japan,* rev. ed. (1982–83).

and 60 percent. However, auto firms in Japan do seem to procure a relatively greater portion of the parts from their subcontractors, relying less on in-house production. On average, it is estimated that 55 percent of a U.S. car's purchased value is provided by external suppliers. For a Japanese car, estimate that 75 percent of its value is supplied by outside subcontractors. (Cole and Yakushiji 1984)

In terms of bank groups there are some legal differences. U.S. banks are not permitted to hold stock of other nonfinancial companies on their own account.[8] In contrast, the antimonopoly law in Japan allows banks to hold up to 5 percent of a particular nonfinancial corporation.[9] As a stockholder of the company, the main bank often sends its representative to the company's board of directors. The main bank is periodically briefed about the company's general business and also often functions as financial rescuer of last resort. If a member company is on the verge of bankruptcy, it is often the main bank that organizes the rescue package to try to save the company. For instance, when Tōyō Kōgyō, the maker of Mazda automobiles, was on the brink of bankruptcy in 1979–80, its main bank, Sumitomo Bank, coordinated the rescue activities. The entire Sumitomo group switched its auto purchases to Mazda. It is estimated that the group members purchased eighteen thousand vehicles over six years (Pascale and Rohlen 1983). Overall, it seems that main banks in Japan play a more significant role in the activities of corporations than do U.S. banks.

5.3 An Oligopolistic Model of Japanese Keiretsu

The U.S. Trade Representative (1985) (USTR) cites three aspects of the oligopolistic behavior that affects U.S.-Japanese trade. First, the government

8. Trust departments of banks do manage pension and trust funds and invest in the stock market. At least legally, the funds are managed on behalf of owners of pension and trust funds, not of the banks.

9. The limit until 1987 was 10 percent of the total stock of any single company.

allows "recession cartels" designed to protect declining industries. As an example, the USTR cites the paper industry, where cartels have existed to cope with the problem of high energy and raw material costs. Second, it is alleged that the Japanese distribution system is a close-knit network of financial and input-output arrangements linking distributors, customers, and suppliers in such a way that nonmembers are excluded. Third, the USTR argues that the *keiretsu* conglomerates of manufacturers, banks and general trading companies, by supporting each others' activities, effectively preclude opportunities for non-*keiretsu* firms.[10]

One prominent industry where U.S. producers charge that oligopoly in Japan restricts imports is semiconductors. In June 1985 the U.S. Semiconductor Industry Association petitioned the president to act under section 301 of the Trade Act of 1974, arguing that the Japanese protected semiconductors through reciprocal buying arrangements among the six large electronics firms. It was alleged that Japanese firms buy their semiconductors needs primarily from each other. The Semiconductor Industry Association requested that the Japanese government force its firms to purchase more U.S. chips to offset the discrimination.

Conceptually, there are two views in the literature of the Japanese groups with very different welfare implications. The first approach focuses on their potential exploitation of joint market power, which tends to be welfare reducing. The second views Japanese groups as a mechanism for risk sharing, which tends to be Pareto improving. In this paper, we will concentrate on a *positive* analysis of how the behavior of groups affects U.S. net exports.[11]

I construct a model of international oligopoly to highlight how members of the Japanese groups may affect industry trade balance. The model is meant to set up some hypothesis for my later empirical work. Following the approach of Brander and Krugman (1983), I assume that the international firms compete both at home and abroad.[12] I start with the competition between a Japanese firm J_1 and an American firm A in the Japanese product market. The analysis for the competition in the U.S. market will be exactly symmetrical. The respective Japanese and U.S. profit functions π^{J_1} and π^A are

$$(1) \qquad \pi^{J_1} = P^{J_1}(x,y)x - C^{J_1}(x,P_m,w^{J_1}),$$

$$(2) \qquad \pi^A = P^A(x,y)y - C^A(y,w^A,t^A).$$

10. This line of argument is really pointing to barriers to entry, whether the potential entrants are foreign or domestic.

11. Note, however, that it is possible for the groups (either due to joint monopoly or risk sharing) to improve the welfare of group members, while reducing the welfare of the Japanese consumers and/or nonmembers, including foreign producers.

12. Brander and Krugman's (1983) original framework focuses on homogeneous products. However, the approach will remain valid if the products are differentiated; see Fung (1991). Furthermore, since the outputs by the international firms are substitutes, the Cournot-Nash setting adopted here is arguably more appropriate because if the firms can choose price setting versus quantity setting, they will endogenously choose the Cournot-Nash strategies; see Singh and Vives (1984).

P^{J_1} and P^A are the product prices; x is the output produced by the Japanese firm, while y is the output produced by the U.S. firm in the Japanese market. The two products are assumed to be imperfect substitutes. C^{J_1} and C^A are the respective cost functions, with w^{J_1} and w^A the labor costs in each country, P_m the price of some material input produced by another member of the same Japanese group (J_2) to which J_1 belongs, and t^A is the transparent trade barriers that the U.S. firms face in Japan.

The model is characterized as a two-stage game with the timing described as follows: J_2 moves first, naming P_m, taking the impact of P_m on the derived demand for m into account. Taking P_m as given, J_1 then sets x, while firm A simultaneously sets y. The equilibrium is subgame perfect.[13] Profit maximization of the international Cournot-Nash firms yields

(3) $$\pi_x^{J_1} = P^{J_1} + xP_x^{J_1} - C_x^{J_1} = 0,$$

(4) $$\pi_y^A = P^A + yP_y^A - C_y^A = 0,$$

(5) $$\pi_{xx}^{J_1} < 0 \quad \pi_{yy}^A < 0.$$

Given P_m, w^A, w^{J_1}, and t^A, the equilibrium market shares and product prices are implicitly determined by (3) and (4) and the inverse demands. The value of U.S. exports to Japan in this industry is given by the equilibrium value of $P^A y$.

Let us now introduce the member of the same Japanese *keiretsu*, J_2, that produces the input m. Being a member of the same group, J_2 will take the interest of the J_1 into account when setting the price P_m. This may be because it holds shares of J_1, has joint investment in projects, or has directors on its board from J_1. To reflect this economic interaction, the profit function of J_2 can be written

(6) $$\pi^{J_2} = (P_m m - km) + g\pi^{J_1} - F^{J_2},$$

where m is the quantity of the material input produced, k is the marginal cost of producing m, and g is the degree of J_2's group affiliation to J_1. More concretely, g can be interpreted as J_2's extent of shareholding over J_1.[14] Maximization of (6) implies

13. The model assumes that there are barriers to entry to these oligopolistic industries; thus entry by other firms is not considered.

14. We can easily accommodate the phenomenon of intragroup cross shareholding if g is interpreted as the extent of shareholding of J_2 over J_1. Let g^* be the extent of sharing of J_1 over J_2. Then

$$\pi^{J_1} = (1 - g)(P^{J_1}x - C^{J_1}(\cdot)) + g^*(P_m m - km - F^{J_2})$$

and

$$\pi^{J_2} = (1 - g^*)(P_m m - km - F^{J_2}) + g(P_x^{J_1} - C^{J_1}(\cdot)).$$

Under the same two-stage game framework, J_2 moves first to set P_m in the first stage. In the second stage, J_1 sets x, given P_m. The analysis proceeds similarly as in the text and yields similar results.

(7) $\qquad \dfrac{\delta \pi^{J_2}}{\delta P_m} \equiv \pi^{J_2}_{P_m} = m + P_m \dfrac{\delta m}{\delta P_m} - k \dfrac{\delta m}{\delta P_m} + g \dfrac{\delta \pi^{J_1}}{\delta P_m} = 0,$

(8) $\qquad \pi^{J_2}_{P_m P_m} < 0.$

Given an exogenous g, the optimal price P_m that J_2 will charge is implicitly defined in (7). From (1)–(8), the equilibrium output and equilibrium price of the U.S. export can be written

(9) $\qquad y = y(w^{J_1}, w^A, t^A, P_m(g)),$

(10) $\qquad P^A = P^A(x, y),$

where $x = x(w^{J_1}, w^A, t^A, P_m(g))$.

To obtain some hypothesis concerning the signs of U.S. export level and export value with respect to their arguments, totally differentiate (3) and (4) to obtain

(11) $\qquad \dfrac{\delta x}{\delta w^{J_1}} = \dfrac{-\pi^{J_1}_{xw^{J_1}} \pi^{J_2}_{yy}}{\Delta} < 0,$

(12) $\qquad \dfrac{\delta y}{\delta w^{J_1}} = \dfrac{\pi^{J_1}_{xw^{J_1}} \pi^{J_2}_{yx}}{\Delta} > 0,$

where $\pi^{J_1}_{xw^{J_1}} = -\delta l/\delta x < 0$ and $\Delta = \pi^{J_1}_{xx} \pi^{J_2}_{yy} - \pi^{J_1}_{xy} \pi^{J_2}_{yx} > 0$ is the standard stability condition for Cournot firms. Equations (11) and (12) tell us that a rise of the wage rate in Japan will raise U.S. export volume but lower Japanese domestic output. The impact on the value of U.S. exports is

(13) $\qquad \dfrac{\delta(yP^A)}{\delta w^{J_1}} = yP^A_x \dfrac{\delta x}{\delta w^{J_1}} + C^A_y \dfrac{\delta y}{\delta w^{J_1}} > 0$

Thus a rise of Japanese wage rate will raise the value of U.S. exports.

Similar calculations show that the U.S. export value is negatively related to the wage in the U.S. and the tariff in Japan, that is, $\delta(yP^A)/\delta w^A < 0$, $\delta(yP^A)/\delta t^A < 0$. To obtain the effect of the strength of the group affiliation, totally differentiate (7),

$\qquad \pi^{J_2}_{P_m P_m} dP_m + \pi^{J_2}_{P_m g} dg = 0,$

(14) $\qquad \dfrac{dP_m}{dg} = - \dfrac{\pi^{J_2}_{P_m g}}{\pi^{J_2}_{P_m P_m}} = - \dfrac{\left[\dfrac{d\pi^{J_1}}{dP_m}\right]}{\pi^{J_2}_{P_m P_m}},$

where $d\pi^{J_1}/dP_m = (xP^{J_1}_y)(dy/dP_m) - m < 0$ and $P^{J_1}_y < 0$. Substituting into (14), we obtain $\delta P_m/\delta g < 0$. The impact of g on the value of Japan's import is:

(15)
$$\frac{d(yP^A)}{dg} = \left[\frac{d(yP^A)}{dP_m}\right]\left[\frac{dP_m}{dg}\right] < 0$$

where the sign of $(d(yP^A)/dP_m)$ can be obtained in a similar fashion as in (13). A higher degree of Japanese group affiliation will lead to a smaller amount of U.S. exports. The reduced form of our model for U.S. export can be written

(16)
$$yP^A = yP^A(w^{J_1}, w^A, t^A, P_m^{J_2}(g))$$

with

$$\frac{\delta(yP^A)}{\delta w^{J_1}} > 0, \quad \frac{\delta(yP^A)}{\delta w^A} < 0, \quad \frac{\delta(yP^A)}{\delta t^A} < 0, \quad \frac{\delta(yP^A)}{\delta g} < 0.$$

Thus the value of U.S. exports to Japan will rise with a higher Japanese wage, a lower U.S. wage rate, lower overt trade barriers in Japan, and lower degree of group affiliation.

For the U.S. market, J_1 exports x_1 and A produces y_1 domestically.[15] Japanese exports are subjected to overt trade barriers t^{J_1}. Group member J_2 supplies quantity of materials m_1 to J_1. Using similar reasoning as before, the analysis of the impact of w^{J_1}, w^A, t^{J_1}, and g on U.S. imports from Japan $x_1 P_1^{J_1}$ can be expressed as $\delta(x_1 P_1^{J_1})/\delta w^{J_1} < 0$, $\delta(x_1 P_1^{J_1})/\delta w^A > 0$, $\delta(x_1 P_1^{J_1})/\delta t^{J_1} < 0$, and $\delta(x_1 P_1^{J_1})/\delta g > 0$. The last comparative static term shows that group affiliation in our model not only restricts U.S. imports but also promotes exports. The reduced form of U.S. net exports $TB = (yP^A - x_1 P_1^{J_1})$ can be written as

(17)
$$TB = TB(w^{J_1}, w^A, t^A, t^{J_1}, g),$$

where $\delta TB/\delta w^{J_1} > 0$, $\delta TB/\delta w^A < 0$, $\delta TB/\delta t^A < 0$, $\delta TB/\delta t^{J_1} > 0$, $\delta TB/\delta g < 0$. U.S. net exports depend on the wage rate in the United States and Japan, the overt trade barriers in both countries, and the intensity of Japanese group affiliation. U.S. industry trade balance is higher with a higher Japanese wage rate, a lower U.S. wage rate, lower extent of Japanese overt trade barriers, higher extent of U.S. overt trade barriers, and a lower degree of Japanese group affiliation.

5.4   Econometric Analysis

The basic econometric equation to be estimated is based on equation (17), which identifies the equilibrium level of U.S. net export value as a function of the wage costs in Japan and the United States, the overt trade barriers (tariffs and tariff-equivalent nontariff trade barriers) in Japan and the United States, and the intensity of group affiliation. The model is meant to explain the inter-industry variation of the value of U.S. industry trade balance with Japan. A linear specification of (17) gives

---

15. Following Brander and Krugman (1983), I have assumed that the profit functions in the United States and Japan are separable.

(18)
$$TB_i = \alpha + \beta_1 USW_i + \beta_2 JW_i + \beta_3 USTQ_i + \beta_4 JTQ_i + \beta_5 g_i + \mu,$$

where USW_i and JW_i are the U.S. and Japanese unit labor costs for industry i, $USTQ_i$ and JTQ_i are the level of overt protection through tariffs and nontariff trade barriers in the United States and Japan for industry i, and g_i is the group affiliation intensity for industry i; μ is the disturbance term. Because some values of TB_i are negative, a log-linear specification in this instance is not appropriate. From previous discussions of this model, it is predicted that $\beta_1 < 0$, $\beta_2 > 0$, $\beta_3 > 0$, $\beta_4 < 0$, and $\beta_5 < 0$. For the purposes of this paper, the main coefficient of interest is β_5.

Like Petri (1990) and Yamawaki and Audretch (1988), my approach departs from the traditional emphasis of factor-intensity approach and focuses on oligopolistic interactions as a determinant of U.S.-Japanese trade. Furthermore, unlike earlier literature on the studies of determinants of trade but in accord with Yamawaki and Audretch (1988) and Petri (1990), I have not confined the explanatory variables to only characteristics of the U.S. industries. Instead, I have explicitly included features of Japanese industries in our equation.

The sources and the method of construction of the variables are given in the appendix. The variable that is most constraining on our choice of industries is the group intensity variable g_i. Due to the availability of g_i, we confine ourselves to the year 1980 for twenty-two industries (compared with twenty-four industries in Yamawaki and Audretch and forty-nine in Petri).[16]

The dependent variable TB_i is the trade balance between the United States and Japan for industry i in 1980. JTQ_i and $USTQ_i$ are the sum of tariffs and tariff-equivalent nontariff barriers for Japan and the United States, respectively, for industry i in 1980. $JULC_i$ and $USULC_i$ represent unit labor costs in Japan and the United States. As a proxy, I follow the literature (e.g., Yamawaki and Audretch 1988) and use the nominal wage divided by value added per worker in each industry. It thus approximates labor costs adjusted by a measure of labor productivity.[17]

Finally, the group intensity variable is given by two proxies. The first is the sales of group-affiliated companies as a percentage of total industry sale (gS_i) and the second is the share of employment accounted for by group-affiliated corporations in industry i (gE_i).[18]

Table 5.7 presents the estimation result of the regression equations based on (17). Equation (A) uses the group affiliation variable gS (percentage of total industry sales); equation (A_1) employs the group affiliation variable gE (percentage of total employment). All equations are estimated by the ordinary least squares method.

Table 5.7 indicates that the extent of group affiliations, either measured by

16. The industries, two-digit and three-digit SIC industries, are listed in the Appendix.

Table 5.7   **Regressions with U.S. Trade Balance**

	Eq. (A)	Eq. (A$_1$)
Constant	9.5001***	9.6204***
	(2.9746)	(3.0283)
Group affiliation	−12.605***	−12.117***
	(−3.9531)	(−4.0177)
U.S. tariffs and	−5.6687	−6.2251
quotas	(−0.27620)	(−0.30598)
Japanese tariffs	0.26146	2.6678
and quotas	(0.31848×10^{-1})	(0.33025)
Japanese unit	−16.804*	−19.071*
labor cost	(−1.7467)	(−1.9391)
U.S. unit labor	1.3657	1.1635
cost	(0.13709)	(0.11799)
R^2	0.540497	0.547856
$\bar{R}^2$	0.396902	0.406562
F	3.76404	3.87740

Note: t-statistics in parentheses.
*Significant at 10 percent level (two-tailed test).
***Significant at 1 percent level (two-tailed test).

sales or by employment, has the expected negative sign and is significant at the 1 percent level. The only other variable (other than the constant) that is significant (at the 10 percent level) is the Japanese unit labor cost. But contrary to our theory, Japan's unit labor costs are negatively related to U.S. net exports to Japan. There can be several potential explanations for this unexpected sign. In studying characteristics of group-affiliated firms, Nakatani (1984) found Japanese group-affiliated firms pay higher wages than independent firms. Thus both group affiliation and high wages in Japan may worsen U.S. net exports to Japan. Alternately, both Yamawaki and Audretch (1988) and Petri (1990) found that Japan's technology intensity and expenditure on research and development are positively related to Japan's exports. It may be that Japan's high wages partly serve as proxies for these variables, and in industries where Japan's wages are high (due to more scientists and engineers), the U.S. trade balance is worse. Other variables such as the overt trade barriers and the U.S. unit labor cost have signs contrary to our model, but they are all insignificant. Using the coefficients of the group affiliation variables in equations (A) and (A$_1$), we can further estimate the percentage decline in U.S. industry net exports due to the Japanese keiretsu. The results are presented in the Appendix, which shows that the industries most affected by Japanese groups are leather and leather products, nonferrous metal and products, shipbuilding, and rubber products. The industries that are typically of the most concern to the U.S. are affected only a relatively small amount. For example, for food and kindred products, the drop in trade balance due to Japanese groups is only 0.301 percent. For such other industries as chemical and allied products, general machinery, and scientific and optical instruments, the impacts are 3.10 percent, 1.19 percent, and 1.17 percent, respectively.

5.5   Further Empirical Analysis

In the last section, I obtained some evidence that Japanese group strength is negatively correlated with U.S. net exports. To test the sensitivity of the results, I conduct several sets of variations of the basic empirical tests. First, I use instrumental variable estimation to correct for biases that may arise if the Japanese group-strength variables are endogenous. I will also estimate the basic equations with the addition of potentially relevant variables, such as transport costs, advertising intensity (as a proxy for product differentiation), and the number of firms in each industry. Lastly I run modified regressions with U.S. gross exports to Japan and the world's trade balance with Japan as the dependent variables.

5.5.1   Instrumental Variable Estimation

In the basic estimation equation I provide estimates of the effects of the Japanese group strengths on U.S. net exports, assuming that g is an independent variable. However, arguments can be made to treat g as endogenous.[19] In this subsection I provide an instrumental variable estimation to correct for potential biases due to the endogenity of group strengths.

The instruments that I have selected are average firm profits in each Japanese industry (JFP_i), proportion of temporary employees in each Japanese industry (JTE_i), proportion of individual proprietorship in each Japanese industry (JIP_i), and percentage of firms with more than three hundred employees in each Japanese industry (JLF_i). If Japanese groups coordinate in their activities, group strengths should be correlated with average profits.[20] Group-affiliated firms with long-term suppliers may use fewer temporary employees. Small subcontractors are also more likely to be individually owned. Finally, suppliers of parts are likely to have smaller numbers of employees.[21] Thus these instruments should be highly correlated with the intensity of group strengths.

17. Since unit labor costs capture differences in productivities, the use of these variables in both countries will partly reflect comparative advantage due to technological differences.

18. Measures of gS_i and gE_i for various industries are constructed from Dodwell Marketing Consultants (1982–83), and Ministry of International Trade and Industry (1981).

19. For example, if Japanese groups are formed for risk sharing, group strength will be determined by how risky a particular industry is.

20. Caves and Uekusa (1976), Nakatani (1984), and Roehl (1983) found that contrary to the view that keiretsu collude, group-affiliated nonfinancial companies did not realize as high an average rate of profits as comparable independent firms for the period 1961–75.

21. Legally, a subcontractor is defined as a firm with three hundred or fewer employees, or with one hundred million yen or less paid-in capital and has a contractual relation with a larger firm for supplying a part, processed product, or material.

Table 5.8   **Regressions with Predicted Values of Group Strengths**

	Eq. ($\hat{A}$)	Eq. ($\hat{A}_1$)
Constant	12.5708***	11.10643***
	(3.7885)	(3.4686)
Group affiliation	− 16.556***	− 13.9195***
	(−4.5630)	(−4.3818)
U.S. tariffs and	− 14.9038	− 13.3667
quotas	(−0.7863)	(−0.6895)
Japanese tariffs	2.4406	1.4447
and quotas	(0.3228)	(0.18632)
Japanese unit	− 16.4802	− 15.1560
labor cost	(−1.8949)	(1.72504)
U.S. unit labor	− 3.5000	− 4.5982
cost	(−0.3908)	(−0.5037)
R^2	0.605187	− 0.587011
$\bar{R}^2$	0.481808	0.457951
F	4.90511	4.54838

Notes: Eq. ($\hat{A}$) uses the predicted values of gS and eq. ($\hat{A}_1$) the predicted values of gE as the group affiliation variables. The values in parentheses are t-statistics.

***Significant at 1 percent level (two-tailed test).

Table 5.8 shows the regression of U.S. net exports with the group variables adjusted by instrumental variables.[22] The group strength variables, both measured by sales and employment, are still significant at 1 percent level. The adjusted R^2 improves from around 0.4 in table 5.7 to 0.48 and 0.45 in table 5.8. Overall, the instrumental variable estimations yield similar results as those with the simple OLS estimations. The degree of Japanese group affiliations remains statistically significant.

5.5.2   Transport Costs as an Explanatory Variable

One interesting variation on the basic regression equation is the addition of transport costs. Lawrence (1987), Saxonhouse (1985), and Balassa (1986) highlight the importance of the cost of transportation as a determinant of the pattern of Japanese trade. In table 5.9, I present results from regressions based on (17) with transport costs TC added. As a representation of TC, I use the unit freight charge calculated by Clark (1981). This proxy pertains only to charges of ocean shipments and does not include costs of air freight.

---

22. As described in the text, first-stage regressions are run with group strengths as dependent variables. The explanatory variables are *JFP, JTE, JIP,* and *JLF.* When group strength is measured by sales, only the intercept is statistically significant at the 1 percent level (adjusted $R^2 = 0.54145$; F-statistic $= 7.199177$). When the group strength is measured by employment, the intercept is significant at the 1 percent level. In addition, *JFP* is significant at 5 percent level (adjusted $R^2 = 0.66225$; F-statistic $= 11.29396$). The predicted values of the group strengths are then used as explanatory variables in the second-stage regressions.

Table 5.9   **Regressions with Transport Cost**

	Eq. (B)	Eq. (B$_1$)
Constant	9.6394**	9.9912**
	(2.5693)	(2.6556)
Group affiliation	−12.691***	−12.347***
	(−3.6539)	(−3.7254)
U.S. tariffs and	−5.3564	−5.4204
quotas	(−0.24833)	(−0.25371)
Japanese tariffs	0.80564×10^{-1}	2.2410
and quotas	(0.91634×10^{-2})	(0.26059)
Japanese unit	−17.043	−19.759*
labor cost	(−1.6389)	(−1.8453)
U.S. unit labor	1.4643	1.4286
cost	(0.14128)	(0.13929)
Transport cost	−0.53057	−1.36715
	$(-0.77873 \times 10^{-1})$	(−0.20052)
R^2	0.540682	0.549605
$\bar{R}^2$	0.356955	0.368691
F	2.94285	3.04404

Notes: Eq. (B) uses gS and eq. (B$_1$) gE as the group affiliation variables. The values in parentheses are t-statistics.

*Significant at 10 percent level (two-tailed test).

**Significant at 5 percent level (two-tailed test).

***Significant at 1 percent level (two-tailed test).

The transport costs variable is insignificant in both cases. However, adding *TC* does not affect the results of the previous basic regression equations. The group affiliation variables (both in terms of sales in eq. [B] or in terms of employment in eq. [B$_1$]) still have the negative sign and are significant at the 1 percent level. One explanation of the insignificance of the added variable is that transport costs reduce U.S. exports as well as U.S. imports. The net impact of the U.S. industry trade balance is thus ambiguous. With net exports as the dependent variable, *TC* does not seem to be an appropriate explanatory variable.

5.5.3   Advertising Intensity and Number of Firms as Explanatory Variables

Adhering to the theoretical model, the only explanatory variables that should be included are USW_i, JW_i, $USTQ_i$, JTQ_i and g_i. However, if we relax our model for empirical implementation and contrast, other relevant variables can reasonably be included. For example, one variable may be the intensity of advertising expenditures in industry i in the United States and Japan. Advertising is an instrument of international oligopolistic rivalry that alters demand for a firm's product. Alternatively, the intensity of advertising can be used as a proxy for the degree of product differentiation between goods sold by the United States and Japan. It is expected that other things being equal, a high advertising intensity by the United States will be positively related to the United States trade balance, while a high advertising intensity by Japan is negatively related to *TB*. In other words, advertising intensity can be interpreted as a proxy for comparative advantage due to product differentiation. As a measure of advertising intensity, we will use the industry advertising expenditure per dollar sale in each country (USD_i and JD_i).

Another variable that may reasonably be included is the number of firms in industry *i* in the United States and Japan. Based on the theoretical literature of Dixit (1984), Eaton and Grossman (1986), Brander and Krugman (1983), and Fung (1987, 1989), we can expect that the number of firms will affect the equilibrium outcome. In particular, increasing the number of firms of a country under symmetry will raise market share and thus exports of that country. Thus with identical firms, the number of U.S. firms in industry *i* should be positively related to the U.S. trade balance, while the reverse sign is expected with respect to the number of firms in Japan.

The results of these expanded regressions are given in tables 5.10 and 5.11. For the regressions that include the number of firms as an explanatory variable, the equations with the group affiliation variable *gE* are not significant overall and are not presented (although the variable *gE* is itself significant).

Equations (C)-(E) essentially confirm the result that in a variety of regres-

Table 5.10   **Regressions with Advertising Intensity**

	Eq. (C)	Eq. (C₁)
Constant	8.6437**	9.3676**
	(2.3758)	(2.5035)
Group affiliation	− 10.519**	− 11.388**
	(− 2.1126)	(− 2.2353)
Japanese tariff	3.1051	4.8146
and quota	(0.35580)	(0.57343)
U.S. tariff and	− 7.3530	− 6.4017
quota	(− 0.34673)	(− 0.30559)
Japanese unit	− 14.184	− 19.574
labor cost	(− 1.0746)	(− 1.3412)
U.S. unit labor	− 1.2885	0.52659
cost	(− 0.11092)	(0.44769×10^{-1})
Japanese adver-	− 92.491	− 8.2067
tising intensity	(− 0.36888)	$(− 0.30340 \times 10^{-1})$
U.S. advertising	38.777	42.432
intensity	(1.2010)	(1.3378)
R^2	0.587881	0.599451
$\bar{R}^2$	0.381822	0.399177
F	2.85297	2.99315

Note: Eq. (C) uses *gS* and eq. (C₁) *gE* as the group affiliation variables. The values in parentheses are *t*-statistics.

**Significant at 5 percent level (two-tailed test).

Table 5.11   Regressions with Number of Firms

	Eq. (D)	Eq. (E)
Constant	9.6805**	9.7642**
	(2.6710)	(2.5361)
Group affiliation	−12.984***	−12.399**
(gS)	(−3.4545)	(−2.3947)
Japanese tariff	−2.6445	−1.2303
and quota	(−0.29950)	(−0.14031)
U.S. tariff and	−13.439	−15.470
quota	(−0.58524)	(−0.69753)
Japanese unit	−18.031*	−19.424
labor cost	(−1.8292)	(−1.4971)
U.S. unit labor	3.6948	3.5263
cost	(0.35987)	(0.30911)
Japanese adver-		−15.497
tising intensity		$(-0.64509 \times 10^{-1})$
U.S. advertising		60.670*
intensity		(1.8237)
No. of Japanese	0.63930×10^{-4}	0.85472×10^{-4}
firms	(1.0629)	(1.4468)
No. of U.S.	-0.83034×10^{-4}	$-0.12730 \times 10^{-3*}$
firms	(−1.2367)	(−1.8281)
R^2	0.587363	0.678098
$\bar{R}^2$	0.381045	0.436671
F	2.84688	2.80871

Note: Eq. (D) regresses gS on the basic equation with variables of numbers of firms. Eq. (E) regresses gS on the basic equation with both numbers of firms and advertising intensifies. The values in parentheses are *t*-statistics.

*Significant at 10 percent level (two-tailed test).

**Significant at 5 percent level (two-tailed test).

***Significant at 1 percent level (two-tailed test).

sions based on equation (17) of our model, the intensity of Japanese groupings is negatively related to the U.S. balance of trade with Japan on an industry basis. Of all the explanatory variables employed, group affiliation is the most consistently significant one.

There are some variables that are significant in one equation but not in others.[23] For example, in (E) the U.S. advertising intensity is found to be positively related to U.S. net exports to Japan. This probably reflects the strategic effect of advertising, which can expand demand as well as shift demand from the firm's rivals. More generally, the advertising to sales ratio may reflect comparative advantage due to product differentiation. Equation (E) then tells

23. Note that in eq. (E) the variable representing number of U.S. firms has the wrong sign and is significant at the 10 percent level. This may be because the assumption of symmetric firms does not hold. If the number of firms can alter the equilibrium solutions (e.g., see Fung 1987), then a smaller number of U.S. firms may increase exports.

us that the more distinctive the U.S. products are, the better the U.S. industry trade balance. Across equations, the degree of explanatory power is fairly consistent and satisfactory, with the adjusted R^2 for all regressions about 0.4.

5.5.4   U.S. Exports as the Dependent Variable

According to (16), an alternative implication of our model is that U.S. exports alone ($USXC_i$) are also negatively related to the degree of Japanese group affiliations. Instead of industry trade balance, I rerun the regressions using U.S. industry exports to Japan as the dependent variable. To adjust for the size of the industries, I divide the exports by Japanese consumption of that industry.

Since Japanese exports to the United States are now excluded, the variable representing U.S. overt trade barriers becomes irrelevant and is omitted. Furthermore, the transport cost variable should be included since its coefficient now has an unambiguous predicted negative sign, unlike the situation where the trade balance is the dependent variable. I have run regressions for both the linear and the log-linear versions, but the linear version performs much better; the results are reported in table 5.12.

Estimates from equations (F) and (F_1) show that the basic results obtained previously are robust with respect to a change of dependent variables. With adjusted U.S. exports to Japan on the left-hand side, the group affiliation variables gS and gE still have the expected negative signs and are significant at the 1 percent level. But as in the trade balance equations, the unit labor costs again have the wrong signs, indicating that again they may act as proxies for other variables such as research and development intensities.[24] The transport cost variable has the expected negative sign but is not significant in either equation.

5.5.5   World Net Exports as the Dependent Variable

A further additional regression analysis uses the world trade balance with Japan (WTB_i) as the dependent variable. The idea is to find out if Japanese group affiliations are also negatively correlated with industry trade balances of countries other than just the United States. World trade balance is defined as the exports from the rest of the world to Japan minus Japan's exports to the rest of the world. To make the analysis meaningful, I omit all variables that pertain to the United States, since these are not necessarily representative of the characteristics of the world. Again, since there are negative values in WTB_i, the log version will not be appropriate. The results, reported in table 5.13, show that Japanese group affiliation is negatively correlated not only with U.S. trade balance but also with the world's trade balance. In this instance, the U.S. data are not unique.[25] Japanese group intensities adversely

24. Note further that Japanese advertising intensity also has the wrong sign.
25. But I also ran similar regressions with world exports adjusted by consumption as the dependent variable. Generally they are not significant. The results are not presented here.

Table 5.12   **Regressions with U.S. Exports**

	Eq. (F)	Eq. (F_1)
Constant	0.18915	0.22628*
	(1.6792)	(1.8630)
Group affiliation	−0.44453***	−0.47427***
	(−3.1740)	(−3.1808)
Japanese tariffs	−0.10193	0.44104×10^{-1}
and quotas	(−0.53593)	(0.24447)
Japanese unit	−0.65638	−0.86965*
labor cost	(−1.7597)	(−2.0224)
U.S. unit labor	0.51807	0.58306*
cost	(1.7307)	(1.8606)
Japanese adver-	25.274***	27.650***
tising intensity	(3.8795)	(3.9123)
U.S. advertising	0.98993	1.0229
intensity	(1.1006)	(1.1369)
No. of Japanese	-0.21596×10^{-6}	-0.13213×10^{-5}
firms	(−0.14541)	(−0.89037)
No. of U.S.	-0.41369×10^{-6}	-0.14102×10^{-5}
firms	(0.22246)	(0.79283)
Transport cost	-0.57358×10^{-1}	-0.82762×10^{-1}
	(−0.32851)	(−0.46711)
R^2	0.692007	0.692608
$\bar{R}^2$	0.461013	0.462063
F	2.99577	3.00423

Note: Eq. (F) uses gS and eq. (F_1) uses gE as the group affiliation variables. The values in parentheses are t-statistics.

*Significant at 10 percent level (two-tailed test).

***Significant at 1 percent level (two-tailed test).

affect U.S. net exports as well as world net exports to Japan. The variable representing the number of firms in Japan has the expected significant negative sign. A larger number of Japanese firms increase Japan's market share and thus reduce the world's trade balance with Japan.[26]

To summarize, I have estimated here a variety of equations generated by my theoretical model. In general, not all the coefficients conform to our predictions. However, there is fairly consistent evidence that the Japanese keiretsu is a factor in U.S.-Japanese trade. This basic conclusion remains robust with alternative specifications of our equation, with different proxies of Japanese group affiliations, and with correction for the possible endogenity of the group-strength variable.[27]

26. As before, the variable representing Japan unit labor costs has the significant sign that is contrary to our model.

27. In addition, alternative functional forms of the regression have also been tested. The results concerning the linear as well as log-linear forms are discussed in the text. To detect the effects of nonlinearities, I also attempted to add the square term of each explanatory variable in turn to the basic equation. The regression results remain qualitatively similar to those of the linear version. The significance of the group-strength variables remain robust.

Table 5.13   **Regressions with World Trade Balance**

	Eq. (K)	Eq. (K₁)
Constant	94.167***	108.61***
	(5.6799)	(7.7224)
Group affiliation	−76.191***	−89.651***
	(−4.5125)	(−6.4039)
Japanese tariffs	0.89182	19.192
and quotas	(0.34071×10^{-1})	(0.91172)
Japanese unit	−172.63***	−212.50***
labor cost	(−5.1220)	(−7.1304)
Japanese adver-	417.67	1005.5
tising intensity	(0.47717)	(1.3855)
No. of Japanese	$-0.39438 \times 10^{-3***}$	$-0.51409 \times 10^{-3***}$
firms	(−2.3291)	(−3.6743)
R^2	0.700389	0.80889
$\bar{R}^2$	0.606761	0.749180
F	7.48052	13.5451

Note: Eq. (K) uses gS and eq. (K₁) uses gE as the group affiliation variables. The values in parentheses are t-statistics.

**Significant at 5 percent level (two-tailed test).

***Significant at 1 percent level (two-tailed test).

5.6 Conclusion

This paper offers an analysis of the role of Japanese *keiretsu* as a potential determinant of U.S.-Japanese trade. Industrial groups in Japan can be classified into three types: those with prewar *zaibatsu* origin, those centered on major banks, and those centered on a prime manufacturer. The Japanese groups are linked economically through many channels. They include cross-holding of shares, intragroup financing by the main banks, subcontracting, regular meeting of presidents of important member firms, and the joint use of general trading companies as agents of imports and exports.

In general, *keiretsu* are still an important component of the Japanese economy, though they are nowhere nearly as powerful as the prewar *zaibatsu*. The links between member firms are also much looser. Perhaps as a way to enhance bargaining power, member corporations do not deal exclusively with other member firms or banks. Even subcontractors, particularly those among the first tier, supply firms other than the prime manufacturer. In the long run, there is a general expectation that *keiretsu* will decline in importance as the Japanese economy becomes more internationalized. One exception, however, is the prime manufacturer-subcontractor relationship, which seems to be increasing in importance over time.

To investigate the impact of *keiretsu* on Japanese-U.S. trade, an oligopoly model of the U.S. and Japanese firms was constructed. It was hypothesized according to this model that a higher degree of Japanese group affiliation will lead to a lower U.S. industry trade balance with Japan. I estimated the focal equation generated by this model and showed that overall there is some evidence that the extent of Japanese *keiretsu* is negatively related to the U.S. trade balance by industry. I estimated similar equations with alternative specifications and different proxies. Furthermore, I also estimated equations where the intensity of group strength was corrected for endogenity. In general, I conclude that the phenomenon of Japanese industrial groups as a factor in U.S.-Japanese trade seems to remain robust.

Since this paper is among the first direct studies of the effects of Japanese *keiretsu*, one must be cautious in drawing policy implications. There are two things to keep in mind, Japanese *keiretsu* may be an important variable explaining the variations of industry-level trade, but they are unlikely to be determinants of overall U.S. trade imbalances. On the aggregate level, macroeconomic conditions remain the most important factors that need to be changed in order for the U.S. trade balances to improve. In addition, the theoretical model as well as the empirical estimations are exercises of *positive* analysis. The model does not tell us what welfare changes may occur if indeed there are changes in the Japanese industrial structures.

Appendix

Industries in the Sample and Percentage Drop of Industry Trade Balance Due to Groups

	Using Eq. (A)(%)	Using Eq. $(A)_1$(%)
1. Food and kindred products	0.301	0.11
2. Fibers and textiles	4.51	3.14
3. Pulp and paper products	3.86	1.99
4. Chemical and allied products	3.10	3.94
5. Petroleum and coal products	2.30	2.07
6. Rubber products	15.44	10.51
7. Iron and steel	2.60	2.52
8. Nonferrous metal and products	16.79	16.38
9. Fabricated metal products	0.85	0.34
10. General machinery	1.19	0.71
11. Electronic and electrical equipment	1.91	1.52
12. Shipbuilding	16.20	11.45
13. Auto parts and components	4.54	3.63
14. Automobile and equipment	1.15	1.13
15. Aircraft and parts	2.54	1.80
16. Watches, clocks and parts	3.71	1.57
17. Scientific and optical instruments	1.17	0.49
18. Stone, clay and glass products	8.64	4.30
19. Lumber and plywood products	0.19	0.04
20. Printing and publishing	0.31	0.22
21. Furniture and fixtures	13.55	6.10
22. Leather and leather products	29.39	30.08

Note: Equation (A) measures the percentage drop of U.S. net exports due to the Japanese groups using the estimated coefficient of the group affiliation measured by sales. Equation (A_1) estimates the same percentage drop using the estimated coefficient of the group affiliation measured by employment.

Definitions of Variables

TB U.S. exports to Japan minus U.S. imports from Japan, 1980.

gS Sales of group affiliated companies as a percentage of total industry sale, 1980.

gE Employment of group affiliated companies as a percentage of total industry employment, 1980.

USULC U.S. nominal wage rate/value added per worker, 1980.

JULC Japanese nominal wage rate/value added per worker, 1980.

JTQ Sum of Japanese tariffs and Japanese tariff-equivalent nontariff barriers, 1989.

USTQ Sum of U.S. tariffs and U.S. tariff-equivalent nontariff barriers, 1989.

USAD U.S. advertising expenditure/total sales, 1980.

JAD Japanese advertising expenditure/total sales, 1980.

USF	Number of U.S. firms, 1980.
JF	Number of Japanese firms, 1980.
TC	Ocean shipments freight charges/f.a.s. import unit values, 1977
USXC	U.S. exports to Japan/consumption of Japan, 1980
WTB	World's exports to Japan minus Japan's exports to the world, 1980
JFP	Value of products minus cost of materials and total wages and salaries in Japan/number of firms in Japan, 1980.
JTE	Number of temporary employees as a percentage of total industry employment in Japan, 1980.
JIP	Number of individually owned firms as a percentage of total number of firms in Japan, 1980.
JLF	Number of firms with more than 300 regular employees as a percentage of total number of firms in Japan, 1980.

Sources of Data

Degrees of group affiliations *gS* and *gE:* constructed from Dodwell Marketing Consultants (1990) and Ministry of International Trade and Industry (1981).

Japanese unit labor costs and number of firms: constructed from Ministry of International Trade and Industry (1981).

U.S. trade balance: U.S. Bureau of the Census, *U.S. Exports: Domestic Merchandise SIC-based Products by World Areas,* Publication FT610 (Washington, D.C., 1980); ibid., *U.S. Imports: Consumption and General SIC-based Products by World Areas,* Publication FT210 (Washington, D.C., 1980).

U.S. unit labor costs and number of firms: U.S. Bureau of the Census, *Census of Manufactures* (Washington, D.C., 1980).

U.S. and Japanese tariffs and nontariff trade barriers: constructed from Saxonhouse and Stern (1989) and Ray (1990).

U.S. advertising/total sales ratio: constructed from U.S. Bureau of Economic Analysis, "Input-Output Structure of the U.S. Economy 1977," *Survey of Current Business* (1984).

Japanese advertising/total sales ratio: constructed from Government of Japan, Administrative Management Agency, 1980 Input-Output Tables (Tokyo, 1980).

Transport costs: Clark (1981).

Unadjusted U.S. exports to Japan: U.S. Bureau of the Census, *U.S. Exports: Domestic Merchandise SIC-based Products by World Areas,* Publication FT610 (Washington, D.C., 1980).

Japanese consumption (production minus exports plus imports): constructed from Ministry of International Trade and Industry (1981) and Japan Tariff Association, *Japan Exports and Imports, Commodity by Country* (Tokyo, 1980).

World trade balance: constructed from Japan Tariff Association, *Japan Exports and Imports, Commodity by Country* (Tokyo, 1980).

Japanese average industry profits, percentage of firms with more than 300 employees, percentage of temporary employees, and proportion of individual proprietorship: constructed from Ministry of International Trade and Industry, *Japan Census of Manufactures: Report by Industries* (Tokyo, 1980) and *Japan Census of Manufactures: Report by Enterprises* (Tokyo, 1980).

References

Aoki, M. 1988. Information, incentives and bargaining in the Japanese economy. Cambridge: Cambridge University Press.

Balassa, Bela. 1986. Japan's trade policies. *Weltwirtschaftliches Archiv,* 122:745–90.

Baldwin, R. 1971. Determinants of the commodity structure of U.S. trade. *American Economic Review* 61:126–46.

Bergsten, C., and R. Cline. 1987. *The U.S.-Japan trade problem.* Washington, D.C.: Institute for International Economics.

Brander, J., and P. Krugman. 1983. A reciprocal dumping model of international trade. *Journal of International Economics,* 15:313–21.

Caves, R., and M. Uekusa. 1976. *Industrial organization in Japan.* Washington, D.C.: Brookings Institution.

Clark, D. 1981. On the relative importance of international transport charges as a barrier to trade. *Quarterly Review of Economics and Business* 21:127–35.

Cline, W., A. Kawanabe, T. Kronsjö, and T. Williams. 1978. *Trade negotiations in the Tokyo Round.* Washington, D.C.: Brookings Institution.

Cole, R., and T. Yakushiji. 1984. The American and Japanese auto industries in transition. Center for Japanese Studies. Ann Arbor: University of Michigan Press.

Dixit, A., 1984. International trade policies for oligopolistic industries, *Economic Journal* 94 (Supplement).

———. 1989. Hysteresis, import penetration, and exchange rate pass-through. *Quarterly Journal of Economics,* 103:205–28.

Dodwell Marketing Consultants. 1982–83. *Industrial groupings in Japan.* Rev. ed.

Eaton, J., and G. Grossman. 1986. Optimal trade and industrial policy under oligopoly. *Quarterly Journal of Economics* 101:384–406.

Fung, K. 1987. Quotas, export trading companies and oligopolistic rivalry. *Journal of International Economic Integration* 2, no. 1 (Spring).

———. 1989. Strategic industrial policy under Cournot and Bertrand oligopoly: Management-labor cooperation as a possible solution to the market structure dilemma. Working Paper, University of California, Santa Cruz.

———. 1991. Collusive intra-industry trade. *Canadian Journal of Economics* 24 (2):391–404.

Helpman, E., and P. Krugman. 1989. *Trade policy and market structure.* Cambridge, Mass.: MIT Press.

Japanese Agency for Small and Medium-sized Enterprises. 1977. A survey of division of labor structure. Tokyo.

Johnson, C. 1982. *MITI and the Japanese miracle 1925–1975.* Stanford, Cal.: Stanford University Press.

Kreinin, M. 1988. How closed is the Japanese market? Additional evidence. *World Economy* 11:529–42.

Krugman, P. 1984. The U.S. response to foreign industrial targeting. Brookings Papers on Economic Activity, no. 1, 77–131.

Krugman, P., and R. Baldwin. 1987. The persistence of the U.S. trade deficit. Brookings Papers on Economic Activities, no. 1, 1–43.

Lawrence, Robert Z., 1987. Imports in Japan: Closed markets or minds? Brookings Papers on Economic Activity, no. 2, 517–54.

McCulloch, R. 1985. Trade deficit, industrial competitiveness, and the Japanese. In *International Trade and Finance,* 3d ed., ed. R. Baldwin and J. D. Richardson. Boston: Little, Brown & Co.

Ministry of International Trade and Industry. 1981. Japan Census of Manufactures, Report by Industries.

Nakatani, I. 1984. The economic role of financial corporate grouping. In *The economic Analysis of the Japanese firm,* ed. M. Aoki. North Holland.

Pascale, R. and T. Rohlen. 1983. The Mazda turnaround. *Journal of Japanese Studies* 9:219–63.

Petri, P. 1984. *Modeling Japanese-American trade: A study of asymmetric interdependence.* Cambridge: Harvard University Press.

———. 1990. Japanese trade in transition: hypothesis and recent evidence. Brandeis University Working Paper 247.

Ray, E. 1981. Tariff and nontariff barriers to trade in the United State and abroad. *Review of Economics and Statistics,* 161–68.

———. 1990. Data on tariffs and nontariff barriers in the U.S. Ohio State University, manuscript.

Roehl, T. 1983. An economic analysis of industrial groups in post-war Japan. Ph.D. diss., University of Washington.

Saxonhouse, G. 1983a. What is all this about industrial targeting in Japan? *World Economy* 6 (September):253–74.

———. 1983b. The micro and macro economics of foreign sales to Japan, in *Trade Policies in the 1980s,* ed. W. Cline. Washington, D.C.: Institute for International Economics.

———. 1985. What's wrong with Japanese trade structure? Seminal Discussion Paper 166, University of Michigan.

Saxonhouse, G., and R. Stern. 1989. An analytical survey of formal and informal barriers to international trade and investment in the United States, Canada, and Japan. In *Trade and Investment Relations Among the United States, Canada, and Japan,* ed. R. M. Stern, chap 9. Chicago: University of Chicago Press.

Scherer, F., and D. Ross. 1990. *Industrial market structure and economic performance,* 3d ed. Boston: Houghton Mifflin Co.

Scott, B., and G. Lodge. 1985. U.S. competitiveness in the world economy. Boston: Harvard Business School Press.

Singh, N., and X. Vives. 1984. Price and quantity competition in a differentiated duopoly. *Rand Journal of Economics* (Winter), 546–54.

U.S. Trade Representative. 1985. U.S. Statement to Japanese Market Access. Addressed to OECD Trade Committee, Washington, D.C.

Yamawaki, H., and D. Audretch. 1988. Import share under international oligopoly with differentiated products: Japanese imports in U.S. manufacturing. *Review of Economics and Statistics* 70:569–79.

Comment   Robert Z. Lawrence

Fung presents an informative summary of *keiretsu* groups, an oligopolistic model of how *keiretsu* could affect net exports, and some empirical tests. My overall impression was that although this is an important topic, the research presented here remains in a very preliminary phase, particularly if it is to be useful to policymakers.

I enjoyed the first section and will not comment on it. I will, however, comment on the theory, the empirical work, and its relevance for the policy debate.

Theory

The strategy in this paper is to come up with a very simple model of the group that allows us to test its effects on trade flows. The methodology is appropriate if the model captures the essential features of the group's behavior, allowing us to place fairly tight constraints on the estimation parameters, and thus to accept or reject the model.

My feeling was, however, that the model fails to capture many of the key questions relating to the existence of groups. The model emphasizes the links between an input supplier and a final producer. The key here is that the supplier holds stock in the firm producing the final product. We know that there can be gains from vertical integration when a supplier has monopoly power. Without vertical integration, when a monopolist supplier raises input prices, his customers are induced to substitute other inputs. A vertically integrated firm, on the other hand, can use shadow prices that reflect marginal cost and thus produce more efficiently and earn higher profits.

Of course, if this is the source of the price advantage given to the Japanese final product producer from exchanging securities with its supplier, it could readily be emulated by vertical integration in the United States. Indeed, as noted by Cline and Bergsten, "Oligopoly behavior in its most intense form will replicate the decisions of a single large firm."[1] So the relationship as captured here does not really *explain* the existence of groups. It assumes them. Moreover, it is not really clear why we should expect Japan to derive a competitive advantage from these groups, unless we make the additional assumption that in the United States there is some constraint on vertical integration.

But it seems to me that the reasons for the existence of groups could go far beyond the effects of cross-holding modeled here. On the one hand, they may

Robert Z. Lawrence is a senior fellow in the Economic Studies Program of the Brookings Institution.

1. C. F. Bergsten and W. R. Cline, *The United States–Japan Economic Problem* (Washington, D.C.: Institute for International Economics, 1985).

simply reflect increased monopoly power. On the other, they could enhance efficiency by achieving the benefits of closer vertical integration while avoiding some of the costs. These benefits relate to the potential gains from reducing risk, improving information flows and perhaps certain economies of scope. There may also be benefits in preserving greater flexibility than full vertical integration would require. In particular, in a system where core firms provide lifetime employment guarantees, they may prefer closely tied suppliers who can lay off their workers to vertical integration. But Fung's model fails to deal with these questions, which could have an important influence on the qualitative nature of the results he obtains.

Finally, let me note that what Fung has modeled is competition in the market for the final product market. The Japanese firm has a *keiretsu* association with its input supplier that gives it access to these inputs more cheaply because it has a share in final product. What many Americans are complaining about, however, is competition in the inputs market. The dispute involves not only the link he models where the supplier has shares in the final producer, but the reverse, where the final buyer has shares in the suppliers who are local.

Empirical Tests

The dependent variable in the test is the bilateral net trade balance. Relying on his model, Fung argues the effects of the group act symmetrically in export competition and in competition within Japan. His model is one where the group allows the Japanese producer access to cheaper raw materials. This allows the final goods producer to charge lower prices at home and abroad, so this mechanism fits his formulation quite naturally. But there are other effects which one might believe are more powerful *in* Japan than they are outside. If the group providing the loans insists on purchases from other group members, for example, indeed this might make a positive contribution to the group share within Japan but hurt export sales abroad. So I would like to see specifications of the dependent variable as imports (or import shares) of particular products.

A second problem with the dependent variable, if I understand it, is surely heteroskedasticity. This means we probably have an equation giving huge weight to autos and electronics.

The dependent variable, unit labor costs, is not clearly defined. How was it derived? What data sources were used? I am not sure the discussion of the variable which implies that it captures *absolute* differences in costs is really justified. Since this is a cross-sectional analysis, you need a purchasing-power parity estimate for each two-digit industry to define these units. How was this done? I missed an explanation in the text, and it is surely critical. Indeed, I suspect that what is really being captured here is the share of labor in overall income. If this is the case, it might help explain the empirical result, but not through the mechanism laid out in the model. In particular, the equation may be telling us of a relationship between trade performance and labor intensity rather than unit costs.

Fung *assumes* the conditions required for a quota to have a negative effect on the (exporters') trade balance. But in theory, of course, the effect is ambiguous. There are higher prices and lower quantities, and when you have imperfect competition, the price response hinges on the demand elasticity. This might explain why the empirical results of the quota are poor. It might simply reflect the fact that his assumption is unwarranted, rather than providing a good test of the effect of groups.

Policy Implications

Simply finding that *keiretsu* has a positive effect on trade fails to sort out the most important dilemma for policy. Are *keiretsu* allowing for an increase in *efficiency* or an increase in *monopoly* power in the domestic market? Either could boost the trade balance, but the welfare effects for the United States and Japan could be very different. This is the key issue on which policymakers need help.

The official U.S. contention in the current negotiations in the Structural Impediments Initiative is, of course, that there are *inefficiencies* due to these groups. These result precisely from the effects on restraining trade. Even if the trade balance is improved, welfare could be reduced, since the groups practices could hurt Japanese consumers and U.S. producers. The perplexing thing to an economist is how such a situation could persist. Why does competition not force some producers to buy cheaper and better foreign goods and thus drive those relying on an inefficient *keiretsu* system out of business? Indeed, the evidence on price differentials between Japan and the rest of the world do seem to suggest such practices exist.

My suspicion is that the groups result in both efficiency gains and losses. In the auto industry, group affiliations seem to have provided benefits. But in other cases, there are suggestions of inefficiency. It is worth recalling, for example, that in an early study, Caves and Uekusa found: "After controlling for other determinants of profitability, we found that profits . . . were if anything negatively related to group affiliation. . . . It remains distinctly possible that rents yielded by group affiliation are consumed in technical inefficiency." [2]

Indeed, it seems to me, one way to sort this out would be to examine performance in third markets rather than in the bilateral balance. We would like to know if given the performance in third markets, the United States tends to do worse in Japan in sectors where there is a *keiretsu* presence.

2. Richard Caves and Masu Uekusa, *Industrial Organization in Japan* (Washington, D.C.: Brookings Institution, 1976).

6 Size Rationalization and Trade Exposure in Developing Countries

Mark J. Roberts and James R. Tybout

6.1 Overview

Economists often argue that exposure to foreign competition should increase plant size and productivity in less developed countries (LDCs). They cite several reasons. First, foreign competition reduces the market power that domestic producers may derive from scale economies, rationed credit markets, or institutional constraints. Consequently, reductions in protection should expand output among these producers and allow better exploitation of scale economies. Similarly, when competitive discipline is absent, the resultant cushion of monopoly profits may allow inefficiently small, wasteful domestic firms to survive. Finally, even if profits are competed away through entry or the threat of entry, limited domestic demand can lead to inefficiently small-scale production in markets for differentiated products, where Chamberlinian competition prevails.

These positive effects of trade exposure are widely held to apply both in developing and in industrialized economies. Nonetheless, analytical models show that they need not obtain. Whether trade liberalization improves efficiency depends critically on the distribution of output adjustments across plants with differing unit costs (Rodrik 1988a). This depends, in turn, on factor intensities, the pattern of demand shifts, the nature of competition, and the extent to which entry and exit are possible (e.g., Buffie and Spiller 1986;

Mark J. Roberts is professor of economics at the Pennsylvania State University. James R. Tybout is associate professor of economics at Georgetown University and a consultant to the World Bank.

Funding was provided by the NBER and the World Bank research project "Industrial Competition, Productive Efficiency, and Their Relation to Trade Regimes" (RPO-674-46). We have benefited from the comments of Robert Baldwin, Ann Harrison, Anne Krueger, Robert Lipsey, Ramon Lopez, Peter Petri, Larry Samuelson, and Marius Schwartz. We also wish to thank Constantina Backinezos, Jin-Sung Park, and Lili Liu for research assistance.

Brown, 1989). When technology and innovation are endogenous, further ambiguities result (Rodrik 1988b).

Simulation models support the received wisdom that in LDCs, liberalization of imperfectly competitive industries results in larger plants and higher efficiency (Condon and de Melo 1986; Devarajan and Rodrik 1989a, 1989b; de Melo and Roland-Holst, chap. 10 in this volume). Disturbingly, however, there is very little micro-econometric evidence confirming the adjustment mechanisms that these models assume. For example, Bhagwati (1988) concludes: "Although the arguments for the success of the [outward-oriented development strategies] based on economies of scale and X-efficiency are plausible, empirical support for them is not available." Pack (1989) goes further, claiming that the link between trade liberalization and productivity growth has not been established at all.[1]

Given the lack of direct evidence regarding industrial adjustment in response to trade liberalization, this paper tackles a very basic question. Specifically, in LDCs, how is trade orientation correlated with the size distribution of plants and with plant-level labor productivity? We begin with a simple model that summarizes some effects of trade exposure on producer size and productive efficiency that have been stressed in the recent analytical and simulation literature. We then examine annual plant-level data from Chile and Colombia to determine whether these effects can be confirmed.

The empirical results indicate that, over the long run, higher trade exposure is correlated with smaller plant sizes, controlling for industry and country effects. However, the mix of high versus low productivity plants is not strongly associated with trade exposure. Both of these findings cast doubt on the mechanisms linking trade, plant size, and productivity in a number of recent analytical and simulation studies.

6.2   Theories Linking Trade Regime and Size Rationalization

6.2.1   The Analytics of Size Rationalization under Imperfect Competition

To motivate our empirical work, we begin with an expository model that generates several predictions familiar from the trade and development literature.[2] First, assume that within each industry, domestically produced goods

1. Pack (1989) writes: "Comparisons of total factor productivity growth among countries pursuing different international trade orientations do not reveal systematic differences in productivity growth in manufacturing, nor do the time-series studies of individual countries that have experienced alternating trade regimes allow strong conclusions in this dimension. . . . Moreover, the firm-level data collected for estimation of production frontiers are quite reliable and confirm the pattern established at more aggregated levels."

2. Buffie and Spiller (1986), Dixit and Norman (1980), Dutz (1990), Lancaster (1984), Helpman and Krugman (1985), Horstmann and Markusen (1986), and Markusen (1981) are among the many relevant references in the analytical literature. Simulation results that reflect at least some of the effects described here include those found in Harris (1984), Rodrik (1988a), Devarajan and

are perfect substitutes, and domestic firms are Cournot quantity competitors vis-à-vis one another. Also, let the domestic product be an imperfect substitute for imports, so that the demand curve faced by domestic producers may be written as $P = P(Q,\Omega)$, where $Q = \Sigma q_i$, q_i is the output of the ith producer, and Ω is the set of factors that determine exposure to world markets.[3] This set includes quantitative restrains (QRs), tariffs, and the real exchange rate. Finally, define $C_i = F + q_i c_i$ to be the total costs of producing q_i borne by the ith plant ($i = 1, n$), where F and c_i are constants. The presence of marginal cost heterogeneity is meant to reflect differences in managerial abilities, credit market access, and capital stocks.[4]

As is well known, the first-order condition for profit maximization under Cournot competition is

(1) $$P(Q,\Omega) + q_i P_Q(Q,\Omega) = c_i \quad i = 1,n,$$

so firms with low marginal costs are relatively large.[5] Also, summing equation (1) over all plants, equilibrium output and price in this market depend only on the *sum* of marginal costs and not on the distribution of marginal costs across plants (e.g., Bergstrom and Varian 1985):

(2) $$nP(Q,\Omega) + QP_Q(Q,\Omega) = \sum_{i=1}^{n} c_i.$$

Given n, and assuming $P_Q < 0$, there is thus a negative monotonic relationship between Σc_i and the equilibrium industry output, Q. In turn, given Q, each plant's output q_i is determined recursively by equation (1).

If market entry and exit are free, the number of firms is endogenous. To characterize equilibrium in this case, we require that the last and least efficient plant (plant n) covers costs, and that all potential firms not in the market anticipate losses upon entry. Sorting plants in order of increasing average cost, this condition amounts to

(3) $$c_{n+1}/q_{n+1} > P(Q,\Omega) > c_n/q_n,$$

Rodrik (1989a, 1989b), Condon and de Melo (1990), de Melo and Roland-Holst (chap. 10, in this volume), and Tarr and de Melo (forthcoming). If there is a novelty to our model, it is that we simultaneously treat cost heterogeneity and entry/exit effects.

3. Domestic markets are small relative to the rest of the world, and foreign producers do not react strategically to domestic producers' behavior.

4. Most models in the trade literature do not allow for marginal cost heterogeneity; we include it here for two reasons. First, it captures the spirit of the X-efficiency arguments found in the development literature. Second, it is an important feature of theoretical models that explain the persistent size heterogeneity one finds in virtually all plant-level census data (e.g., Jovanovic 1982).

5. We do not believe the link between size and efficiency is well established in the empirical literature on developing countries. However, as this link is assumed in most analytical and simulation models, we assume it holds here to demonstrate how these models work.

where q_{n+1} is the output level the $n + 1$th (potential) plant would choose if it were to enter the market.

6.2.2   Demand Shifts and Rationalization

We can now review predictions about the link between demand shifts and the size distribution of plants. Hereafter, any shift that results in plant size adjustments that reduce the industry-wide average cost will be said to have "rationalized" industry. In our framework this can occur two ways—either by increasing output levels overall and reducing average fixed costs, or by shifting market shares toward large, low marginal cost plants and reducing average variable costs.

To describe the conditions under which trade liberalization induces such shifts, it is convenient to assume a linear demand schedule with both the intercept and the slope dependent upon trade regime:

$$(4) \qquad\qquad P = \alpha - \beta Q,$$
$$\alpha = \alpha(\Omega), \quad \beta = \beta(\Omega).$$

Then, if entry is not possible, equilibrium is described by the follow $n + 2$ conditions:

$$(5.1) \qquad\qquad Q = \frac{n\alpha - \Sigma c_i}{\beta(n + 1)},$$

$$(5.2) \qquad\qquad P = \frac{\alpha + \Sigma c_i}{(n + 1)},$$

$$(5.3) \qquad\qquad q_j = \frac{\alpha + \Sigma c_i - c_j(n + 1)}{\beta(n + 1)}, \quad j = 1, n.$$

From these equations, the effect of demand shifts induced by trade reforms follow easily. Suppose that, beginning from autarky and binding QRs, trade is liberalized. This type of reform has the effect of placing domestic producers in large world markets where there are many other producers and substitute products. Regardless of whether the domestic product is exportable or import competing, one would expect its demand elasticity to rise. We isolate the consequences of such an elasticity increase by pivoting the demand curve through the pre-reform equilibrium point, reducing both α and β. By equation (5.2) P must fall, so Q must rise, and industry-wide average fixed costs must fall. The market share of plant j, q_j/Q, does not depend on β. However, reductions in α increase the market share of large, low-cost plants, and thereby reduce average variable costs for the industry.[6] So trade reforms that increase the elasticity of demand without shifting it inward reduce average costs, both by shifting production toward low-cost producers and by increasing industry-wide output.

6. More precisely, the market share of the jth plant expands as α falls if c_j is less than $\Sigma c/n$.

Of course elasticity effects are not the only possible effect of increased foreign competition. Trade reforms that amount to tariff reductions or real currency appreciation may act mainly to reduce domestic demand for import-competing products. If this causes a contraction in total output, average fixed costs will rise for the affected industries, at least partly offsetting any fall in average variable costs. Although many simulation models allow for this contractionary effect of liberalization, it has not usually proved to be dominant.[7]

Now consider the adjustments that occur when entry and exit are possible. Suppose trade liberalization shifts demand inward (reduces α), with or without an increase in elasticity. By equation (5.2), P must fall, so the smallest, least efficient firms will begin to take losses and exit, reducing both n and Σc_i.[8] In the initial equilibrium $c_n \leq P$ (eq. [3]), so before price adjusts this exit will have reduced nP more than it reduced Σc_i. Accordingly, to restore equilibrium Q must contact more and P must fall less than they would have if exit were not possible (eq. [2]). In sum, compared to the case of no exit, efficiency effects are stronger for two reasons: The least efficient plants leave the market entirely, and remaining plants face less contractionary pressure. By analogous logic, free entry and exit exacerbate the reduction in productive efficiency associated with *outward* shifts of the demand curve, as might accompany quotas or increases in the tariff rate: Small, inefficient firms are induced to enter and take market shares from incumbents. This consequence of market expansion through protection is another familiar story in the literature.[9]

6.2.3 Robustness

Though far from comprehensive, the exposition above gives an idea of the size rationalization effects that have recently been stressed in literature. In particular, exposure to foreign competition can increase plants' size by increasing the elasticity of demand. Even if exposure to competition reduces plant size by contracting demand, it is likely to hit the most inefficient plants hardest. Hence, unless returns to scale are important, efficiency gains are still likely. Finally, the positive effects of liberalization are larger when entry and exit are possible because inefficient plants will be forced out of the market, allowing those producers who remain behind to operate on a larger scale.

Although these effects are often stressed, they are not guaranteed. There is no reason why liberalizations might not contract demand for domestic products so severely as to increase average costs—particularly when fixed costs and entry barriers are significant. Moreover, as various authors have shown, alternative analytic frameworks expand the range of possible outcomes. For

---

7. An exception is de Melo and Tarr (forthcoming).

8. To see this, note that the demand function (4) and the profit maximization condition (1) imply $q_j = (p - c_j)/\beta, j = 1, n$. If P falls, q_j must fall, and so average costs at the ith plant must rise.

9. Although their models are different, the same conclusions are stressed in Eastman and Stykolt (1966), Dixit and Norman (1980), and Harris (1984).

example, if static Cournot quantity competition is replaced with another type of competition, firms adjust their output levels differently in response to demand shifts. The monotonic negative relationship between plant size and average variable costs might then be broken, and it would no longer necessarily hold that shifting production toward large plants improves efficiency. Still more outcomes are possible if one endogenizes marginal costs, allowing for changes in factor prices, X-efficiency, and learning-by-doing. Finally, domestic product differentiation can be introduced. This not only opens the possibility of cross-plant variation in the degree of competition from foreign substitutes, it also allows endogenous adjustments in the length of production runs.

Given these qualifications, it is clearly an empirical question whether trade liberalization will (1) increase the average scale of production, (2) shift market shares toward large producers, and (3) bring with it productivity improvement. The remainder of this paper is devoted to an econometric examination of these issues.

6.3   Empirical Methodology

6.3.1   The Data and Country Backgrounds

In this section we examine cross-country and intertemporal contrasts in trade exposure, plant size distributions, and labor productivity distributions for evidence on the empirical relevance of the theoretical effects reviewed in section 6.2. To do this we utilize annual census data covering all manufacturing plants with at least ten workers in Colombia and Chile.[10] But before turning to the empirical models these data support, it is useful to review the cross-country differences and within-country time series fluctuations in trade policies and industrial performance that allow us to identify parameters.

Chile

The Chilean data used in this paper cover the period 1979–85; we begin our overview with the years immediately preceding. Like much of Latin America, Chile pursued an inward-oriented development strategy in the 1960s. The system of incentives—including tariffs, quotas, exchange rate policy, and domestic market regulations—favored manufacturing at the expense of agriculture and import-competing producers over exporters (Corbo 1985). This bias intensified in the early 1970s. By 1973 average tariff rates exceeded 100 percent, prior deposit requirements for importers created heavy

---

10. The governments of Chile and Colombia have recently made these data available to the World Bank in connection with the World Bank research project "Industrial Competition, Productive Efficiency, and Their Relation to Trade Regimes" (RPO 674–46). They are described in Roberts (1989) and Tybout (1989). Our discussion of Chile is based on Tybout (1989); our discussion of Colombia is based on Roberts (1989).

additional surcharges, and a complex system of multiple exchange rates prevailed.

In 1973, the military seized power and began implementing radical policy changes. In addition to fiscal austerity and price stabilization programs, the new government rapidly implemented laissez-faire micro reforms. The new administration sold public enterprises, decontrolled prices and interest rates, and dismantled trade barriers. The average nominal tariff rate fell from 105 percent in 1974 to 12 percent in 1979.

Although the industrial sector initially suffered from recessionary macro conditions, recovery began in 1976 and continued into 1981. Several features of this recovery were noteworthy. First, the reductions in industrial employment that accompanied the 1974–75 recession continued during the 1976–81 recovery, so that labor productivity increased dramatically. Second, the balance of trade in industrial products worsened considerably during the latter part of the recovery period. The trade liberalization was partly responsible, but there was also considerable exchange-rate appreciation beginning in 1979. Third, during 1976–81 a handful of powerful conglomerates (*grupos*) emerged and consolidated control over both financial and industrial enterprises.

By the end of 1982, the Chilean economy was again in serious trouble. The exchange rate had been overvalued for some time, and tradable sector producers had undergone a protracted profit squeeze. Large capital inflows were necessary to finance the current account deficit, yet international credit was evaporating, exacerbating firms' financial stress with very high interest rates. The government finally devalued, but the financial soundness of the economy had already been undermined, and a major recession followed. Unemployment reached roughly 30 percent in 1983.

To help the economy recover, the government took various steps to ease firms' financial problems. This relief, in addition to devaluation, a mild increase in tariff protection, and a reduction in the corporate income tax from 38 percent to 10 percent, facilitated a quick industrial sector recovery. As the recovery continued, average tariff levels were gradually dropped, falling from a peak of 36 percent in September 1984 to 15 percent in 1988.

To summarize, our sample period includes the end of a major trade liberalization and economic recovery (1979–81), a severe recession that was accompanied by devaluation and mild increases in protection (1982–83), and a sustained recovery with a return to very low levels of protection. Table 6.1 presents time series on trade exposure and average workers per plant (an index of average plant size). Note that the ratio of imports to output grew substantially over the period 1979–82, then fell (with devaluation and increased protection) after 1982. Both total manufacturing employment and average plant size declined continuously after 1979 until the recovery began in 1984.

Popular sentiment has it that the Chilean industrial sector is now one of the most efficient in Latin America. Although the government's approach to antitrust policy is essentially laissez-faire, it is commonly held that the discipline of foreign competition prevents firms from exercising much market power and forces inefficient firms to reform or shut down. The grupos are still in evidence, but they too are considered efficient competitors by most observers.

Colombia

The Colombian data base spans 1977–87 but, as with Chile, it is instructive to begin with a review of years preceding. In 1967, the Colombian government began to abandon its traditional inward-looking development strategy in favor of export promotion policies, a modest degree of trade liberalization, and greater exchange-rate flexibility. Exports were encouraged with duty-drawback schemes, tax incentives, and special credit facilities. Imports were liberalized by scaling back prior licensing requirements, eliminating prohibited lists, and reducing average nominal tariff rates.[11]

During this period of export promotion and trade liberalization there was growth in the aggregate economy as well as in the volume of imports and exports. Real GDP grew at an annual average rate of 6.3 percent over the 1967–75 period, and the manufacturing sector grew at an annual rate of 8.8 percent. But beginning in late 1975, significant changes in Colombia's macroeconomic environment began to influence trade policy and the real exchange rate. Specifically, substantial increases in world coffee prices and increased foreign borrowing contributed to large foreign exchange inflows, which resulted in increased inflation. Substantial real appreciation resulted, which tended to hurt tradable goods producers in the industrial sector. Accordingly, between 1976 and the early 1980s, efforts to liberalize the trade regime proceeded at a slower pace.

The trend toward liberalization stalled completely in the early 1980s. In 1980, approximately 69 percent of all commodities did not require import licenses. But in 1981 only 36 percent of all commodities were classified in the free import category, and this percentage fell continuously through 1984. By that time only 0.5 percent of all commodities could be freely imported, 83 percent required licenses, and 16.5 percent were prohibited. Liberalization resumed in 1985 and 1986 but not enough to return to 1980 levels.

The time series patterns in Colombian trade exposure are reported in table 6.1. There is a marked increase in import penetration and a marked decline in export shares over the period of currency appreciation, 1977–82. Over the same period, total manufacturing employment and average plant size declined. Finally, note the contrasts between Chile and Colombia in terms of

11. In 1971 approximately 3 percent of all commodities could be freely imported, 81 percent required licenses, and the remaining 16 percent were prohibited. By 1974 approximately 30 percent of all commodities on the tariff schedule could be freely imported and the remaining 70 percent required prior licensing (Garcia 1988, table 2.1). Also, nominal tariff rates had fallen to an average of 32 percent.

Table 6.1 **Trade Exposure and Market Size in Colombia and Chile**

Year	Import Share[a]		Export Share[b]		Total Employment[c]		Plant Size[d]	
	Colombia	Chile	Colombia	Chile	Colombia	Chile	Colombia	Chile
1977	.246		.100		402.7		77.0	
1978	.262		.088		410.7		79.0	
1979	.250	.528	.092	.086	420.8	229.0	78.7	55.6
1980	.328	.600	.108	.105	419.8	209.8	77.2	56.4
1981	.363	.762	.055	.060	404.3	194.2	75.0	57.5
1982	.375	.758	.053	.088	394.2	155.2	69.9	51.3
1983	.329	.637	.047	.088	374.5	147.3	74.6	52.9
1984	.297	.762	.047	.081	372.6	164.2	74.4	56.6
1985	.264	.701	.051	.072	360.0	174.2	69.7	60.9
1986	.289		.061		368.6		68.5	
1987	.287		.065		397.5		71.0	
Average	.299	.678	.070	.083	393.2	182.0	74.1	55.9

[a]Manufactured imports as a share of domestic manufactured output.
[b]Manufactured exports as a share of domestic manufactured output.
[c]Total manufacturing employment, in thousands.
[d]Average number of workers per plant in the manufacturing sector.

trade exposure, total industrial employment, and average plant size. Both the total manufacturing sector and the average plant size are larger in Colombia. Moreover, imports, and to a lesser degree exports, are small in Colombia as a share of domestic production. This partly reflects differences in the size of the two countries but probably also reflects Colombian trade policy, which never came close to the degree of openness found in Chile.[12] For example, while Chile essentially eliminated QRs, they remained a prominent feature of Colombian trade policy throughout the sample period. Similarly, while Chile had achieved uniform 10 percent tariffs by 1979, Colombian tariffs remained around 30 percent after substantial cuts in 1974.

6.3.2 An Empirical Framework for Plant Size and Productivity Analysis

As noted in section 6.2, theory alone cannot tell us the qualitative, much less quantitative, relationship between trade exposure and cross-plant distributions of size or productivity. Yet econometric evidence on the association between these variables is almost nonexistent. Therefore, to generate some new "stylized facts," we now develop empirical models that summarize the correlations between these variables using country- and time-specific data on three-digit manufacturing industries in Chile and Colombia. To distinguish short-run and long-run correlations, two types of models will be used—those that exploit cross-country variation in trade exposure and size or productivity

12. Colombian per capita income is a bit lower than that of Chile, but Colombia has more than double Chile's population.

distributions, and those that exploit variation within countries over time. Both types of models will control for industry effects, domestic market size, and ease of entry and exit.

We begin by constructing some measures of the plant size distribution for industry i, country j, and year t. For each (i, j, t) combination we rank plants by ascending employment level and find the employment levels of plants at the 10th, 25th, 50th, 75th, and 90th percentiles.[13] Similarly, to summarize productivity distributions for each observation, we rank plants by output per worker and find cut-offs for the same percentiles. We thereby generate five summary measures of the cross-plant size distribution, and five summary measures of the cross-plant labor productivity distribution:

$\ln(\text{EMP}k_{ijt})$ = Logarithm of the kth percentile of the employment size distribution ($k = 10, 25, 50, 75, 90$)

$\ln(\text{PRD}k_{ijt})$ = Logarithm of the kth percentile of the productivity (output per man) distribution ($k = 10, 25, 50, 75, 90$)

One by one, each of these summary measures is regressed on proxies for product market conditions, *inter alia*. This approach permits us to analyze changes in the *shape* of the size and productivity distributions as well as changes in the median size. We express all percentiles in logarithms to facilitate analysis of their rates of change and the associated shifts in output shares. For industry i, country j, year t, the explanatory variables we work with are:

$\ln Q_{ijt}$ = Log of real industry output

$\ln (M/Q)_{ijt}$ = Log of the ratio of imports to output

$\ln (X/Q)_{ijt}$ = Log of the ratio of exports to output

$\overline{\text{TUR}}_{ij}$ = Mean turnover rate. The turnover rate is the sum of the industry's entry and exit rates. These rates are averaged across all years for each industry in each country to get a "long-run" value that is specific to each industry in each country.

$\overline{\text{ERP}}_{ij}$ = Log of the mean effective rate of protection. Given that Chilean protection was essentially uniform during the sample period, variation in this protection measure is due only to Colombia. For Chile, we set this variable at 0. Colombian figures are averages of effective protection measures for 1979, 1984, and 1985 reported in Cubillos and Torres (1987).

Hence, for example, the kth employment percentile is explained by the following regression:

---

13. Because of various data problems, the manufacturing industries 311, 312, 314, 353, 354, 361, 372, and 385 are not included in the analysis. This leaves twenty-one three-digit industries in each country to support our regressions.

(7) $EMPk_{ijt} = \beta_1 lnQ_{ijt} + \beta_2 ln(M/Q)_{ijt} + \beta_3 ln(X/Q)_{ijt} + \beta_4 \overline{TUR}_{ij} +$
$\beta_5 \overline{TUR}_{ij} lnQ_{ijt} + \beta_6 \overline{TUR}_{ij} ln(M/Q)_{ijt} + \beta_7 \overline{TUR}_{ij} ln(X/Q)_{ijt} + \lambda_{ij} + \mu_{jt} + \varepsilon_{ijt}.$

Here lnQ proxies total market size, while $ln(X/Q)$ and $ln(M/Q)$ proxy exposure to international markets. (When interpreting coefficients on these latter variables, it must be kept in mind that the regression has already controlled for total output.) The average turnover rate, $\overline{TUR}$, is used as a measure of the extent, and thus the ease, of entry and exit into an industry over time. High turnover rates are consistent with low sunk costs of entry and hence should reflect the potential for competitive pressures from domestic rivals. As discussed in section 6.2, the sensitivity of size distributions to demand shifts should depend on the ease of entry and exit. We therefore interact our turnover variable with the trade variables in the regression equations. Finally, to control for the industry-specific technology effects and country-specific macro conditions, represented by λ and μ, respectively, industry and time dummies are included.[14] Equation (7) can also be estimated using productivity percentiles, $ln(PRDk)$, as dependent variables.

As seen in table 6.1, there are fairly significant and persistent cross-country differences in trade exposure and average plant size, but plant size fluctuations within each country over time are smaller. This suggests that the patterns of correlation will depend upon the type of estimator applied to the panel data. For example if we use a "between" estimator, parameters are identified with cross-country differences in the (temporal) mean values of the variables. These estimates are obtained with OLS on equation (7) averaged across time:[15]

(8) $\overline{EMPk}_{ij} = \beta_1 \overline{lnQ}_{ij} + \beta_2 \overline{ln(M/Q)}_{ij} + \beta_3 \overline{ln(X/Q)}_{ij} + \beta_4 \overline{TUR}_{ij}$
$+ \beta_5 \overline{TUR}_{ij} \overline{lnQ}_{ij} + \beta_6 \overline{TUR}_{ij} ln(M/Q)_{ij} + \beta_7 \overline{TUR}_{ij} \overline{ln(X/Q)}_{ij} + \lambda_i + \bar{\mu}_j + \bar{\varepsilon}_{ij}.$

Parameter estimates of $\bar{\mu}_j$ in this model will reflect country-wide contrasts between the Chilean and Colombian size distributions, while λ_i estimates will reflect technological and other industry-specific factors common to both countries that determine the size distribution for industry i. The remaining parameters reflect correlations once these factors are controlled for. Because variables are averaged over time, the estimates might be viewed as reflecting long-run correlations.[16] To examine the robustness of our findings to alternative measures of trade exposure, we will also estimate the model using the effect rate of protection (ERP) rather than $ln(X/Q)$ and $ln(M/Q)$.

---

14. Because the turnover rate we construct has no time variation, the coefficient β_4 cannot be identified separately from λ_{ij}. Thus no β_4 values are reported with eq. (7) estimates.

15. Here it is not possible to identify separate country effects for each industry because observations have been averaged over time. Hence the industry effects, λ_i, do not have a j subscript.

16. Recall, however, that the sample countries underwent significant changes in trade orientation from the presample to the sample years; so if adjustment is slow, even the "between" estimates may not reflect steady states.

An alternative estimator of equation (7) does not involve averaging over time. Rather, it identifies parameters by treating a single industry, country, and *year* as the unit of observation. If we control for technology differences with country-specific industry dummies, and we control for macro effects with country-specific time dummies, the resultant "within" estimates will reflect the time-series correlations of the size and productivity distributions with industry-specific trade policy. These estimates address the question of how much rationalization occurs *within* a country in the short run as trade exposure changes. They will be more sensitive to hysteresis effects than the "between" estimates, so entry and exit are likely to play a smaller role in the short run. Bear in mind also that this estimator will not pick up the dynamics of adjustment processes—all correlations are contemporaneous. Finally, given that the variable ERP does not vary through time, we are unable to check the robustness of our "within" regression by replacing $\ln(X/Q)$ and $\ln(M/Q)$ with the effective rate of protection.

6.4   Results: Between-Country Estimates

6.4.1   The Employment Size Distribution

Table 6.2 presents regression coefficients for the employment size distribution using the "between" estimator. Explanatory variables are listed on the left-hand side of the table and percentiles across the top. Each column in each panel summarizes a separate regression. The top panel was estimated using import and export shares as the measure of trade exposure and the bottom panel was estimated using effective rates of protection. Note that, overall, the fit as measured by adjusted R^2 is very tight, and both trade patterns and turnover appear to matter a great deal.[17] (*F*-statistics test the null hypothesis that all variables listed and industry dummies have zero coefficients.)

Looking across columns in the top half of table 6.2, one sees that an increase in import share is associated with a reduction in all size percentiles, controlling for the level of industry output. These results suggest that, contrary to the findings of many simulation models, the elasticity effects of import competition on plant size are not dominant. Rather, demand contraction, factor market effects, and other forces associated with increased import competition apparently lead to *smaller* plants.[18] We defer the issue of whether this means efficiency losses accompany liberalization to section 6.4.3 below.

Notice next that large plants appear to contract relatively *more* in the face

17. Interestingly, the country dummy is insignificant in the employment regressions, suggesting that any cross-country contrast in the size distribution is associated with contrasts in the explanatory variables. (Country dummies in the productivity regressions of table 6.4 reflect differences in units of measurement, *inter alia*.)

18. Baldwin and Gorecki (1983) found similar effects in Canadian data, although they did not stress them in their analysis.

Table 6.2   **Between Estimates of Employment Size Distribution**[a]
(absolute values of *t*-statistics in parentheses)

	Percentile				
	10th	25th	50th	75th	90th
	Trade Exposure Measured with Import and Export Shares				
ln(M/Q)	− .184*	− .317*	− .432	− .573*	− 1.10*
	(2.59)	(2.78)	(2.03)	(2.24)	(2.98)
ln(X/Q)	− .204*	− .333*	− .367*	− .168	.004
	(6.24)	(6.36)	(3.76)	(1.43)	(.022)
ln(Q)	− .268*	− .496*	− .414	− .251	.129
	(3.81)	(4.40)	(1.97)	(1.00)	(.353)
TUR	− 7.60*	− 14.17*	− 10.02	13.43	14.72
	(3.31)	(3.86)	(1.46)	(1.63)	(1.23)
TUR * ln(M/Q)	.446*	.663*	1.11*	1.39*	2.72*
	(3.04)	(2.82)	(2.31)	(2.64)	(3.56)
TUR * ln(X/Q)	.772*	1.29*	1.51*	.695	.188
	(5.43)	(5.67)	(3.54)	(1.36)	(.254)
TUR * ln(Q)	.691*	1.21*	.974*	− .564	− .722
	(4.65)	(5.09)	(2.19)	(1.06)	(.935)
Chile dummy	− .019	.055	− .039	− .291	− .037
	(.260)	(.473)	(.179)	(1.12)	(.097)
Mean of dependent variable	2.47	2.80	3.37	4.15	4.99
$\bar{R}^2$	.887	.903	.842	.866	.765
$\hat{\sigma}$	.046	.074	.139	.167	.242
F (28,13)	12.45	14.57	8.80	10.46	5.76
	Trade Exposure Measured with Effective Protection Rates				
ERP	.244*	.352*	.361	.332	.368
	(3.41)	(2.52)	(1.78)	(1.97)	(1.36)
ln(Q)	.296*	.422	.545	1.15*	1.24*
	(2.39)	(1.78)	(1.58)	(4.03)	(2.70)
TUR	14.05*	19.08	21.96	43.73*	45.28
	(2.33)	(1.64)	(1.31)	(3.13)	(2.03)
TUR * ERP	− .707*	− 1.05*	− 1.01*	− 1.04*	− 1.11
	(4.45)	(3.43)	(2.29)	(2.84)	(1.89)
TUR * ln(Q)	− .876*	− 1.18	− 1.41	− 2.67*	− 2.73
	(2.29)	(1.62)	(1.32)	(3.03)	(1.93)
Chile dummy	.003	− .038	− .113	− .517	− .474
	(.014)	(.097)	(.198)	(1.09)	(.623)
Mean of dependent variable	2.47	2.80	3.37	4.15	4.99
$\bar{R}^2$	.664	.587	.596	.836	.647
$\hat{\sigma}$	.080	.153	.222	.185	.296
F (26,15)	4.12	3.24	3.33	9.02	3.89

[a]Industry dummies were included in the regressions but are not reported.

*Significantly different from zero at the .05 level using a two-tail test.

of import competition, so even the market share effects of trade liberalization appear to be absent. This result is not as robust as the negative correlation between trade exposure and size, as will be seen presently. Nonetheless, possible explanations are worth listing. First, drawing on the simple analytics of section 6.3, it is possible that trade exposure actually reduces demand elasticities. Second, and more plausibly, it may be that imported goods do not compete with the kinds of goods small plants produce, so large plants bear most of the adjustment burden. Third, industries with large plants may be more effective at lobbying for import protection.

The coefficients on the interaction between TUR and $\ln(M/Q)$ are significantly positive, which implies that the size effect of trade exposure is more substantial in low-turnover industries. Given that import expansion is associated with output contraction, this is consistent with the theory reviewed earlier: More size adjustment occurs when exit is not easy. Alternatively, the results might be interpreted to mean simply that the discipline of foreign competition matters more in industries where the discipline of potential entry is less important. Here again, the larger effect for the higher percentiles is consistent with the hypothesis that imports compete more directly with big plants. In either case, the data support Buffie and Spiller (1986), Rodrik (1988a), and others who have argued that it is critical to take ease of entry into consideration when predicting the effect of regime changes on size distributions.

Turning next to export shares, one finds the direction of the effects is similar: High trade exposure is associated with smaller plant sizes, and the effect is strongest in industries with low turnover. This pattern is generally supportive of the premise that both $\ln(X/Q)$ and $\ln(M/Q)$ measure exposure to foreign markets. However, the effect of $\ln(X/Q)$ now weakens as we move to higher percentiles, so most of the contrast between "open" and "closed" markets appears to be showing up among small plants. This same pattern holds for the interaction between $\ln(X/Q)$ and TUR. We have no ready explanation for this finding, but it may indicate that small plants are relatively more important export suppliers.

Given import and export shares, larger industry-wide output levels have an effect on the size distribution that is qualitatively identical to that of trade exposure. Larger domestic production is associated with relatively more small producers, especially in low-turnover industries. However, it must be remembered that $\ln(Q)$ enters the variables $\ln(X/Q)$ and $\ln(M/Q)$ negatively. Hence, the total effect of an increase in output holding M and X fixed is given by the sum of the output coefficient and the negative of the import and export coefficients. For example, a unit increase in $\ln(Q)$ holding X and M fixed shifts the 10th percentile rightward by $.184 + .204 - .268 > 0$. The negative coefficient on output in the regression equations implied that a *proportionate* increase in Q, X, and M is associated with a smaller size distribution of plants.

Since industry dummies are already included, the level of turnover only controls for country-specific differences in turnover rates. These can be due to cross-country differences in product mixes within given industries, or to differences in credit markets and other determinants of sunk costs.[19] The pattern that emerges is expected: High turnover is associated with a relatively large number of small plants.

To check the robustness of the findings concerning trade exposure and plant size, we next replace the trade exposure measures $\ln(X/Q)$ and $\ln(M/Q)$ with the effective protection measure ERP.[20] The coefficient on ERP in the regressions can be interpreted as the difference in size distributions that is correlated with differences in effective protection rates, controlling for country-wide plant-size differences, and for industry-specific effects.

Results are reported in the bottom half of table 6.2. Note first that there is a positive correlation of the employment size distributions with effective protection. Just as with the X/Q and M/Q measures of trade exposure, higher rates of effective protection are associated with larger plant sizes. Moreover, the size effect is less extreme in high turnover industries. In both these senses the results conform to the findings in the top half of table 6.2: Demand contraction and other effects associated with high trade exposure appear to dominate elasticity effects.

However, comparing the different size percentiles, one finds that the statistically significant effects of increased protection appear in the lower percentiles, which suggests that small plants expand at a relatively rapid rate when protection is increased. Contrary to our earlier findings, these results are consistent with the hypothesis that trade exposure increases demand elasticities, thereby inducing rationalization by forcing small plants to contract relatively more.

Finally, in the ERP regressions we see that larger domestic production and higher turnover are both associated with rightward shifts in the size distribution. Both of these patterns are present across all the percentiles. This same pattern was reported in the top half of table 6.2 for the 75th and 90th percentiles. However, the 10th through 50th percentiles tended to decline with increased output or turnover in the regressions based on $\ln(X/Q)$ and $\ln(M/Q)$. These do not strike us as important anomalies because, as discussed above, the size shift associated with output increases is positive for all table 6.2 percentiles when X and M are held fixed. Also, our turnover variable is mainly useful in interaction terms; the level effects of entry barriers are essentially controlled for with industry dummies.

To summarize the robustness of the "between" estimates, we conclude that

19. Recall that Chile underwent a major financial crisis and restructuring in the early 1980s.

20. We also repeated these regressions using real output, rather than employment, as the measure of plant size. The qualitative results are very similar for the two measures. Overall, shifts toward smaller plants are associated with high trade exposure, especially in low-turnover industries. In the output size distribution, however, only the effect of export share was consistently significant.

the correlation between trade exposure and the employment size distribution is clearly negative in the long run, and the magnitude of the effect is clearly moderated by ease of entry or exit.[21] However, whether small or large plants adjust more in percentage terms to increases in exposure depends on the measure of exposure that is used. Perhaps effective protection measures are most relevant for policy analysis, since these are most directly controlled by the government.

6.4.2 Predicted Employment Size Distribution under Alternative Trade Regimes

Given that the regression models use interaction terms between turnover and trade exposure, it is difficult to infer the magnitudes of predicted differences in the employment size distribution under alternative trade regimes. Accordingly, table 6.3 presents predicted values of the employment size distributions based on regression results from table 6.2.

The top panel illustrates how the employment size distribution shifts as the import share rises, the middle panel illustrates how it shifts as the export share rises, and the bottom panel illustrates shifts with changes in effective protection. The left side of the table describes a low turnover industry while the right side corresponds to a high turnover industry. Within each panel, columns present "low", "medium," and "high" export or import shares.[22] Finally, rows of the table give predicted employment levels for the 5th through 95th percentiles, as well as the mean and standard deviation of the employment distribution.

First, focusing on the size distribution for low-turnover industries, the leftward shift in the size distribution as import shares increase is marked. For example, the median plant size falls from 31.9 to 20.5 employees as the import share rises. This leftward shift is particularly large for the 75th, 90th, and 95th percentiles. Similarly, both the mean and the standard deviation drop substantially with increases in import share. Recall, however, that high turnover moderates the extent to which import shares reduce plant size. This appears in table 6.3 when one moves from the low-turnover to the high-turnover figures, especially among large plants.

Relative to import shares, export shares appear to covary less with the employment size distribution. For example, among low-turnover industries, the median plant size declines only from 27.3 to 26.5 employees as the export share increases. Also, although plants in high-turnover industries are generally

---

21. Similar results were obtained when plant-level output was used as a size measure instead of employment (see n. 20).

22. The "low-turnover" predictions assume the turnover rate associated with the 25th percentile of the turnover distribution, and "high-turnover" predictions assume the turnover rate of the 75th percentile. Low, medium, and high trade exposure measures correspond to the 25th, 50th, and 75th percentiles of their respective distributions.

Table 6.3   **Predicted Employment Size Distribution under Alternative Levels of Trade Exposure**

	Low-Turnover Industries			High-Turnover Industries		
	Low	Moderate	High	Low	Moderate	High
	Import Share					
Percentile:						
5th	10.6	10.1	9.4	9.6	9.6	9.5
10th	11.7	10.9	9.8	10.8	10.5	10.1
25th	16.7	14.5	11.6	13.9	12.9	11.5
50th	31.9	26.8	20.5	23.0	21.5	19.4
75th	73.6	59.0	42.1	61.4	57.0	50.8
90th	199.2	131.0	69.2	110.8	97.0	79.3
95th	276.8	188.2	104.6	222.4	188.3	146.1
Mean	73.4	52.1	31.1	56.7	48.0	37.3
Std. Dev.	93.0	61.1	32.2	87.1	65.7	42.7
	Export Share					
Percentile:						
5th	10.2	10.1	10.1	9.2	9.6	9.7
10th	11.2	10.9	10.8	9.8	10.5	10.9
25th	15.0	14.5	14.2	11.5	12.9	13.7
50th	27.3	26.8	26.5	18.3	21.5	23.3
75th	59.4	59.0	58.7	52.8	57.0	59.2
90th	124.9	131.0	134.1	90.5	97.0	100.6
95th	200.2	188.2	182.4	188.2	188.3	188.3
Mean	54.2	52.1	51.1	47.3	48.0	48.4
Std. Dev.	66.7	61.1	58.4	70.9	65.7	63.2
	Effective Rate of Protection					
Percentile:						
5th	11.7	11.8	11.9	10.2	10.2	10.2
10th	14.2	14.5	14.7	11.3	11.3	11.3
25th	21.2	21.7	22.2	15.1	15.1	15.1
50th	41.1	42.3	43.4	28.2	28.3	28.3
75th	79.7	81.4	82.9	70.1	69.6	69.1
90th	173.3	177.7	182.0	159.7	159.0	158.4
95th	324.3	339.2	354.1	278.6	281.2	283.7
Mean	76.3	78.6	80.9	67.7	67.9	68.1
Std. Dev.	86.3	88.9	91.4	95.8	96.8	97.7

Note: Table entries are number of employees in kth percentile plant.

more concentrated in the lower employment ranges, changes in export shares appear to have little effect on location or shape of the distribution.

The bottom panel of table 6.3 reports predicted percentiles of the size distribution when the effective rate of protection is varied. The most substantial change occurs in the upper percentiles of the size distribution for low-turnover industries. Increases in the effective rate of protection are correlated with an increase in the size of the larger plants, but the increase is not as large as that associated with changes in import penetration.

6.4.3   Distribution of Labor Productivity

The empirical results thus far have shown that high trade exposure is associated with relatively small-scale production, controlling for other factors. Does this mean that trade exposure worsens productivity? To examine this issue more directly, we next apply our empirical model to the distribution of labor productivity across plants. This not only allows us to determine the overall direction of productivity shifts with trade exposure, it also speaks to such questions as whether shifts are concentrated among the least productive plants.

Table 6.4 reports "between-country" regression results for the percentiles of the labor productivity distribution. The top half of the table measures trade exposure with import and export shares while the bottom half uses effective rates of protection. The first result to notice is that significance levels are much lower than those associated with size distributions. Hence reductions in labor productivity do not obviously accompany reductions in scale. Notice next that differences in the import share between countries are positively correlated with differences in the percentiles of the productivity distribution, while the export share is negatively correlated. This negative correlation of exports and productivity could reflect the limitations of single-factor productivity measures: low labor productivity may be due to high labor intensity without implying low total factor productivity, since capital is not controlled for. Moreover, the Heckscher-Ohlin models suggests that trade liberalization should stimulate exports of labor-intensive products, so this omitted variable bias in our productivity measure will be correlated with trade patterns.

Larger levels of industry output, holding import and export shares fixed, are correlated with a rightward shift in the labor productivity distribution. This could reflect increased capacity utilization or exploitation of scale economies in the larger market. High-turnover industries also have higher productivity levels. As was seen in the employment distributions, high turnover tends to reduce the magnitude of the import, export, and output correlations. Finally, the country dummy variable is positive and significant. This can simply reflect differences in the units of measurement of output. However, with the exception of the country dummy and output level among higher productivity plants, virtually none of the remaining coefficients is statistically significant. Unlike the employment size distribution, there is little evidence

Table 6.4   **Between Estimates of Labor Productivity Distribution[a]**
                      (absolute values of t-statistics in parentheses)

	Percentile				
	10th	25th	50th	75th	90th
	Trade Exposure Measured with Import and Export Shares				
$\overline{\ln(M/Q)}$	.158	.239	.230	.289	.398
	(.474)	(.898)	(.890)	(1.08)	(1.58)
$\overline{\ln(X/Q)}$	−.271	−.258*	−.089	−.045	−.186
	(1.81)	(2.16)	(.764)	(.372)	(1.64)
$\overline{\ln(Q)}$	.260	.387	.490	.643*	.619*
	(.775)	(1.44)	(1.88)	(2.38)	(2.44)
TUR	8.26	8.81	7.26	9.27	6.46
	(.754)	(1.01)	(.854)	(1.05)	(.780)
$\overline{TUR} * \overline{\ln(M/Q)}$	−.389	−.592	−.644	−.667	−.824
	(.550)	(1.05)	(1.18)	(1.17)	(1.54)
$\overline{TUR} * \overline{\ln(X/Q)}$	.910	.806	.107	−.064	.513
	(1.40)	(1.55)	(.213)	(.122)	(1.04)
$\overline{TUR} * \overline{\ln(Q)}$	−.495	−.516	−.547	−.618	−.312
	(.708)	(.926)	(1.01)	(1.10)	(.589)
Chile dummy	1.91*	1.88*	1.85*	1.72*	1.55*
	(5.65)	(7.00)	(7.09)	(6.32)	(6.06)
Mean of depen-dent variable	4.56	5.02	5.52	6.07	6.58
$\bar{R}^2$	.963	.978	.981	.980	.983
$\hat{\sigma}$	.224	.177	.174	.181	.170
$F(28,13)$	38.94	67.28	75.56	73.14	83.32
	Trade Exposure Measured with Effective Protection Rates				
ERP	.392	.296	.161	.143	.204
	(2.04)	(1.73)	(1.01)	(.851)	(1.21)
$\overline{\ln(Q)}$	.788*	.715*	.493	.479	.552
	(2.46)	(2.50)	(1.86)	(1.71)	(1.96)
TUR	36.08*	28.30	11.44	8.44	12.05
	(2.31)	(2.03)	(.884)	(.618)	(.879)
$\overline{TUR} * \overline{ERP}$	−.872	−.588	−.031	.104	−.147
	(2.07)	(1.56)	(.089)	(.281)	(.399)
$\overline{TUR} * \overline{\ln(Q)}$	2.49*	−1.97*	−.880	−.628	−.868
	(2.51)	(2.24)	(1.08)	(.726)	(1.00)
Chile dummy	2.51*	2.48*	2.52*	2.56*	2.45*
	(4.65)	(5.13)	(5.63)	(5.43)	(5.18)
Mean of depen-dent variable	4.56	5.02	5.52	6.07	6.58
$\bar{R}^2$	.967	.976	.981	.980	.979
$\hat{\sigma}$	.210	.187	.174	.183	.184
$F(26,15)$	47.80	65.73	81.35	76.25	76.12

[a]Industry dummies were included in the regressions but are not reported.

*Significantly different from zero at the .05 level using a two-tail test.

here that productivity differences across the two countries are related to trade exposure.

The bottom half of table 6.4 reports regression results using the effective rate of protection as the measure of trade exposure. Again, output and turn-over are correlated with a rightward shift in the productivity distribution. Increased trade protection is correlated with higher productivity, especially for the least productive plants, but once again, none of these coefficients is statistically significant. In short, there is no clear evidence that differences in trade exposure between sectors in Colombia and Chile are correlated with differences in the distribution of plant-level labor productivity.

6.5   Results: Within-Country Estimates

As reviewed in section 6.3, an alternative way to identify our model is to use the within-country temporal variation in the data. This approach picks up the short-run associations between trade exposure, output levels, and the size and productivity distributions. The top panel of table 6.5 presents results for the employment size distribution and the lower panel presents results for the productivity distribution.[23] (F-statistics test the null hypothesis that all reported variables, time dummies, and industry dummies have zero coefficients.)

6.5.1   Employment Size Distribution

Fluctuations in import shares show a negative association with plant sizes, just as in all the "between" country regressions. Now, however, this association is so weak statistically that it makes little sense to talk of short-run rationalization effects. Because we are limiting the "within" model to contemporaneous effects, we find this low significance unsurprising.

More surprisingly, time series fluctuations in export shares correlate positively with the percentiles of the size distribution, although they are negatively correlated with percentiles in the "between" regressions. Though weaker than in table 6.2, these correlations are still statistically significant. So in the short run, output growth due to export share expansion is associated with relatively rapid employment growth. In terms of rationalization, the growth in employment is concentrated among large plants. We see no obvious explanation for this contrast between the "within" and the "between" results.

The coefficients on the output variable indicates that the correlation of in-

---

23. The "within" estimator, unlike the "between" estimator, permits us to test the null hypothesis that the same relationship between size and trade exposure holds in all industries. But to do so, we must drop our time dummies and our turnover index. Not surprisingly, for this restricted version of the model the hypothesis of common slope coefficients across industries can be rejected for all the employment and productivity percentiles. Specifically, the $F(120, 210)$ statistics for the 10th, 25th, 50th, 75th, and 90th employment percentiles are 5.12, 9.03, 10.60, 9.10, and 7.63, respectively. The same statistics for the productivity percentiles are 2.81, 2.70, 1.94, 2.47, and 3.27.

dustrial output with plant sizes is generally positive. This reflects a combination of output adjustments by incumbents and entry or exit. However, given that most turnover takes place among small plants, shifts in the higher percentiles reflect mainly the expansion and contraction of incumbents (Roberts 1989; Tybout 1989). Finally, in industries where turnover is high, the positive correlation between output and size is relatively muted.

Overall, the patterns of contemporaneous correlation between the percentiles of the employment size distribution are much less systematic than the between country estimates. Systematic rightward or leftward movements of the size distribution are not obvious in the regression results. This suggests that while the across-country differences in trade exposure are correlated with differences in the entire size distribution of plants, the time-series differences in trade appear to have a more random effect on plants within the size distribution. This may mean that differences in the plant-size distribution between the countries reflect underlying structural differences in the size of markets, openness to trade, and other factors. In contrast, time-series fluctuations in the size distribution within each industry and country reflect idiosyncratic aspects of the market and time period.

6.5.2   Labor Productivity Distribution

The bottom half of table 6.5 reports results for the labor productivity distribution using the within-country variation. Import share has no significant effect on the shape of the distribution. In contrast, an increase in the export share is positively and significantly correlated with the 10th, 25th, and 50th percentiles of the productivity distribution but negatively correlated with the 75th and 90th percentiles. That is, higher export shares are correlated with higher productivity for the less productive plants but lower productivity for higher productivity plants.

Expansion in output over time leads to productivity improvements. This can result from either increased use of capital or scale economies in high output periods. Finally, as we have seen throughout this paper, the import, export, and output correlations are lower in magnitude in high-turnover industries. In particular, the turnover results could arise if high-turnover industries are less capital intensive or have technologies with less scale economies. Demand fluctuations in these industries then have less effect on an individual plant's labor productivity and thus less effect on the distribution across plants.

Overall, the "within" estimator indicates little evidence of rationalization with variation in trade exposure over time. The productivity changes over time are largely explainable with variation in capital utilization.

6.6   Summary

It is often argued that when domestic markets are imperfectly competitive, increased exposure to global markets should rationalize production. Such ex-

Table 6.5   **Between Estimates of Employment Size and Productivity Distribution[a] (absolute values of t-statistics in parentheses)**

	Percentile				
	10th	25th	50th	75th	90th
	Employment Size Distribution				
$\ln(M/Q)$	−.048	.010	−.168*	−.115	−.120
	(.812)	(.144)	(2.06)	(1.03)	(1.09)
$\ln(X/Q)$	.035*	.007	−.042*	.071*	.061*
	(2.35)	(.417)	(2.04)	(2.57)	(2.19)
$\ln(Q)$	.163	.270*	.165	.349	.624*
	(1.58)	(2.27)	(1.17)	(1.82)	(3.26)
$\overline{TUR} * \ln(M/Q)$	.226	−.047	.463	.195	.178
	(1.19)	(.215)	(1.77)	(.551)	(.502)
$\overline{TUR} * \ln(X/Q)$	−.091	−.026	.146*	−.243*	−.214
	(1.83)	(.452)	(2.12)	(2.61)	(2.30)
$\overline{TUR} * \ln(Q)$	−.577	−.776*	−.306	−.784	−1.25*
	(1.76)	(2.05)	(.679)	(1.29)	(2.07)
Mean of dependent variable	2.48	2.82	3.40	4.19	5.02
$\bar{R}^2$	.805	.902	.932	.925	.936
$\hat{\sigma}$	.072	.083	.099	.133	.133
F (63,314)	25.66	56.06	82.78	74.98	88.76
	Labor Productivity Distribution				
$\ln(M/Q)$	.007	−.066	−.011	−.046	.044
	(.066)	(.712)	(.120)	(.520)	(.432)
$\ln(X/Q)$	.053	.076*	.069*	−.056*	−.055*
	(1.89)	(3.25)	(2.95)	(2.55)	(2.12)
$\ln(Q)$	.714*	.686*	.982*	.896*	1.29*
	(3.68)	(4.26)	(6.07)	(5.89)	(7.25)
$\overline{TUR} * \ln(M/Q)$	−.003	.182	.067	.280	−.017
	(.008)	(.612)	(.225)	(.995)	(.052)
$\overline{TUR} * \ln(X/Q)$	−.101	−.187*	−.187*	.258*	.149
	(1.07)	(2.39)	(2.38)	(3.50)	(1.73)
$\overline{TUR} * \ln(Q)$	−.890	−.837	−1.85*	−1.55*	−2.93*
	(1.44)	(1.63)	(3.59)	(3.21)	(5.18)
Mean of dependent variable	4.33	4.78	5.27	5.83	6.35
$\bar{R}^2$	.986	.991	.992	.993	.990
$\hat{\sigma}$	.135	.112	.133	.106	.124
F (63,314)	418.55	668.55	706.12	837.12	620.30

[a]Separate industry dummies and time dummies for each country were included in the regressions but are not reported.

*Significantly different from zero at the .05 level using a two-tail test.

posure is believed to increase the elasticity of demand perceived by domestic producers, which in turn should shift production toward the large, efficient plants. The rationalization effects should be especially marked when there are low barriers to entry and exit because inefficiently small plants will be induced to shut down. This paper is the first attempt we know of to confront these theories of rationalization with actual data on the size distribution of plants from developing countries.

Several striking results emerge. First, increased exposure to import competition appears to clearly *reduce* the size of all plants in both the short run and the long run, but especially in the latter. Whether large plants shrink relatively less depends on the way in which we measure exposure to world markets: Increases in import shares are associated with relatively rapid shrinkage by large plants, but reductions in effective protection correlate with relatively little shrinkage by large plants. Either way, it appears that models that predict trade liberalization will increase average plant size in import-competing sectors do not describe recent Chilean and Colombia experiences. This may mean that productivity improvements have not accompanied liberalization, but our findings on this issue are not strong enough to warrant much confidence in this conclusion.

Second, as theory suggests, it makes a great deal of difference whether one is analyzing industries with high or low entry barriers. The effects of changing output levels, import shares, export shares, and effective protection rates are systematically moderated by the possibility of easy entry or exit. One interpretation is that there is less role for output adjustment by incumbent plants when the number of plants adjusts to demand shifts. Alternatively, our results could simply mean that high turnover reflects competitive pressure and reduces the marginal impact of foreign competition on market structure.

Third, the "long-run" correlations of trade regimes and size distributions are quite different from the short-run year-to-year correlations. Not only are the effects of trade exposure stronger in the long run, but the correlations of export shares change sign. The short-run correlations show exports associated with relatively small plants. We trust the long-run figures more, because we limited our short-run analysis to simultaneous correlations and have not attempted to model the dynamics of adjustment. Nonetheless, the short-run findings suggest caution in extracting policy recommendations from our figures.

This paper is a first step in the direction of micro-based examinations of the rationalization hypothesis. Though suggestive, much remains to be done. Aside from modeling the dynamics of adjustment, we hope to study the relationship between average costs and size and the degree to which plants adjust costs endogenously with changes in the trade regime.

References

Baldwin, J. R., and P. K. Gorecki. 1983. Trade, Tariffs, and Relative Plant Scale in Canadian Manufacturing Industries: 1970–1979. Economic Council of Canada, Discussion Paper No. 232.

Bergstrom, T., and H. Varian. 1985. When are Nash Equilibria Independent of the Distribution of Agents' Characteristics? *Review of Economic Studies* 52: 715–18.

Bhagwati, J. 1988. Export Promoting Trade Strategy: Issues and Evidence. *World Bank Research Observer* 3:27–58.

Brown, D. 1989. Tariffs and Capacity Utilization by Monopolositically Competitive Firms. Tufts University Discussion Paper No. 89–108.

Buffie, E., and P. Spiller. 1986. Trade Liberalization in Oligopolistic Industries. *Journal of International Economics* 20:65–81.

Condon, T., and J. de Melo, 1990. Industrial Organization Implications of QR Trade Regimes: Evidence and Welfare Costs. World Bank. Typescript.

Corbo, V. 1985. Reforms and macroeconomic adjustments in Chile during 1974–84. *World Development* 13:893–916.

Cubillos Lopez, Rafael, and Luis Alfonso Torres Castro. 1987. La Proteccion a la Industria en un Regimen de Exenciones. *Revista de Planeacion y Desarrollo* 19:45–100.

Devarajan, S., and D. Rodrik. 1989a. Trade Liberalization in Developing Countries: Do Imperfect Competition and Scale Economies Matter? *American Economic Review, Papers and Proceedings* 79: 283–87.

———. 1989b. Pro-competitive Effects of Trade Reform: Results from a CGE Model of Cameroon. Harvard University. Typescript.

Dixit, A., and V. Norman. 1980. *Theory of International Trade.* Cambridge: Cambridge University Press.

Dutz, M. 1990. Firm Adjustment to Trade Liberalization. Princeton University. Typescript.

Eastman, H. C., and S. Stykolt. 1966. *The Tariff and Competition in Canada.* Toronto: University of Toronto Press.

Garcia, J. 1988. The Timing and Sequencing of a Trade Liberalization Policy: The Case of Colombia. World Bank. Typescript.

Harris, R. 1984. Applied General Equilibrium Analysis of Small Open Economies with Economies of Scale and Imperfect Competition. *American Economic Review* 74: 1016–33.

Helpman, E., and P. Krugman. 1985. *Market Structure and Foreign Trade.* Cambridge, Mass.: MIT Press.

Horstmann, I., and J. R. Markusen. 1986. Up the Average Cost Curve: Inefficient Entry and the New Protectionism. *Journal of International Economics* 20: 225–48.

Jovanovic, B. 1982. Selection and the Evolution of Industry. *Econometrica* 50, 649–70.

Lancaster, K. 1984. Protection and Product Differentiation. In *Monopolistic Competition and International Trade,* ed. H. Kierzkowski, 137–56. Oxford: Oxford University Press.

Markusen, J. 1981. Trade and the Gains from Trade with Imperfect Competition. *Journal of International Economics* 11:531–51.

Melo, J. de, and D. Tarr. Forthcoming. *A General Equilibrium Analysis of U.S. Trade Policy.* Cambridge, Mass.: MIT Press.

Pack, H. 1989. Industrialization and Trade. In *Handbook of Development Economics,* ed. H. Chenery and T. N. Srinivasan, vol. 1. Amsterdam: North-Holland.

Roberts, M. 1989. The Structure of Production in Colombian Manufacturing Industries. World Bank. Typescript.

Rodrik, D. 1988a. Imperfect Competition, Scale Economies and Trade Policy in Developing Countries. In *Trade Policy Issues and Empirical Analysis*. ed. R. Baldwin. Chicago: University of Chicago Press.

————. 1988b. Closing the Technology Gap: Does Trade Liberalization Really Help? Harvard University. Typescript.

Tybout, J. 1989. Entry, Exit, Competition and Productivity in the Chilean Industrial Sector. World Bank. Typescript.

Comment   Robert E. Lipsey

The basic question that motivates this study is whether trade liberalization in developing countries, or liberalization of the economy in general, increases the efficiency of production. That is the issue the authors raise in the introduction, it is of great interest to development and trade economists, and it was apparently the question that motivated the World Bank study from which this paper is derived.

A major novelty of the paper is the use of establishment data from censuses of manufactures for Chile and Colombia, data that are rarely available to researchers outside the statistical agencies themselves. They are the only type of data that could be used to study size distributions, as is done in this paper, and they have the potential for examining many other broader issues involved in the study of the effects of trade policy.

This paper, described by the authors as a first step in the analysis of their exceptionally rich data set, focuses on one aspect of that broader topic: an attempt to explain the shape of the distribution of manufacturing plants by size and the distribution by output per worker.

One reason for relating trade policy to the size distribution of firms is that much of the theoretical literature and simulation models of trade policy assume the importance of scale economies. Yet, as the authors point out, the empirical literature has not confirmed the efficiency effects of trade liberalization and, in particular, has not confirmed the channel of efficiency gains through effects on the size distribution of firms.

The description of the data brought my mind back to a paper by Patricio Meller, based on the 1967 Chilean Manufacturing Census, that confirmed for that country what had been found for the United States: great heterogeneity of establishments with respect to size and measured productivity within appar-

Robert E. Lipsey is a professor of economics, Queens College and the Graduate School and University Center, the City University of New York. He is also a research associate and director, New York Office, of the National Bureau of Economic Research.

ently narrowly defined industries.[1] Striking findings there were that 75 percent of establishments operated at a level of efficiency more than 50 percent below that of the most efficient in their four-digit industries and that neither size, nor capital/labor ratios, nor skill ratios were systematically different between efficient and inefficient firms in the same industry. However, the dispersion was much smaller among large firms. In the small firm group (5–9 persons), 46 percent of establishments were less than a third as efficient as the most efficient establishments in their size group. Among large firms (100 or more), only 6 percent were less than a third as efficient as the firms on the efficiency frontier.

What can explain the survival of apparently inefficient enterprises? Meller suggested various imperfections of factor and commodity markets, especially in the circumstances of 1967, but also pointed out that even within four-digit industries, establishments are producing goods that are not substitutes. That is partly a matter of geographical isolation, but also includes differences in quality of product and in the range of products produced.

Two of the assumptions in the theoretical presentation in the Roberts and Tybout paper seem to contradict Meller's interpretation of his results. One is the assumption that "domestically produced goods are perfect substitutes." The other is the assumption that "firms with low marginal costs are relatively large." The authors disavow the size-marginal cost relation as an empirical regularity but use it because it illustrates the working of "most analytical and simulation models." Meller reported that "it cannot be established empirically that one size group of industrial establishments is more efficient from a technical viewpoint than another size group. . . . [L]arger establishments are more technically efficient than smaller establishments only in two industries." The present paper deals with a period in which the Chilean economy was much less protected from foreign competition and in which domestic markets were far less regulated than in 1967,[2] but it would be useful for interpreting the present results to know whether these earlier findings still applied.

I did not find the theoretical framework that begins the paper very helpful in interpreting the results. The authors, too, need to step outside it from time to time in order to arrive at more intuitive interpretations of their results. An example is the assumption in the theoretical framework that while domestic products are imperfect substitutes for imports, all domestic goods in a three-digit industry are perfect substitutes. In explaining why import liberalization appears to affect large firms more than small ones, Roberts and Tybout sug-

---

1. Patricio Meller, "Efficiency Frontiers for Industrial Establishments of Different Sizes," *Explorations in Economic Research,* vol. 3, no. 3 (New York: National Bureau of Economic Research, 1976).

2. James Tybout, Jaime de Melo, and Vittorio Corbo, "The Effects of Trade Reforms on Scale and Technical Efficiency: New Evidence from Chile," World Bank, Washington, D.C. (June 1989), manuscript.

gest, quite plausibly but in contradiction to the assumption, that imported goods do not compete with the kind of goods small plants produce but do compete with the output of large plants.

The main substantive results are from what is referred to as "between-country estimates." These compare the size of plant at each of five percentiles in Colombia with the size of the plant in the same industry at the same percentile in Chile. Plant size in an industry at a percentile, such as the 10th or the 50th, is then related to a number of industry variables that may differ between the countries. These includes measures of trade exposure (export/production and import/production ratios and effective protection rates), of industry output, and of the turnover of firms in an industry.

The between-country results are described in the text as if they involved changes in the variables but they are, of course, differences between the countries. The authors interpret these as the long-run effects that would follow from changes in the independent variables, but it is not always obvious that another interpretation would not be as plausible. For example, higher import ratios in an industry in a country seem to be associated with smaller plant sizes. That association is referred to as resulting from a contraction of plants in the face of greater import competition. Another explanation that is equally plausible, I think, is that imported components can be a substitute for labor input, and therefore the higher the ratio of imports to output in an industry, the smaller the employment for a given output.

High ratios of exports to output are also associated with smaller plant employment size, particularly among smaller plants. The authors suggest that small plants may be "relatively more important export suppliers." While that is a possibility, it would be surprising in view of the common belief that large firms are responsible for a disproportionate share of exports in most countries. Another possibility is that the plants at the low end of the employment size scale are more often assembly-type operations with large imports of components and large exports of finished products, but small employment relative to their output.

I do not mean to suggest that these interpretations are particularly more convincing than those offered by the authors. My point is that results of comparisons of size distributions are subject to a variety of equally plausible interpretations.

The measures of turnover used in the analysis here are industry characteristics rather than variables to be affected by liberalization. Exits and entrances would be extremely interesting to observe and study as a consequence of liberalization rather than only as an industry characteristic. Who exits the industry? If they are small firms, are they inefficient small firms? Are new entrants small when they enter? It would also be interesting to study the relation of exits and entrances to the size distribution of establishments. A rise in the average output at the 10th percentile could reflect gains in output by all the firms in the lowest 10 percent. That seems to be the author's usual interpretation of the numbers. However, it could also reflect the disappearance of a large number of small firms, so that the ones now at the 10th percentile are the ones that were at the 20th percentile before. Those would be very different events, and it would be worth while to distinguish between them. Some of these issues are discussed elsewhere by Tybout,[3] but the results do not seem to get incorporated into the present discussion.

Another section of the paper deals with between-country differences in what is referred to as productivity or labor productivity. The authors point out that this is a partial productivity measure, but the point deserves emphasis. Since capital intensity is not controlled for, variations in labor productivity imply nothing about efficiency or about the marginal costs referred to earlier in the paper. It is conceivable that high labor productivity plants are simply capital-intensive operations, and there is no assurance that high capital intensity represents efficiency, particularly in a developing country. As the authors point out in commenting on the negative correlation between export shares and labor productivity, "trade liberalization should stimulate exports of labor-intensive products," that is, by this measure, low productivity products. What can we conclude, then, from this analysis?

Another aspect of liberalization that might be considered in future work is the degree of openness to foreign direct investment. Studies for Mexico seem to suggest that the presence of foreign firms in an industry can have a substantial effect on the rate of growth of productivity or convergence toward developed-country productivity levels.[4] Foreign direct investment does not play the same role in manufacturing in Chile and Colombia as it does in Mexico, but the effect may be worth investigating, especially if the census data distinguish foreign-owned establishments.

On the whole, the results presented here whet one's appetite for further study of these data. My feeling is that not much can be squeezed from further study of distributions of firms and that the most interesting results will come from the future work that will take advantage of the longitudinal aspect of the data. One would like to know which firms and establishments are growing and declining with trade liberalization or other changes in economic policy or external economic forces. The studies that have come from the U.S. Census Bureau's program of analysis of longitudinal census data encourage me to believe that this project has potential payoffs that are not yet evident in this first report, and that is something to look forward to.

3. James Tybout, "Entry, Exit, Competition, and Productivity in the Chilean Industrial Sector," World Bank, Washington, D.C. (May 1989), manuscript.
4. See Magnus Blomström and Edward N. Wolff, "Multinational Corporations and Productivity Convergence in Mexico," NBER Working Paper no. 3141, October, and Magnus Blomström, *Foreign Investment and Spillovers: A Study of Technology Transfer to Mexico* (London: Routledge, 1989).

Comment   Peter A. Petri

This is a novel and interesting paper, one of the few studies that I know that examine the effects of trade exposure using a firm-level, microeconomic dataset. It is also timely and important, given how much money and effort is currently being invested by developing countries and the "terrible twins" (the IMF and the World Bank) in outward-oriented development strategies. Finally, it seems to produce a very surprising (though frankly not entirely convincing) result.

Broadly, three types of static production gains can follow from trade liberalization: intersectoral resource shifts from inefficient to efficient sectors, intrasectoral resource shifts from inefficient to efficient firms, and intrafirm resource shifts from inefficient to efficient activities. This paper addresses the middle tier of these effects, the efficiency gains associated with changes in the market share of different firms. The authors use a theoretical model to associate efficiency with firm size, and they then check to see whether trade exposure leads to higher market shares for larger firms (i.e., greater concentration).

The surprise is that greater trade exposure tends to shift the size distribution toward smaller rather than larger firms. This runs against the predictions of the paper's simple oligopoly model, which suggests that demand changes that represent greater openness should lead to a consolidation of industry output in the hands of larger, more efficient firms. There are two alternatives: The results may be wrong, or the theory may be inappropriate.

Consider first the strength of the evidence. The authors examine the effect of trade exposure on industry structure by running regressions of firm size (the independent variable) on various measures of trade exposure, both entered separately and in interaction with a "turnover" (ease-of-entry) variable. One factor that makes the results difficult to interpret is that the direct and interaction terms for a given trade exposure measure typically have opposite signs, and therefore the net effect of trade exposure on concentration is smaller than suggested by its direct coefficient alone. Fortunately, the authors do show net effects in table 6.3, which simulates changes in trade exposure holding other things constant. It shows that in low turnover industries (where the strongest effects are found), shifting from low to high trade exposure reduces the median firm's employment from 31.9 to 20.5 using the import penetration measure, from 27.3 to 26.5 using the export-output measure, but increases it from 41.1 to 43.4 using the ERP measure. No statistical brackets are given for these estimates, but it would seem that only the import penetration results imply statistically significant changes. This raises the question, to

Peter A. Petri is the Carl Shapiro Professor of International Finance, and Director of the Lemberg Program in International Economics and Finance, in the Department of Economics, Brandeis University.

which I return later, whether something else might explain the relationship between high import exposure in particular and the absence of large firms.

A second point concerns the nature of the dataset. The long-term analysis, which is the only one that appears to provide statistically significant results, essentially compares industry size distributions in Colombia and Chile, rather than changes in the size distribution that might have resulted from a liberalization program. Both Colombian and Chilean data exclude firms with fewer than 10 employees. Consider the implications of this floor in the following thought experiment. Assume that before Chile liberalized its trade, firms in both Chile and Colombia were distributed uniformly between 10 and 100 employees. Suppose now that the Pinochet "treatment" reduced employment *equally* (say, by one half) in firms of every size category. We would therefore expect to see firms ranging from 5 to 50 employees in Chile—but the Chilean census forces all firms below 10 employees to "exit"! Comparing the tops of the distributions across the two countries, we will see the full 50 percent decline, but at the bottom both Chile and Colombia have 10-employee firms (0 percent decline). In between, the 25th percentile firm will appear to shrink by 38 percent, and in general, the decline will appear smaller near the bottom of the distribution. Since table 6.3 suggests that many firms are clustered near the 10-employee floor, one wonders to what extent the results are an artifact of censoring.

Now consider the appropriateness of the theory. Were the large firms that may have disappeared in Chile more efficient than small firms? Unfortunately, there are apparently not enough data to examine the relationship between total factor productivity and firm size, and since factor proportions typically vary with firm size, labor productivity cannot serve as a proxy. Meanwhile, as the authors carefully note, the theoretical connection between size and efficiency is established only for the rather narrow specification of the paper—Cournot interactions in a homogeneous product oligopoly model.

The authors propose several sensible alternative explanations based on the assumption that the products produced by different-sized firms are heterogeneous—a very plausible explanation in light of the great variability that we observe in various firm statistics even within four-digit industrial classifications. One possibility is that smaller firms are better able to survive foreign competition because they occupy niche markets, protected by natural barriers such as geography. This point nicely complements the analysis of U.S. steel markets elsewhere in this book; minimills have fared much better against imports than large integrated producers. A further related possibility is that the "missing" large firms in Chile are not missing *because* of greater import penetration, but because of third factors (say, the absence of some local raw material) that make the country uncompetitive in that product that the large firms would have made and that therefore also lead to higher import penetration.

Finally, consider the implications of the paper for liberalization. Methodological quibbles aside, there seems to be evidence here to support the paper's central point, that it is futile to expect large gains from scale effects in import-besieged industries. But should we be looking for large gains from trade *within* industries that are knocked out by foreign competition? The real gain here is that resources are released. There may still be plenty of rationalization elsewhere—across firms classified by a better correlate of efficiency, within firms, and across sectors. The paper does not address these questions directly, but it presents intriguing evidence that such rationalization is happening. The shrinkage of the manufacturing sector analyzed in the paper suggests that the action is elsewhere—perhaps in grapes in Chile and other, more troublesome agricultural products in Colombia. I hope that in future work the authors will look deeply into these and other data to address the issue of efficiency. This is a stimulating beginning for an important, if difficult, journey.

7 Estimating the Effect of Quantitative Restrictions in Imperfectly Competitive Markets: The Footwear Case

Bee-Yan Aw

7.1 Introduction

Over the past decade and a half, U.S. manufacturing industries have come under increasing pressure to adjust to forces of change in the world economy. The rapid rate of growth of imports from the developing and newly industrialized countries (NICs), in particular, has given greater significance to the question of import competition. The NICs' explosive export growth in such labor-intensive and thus "sensitive" (from a developed country viewpoint) industries as footwear, clothing, and electronics has led to impositions and renewals of trade policies aimed at protecting domestic U.S. producers in these industries. The most popular of these policies is the voluntary export restraint (VER). A VER is a quantitative restriction imposed on the exports of selected foreign suppliers and is administered by the exporting country. VERs have limited U.S. imports of textiles and clothing, footwear, autos, carbon and some specialty steel, and machine tools.

There is a substantial body of theoretical and empirical literature looking at the upgrading effect of VERs as well as their effect on import prices and hence, implicitly, the welfare of the importing country.[1] Little, however, has been done to model empirically the effect of a VER on the domestic industry that the policy is aimed at protecting. While a VER, like any trade-distorting instrument, has its obvious economic costs, its beneficiaries, at least in principle, are the domestic producers of the constrained import. The VER also directly affects the foreign producers whose exports are being constrained.

Bee-Yan Aw is an assistant professor of economics at the Pennsylvania State University.

1. For theoretical work on the effect of VERs, see Falvey (1979) and Rodriguez (1979). For empirical work related to this issue, see Anderson (1985), Aw and Roberts (1986, 1988), and Feenstra (1984).

The primary goal of this paper is to examine the actual effects of the VER on domestic producers and compare these with the effects on foreign producers of footwear.

In the empirical literature on international trade, the conventional approach to modeling the demand and supply of a traded good is to assume that the market under consideration is perfectly competitive. In reality, relatively few markets for manufactured goods and services meet the assumptions of perfect competition. Although there has been considerable development in the theory of trade under imperfect competition in the last decade, the same cannot be said about empirical work on trade in imperfectly competitive markets. Helpman and Krugman (1989) offers a synthesis of the new theory of trade policy that arises specifically from the presence of imperfect competition. They conclude that allowing for imperfectly competitive markets leads to nonstandard impacts of trade policy and that the evaluation of trade policy should take imperfect competition into account from the start.

This paper utilizes an empirical model of the footwear industry in which imperfect competition is allowed. It proceeds to quantify the effect of the VER on footwear from the perspective of U.S. footwear producers. Drawing from recent tools developed in the industrial organization literature, the traditional approach assuming perfect competition is generalized to allow for imperfect competition in the market for U.S. domestic footwear over the 1974–85 period. A simultaneous equation model of demand and supply is specified and estimated for domestic footwear. The generalized supply relation allows us to identify deviations from competitive pricing in this market.

The U.S. footwear VER offers domestic footwear producers protection by directly raising price of domestic output as a result of the supply constraint. In addition, by limiting competition, the VER could lead to or enhance non-competitive behavior by domestic footwear producers, enabling these producers to charge or alter the markup over the competitive prices in the market.[2] Thus, in the domestic market, deviations from competitive pricing may differ during the VER and non-VER periods. The empirical model developed in this paper allows us to estimate the effect of the supply constraint on domestic price and any change in price due to changes in noncompetitive behavior.

The traditional conclusions about the effects of trade policies on perfectly competitive foreign firms also breaks down when these firms are in fact not competitive.[3] The issues of the pricing behavior of foreign firms and the effect of the VER on import prices are examined in Aw (1991), which focuses on U.S. imports of footwear from Taiwan. Even with the VER in place, Taiwan's

---

2. This is a familiar argument: that protection of domestic industries is anticompetitive, allowing domestic firms to increase their markups at the expense of domestic consumers. The extent of this anticompetitive effect depends both on the form as well as the level of protection. Bhagwati (1969) shows that quotas in some sense are more anticompetitive than tariffs.

3. As Helpman and Krugman (1989) show, if tariffs or quotas are applied against foreign firms with market power, the importing country may gain by recapturing some of the monopoly rents the foreign firms extract from domestic consumers.

exports to the United States in 1980 were more than triple those of the next largest foreign supplier.[4] Results on the effects of the VER in the domestic footwear market are compared and contrasted with those for Taiwanese footwear exporters in Aw (1991).

The empirical results from this paper suggest that the direct effect of the VER on the U.S. domestic footwear price is significantly different from zero but small. The VER is associated with a 5 percent increase in the price of domestic footwear in contrast to a 22 percent increase in the price of imported footwear from Taiwan. On the supply side, the parameters representing the index of competitiveness are not significantly different than zero, implying that domestic footwear producers priced competitively during both the non-VER and VER periods. Taiwanese footwear exporters also priced competitively during the unconstrained period. Overall, while the VER did result in higher footwear prices, the footwear market in the United States is characterized by competitive pricing behavior on the part of both foreign and domestic suppliers, even during the constrained period.

Section 7.2 contains information of the changing condition of the U.S. footwear industry and the context in which the VER was granted to the industry. In section 7.3 the empirical model used to estimate the different effects of the VER on the domestic market is developed. Section 7.4 discusses the necessary data and estimation techniques and is followed by a discussion of the empirical results in section 7.5. A summary and conclusions are offered in section 7.6.

7.2 The Footwear Industry

The features of easy entry and exit, constant technology, and a large number of small firms have led economists to assume that the U.S. footwear industry is perfectly competitive. This assumption is often made despite the fact that a relatively small number of producers account for a large share of annual U.S. production. In 1976, about a quarter of the firms produced 82 percent of the output.

Footwear production is one of the relatively labor-intensive, technologically unsophisticated industries in which developing countries have held a comparative advantage over the developed countries for the past twenty years. The less developed countries' (LDCs') share of world footwear exports increased from 11 percent during the mid-1960s to almost 50 percent in 1985, with a significant and growing share of these exports destined for the U.S. market. The LDCs' quantity share of consumption of nonrubber footwear in the United States increased from 11 percent in 1971 to about 60 percent in 1985. By 1980, Taiwan alone accounted for over 40 percent of the total vol-

---

4. From the perspective of Taiwan, about 50–70 percent of Taiwan's footwear exports during the sample period were absorbed by the United States. From the U.S. perspective, Taiwan's share of total U.S. footwear imports ranged from 30 to 40 percent in the decade of the 1970s.

ume of U.S. footwear imports, an increase of more than 30 percentage points since the 1960s (see U.S. International Trade Commission 1981).

American production of nonrubber footwear declined 21.2 percent from 1971 to 1976, while the ratio of domestic shipments to U.S. consumption fell from 67.2 percent to 53.1 percent in the same period. Average annual employment in the industry declined 13.2 percent from 1973 to 1976. Footwear-worker wages relative to all manufacturing employees fell from 66.7 percent in 1973 to 62.6 percent in 1976. Thus, the performance indicators during the first half of the 1970s show a rapid decline of the domestic industry.

Consequently, the pressure to grant some form of protection to the U.S. domestic industry was high. In late 1977, VERs were negotiated with Taiwan and Korea to restrict their nonrubber footwear exports to the United States through 1981. In principle, the VER can offer protection to domestic producers by raising prices for imported footwear. Moreover, by directly limiting foreign competition, the VER may enable domestic producers to charge markups of price above marginal cost.

Empirical work on footwear has indicated that the VER-constrained countries responded by substituting into rubber footwear exports and upgrading the quality of the nonrubber footwear exported to the U.S. market (see Aw and Roberts 1986). To the extent that U.S. production concentrated on higher quality footwear, the VER led to increased competition for domestic producers. Furthermore, the major complaint of U.S. nonrubber footwear producers was that the relief provided by the VER was largely negated by import surges from noncontrolled sources. These imports rose from 141 million pairs in 1977 to 225 million in 1978 and 255 million in 1979. It is therefore not clear that competition from imports was in fact reduced by the VER.

7.3 The Empirical Model

In this section, we develop a model of the domestic footwear market in which deviations from perfectly competitive pricing are allowed. The model is used to test parametrically the hypothesis of competitive behavior in the market for U.S. domestic footwear over the 1974–85 period and to quantify the markup over marginal cost that accrues to U.S. footwear producers from the imposition of the VER.

The purpose of the model developed here is to estimate simultaneously an industry's demand and supply relations in the context of imperfect competition.[5] For this purpose we extend an empirical model formulated by Appelbaum (1982) for testing various hypotheses about noncompetitive behavior by explicitly incorporating the effect of VERs in order to empirically analyze the domestic footwear market.

---

5. An overview of the empirical techniques that have been applied in this area is provided by Bresnahan (1989).

Consider a noncompetitive industry producing a homogeneous output Q that faces an inverse market demand schedule

(1) $P = D(Q, Z)$,

where P is the price of Q and Z represents the exogenous variables that shift the demand function. Let the producers' cost function be represented by

(2) $C = C(Q, W)$,

where W are exogenous variables such as input prices or fixed factors of production. While the cost function (2) contains all the information on the firm's technology, more precise parameter estimates can be obtained by including additional equations summarizing the firm's input choice. A set of estimable factor demand equations can be derived from (2) by applying Sheppard's Lemma,

(3) $X = \partial C(Q, W)/\partial W$,

where X is the vector of input demands.

When producers are not price takers in the output market, the generalized supply relationship is represented by the equality of marginal revenue and marginal cost. This can be written as

(4) $P\left(1 - \dfrac{\theta}{\eta}\right) = \partial C(Q, W)/\partial Q$,

where η is the price elasticity of market demand and θ is the index of the degree of competitiveness in the domestic market. The markup of price over marginal cost depends on both the elasticity of demand and a market structure parameter θ which varies between zero (perfect competition) and unity (monopoly). Bresnahan (1989) explains the equivalence between this form and the markup commonly derived from a homogeneous product oligopoly model using conjectural variations.

This model is applied to the U.S. domestic footwear industry for the sample period 1974–85. From 1977 to 1981, the United States imposed VERs on footwear imports from Taiwan and Korea. The model is modified to take into account the effect of the VER on both the demand and supply sides. Under imperfect competition, a trade policy such as a VER may alter the markup of price over marginal cost.

The demand function is estimated in log-linear form and written as

(5) $\ln P_t = \gamma_0 + \gamma_1 \ln Q_t + \gamma_2 \ln GDP_t + \gamma_3 \ln I_t + \xi D_t + \varepsilon_t$,

where P_t and Q_t are the price and quantity indexes of domestic footwear in period t. GDP_t is per capita U.S. real gross domestic product, I_t is a price index of U.S. imports of footwear, while D_t is a dummy variable that takes on the value of zero during the non-VER years and unity during the VER years.

It is important that the functional form chosen in estimating marginal cost not place severe restrictions on these estimates. The translog cost function satisfies this criteria, since it places no a priori restrictions on the first or second derivatives of the cost function. Due to data availability, the empirical function estimated is a short-run cost function. Labor and materials are variable inputs purchased in competitive markets and capital is fixed. The short-run cost function is assumed to take the translog form

$$
\begin{aligned}
(6) \quad \ln VC_t = \delta_o &+ \delta_L \ln PL_t + \delta_K \ln K_t + \delta_Q \ln Q_t^p + (.5)\,\delta_{LL} \\
\ln PL_t \ln PL_t &+ (.5)\,\delta_{KK} \ln K_t \ln K_t + (.5)\,\delta_{QQ} \ln Q_t^p \ln Q_t^p + \delta_{LK} \ln PL_t \\
\ln K_t &+ \delta_{LQ} \ln PL_t \ln Q_t^p + \delta_{QK} \ln Q_t^p \ln K_t,
\end{aligned}
$$

where VC_t is normalized variable cost (measured as the ratio of the sum of labor and material costs to the price of materials), Q_t^p is the output produced in period t, PL_t is the price of labor relative to the price of materials, and K_t is the volume of capital stock.[6]

From (6), the marginal cost of footwear output is given by

$$
(7) \quad \frac{\partial VC_t}{\partial Q_t^p} = \frac{VC_t}{Q_t^p}\,(\delta_Q + \delta_{QQ} \ln Q_t^p + \delta_{LQ} \ln PL_t + \delta_{QK} \ln K_t).
$$

The labor demand equation, written in cost-share form, can be constructed from (6):

$$
(8) \quad \frac{\partial \ln VC_t}{\partial \ln PL_t} = S_L = \delta_L + \delta_{LL} \ln PL_t + \delta_{LK} \ln K_t + \delta_{LQ} \ln Q_t^p,
$$

where S_L is labor's share of the total expenditure on variable inputs.

Finally, (4), the supply equation, can be written as

$$
(9) \quad P = \frac{\partial VC_t}{\partial Q_t}\,(1 - \frac{\theta}{\eta})^{-1}.
$$

Substituting the expression for marginal cost (eq. [7]) into (9) yields

$$
(10) \quad \frac{PQ_t}{VC_t} = (\delta_Q + \delta_{QQ} \ln Q_t^p + \delta_{LQ} \ln PL_t + \delta_{QK} \ln K_t)(1 - \frac{\theta}{\eta})^{-1},
$$

which expresses the ratio of revenue to total variable cost as the product of the output-cost elasticity and a markup factor which depends on the demand elasticity, η, and θ, the index of the degree of competitiveness.

Equation (11) modifies (10) by incorporating the effects of the VER during the 1977–81 years of the sample period.

$$
\begin{aligned}
(11) \quad \frac{PQ_t}{VC_t} = (\delta_Q &+ \delta_{QQ} \ln Q_t^p + \delta_{LQ} \ln PL_t + \delta_{QK} \ln K_t) \\
&(1 - [\theta_V D_t + \theta_{NV} (1 - D_t)]/\eta)^{-1},
\end{aligned}
$$

6. Normalizing the price of labor and variable cost by the price of materials imposes linear homogeneity in factor prices on the short-run cost function.

where D_t is the dummy variable that equals one during the VER years and zero otherwise and η is the demand elasticity, which equals the inverse of γ_1 from the demand equation (5).

Equation (11) allows the competitiveness index for the restricted and unrestricted periods to be estimated parametrically together with the parameters of the cost function. A familiar argument is that protection of domestic industries may be anticompetitive, allowing domestic producers to increase their markups at the expense of domestic consumers. Bhagwati (1969) argues that the degree of anticompetitiveness is higher with a quantitative restriction like a VER than with tariffs. The complete estimating system for the U.S. domestic footwear industry consists of the market demand equation (5), short-run cost function (6), labor share equation (8), and the output supply equation (11). From this set of equations we can estimate the effect of the VER on the price of domestic footwear as well as on the degree of competitiveness in the domestic footwear market.

7.4   Data

The basic data set to be analyzed consists of observations on prices and quantities of domestic U.S. footwear from 1974 to 1985. This section describes the measurement and specification of these variables as well as the exogenous variables in the demand and supply relations in the U.S. domestic market.

The price and quantity of domestic and imported footwear are measured using index number techniques that avoid the well-known bias contained in unit-value indexes. The enhanced incentive to upgrade the quality of the import bundle when a VER is imposed and the spillover effect on producers of the competing domestic product make it important to account for changes in the underlying mix of commodities in the domestic and import bundles over time. This paper relies on Törnqvist price indexes (see Aw and Roberts 1986) to control for these changes. The value and volume data needed to construct the price and quality indexes for domestic footwear are from the NBER four-digit manufacturing *Productivity Database, 1958–86,* which reports value and price of shipments for five product categories of footwear. The import price index in the demand equation for the domestic market is based on the footwear exports of the six major U.S. suppliers—Taiwan, Korea, Italy, Spain, Brazil, and Hong Kong.

In the domestic market, there are three exogenous variables in the demand equation (5). GDP_t, the U.S. gross domestic product in real terms per capita, is obtained from the IMF's *International Financial Statistics* 1986. The price of the substitute to the domestic output, I_t, consists of the Törnqvist price indexes of footwear imports from Italy, Spain, Taiwan, Korea, and Hong Kong and is based on data obtained from the Census Bureau's *U.S. General Imports: General and for Consumption,* Schedule A, FT 135 (1974–85). This publication reports values and quantities of U.S. footwear imports by destination countries disaggregated into thirteen seven-digit product categories. The third exogenous variable in equation (5) is the dummy variable indicating the presence, or absence of the VER.

The exogenous variables in the domestic producers' cost function, namely, total output of footwear production Q_t^p, input prices for labor and materials, and capital stock data, are all obtained from the NBER *Productivity Database*.

7.5   Estimation Results

The domestic market model is estimated for the sample period 1974–85 using the three-stage least squares estimator. The endogeous variables are the price and quantity of domestically produced footwear.

7.51   Domestic Market Estimates

The parameter estimates for the demand and supply functions for the domestic footwear market are presented in table 7.1. Two main inferences can be drawn from these estimates concerning the effects of the voluntary export restraint imposed on footwear imports from Taiwan and Korea. Firstly, the indexes representing the degree of competitiveness (θs) do not differ significantly from zero during the non-VER or the VER years. This suggests that the

Table 7.1   **Parameter Estimates for the Demand and Supply of U.S. Footwear Industry (standard errors in parentheses)**

Supply parameters:		
δ	7.794	(.014)**
δ_L	.330	(.004)**
δ_K	.178	(.372)
δ_Q	1.545	(.093)**
δ_{LL}	.084	(.026)**
δ_{KK}	.992	(.440)
δ_{QQ}	.407	(.160)*
δ_{LK}	.119	(.045)*
δ_{QK}	−.858	(.255)**
θ_V	.035	(.048)
θ_{NV}	.017	(.037)
Demand Parameters:		
γ_0	7.167	(2.847)*
γ_1	−.638	(.028)*
γ_2	−1.254	(.349)**
γ_3	.258	(.072)**
ξ	.053	(.021)*

*Rejects the hypothesis that the parameter equals zero at the 0.05 significance level using the two-tail test.

**Rejects the hypothesis that the parameter equals zero at the 0.01 significance level using the two-tail test.

Table 7.2   **Mean Marginal Cost, Price, and Markup**

Years	Marginal Cost	Price	Markup
1974–76	$4.442	$4.698	.056%
1977–81	$6.153	$6.545	.0637%
1982–85	$7.311	$7.858	.0748%

domestic footwear market was competitive not only during the period in which footwear imports were unrestricted but also during the VER period. Perhaps the fact that the VER was country-specific and that footwear imports surged from unrestricted sources meant that competitive pressures from imports continued to prevail despite the VER. Consequently, the price of domestic footwear generally reflects marginal cost throughout the sample period.

This becomes clear from examining the trend of marginal cost estimates and price over the three subperiods (pre-VER, 1974–76, during VER, 1977–81, and post-VER, 1982–85) in table 7.2. The price per pair of shoes averaged $4.7 before 1977 and rose by almost 40 percent to $6.6 during the VER years. After the VER, footwear price rose by 20 percent to reach $7.9 over 1982–85. These price increases are matched very closely by increases on the cost side. Estimates of the supply parameters in table 7.1 indicate that these increases are significantly related to increases in labor costs. Marginal cost per pair of shoes rose by 39 percent from an average of $4.4 in 1974–76 to $6.2 during the VER period. This rate of increase tapered off to 19 percent during the 1982–85 subperiod when the marginal cost averaged $7.3 per pair. It is not surprising, therefore, that the markup, calculated as the ratio of the difference in the price and marginal cost to price per pair of shoes, is small (6 to 7 percent) and does not vary significantly across the subperiods.

The second inference from table 7.1 concerns the price effect of the VER as reflected in the parameter estimate for ξ in the demand equation. By raising the price of imports which substitute for domestic footwear, the VER shifts up the demand curve for the latter and thus raises its price. The results indicate that this demand side effect is significantly different than zero and is slightly above 5 percent.

Except for the parameters measuring the competitiveness index and the capital stock, the other parameters in the supply and demand equations are significantly different from zero. The first-order parameters in the cost function all carry the expected signs. The elasticity of supply of domestic footwear is estimated at 1.6.

The inverse of the demand parameters, γ_1, γ_2, and γ_3 reflect the average price, income, and cross-price elasticities of demand for domestic footwear respectively, and are given in table 7.3. The demand elasticities for domestic footwear with respect to its own price and the price of imported footwear are estimated at -1.57 and 3.87, respectively. These estimates suggest that purchases of domestic footwear are generally more sensitive to changes in its own

Table 7.3   Mean Elasticities for Domestic and Imported Footwear[c]
              (standard errors in parentheses)

	Domestic	Imports
Own price	− 1.57	− 2.59
	(.028)*	(.348)**
Income	− .80	1.36
	(.349)**	(.239)**
Cross-price	3.87	6.01
	(.072)**	(.583)**
VER markup	.053	.22
	(.021)*	(.044)**

*Rejects the hypothesis that the parameter equals zero at the 0.05 significance level using the two-tail test.
**Rejects the hypothesis that the parameter equals zero at the 0.01 significance level using the two-tail test.

price and the price of imported footwear than previously thought. In their work on the footwear industry, Bale and Mutti (1981) estimated that the own and cross-price elasticities for domestic footwear from 1947 to 1972 are − .7 and .7, respectively. The negative sign on the income variable in the demand equation suggests that footwear is an inferior good.[7]

7.5.2   Contrasting the Domestic and Import Markets

In this section comparisons are made between the empirical estimates on the domestic market in this paper with those in the market for Taiwanese footwear imports analyzed in Aw (1991).

Aw (1991) estimated a model of Taiwanese export supply of high and low-quality footwear to the United States allowing for imperfect competition in that market. However, unlike the model for the U.S. industry where the availability of better cost data permits a more straightforward identification of market power, identification of the degree of competitiveness for Taiwanese exporters involves an appropriate specification of the market demand curve.[8] The empirical estimates on the market for U.S. imports from Taiwan used in this section are based on the estimation of a simplified single-quality version of Aw's model.

Estimates on the supply side of the import market model indicate that, like their domestic counterpart, prices of Taiwanese footwear exports to the United States were priced competitively during the unconstrained period of the

7. This result appears odd in light of the high cross-price elasticity and the positive income elasticity for shoes imported from Taiwan reported later. As suggested by the discussant of this paper, despite the use of the Törnqvist price index to account for quality changes, it is possible that not all of these changes have been fully expunged from the data.
8. More specifically, the demand function has to fulfill certain nonseparability conditions.

sample.[9] However, in contrast to the small price effect of the VER on the price of domestic footwear of 5 percent, there was a markup of about 22 percent on the price of Taiwanese footwear exports to the United States due directly to the supply restriction created by the VER. This figure represents the scarcity premium for a quota ticket in Taiwan, since the Törnqvist price index used to obtain the estimate corrects for any quality upgrading of the import bundle due to the VER. This percentage is at least double the estimate of 7–11 percent given by the Taiwanese Footwear Manufacturers Association.

Estimates of mean own-price, income, and cross-price elasticities of demand for U.S. imports from Taiwan are reported in the second column of table 7.3. The average own-price elasticity of demand for Taiwanese imports is estimated at -2.6. This is not only much higher than the estimate for the domestic market counterpart but exceeds most previous estimates of the responsiveness of imported U.S. footwear.[10] The cross-price elasticity is 6, implying that imports are very responsive to changes in the price of the domestic substitute. On the other hand, the income elasticity in the import market is 1.36 and statistically significant. This figure is considerably less than the previous estimates of 5.2 by Szenberg, Lombardi, and Lee. (1977) and 2.5 by Bale and Mutti (1981). Taken together with the estimate of income elasticity for the domestic market, these results suggest that the demand for footwear in the U.S. is not as sensitive to changes in income as previously thought.

7.6 Summary and Conclusions

The theory that free trade is not optimal in imperfectly competitive industries has increasingly been used to argue for government intervention in international trade. The results from this paper indicate that the justification for the imposition of the VER on footwear imports must lie in sources other than imperfect competition. There was competitive pricing behavior on the part of both domestic and foreign producers of footwear throughout the sample period. The distortion arising from the deviation of price from marginal cost in this industry was the result of the pure scarcity effect of the VER.

The results from this paper indicate that the direct effect of the VER on the price of domestic footwear, while significant, was much smaller than that on the price of the imported counterpart from Taiwan. The restraint on Taiwanese and Korean footwear exports resulted in a 5 percent increase in the price of domestic footwear but a 22 percent scarcity premium for Taiwanese exporters.

On the supply side, domestic footwear producers priced competitively not

9. Given that the VER on Taiwanese footwear was binding, the degree of competition in the output market does not matter during the constrained period.

10. For example, these estimates range from -1.33 in U.S. International Trade Commission (1977) to -1.5 in Szenberg et al. (1977). However, Bale and Mutti (1981) estimated the elasticity to be -3.1.

only during the non-VER period but when imports from Taiwan and Korea were restricted. Such competitive pricing behavior was probably the consequence of the availability of close substitutes from numerous U.S. suppliers and the existence of many noncontrolled foreign suppliers.

References

Anderson, James E. 1985. The Relative Inefficiency of Quotas. *American Economic Review* 75 (1): 178–90.

Appelbaum, Elie. 1982. The Estimation of the Degree of Oligopoly Power. *Journal of Econometrics* 19:287–99.

Aw, Bee Yan. 1991. An Empirical Model of Mark-ups in a Quality Differentiated Export Market. *Journal of International Economics,* forthcoming.

Aw, Bee Yan, and Mark J. Roberts. 1986. Measuring Quality Changes in Quota Constrained Import Markets: The Case of U.S. Footwear. *Journal of International Economics* 21:45–60.

———. 1988. Price and Quality Comparisons for U.S. Footwear Imports: An Application of Multilateral Index Numbers. In *Empirical Methods for International Trade,* ed. Robert C. Feenstra, 257–75. Cambridge, Mass.: MIT Press.

Bale, Malcolm, and John Mutti. 1981. Output and Employment Changes in a Trade Sensitive Sector: Adjustment in the Footwear Industry. *Weltwirtschaftliches Archiv* (Kiel). 117 (2).

Bhagwati, Jagdish. 1969. On the Equivalence of Tariffs and Quotas. In *Trade, Tariffs, and Growth,* ed. J. N. Bhagwati, 248–65. Cambridge, Mass.: MIT Press.

Bresnahan, Timothy F. 1989. Empirical Studies of Industries with Market Power. In *Handbook of Industrial Organization,* ed. Richard Schmalensee and Robert Willig. Amsterdam: North-Holland Publishers.

Falvey, Rodney E. 1979. The Composition of Trade within Import-restricted Product Categories. *Journal of Political Economy* 87:1105–14.

Feenstra, Robert C. 1984. Voluntary Export Restraints in U.S. Autos, 1980–1981: Quality, Employment, and Welfare Effects. In *The Structure and Evolution of Recent U.S. Trade Policy,* ed. R. E. Baldwin and A. O. Krueger, 35–59. Chicago: University of Chicago Press.

Helpman, Elhanan, and Paul R. Krugman. 1989. *Trade Policy and Market Structure.* Cambridge, Mass.: MIT Press.

International Monetary Fund. 1986. *International Financial Statistics: Yearbook 1986.* Washington, D.C.

National Bureau of Economic Research. *Productivity Database, 1958–86.* Cambridge, Mass.: National Bureau of Economic Research.

Rodriguez, Carlos. 1979. The Quality of Imports and Differential Welfare Effects of Tariffs, Quotas, and Quality Controls as Protective Devices. *Canadian Journal of Economics* 12:439–49.

Szenberg, Michael, John W. Lombardi, and Eric Y. Lee. 1977. *Welfare Effects of Trade Restrictions: A Case Study of the U.S. Footwear Industry.* New York: Academic Press.

U.S. Department of Commerce, Bureau of the Census. 1974–86. *Current Industrial Reports, Footwear.* Washington, D.C.

———. 1974–85. *U.S. General Imports: General and for Consumption,* Schedule A, FT 135. Washington, D.C.

U.S. International Trade Commission. 1981. *Non-Rubber Footwear.* USITC Publication 1139. Washington, D.C.

Comment   Keith E. Maskus

Bee-Yan Aw's paper is a nice example of how we can advantageously use straightforward partial-equilibrium models and sensible econometric techniques to examine basic questions about the effects of trade policy on domestic and foreign firms competing in the home market. Her approach is a simple modification of the standard textbook model of protection. Consider the home market for a standardized and rather homogeneous product, such as footwear, facing a high degree of import competition from price-elastic foreign suppliers. The modification comes in allowing for two possibilities that are not in the simple textbook model. The first possibility is that imported and domestic products may be differentiated in some way, allowing us to treat them in separated markets. The second, and related, possibility is that domestic and foreign suppliers may have some power to extract monopoly profits through imperfectly competitive pricing behavior. Aw's analysis shows that these issues may be incorporated analytically without much difficulty and that the payoff to doing so in terms of understanding the underlying form of competition can be rewarding.

The main purpose of the paper is to infer the effects of the voluntary export restraint (VER) negotiated between the United States and Korea and Taiwan on competition and prices in the U.S. markets for domestic and Korean and Taiwanese footwear. One might wonder about the choice of footwear for such an analysis, since there is likely to be a strong prior expectation that these markets come close to the perfectly competitive extreme. Both the domestic and Korean and Taiwanese sources of supply face strong competition from each other and from additional international suppliers. Footwear technology is highly standardized and stable so there is little scope for generating any dynamic forms of comparative advantage. Significant import penetration is simply the result of high costs in the U.S. industry. In short, the standard textbook model is probably the right one for this industry, implying that our conventional notions of the costs and benefits of trade barriers are also substantially correct.

Nonetheless, in any industry, market structure and the degree of competition are ultimately empirical issues that deserve investigation, as Aw has competently done. Further, as is well known, the imposition of the VER itself could have an impact on competitive behavior in U.S. markets, making it a worthy episode for study. In this context, Aw's results are reasonably clear

Keith E. Maskus is associate professor of economics at the University of Colorado, Boulder.

and would, I believe, stand up well to alternative specifications. In particular, prior expectations are borne out: the U.S. industry is forced to price competitively whether or not there is a VER in place against the major foreign supplier. The VER rents are transferred completely to foreign exporters. There was no strategic rent capture, and the VER clearly worsened the U.S. terms of trade. The main benefit of the program was that it offset the cost advantage of Taiwanese and Korean footwear suppliers, which presumably is precisely what the U.S. industry desired. Otherwise, the VER can only be considered to have been harmful to U.S. interests in the most damaging way possible. These results provide a sense of reassurance that economists are not misleading their students and themselves about the dangers of protection. After all, if Aw had discovered that the United States had somehow increased its welfare by imposing a VER on an apparently competitive industry, the profession would have been confronted with a surprising, and therefore noteworthy, result.

Thus, Aw's analysis has confirmed basic expectations, which fact may be sufficiently convincing of the correctness of the exercise. However, a few cautionary notes must be sounded before the conclusions are accepted wholeheartedly. These comments relate to both the adequacy of the model for capturing the true complexities of competition in footwear and to the empirical research design.

Four issues may be raised about aspects of competition in footwear markets that go unconsidered here. First, the model lacks any specification of what is thought to be the potential source of imperfect competition among domestic and foreign shoe producers. Each industry produces a homogeneous product, though there is differentiation between U.S. and foreign footwear. In itself, this assumption is uncomfortable, since presumably differentiation is greater across types of shoes (e.g., rubber versus nonrubber or finer classifications of characteristics), regardless of geographical source, than across country of origin. Aw's approach is thus reminiscent of trade models employing the Armington assumption, which has been shown to be of dubious value. The form of product differentiation is, in principle, significantly related to competitive decisions. For example, if U.S. firms consider their main competition to be other U.S. firms, which would be appropriate under the nation-specific differentiation hypothesis assumed in Aw's paper, they would likely perceive themselves to have fewer competitors than they would under the product-specific differentiation hypothesis with its global supply sources. The VER may then induce more, presumably inefficient, entry by U.S. firms in the former case. Perhaps more fundamentally, the notion that each national industry produces a homogeneous product leaves little scope for explaining uncompetitive behavior in the absence of further assumptions about entry barriers or the distribution of firm sizes and resulting strategic activity. In short, what is supposed in this analysis to induce, even potentially, collusive behavior by U.S. firms?

A second competitive issue stems from the first. Aw's model is designed exclusively to consider pricing behavior. It is clear, however, that competitive pressures and the imposition of the VER could affect markets equally through output responses. No mechanism for entry, exit, or investment decisions is allowed here, which is understandable given the limited amount of data available. Nonetheless, as the author notes, the introduction of a quantitative import limitation in an imperfectly competitive market could result in greater or lower domestic output, depending on the competitive responses. The paper finesses this issue by considering only the estimation of a short-run cost function with fixed capital stock for the U.S. industry, which practice conditions the results of estimates of price-marginal cost gaps. It is likely that over the twelve-year period considered, new investments were undertaken by U.S. footwear firms, perhaps inefficiently, which would be an interesting question for subsequent analysis to consider.

A third concern is the absence of serious consideration of additional international supply sources. The issue is often raised in the paper but is not dealt with satisfactorily due to the strict focus on bilateral competition. The welfare effects of the VER depend on relevant trade elasticities from other footwear sources, both directly and because the behavior of U.S. and Taiwanese firms is affected by third-country competition. In the simplest view, it seems likely that, in lobbying for the VER, the U.S. industry succeeded only in making Taiwanese exporters richer while inviting greater imports from elsewhere, with few benefits to themselves. Indeed, in that context one wonders what the motivation for the VER, as opposed to, say, a nondiscriminatory tariff, could have been in the first place.

A final competitive issue is perhaps the least relevant for the modeling exercise, but an intriguing one all the same. Perhaps an important layer of competition has been missed here. Specifically, footwear producers in the United States, for whose benefit the VER was presumably erected, are not typically the final sellers of their products. Footwear retailers sell both American and imported products and may be in a position to exploit market power of their own through oligopsonistic procurement. This possibility could be significant both in considering the welfare effects of the VER, specifically the disposition of its rents, and in explaining the inability of U.S. producers to raise prices above marginal costs.

Turning to the empirical methods, which are generally sensible given the inevitable tradeoffs between analytical rigor and empirical tractability in these exercises, several concerns may be voiced as well. First, there are only twelve years of data. Yet sixteen parameters are estimated in one market and eleven parameters in the other market, and there is the subsequent desire to make inferences about market structure and associated demand and supply elasticities. Thus, the data are asked to reveal more information than they may legitimately contain. It might have been better to increase the sample size by considering some pooling possibilities across several footwear categories, which approach seems feasible given the prior categorical aggregation.

Second, the simultaneous-equations framework adopted in Aw's paper is a decided improvement over most other empirical efforts in the field of trade policy and imperfect competition. However, it is doubtful that all relevant relationships have been captured in the model. For example, it seems that some parameters should be codetermined in principle. Consider Θ (the competitiveness parameter in the U.S. market), η (demand elasticity), and ξ (the effect of the VER on demand for domestic footwear). The VER could influence not only the size of the demand for U.S. shoes, but also its elasticity, which would in turn affect the competitive behavior of U.S. producers. Similarly, since the prices of imported Taiwanese footwear are included in I_t, the price index of imported shoes in the U.S. demand equation, the VER on Taiwanese footwear products may dominate the estimated cross-price demand elasticity γ_3, implying that γ_3 and ξ may be codetermined. This latter problem could be handled simply by interacting the VER dummy variable with I_t. On a different plane, it is doubtful that modeling the markets for U.S. and Taiwanese footwear separately adequately captures their interrelationships, even allowing for the shift parameter in U.S. demand.

Third, the markedly different modeling strategies in the two markets are hard to understand. Aw has specified a log-linear demand for U.S. shoes with a VER dummy but a "linear" U.S. demand for Taiwanese shoes that incorporates an interaction term between imports and the prices of substitute footwear. It is difficult to make meaningful elasticity comparisons across markets in this context. At the same time, she has adopted a translogarithmic short-run cost function for U.S. producers and a linear long-run cost function for Taiwanese producers. There is no explanation for this rather marked conceptual difference between cost structures, a difference that conceivably could color the size of the relative markups.

A final small comment is in order. The author has taken pains to control for quality changes in the data in order to focus strictly on price competition. Yet a striking result in the paper is that the income elasticity for U.S. shoes is negative while that for Taiwanese imports is positive. Could it be that quality changes have not been fully expunged from the data?

Comment   J. David Richardson

I like the spirit of this paper a great deal: specify an econometric model with careful attention to theory, apply it to a data set that the author herself has painstakingly validated for the purpose, and see how well the specification stands up against the data.

J. David Richardson is professor of economics at the Maxwell School of Citizenship and Public Affairs, Syracuse University, and a research associate of the National Bureau of Economic Research.

I find the conclusions from these procedures quite credible. The data suggest that VERs on Korean and Taiwanese footwear exports to the United States generated modest rent transfers. The data support no trace of imperfect competition in any footwear market, either before or after the VERs.

I am persuaded that these conclusions are robust, too, given our knowledge of the industry's structure. The paper motivates its search for indications of imperfect competition by observing that 82 percent of U.S. footwear output was produced by one quarter of the firms. But there are a lot of firms in that one quarter! So it does not surprise me that the results come out looking pretty competitive.

I was disappointed that the paper itself did not reinforce my sense of robustness that rent transfers would be everything and imperfectly competitive effects (on price/cost margins, on profits, on scale, on entry or exit, etc.) would be nil. The paper could have driven home that point by more imaginative experimentation with alternative specifications. It selects one specification only—and not a very compelling one at that, because of peculiarities and undefended asymmetries.

I can illustrate what I mean by abstracting from third-country suppliers and from other important detail that the paper includes but that is extraneous for my purpose. At its core, the model is made up of two inverse demand functions,

$$(1) \qquad\qquad p_1 = p_1\,(q_1, p_2, \ldots),$$

$$(2) \qquad\qquad p_2 = p_2\,(q_2, p_1, \ldots),$$

where p's are prices, q's are quantities, and 1 and 2 denote countries whose footwear competes as imperfect substitutes; and two marginal cost functions,

$$(3) \qquad\qquad c_1 = c_1\,(q_1, \ldots),$$

$$(4) \qquad\qquad c_2 = c_2\,(q_2, \ldots),$$

where c's are marginal costs.

This is where the asymmetries begin. Equation (1) is specified as a log-linear function but (2) is a conveniently nonlinear "linear" function—the product $p_1 q_2$ enters linearly and conveniently in addition to other variables, on the right-hand side. I would have preferred for close substitutes to have consistent functional forms. Equation (3) is specified as a translog short-run cost function (capital held constant), but (4) is a linear long-run cost function (capital costs included on the right-hand side). The author comments soberly at one point that "it is important that the functional form chosen in the estimation of the cost relation not place severe restrictions on the estimates of marginal cost." But she seems unable to apply the spirit of that rule to (4) for lack of data, and unwilling to apply it to (1) and (2) despite the well-known hypersensitivity of results in imperfect competition to the curvature of the demand curve.

Another all-important specification question is how a VER should enter equations (1)–(4). Does it make the constrained supplier's cost curve vertical after a point? Does it introduce a vertical segment to one demand curve, with a consequent discontinuity in its marginal revenue curve? Does it shift the other demand curve, and if so exactly how—horizontally, linearly, . . . (the functional form question again)? The author opts for the first choice alone, and leaves it at that. In equation (11) of the paper, for example, there seemed to be a fairly simple opportunity to allow a VER dummy variable to shift both the "degree-of-competition" parameter and the demand elasticity. Only the former is permitted; the demand elasticity is assumed to be unaffected by the VER.

There are in addition two questions that the paper leaves peculiarly unresolved. One is whether product differentiation across varieties (rubber/non-rubber, and so on) is empirically more important than product differentiation across nationalities. The answer provided (in note 8) seems inadequate and at variance with common sense; countries produce many overlapping varieties, and casual observation suggests that shoe consumers do not put a great deal of weight on national origin, say, by comparison with consumers of automobiles and other consumer durables. A second unresolved question is whether the estimated cross-price elasticity of U.S. demand for imported footwear can credibly be 6, while the own-price elasticity is far smaller, and whether domestic footwear can be credibly considered an inferior good, as the paper maintains. Once again, the paper's answer seems inadequate. I would have appreciated some attention to how robust these results were to alternative specifications.

III

A New Measure of Trade
Restrictiveness and Estimates
of Trade Policy Effects
with CGE Models

8   The Coefficient of Trade Utilization: The Cheese Case

James E. Anderson

It has long been recognized that the opportunity to trade is a technology, but it has not been possible to compare trading efficiency across time and space in the manner of the productivity literature. Anderson and Neary (1989) provide a rigorous general equilibrium theory of index numbers for quotas, the coefficient of trade utilization, which is the basis for intertemporal (and international) comparisons of trade restrictiveness. This paper further develops the new index and demonstrates its operation and significance to the partial equilibrium evaluation of U.S. cheese import policy from 1964 to 1979.

There are three accomplishments. First, the operationality of the new index is established. Second, the time-series analysis of restrictiveness of the quota system reveals that the coefficient of trade utilization and the standard average tariff-equivalent measure of restrictiveness yield opposite implications in over half the observations. The coefficient of trade utilization reveals wide fluctuations in restrictiveness dominated by a significant reduction in the coefficient of trade utilization (a tightening of the average effective quota), at an average annual rate of (minus) 14 percent per year. The conventional measure, a trade-weighted average of tariff equivalents, rises by an average of 4 percent per year, which is very roughly consistent with the average quota change and the aggregate price elasticity of -3.5 reported in Anderson (1983). In contrast, in eight out of the fifteen years, the average tariff equivalent moved in the same direction as the coefficient of trade utilization; that is, it had opposite implications for the direction of restrictiveness. Third, the use of the new index is shown to make a considerable difference to the interpretation of quota reform. The new method reveals a different structure than was shown in the Anderson (1985) study of the inefficiency of the U.S. cheese quota allocation

James E. Anderson is professor of economics at Boston College.

policy, which distributes imports on a by-commodity-by-country basis.[1] The reform reallocates the quota to equalize the unit rent subject to the same aggregate import of cheese. In the earlier study, the gain from an efficient policy was calculated to be about 15 percent of base expenditure on imported cheese, which was about 30 percent of the total gain possible from a move to free trade. Using the new method of evaluation, the reform is equivalent to a 90 percent increase in the average quota, which in turn is about 25 percent of the increase implied by a return to free trade. Also, using evaluation methods ill-suited to the comparison, the earlier study showed that the efficiency gain from a commodity reallocation with country allocations frozen was 1.8 percent of the gain from a reallocation over both commodities and countries. In the present study, commodity reallocation alone picks up 15.6 percent of the gain from a full reallocation, nearly an order of magnitude more.

In a world where the only trade distortions are tariffs or subsidies, comparisons of protection levels over time and space appear simple. A rough measure of the trend in protectionism or liberalization is seen in the time series of the trade-weighted average tariff or subsidy, while a cross section of average tariffs compares national distortions. Despite the common use of such measures, economists have long realized that their comparability is unfounded, as is the use of trade weights. The proliferation of nontariff barriers in the past twenty years has made it especially important to arrive at a full theory of index numbers for trade distortions, since the methods to be used when new distortions are introduced are unknown, as are the appropriate weights. Using the methods illustrated below, proper indices of partial and overall trading efficiency can be constructed for use in international trade negotiations and reform evaluations. The present paper is confined to quota evaluation albeit in the presence of tariffs (but see Anderson and Neary (1991) for development of tariff and tariff cum quota indices).

If a single quota is to be evaluated, its restrictiveness could be measured by the rate of contraction of quantity below the free trade level or by the rate of increase of price above the free trade level (the tariff equivalent of the quota). With several quotas, the index number problem arises: What average quantity restriction or price increase represents the restrictiveness of the system? The coefficient of trade utilization is a solution to the index number problem. It is defined to be the *uniform* contraction factor applied to free trade quantities which is equivalent in welfare to the actual quota vector. The general equilibrium structure of the trading economy provides the weights to be used in constructing this index, and these turn out to be operational.

Current methods of evaluation require information on quota premia, an elasticity of import demand, and the trade data. The new method uses only these data and a new variable indicating the share of quota rents transferred to

---

1. In 1980, a partial reform allowed national cheese quotas to be shifted across cheese categories.

foreigners. Quota rents are usually shared, and the rent retention rate is important; the cheese results show that including it alters the reform evaluation measure by 40 percent. Since rent retention will be needed in any correct analysis, the new measure places no added burden on the empirical worker; it is a practical measure. However, to evaluate quotas, it is critical to obtain information on the notoriously elusive quota premia.

Section 8.1 reviews the coefficient of trade utilization concept, following Anderson and Neary (1989, 1991), and presents some extensions. Section 8.2 reviews the structure of U.S. cheese imports, very closely following Anderson (1985). Section 8.3 presents the results of applying the new concept to the U.S. cheese market. Section 8.4 concludes with suggestions for further work.

8.1   The Coefficient of Trade Utilization

This section reviews the coefficient of trade utilization concept of Anderson and Neary in 8.1.1, and applies it by (1) spelling out a partial equilibrium version and (2) extending its use to time-series evaluations in the manner of the productivity literature. Section 8.1.2 makes clear the relative advantage of the coefficient of trade utilization over previous methods.

8.1.1   Review

The coefficient of trade utilization is the *uniform* contraction factor applied to free trade quantities (or any reform quantities) which is equivalent in welfare to the actual quota vector (see eq. [5] below). This is also the ratio of the shadow value of the new quota bundle—the free trade bundle—to the shadow value of quotas needed to maintain the initial level of welfare. Anderson and Neary identify the proper weights and thus provide a rigorous foundation for distortion averages, such as have been attempted without an adequate theory in the form of tariff averages.[2]

It is necessary to be precise about the sense in which the distortion index values are comparable internationally or intertemporally. Ordinal utilities are not comparable. A legitimate comparison of the effect of distortions can nevertheless be made. Suppose a trade reform improves the efficiency of trade utilization by more in country A than country B. Then country B would have a greater real income increase if it reduced trade distortion at the rate of country A, while country A would have a smaller real income increase if it cut trade distortion at the rate of country B.

Anderson and Neary (1989) deal with a general equilibrium measure that incorporates all quotas, but it is possible to restrict the set of instruments to those regarded as feasible to reform in a trade negotiation. The present paper defines a partial coefficient of trade utilization for trade reform in one sector and applies it to cheese. Partial distance measures of distortion are of course

---

2. Anderson and Neary (1991) provide a version for tariffs as well.

subject to the difficulty that welfare may not always increase with a cut in the distortion.[3]

The coefficient of trade utilization will be defined in three stages. First, the Dixit and Norman (1980) textbook description of a distorted trading equilibrium is amended to allow quotas with rent sharing. Second, the distorted trading equilibrium implicitly relates a utility level for the representative consumer to the quota levels. This relation is made explicit in the distorted trade utility function. Finally, Deaton's (1979) distance function concept is used to relate a reform value of the quota to the current level of the distorted trade utility function. This is the coefficient of trade utilization.

The foundation is the trade expenditure function $E(p,\tau,u)$, where p is the domestic price vector of quantity-constrained trade, π is the domestic price vector of unconstrained trade, and u is the utility level of the representative consumer. Shepard's Lemma implies that the desired trade quantities (excess demands) are E_p for the constrained goods and $E\pi$ for the unconstrained goods. A fundamental requirement of trade equilibrium is the external budget constraint, with the simplest textbook case arising with free and balanced trade: $E(p,\pi,u) = 0$. For distorted trade, the external budget constraint is in external prices, p^* and π^*, differing from p and π. Thus

(1) $$E(p,\pi,u) - (1 - \omega)[p - p^*]Q - tE_\pi(p,\pi,u) = R,$$

where R is a net deficit or surplus (equal to zero in the textbook case), t is the specific tax vector for the unconstrained goods (equal to $\pi - \pi^*$, where π^* is the foreign price), Q is the quota vector, and ω is the fraction of the quota rent transferred to foreigners. The term $(1 - \omega)[p - p^*]Q$ is the quota rent retained at home, while $tE\pi$ is the tariff revenue. Equation (1) implies that net trade expenditure in domestic price equals the transfer R plus the tariff revenue plus the retained quota rent. The quantity constraints imply market clearing relations

(2) $$E_p(p,\pi,u) = Q.$$

The system of equation (1)–(2) defines the equilibrium domestic price vector p and the equilibrium utility u as functions of the trade distortions Q, ω, and t and of the exogenous net surplus R.

Anderson and Neary (1989) build a general equilibrium basis for reform evaluation setting R equal to zero. The distorted trade utility function is defined implicitly as the level of utility attained when (1)–(2) hold in equilibrium:

(3) $$v(Q;t, \omega,p^*,\pi^*,R) \equiv \{\, U \mid E(p,\pi,u) - (1 - \omega)[p - p^*]Q$$
$$- tE_\pi(p,\pi,u) = R, E_p(p,\pi,u) = Q, \pi = \pi^* + t\}.$$

---

3. The difficulty is reduced but not eliminated when the full distance measure is used.

The derivatives of this function with respect to the policy variables Q are developed in Anderson and Neary (1989). In particular, v_Q is proportional to the general equilibrium shadow price of a quota, ρ. A very important special case for practical work, illustrated in the application below, is implicit separability:

$$E(p,\pi,u) = \xi(\phi(p,u),\eta(\pi,u),u),$$

where ϕ and η are subexpenditure functions for the quota and nonquota goods, respectively. In this case, Anderson and Neary (1992) show that the shadow price of quotas has the particularly simple form:

$$(4) \qquad \rho = (1 - \omega)[p - p^*] - \frac{\omega}{\varepsilon}p - \tau p,$$

where ε is the aggregate elasticity of demand for the constrained group and τ is the import-weighted average ad valorem tariff on the unconstrained goods.

For the present paper it is not necessary to consider the derivatives v_t since "other tariffs" are assumed to be fixed. But it is necessary to extend Anderson and Neary's (1989) measure to the case where some quotas (such as those on textiles) are not under control or study. This is easy, since under separability (4) continues to hold for any single quota. Let Q denote the focus group of quotas, and let X denote all other quotas; $v(Q\cdot)$ becomes temporarily $v(Q,X,\cdot)$, and the vector ρ has elements restricted to those dual to Q. Thus there is no extra generality in carrying around terms in X. If separability does not hold (i.e., suppose the X goods enter via a subexpenditure function such that there is a difference in the cross-price elasticities between Q and Z on the one hand and between X and Z on the other hand), the formula analogous to (4) contains in addition a composition effect term driven by the difference in cross-price elasticities. This possibility is suppressed below due to lack of information and a belief that it is not a significant source of bias.

Now the coefficient of trade utilization can be defined. Figure 8.1 illustrates it for the case of two quotas. The term $v(Q_1,Q_2, \ldots) = u$ is an indifference curve in the quota space, with the subscript denoting an element of the quota vector, $Q' = (Q_1,Q_2)$. (Ignore the K and L labels on the two axes and the y label on the indifference curve at this point.) Point A is a quota point not on the indifference curve, possibly associated with a reform. Following Deaton (1979), point A is evaluated relative to the quota setting necessary to maintain u by using the distance function: the radial expansion or contraction necessary to move from A onto the indifference curve. On the diagram, the scalar factor Δ equal to OA/OB is the distance measure of the value of point A: the coefficient of trade utilization.

An alternative equivalent definition is important for interpretation and empirical work. Note that at B, there is a supporting "budget" plane tangent to the indifference curve there. Its slope is equal to minus the ratio of the shadow prices of the quotas, and the value of the budget is the shadow value of dis-

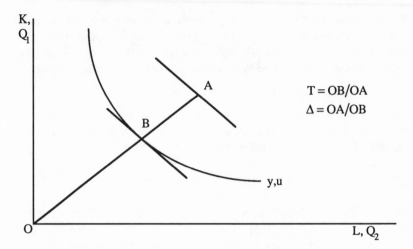

Fig. 8.1   The distance function

torted trade which supports u. The shadow value of the quota bundle at A is represented on figure 8.1 by a plane through A with slope equal to the slope of the indifference curve at B. The alternative definition of the coefficient of trade utilization is the shadow value of the bundle at A relative to the shadow value of distorted trade necessary to support u. Intuitively, a higher budget implies a potential increase in welfare.

For perspective, it is important to relate the coefficient of trade utilization to two other literatures. First, the theory of trade distortions, following Meade, essentially explored conditions under which the budget line could be shown to shift out. The shadow price of quotas result (4) is in that spirit: a rise in an element of the quota vector raises the budget line if the shadow price is positive. The post-Meade literature, reflecting its theoretical orientation, was not concerned with scaling the shift. Practically oriented approaches to trade policy require comparability of one shift with another, however, and thus the applied literature has made do with inappropriate scaling factors. Since the shadow prices are determined only up to a factor of proportionality, the scaling factor can be called a normalization. The coefficient of trade utilization defines an appropriate normalization and thus opens the way to comparability.

Second, in sharp contrast, the theory of productivity measurement from its inception has been empirically oriented and has always used what are now known to be distance function methods. Thus on figure 8.1 the axes can be relabeled with the inputs K and L on the axes, and the contour can be an isoquant: $y = f(K,L)$. Point A is an inefficient point (using outmoded technology, or reflecting some inefficiency due to policy). The scale factor $T = OB/OA$ represents the factor by which the input bundle at A can be shrunk and still maintain output of y. The slope of the isoquant at B represents minus the ratio of the factor prices and the level of the budget line the minimum cost.

The distance measure of technical efficiency is the ratio of the cost associated with A to the minimum cost needed to produce y. The main practical use of T is in its rate of change form

$$\hat{T} = \hat{y} - (\alpha\hat{K} + (1 - \alpha)\hat{L}),$$

where $\hat{T}$ is the famous rate of growth of total factor productivity, $\hat{y}$ is the rate of change of output, α is the competitive cost share of payments to K, $(1 - \alpha)$ is the cost share of payments to L, and $\hat{K}, \hat{L}$ are the input rates of change.

Now consider the connection of the two uses of the distance concept. In levels, the same operation (inverted, reflecting the difference between consumption of Q_1 and Q_2 and input demand for K,L) obviously defines both. The practical use of T is in its rate of change form, where the shares and the input rates of change are observable.[4] The coefficient of trade utilization has an entirely analogous rate of change form developed below, where the role of competitive cost share is taken by "shadow value of quotas share." Using equation (4), these also are observable, as are the $\hat{Q}$s.[5] The same techniques and means of interpreting and comparing total factor productivity growth rates are thus immediately available for interpreting and comparing the rate of change of trading efficiency as measured by the coefficient of trade utilization.

To return to a formal development of the coefficient of trade utilization, the distance in Q space from an arbitrary bundle Q to an arbitrary general equilibrium utility contour $v(\cdot) = u$ is its basis. Paralleling Hicks, there are "compensating variation" (the distance from the new bundle to the old utility contour) and "equivalent variation" (the distance from the old bundle to the new contour) measures of the total trade inefficiency. I assume $v_\Delta = -v_Q{}'Q/\Delta^2$ is negative.[6] First, the compensating variation form of the coefficient of trade utilization is implicitly defined as the value of Δ such that

$$(5) \qquad v(Q^1/\Delta,\omega;t,p^*,\pi^*,R) = u^0.$$

Δ exceeds unity for a reform in restricted trade when Q^1 is the new trade bundle and u^0 is the old trade utility (associated with trade restraint Q^0). Δ is

---

4. Strictly speaking, the distance operation picks up technical efficiency change only for fixed factor prices. When factor prices vary, it is necessary to use for $\hat{K}$, $\hat{L}$ that portion of the change in input usage that is econometrically explained by changes in the factor prices. The residual changes in factor usage (in an estimated factor demand system) are the "factor augmentation rates." $\hat{T}$ is alternately the share-weighted average of the factor augmentation rates.

5. A careful reader, in light of the previous note, will observe that the coefficient of trade utilization could claim a greater degree of accuracy than the standard productivity measure. The $\hat{Q}$s are directly measured, while the input rate of change residuals needed for productivity measurement reflect measurement error, misspecification of all sorts, estimation bias, and so forth. Much of the last thirty years of the productivity literature is devoted to explaining the residual in terms of underlying elements, a development that is entirely bypassed here.

6. The assumption that the shadow value of trade distortions be positive is analogous to a more familiar condition that trade revenue be positive but is more restrictive. The distance function method could still be used when v_Δ can change sign, but considerable care must be taken to avoid regions where Δ cannot be defined, as well as the obvious issues with multiple solutions.

equal to 1 when Q^1 is equal to Q^0. Δ bears a close relation to Debreu's coefficient of resource utilization, hence its name. Second, the equivalent variation form is implicitly defined as the value of Δ^* such that

(6) $$v(Q^0/\Delta^*,\omega;t,p^*,\pi^*,R) = u^*$$

for some arbitrary feasible reform utility u^*. Defining Δ^* in this way implies that a value less than one is a welfare improving reform.[7] The equivalent variation measure Δ^* is in principle superior to Δ because of its transitivity property. It is a "quota-metric" utility function since it compares the new utility level to the old bundle Q^0 and, due to ordinality, Δ^*_u can be set equal to 1. The compensating variation measure need not be transitive, but it is more practical since it compares the new bundle to the old utility, whereas the equivalent variation requires using the complete general equilibrium model to compute the new level of real income. Transitivity of Δ is guaranteed in the special case of homothetic preferences (see Chipman and Moore 1980), which obtains in the application below. In the remainder of this discussion I stick to the compensating variation form. Equation (5) uses the bundle Q^1 as a reference, standing for a reformed Q, with rises in Δ measuring improvements in the efficiency of utilization of the trade opportunity. For a reform going all the way to free trade, Q^1 is equal to the free trade bundle.

From its implicit solution in (5), Δ is homogeneous of degree one in Q, and it has derivatives proportional to the shadow price of quotas vector, ρ. This allows a further refinement, following Deaton. The alternative measure of Δ suggested by figure 8.1 is the shadow value of Q relative to the shadow value of distorted trade needed to support u. How is the normalization factor, the denominator of the distance measure, to be defined? An "expenditure function" is suggested by the diagram: the Q bundle can be regarded as the "shadow-expenditure-minimizing" selection of Q subject to given shadow prices ρ and given u. If v is quasi-concave in Q, this is unexceptionable. Unfortunately, as is well known, v need not always be quasi-concave in Q. A further hypothesis of "efficient protection" might then be applied to rule out selection of points in Q space which are in the nonconcave portions of the indifference curves. Let G be the minimum value of distorted trade revenue:

(7) $$G(\rho,u;\omega,t,p^*,\pi^*,R) = \min_{Q} \{ \rho'Q \mid v(Q,\omega;t,p^*,\pi^*,R) = u \} .$$

$G(\cdot)$ has all the standard expenditure function properties in ρ. Dual to G is a distance function (Deaton 1979):

---

7. Δ^* can be used for partial reform evaluation, but it is not generally defined in the move all the way to free trade, since Q^0 is not generally a radial contraction of the free trade trade vector. (The two measures are trivially identical in the two good case.) This means that v_Δ^* passes through zero somewhere, violating the assumption needed for use of the implicit function theorem. Stern (1986) discusses similar problems which arise when the distance function is used in consumer theory with labor supply as a choice variable.

(8) $\Delta(Q,u;\omega,t,p^*,\pi^*,R) = \min_{\rho} \{\rho'Q \mid G(\rho,u;\omega,t,p^*,\pi^*,R) = 1\}$,

where $G(\cdot) = 1$ is the normalization rule for quota shadow prices. Due to its derivation in (8), Δ is homogeneous of degree one in Q and concave.[8] The concavity of Δ is especially useful in index number construction over discrete changes, since it justifies simple operational approximations which are an average of the Paasche and Laspeyres indices[9] (see, e.g., Caves, Christensen, and Diewert 1982).

The two principal uses of Δ applied below are (i) the evaluation of actual quota policy over time and (ii) the evaluation of trade reform. In other work it will also be useful to compare the index of trading efficiency across countries. For the first use of (18),

(9) $\hat{\Delta} = \Sigma\beta_i\hat{Q}_i + (u\Delta_u/\Delta)\hat{u} + (R\Delta_R/\Delta)\hat{R} + (\pi\Delta_\pi/\Delta)\hat{\pi} + \ldots$,

where β_i is the shadow quota rent share for quota i, $\rho_iQi/\rho'Q$, and the sum of the β's is unity (it is not necessarily true that all are positive, although positive shadow prices were found in the work below). Equation (9) allows for the influence of other price changes $\hat{\pi}$, the capital transfer $\hat{R}$, and real income $\hat{u}$. The latter is assumed to be growing exogenously to the process of quota policy, which is surely reasonable for the case of U.S. imported cheese. For simplicity in the calculations, the influence of all changes save real income are suppressed. Fortunately, for the case of homothetic preferences, the elasticity of Δ with respect to real income is -1.[10] Thus,

(9') $\hat{\Delta} = \Sigma\beta_i\hat{Q}_i - \hat{Y}$.

This has the intuitive implication that a quota vector which grows less fast than the real income growth rate is increasing trade restrictiveness.

The second important use of equation (8) is to evaluate trade reform:

(10) $\hat{\Delta} = \Sigma\beta_i\hat{Q}_i$,

where the same condition on the shares holds. In this case the proportional changes in the quotas are imposed by the reform structure.

---

8. Since $v(Q,\pi)$ need not be concave in Q, the minimizing assumption "concavifies" the underlying preferences. In the proposed use of Δ in evaluating trade reform, this is appropriate because we regard the planner or analyst as evaluating proposed bundles Q relative to the minimum value of distorted trade needed to support u^0. In the equivalent variation form, proposed reforms resulting in utilities u^* are evaluated by comparing the value of bundles Q^0 to the minimum value of distorted trade needed to support u^*.

9. In practice, when $v(\ )$ is not concave in Q, the change in the true index need not lie between the conventional measure of the change in the Paasche and Laspeyres indices. The true measure requires calculations of the minimizing shadow prices.

10. The market-clearing relations are $E_p = Q$. For homotheticity, $E_p(p,\pi,u) = uE_p'(p,\pi)$. Then $Q/\Delta = uE_p'(p,\pi)$. Constant restrictiveness (constant Δ with no change in p) is possible only if Q grows at the same rate as u.

It is important to emphasize that $\hat{\Delta}$ is conceptually identical to the productivity measures like $\hat{T}$ used to track the behavior of economies over time and space. It converts the actual or proposed changes into a uniform equivalent change in trade, just as the productivity index is a uniform equivalent growth in factors. Also, like the productivity measure, it is operational and offers a basis of comparison of trade policies. The natural units of the coefficient of trade utilization and the public's familiarity with productivity measures give it an added advantage in communicating the results of policy evaluations.

8.1.2   Comparison with Current Methods

The coefficient of trade utilization is a proper index of trade distortions. The index which is commonly used by default for intertemporal comparisons is a trade-weighted average of tariffs, or in the present case of "tariff equivalents" of quotas. It has well-known defects due to the substitution effect: a high tariff equivalent will be associated with a small quota, other things equal. In section 8.3 an index of this type is constructed for cheese imports in the U.S. from 1964 to 1979 and its rate of change is contrasted with the rate of change of te coefficient of trade utilization. If the two measures agree in their implication for restrictiveness, a rise in the average tariff equivalent should coincide with a fall in the coefficient of trade utilization. It is highly significant that for eight of the fifteen observations on one-year changes, protection measured by the average tariff equivalent moved in the same direction as the coefficient of trade utilization.

Other measures of the effect of trade distortions have different purposes and thus do not permit comparison over space and time. For example, when correctly applied the standard measures of the effect of trade reform (compensating and equivalent income variations) give correct measures of the shift in the relevant general equilibrium budget constraint (the shift from B to A), but they lack a scale (normalization) that would permit comparisons. Some analysts report the unscaled compensating or equivalent variation numbers. This biases the measure upward for large countries in cross-country comparisons and for later periods in intertemporal comparisons. Several varieties of scale have been attempted. For large reforms such as complete free trade, it is usual to report the compensating variations as fractions of national income. This biases the measure downward in cross-country comparisons for "naturally" less open economies like that of the United States. A more sophisticated version of the expenditure function model, which appears to allow comparability, arises when the effect of the reform is scaled by the trade expenditure or by the total gain from trade. I used both expedients in partial equilibrium in my 1985 cheese paper reviewed in the next section.

While the ratios of compensating variations to either the trade expenditure or the gain from trade are natural, they are not appropriate for comparison purposes. With the compensating variation methods that typically would be used, let Q^0 and Q^1 be two quota vectors with associated domestic prices p^0

and p^1. Suppose for simplicity that all rent is retained domestically. The gain from trade reform measure relative to base expenditure is

(11)
$$\frac{E(p^1,\pi,u^0) - E(p^0,\pi,u^0) + \text{net rent change}}{E(p^0,\pi,u^0)}.$$

For proper applications, the numerator is a legitimate measure of the income which could be deducted from the representative consumer facing the new prices while maintaining u^0. The denominator measure is the net trade expenditure, equal in general equilibrium to the base quota rent plus any transfer. The ratio (11) is the proportion of base expenditure (rent plus transfer) that could be deducted from the representative consumer facing the new prices while maintaining u^0. Thus far, all is well. But consider a new initial point p^2, associated, for example, with a more restrictive initial condition and hence a lower u^2. If the compensating variation is transitive, the value of the numerator in the move from 2 to 1 will exceed the value of the numerator in the move from 0 to 1; that is, the two values of the numerator will correctly sign the welfare comparison. But the two proportionate changes are no longer comparable; they do not have the same base. In Anderson (1985), reviewed in the next section, equation (11) was used with the wrinkle that the partial equilibrium nature of the study meant that the denominator was total expenditure on cheese.

The alternative measure used in Anderson (1985) and sometimes applied elsewhere is the relative inefficiency measure for quota reform:

(12)
$$\frac{E(p^1,\pi,u^0) - E(p^0,\pi,u^0) + \text{net revenue change}}{E_p(p^0,\pi,u^0)p^* - E(p^*,\pi,u^0)},$$

where the denominator is the gain from a complete liberalization of trade (the gain from free trade in the cheese sector in the application below). Once again the denominator shifts with the initial condition and vitiates comparability. Finally, it is conceivable to scale by the value of the leap from autarky to free trade: p^0 is set equal to the autarky level. This does resolve the noncomparability issue of the preceding two scales but is infeasible, since calculation of autarky prices is rarely credible.

In contrast, the coefficient of trade utilization is a proper index for trade distortions. In all cases, the practitioner can use an appropriate transformation to accommodate shifts in the nondistortion variables (note that there is no apparent way to extend the measures above) and can be certain that all trade distortions are evaluated using true shadow prices. The comparability problem is solved in principle.

8.2   The Cheese Import Model

I review here a portion of my (1985) paper, in order to provide a self-contained treatment. The purpose of my earlier paper was to document the potential large welfare inefficiency implied by the common practice of allocating quotas at a detailed by-commodity-by-country level and prohibiting resale. U.S. cheese imports were selected for study because the data were good, the quotas were so allocated, and the domestic policy objective in limiting cheese imports apparently did permit a reallocation over types, while preserving the same aggregate level of imports. An econometric model of cheese demand was fitted to use in the welfare evaluation.

In this paper the data are used for two applications. First, the data for the earlier study are used along with the estimated aggregate elasticity of cheese demand to form a time series of the rate of change of the coefficient of trade utilization. Second, the 1985 exercise is repeated but with the coefficient of trade utilization as the welfare measure.

I first describe the market for imported cheese in the United States and then explain the computation of reform magnitudes for the second exercise.

8.2.1   The U.S. Dairy Industry and the Quota System

The U.S. dairy quota system originated as a by-product of the dairy price support system. The main element is support of a manufacturing-grade milk price, but there are also butter and American-type cheese support prices. To avoid supporting foreign farmers, quotas have been imposed on a variety of cheeses under executive authority, which is very broad.

The essential principle of the quota system is, however, to set detailed levels of imports on a basis consistent with historic proportions. The presidential quota authority does not stipulate that this principle is to be carried through to allocation by country of origin, but the quota administrators have so proceeded. In contrast, quota administrators appear to regard their objective as a target level of milk-equivalent tonnage in groups identified as substituting for domestic milk products (see, e.g., Emery 1969, 9–11).

Thus the stated objective of the quota administrators supports a noneconomic constraint of the simple form in which individual by-commodity-by-country quotas could be reallocated subject to a constant total. Despite this, the current allocation system creates detailed binding quotas. The USDA (U.S. Department of Agriculture) quota system administrators develop license allocations by commodity by country from base-year allocations in the legally mandated categories. They claim to have effective auditors who implicitly frustrate resale of licenses. Measured differences in average quota rent margins, reported in Anderson (1985), bear out the claim.

The Census trade data have nine commodity categories of continuously imported cheese plus a catch-all, with six of the nine plus a part of the catch-all category subject in part or whole to quota constraint. This creates the circumstances for a case study of quota inefficiency when the quota constraints are converted into an overall constraint on the six categories. Inefficiency arises due to (1) inefficient allocation by country within the same cheese type (a matter of administrative discretion) and (2) inefficiency allocation over types (partially mandated in current presidential proclamations, but presumably easily changed within the spirit of presidents' previous exercises of authority).

I now rationalize a partial equilibrium approach to the U.S. market for imported cheese. The United States is a small consumer of foreign cheese; hence the foreign price of foreign cheese is reasonably taken to be exogenous. Its domestic price in quota constrained categories is of course endogenous. U.S. consumption of cheese is a tiny fraction of total food consumption, so ignoring spillover effects onto noncheese prices may be reasonable; the prices are assumed to be exogenous. The domestic price of domestic cheese is endogenous save when the government is maintaining a floor price through large purchases. Endogenous domestic prices of both imported and domestic cheese were fitted to an implicit reduced form in the econometric work on cheese demand discussed in Anderson (1983). The "fitted prices" were used as instruments in estimation of the demand system.

In principle, it is possible to model the supply side of the domestic cheese industry. Domestic cheese production and sale is dominated by and large by the government's milk, cheese, and butter price supports. Successfully dealing with the supply side of the domestic cheese markets probably requires a model of how the government sets its supports. Fortunately, in the welfare (as opposed to the econometric) analysis it is permissible to treat the U.S. price of U.S. cheese and related dairy products as independent of import policy changes, since it can be assumed that the government will offset any domestic price effect by support purchase. This is effectively true in a large part of the sample (1964–79), particularly in the later years.

A nine-equation model of imported cheese demand was estimated for the years 1964–79. An implicitly separable food and beverage expenditure function is assumed to exist for a representative U.S. consumer identifiable in the aggregate data (see Anderson 1983 for discussion of the implied assumptions). The almost ideal demand system (AIDS) expenditure function is used, with the further wrinkle that only a tiny portion of total food and beverage consumption is estimated—that for nine imported cheeses (see Deaton and Muellbauer 1980 for a general treatment of AIDS). AIDS is used because it is a flexible function form with particularly simple capability for allowing nonhomothetic preferences while permitting exact linear aggregation.

The results reported in Anderson (1983) were reasonably "good," with sensible elasticities, absence of obvious specification bias, and a good fit. The null hypothesis of homotheticity could not be rejected in a joint test. As is common in flexible functional form estimation, however, concavity of the demand system was rejected in unconstrained estimation, and had to be enforced about the point of means. The main additional sources of possible specification error are in aggregation over consumers and over cheeses. The data do not permit an attack on these problems. To give some feel for the demand structure that results, appendix table 3.A1 in Anderson (1988) presents point estimates of compensated price elasticities. The elasticities are evaluated at the point of means of the shares. These imply an aggregate price elasticity of demand for imported cheese as a group of -3.54, which is plausible for a product group with good domestic substitutes. A reader skeptical of the econometric methods used is free to regard these and the underlying parameters as plausible guesses to be used in simulation.

8.2.2   The Cheese Quota Reform Exercise

The essential ingredients of the study of cheese import inefficiency are the trade quantities and prices (see Anderson 1983, 1985, for more details on these data). Domestic auction prices and foreign port values of imported cheeses were obtained from USDA and Census data. The domestic part of the total quota premium equals the difference between these less a marketing margin based on similar unconstrained imported cheeses. These are converted to annual averages for the calculations below. The foreign part of the quota premium is based on data reported in Boisvert, Hornig, and Blandford (1988). The trade quantities come from Census data.

The theoretical analysis of my earlier paper (1985) derives the efficient[11] reallocation of existing quotas policy as equivalent to a uniform specific tariff that would achieve the same aggregate quantity of constrained cheese. The estimated demand functions evaluated at the point of means can be substituted into the constraint and the resulting equation solved for the efficient tariff. Thus the model solves for t in

$$\Sigma E_{p_i}(p^* + t, u) = \bar{Q},$$

where $\bar{Q}$ is the aggregate quota constraint, and, by Shepard's Lemma, E_{pi} is the demand for the ith quota-constrained cheese. (Strictly speaking, u changes with the reform, but the change is trivial.) The estimated AIDS demand function is used for E_{pi}. After t is solved, a welfare analysis of the reform is calculated. The replication of these results is reported in the next section.

8.3   The Results

Two uses of the new concept of trading efficiency are made here. I first present the time-series results. The sixteen-year period of the data was marked by considerable fluctuation in the restrictiveness of the various quotas, with an overall dramatic increase in restrictiveness. Most notably, the coefficient of trade utilization and the average tariff equivalent give opposite implications in over half the observations. Second, I reevaluate the potential improvement in trade efficiency due to an efficient allocation of cheese imports as in Anderson (1985). The surprise here is that the by using the coefficient of trade utilization measure, the relative importance of the commodity-alone reallocation grows from less than two per cent to over a fifteen per cent of the commodity-and-

---

11. Based on eq. (4), I now know what I did not in 1985, that the implied reform, while more efficient, is not optimal, since the shadow price of the quota is not equal to the unit rent.

country reallocation gain. The inefficient allocation is equivalent to 14 (89) percent reduction in average constrained cheese imports under commodity-alone (commodity-and-country) reallocation.

8.3.1 The Increase in Restrictiveness, 1964–1979

Using equation (9′), we can readily calculate the local rate of change of the coefficient of trade utilization. For discrete changes, it is customary to use β shares that are the arithmetic average of the shares at the two end points. This procedure is exact for the translog form of the underlying function Δ and is appropriate for any concave function Δ in the sense that the true value of the change in Δ must lie between the values formed using the new and old shares.[12] Thus, while Δ is not a translog (despite the essentially translog structure of the AIDS system), and indeed has no closed form, I assume the usual procedure, which would generally be used by other practitioners, is close enough.[13]

To control for noise in such disaggregated data, the $\hat{Q}$ series is based on the calculated demands rather than the measured imports.[14] The tariff rate used in constructing the shadow price of quotas, ρ, is set at the import-weighted average ad valorem rate on all imports in each year. The aggregate elasticity of demand for constrained imports is obtained from the AIDS system and the standard formula

$$(13) \qquad\qquad \varepsilon = \Sigma\Sigma w_i \varepsilon_{ij},$$

where the ε_{ij}'s are the partial elasticities of demand, estimated in Anderson (1983). At the point of means, ε is equal to -3.54. The results reported below hold it constant rather than the more refined version allowing the elasticity to vary endogenously. The differences are minor. The data series reported in section 8.2 yield the quota premium based on the average eternal f.a.s. price.

---

12. This follows from a straightforward application of the mean value theorem for a concave function. By concavity,

$$\Delta_Q(Q^0)[Q^1 - Q^0] \geq \Delta(Q^1) - \Delta(Q^0) \geq \Delta_Q(Q^1)[Q^1 - Q^0].$$

See Caves, Christensen, and Diewert (1982) for more discussion.

13. In principle, it is possible to check the appropriateness of the assumption by calculating Δ from the nonlinear system

$$(i) \qquad\qquad \frac{Q^1}{\Delta} = E_p(p,\pi,u),$$

$$(ii) \qquad\qquad R = E(p,\pi,u) - (1 - \omega)[p - p^*]\frac{Q^1}{\Delta} - tE_\pi(p,\pi).$$

Equations (i) and (ii) solve for p,Δ in terms of $R,u,\pi^*,p^*,t,$ and ω, using $\pi = \pi^* + t$. This can be done for the specific AIDS system estimated by Anderson. Time did not permit resolution of the convergence problems encountered here.

14. The measured imports do not correspond exactly to the quotas due to (1) the Commerce Department's practice of reporting the import data in the month in which the information arrives from the Customs Bureau rather than the month of shipment, and (2) minor inconsistencies in the statistical classification schemes.

This lies above the foreign marginal cost due to rent captured by foreigners, as Boisvert et al. (1988) show. Following their data, the rent retention rate ω is set equal to .50.

In contrast, the standard approach to summarizing developments in the import of cheese would be based on tariff equivalents of quotas, or quota premia. There is a great deal of variation in the quota premia over time, and a rising trend predominates. While the correlation between the six premia time series is high, it is not perfect. Thus a highly diverse picture presents itself to the analyst, and prior to the methods of this paper there was no adequate way to summarize the developments. The main alternative would be the annual percentage change in the trade-weighted average tariff equivalent of the quotas, which is reported below.

The average annual rate of change of trade utilization, $\hat{\Delta}$, calculated using equation (9′) as explained above is − 14 percent, effectively cutting in half the imports of cheese every six years. This average masks some spectacular annual variations. Table 8.1 presents the annual percentage changes in the coefficient of trade utilization for cheese imports from 1965 to 1979 in the first column. Notice the very restrictive policies followed in the mid and late 1970s with a break in 1976, a year in which a temporary relaxation of the quota was permitted to help in the political struggle against food price inflation.

The annual percentage change in the trade-weighted average tariff equivalent of the quotas, $\hat{T}$, (T.E.) is presented in the second column. The average change over the fifteen years is 4 percent, doubling the average tariff rate every eighteen years, and similarly implying a sharp rise in restrictions. To provide

Table 8.1   **The Rate of Decline of Cheese Trade Efficiency, 1965–1979**

Year	Rate of Change of Average T.E.	Rate of Change of CTU
1965	.10	− 0.17
1966	**.26**	**0.13**
1967	.05	− 0.03
1968	**.40**	**0.06**
1969	**− .47**	**− 0.11**
1970	**− .02**	**− 0.16**
1971	.13	− 0.18
1972	**− .04**	**− 0.09**
1973	**− .08**	**− 0.08**
1974	**− .05**	**− 0.33**
1975	**− .03**	**− 0.40**
1976	− .006	0.02
1977	.12	− 0.26
1978	.06	− 0.19
1979	.15	− 0.28
Average	.04	− 0.138

Note: Bold type indicates that the observations for the two measures have the same sign.

contrast, the observations for which the two measures have the same sign (diverge in implication) are printed in boldface. This occurs in eight of fifteen cases. Another way to describe the result is with correlation analysis. One might expect the two series to be perfectly negatively correlated in a rank sense. Spearman's rank correlation coefficient for the two series is 0.34, which does not permit rejection of the null hypothesis of no relation between the series.

The level of restrictiveness on average in the sample period is high according to either measure. The average level of *ad valorem* tariff equivalent is around 25 percent (the basis for the changes in table 8.1). It should be noted that this figure corresponds to the retained rent concept $(1 - \omega)(p - p^*)$. The coefficient of trade utilization for the move to free trade is 2.3, meaning that a 130 percent average rise in quantity can be achieved. The two percentages are very roughly connected via the aggregate elasticity of -3.5.

Since all time series are substantially driven by cyclical phenomena, it is worth noting that cyclic disturbances are purged by the device of using Qs calculated to lie on the demand functions, which should take care of much of the problem. A complete accounting of cyclic versus other reasons for the behavior of effective trade policy is beyond the scope of this paper, but something like 1966 to 1976 is a complete cycle, and the data do not suggest the dominance of cyclic phenomena in cheese policy.

8.3.2   Reform Evaluation

Section 8.2 reviews the background of my (1985) evaluation of the efficiency gain from a reallocation of quota licenses subject to the constraint that the total import of cheese in constrained categories did not change, all evaluation being done at the point of means. Two variants were assessed. In one, the country allocations were frozen, so that the average foreign price of cheese in each category remained constant. A reallocation over the six types resulted in the gain shown in table 8.2, first row of column (1) (adapted from Anderson). The other variant permitted reallocation to a (conservatively chosen) low-cost supplier, with results shown in the second row of column (1). Two features of this study should be noted, because they contrast with the methods used below. First, while apparently reasonable, the scaling methods used in table 8.2 have no real foundation in theory and can be misleading in reform evaluation because they do not use shadow prices. They result in rather modest measures of gain which are not readily comparable with other reforms under other circumstances. Second, a notable implication of table 8.2 appears to be that the gain from a commodity reallocation is modest compared to the gain from picking a more efficient supplier, since .0028 (in the first row) is less than 2 percent of .152 (in the second row). The coefficient of trade utilization permits a more appropriate scale that is quite intuitive. Its use turns out to revise upward the estimation of the efficacy of a commodity-alone reallocation by almost an order of magnitude.

Table 8.2   Efficiency Gains from Cheese Quota Reform

| | Welfare/Base Expenditure | | Relative |
| | Efficient Tax | Free Trade | Inefficiency |
	(1)	(2)	(1)/(2)
No supply reallocation	.0028	.087	.103
Supply reallocation	.152	.497	.306

Table 8.3   CTU Measure of Gains from Cheese Quota Reform

| | % Change in CTU | | Relative |
| | Efficient Tax | Free Trade | Inefficiency |
	(1)	(2)	(1)/(2)
No supply reallocation	.139	1.278	.109
Supply reallocation	.891	3.623	.246

Table 8.3 contains the calculated gain in the coefficient of trade utilization under the same circumstances. The entries have the interpretation of an average percentage increase in the aggregate quota. Thus moving to an efficient quota (equivalent to that implied by a uniform specific tax) under no supply reallocation is effectively a 14 percent increase in the aggregate quota, while under country reallocation the efficient quota is effectively a 90 percent increase in the average quota.

Assessing the relative significance of country reallocation, .139 (in the first row) is about 16 percent of .891 (in the second row), so that commodity reallocation alone is seen to be much more (almost ten times more) significant than with the methods of table 8.2. It is important to understand why the results differ.

The difference in results is mainly due to the difference in scaling factors: the results in table 8.2 are scaled by base expenditure, while the results in table 8.3 use a proper normalization as a scaling factor. For example, in the first column of table 8.2, the ratio (1.11) is evaluated under commodity-alone and commodity-by-country reallocations. The denominator (base expenditure) is the same in both cases, while the numerator of the expression evaluated in the second row of table 8.2 is greater than that evaluated in the first row by $(.152 - .0028) * (\text{base expenditure})$. In contrast, for the results reported in table 8.3, the coefficient of trade utilization concept normalizes the change in distortion revenue implied by the new quota bundle minus the old bundle. The normalization factor is the shadow rent needed to support initial utility (or, the marginal shadow rents used to evaluate quota changes are normalized), so that the expressions evaluated in the second row of table 8.3 have a different denominator as well as a different numerator from those in the first

Table 8.4   **Effect of Tariffs and Rent Sharing on CTU Gains**

	% Change in CTU		
	Pure Import Q (1)	Tariff Effect (2)	Shadow Price (3)
No supply reallocation	0.132	0.102	.139
Supply reallocation	1.351	1.314	.891

row. In this application the normalization reduces greatly the difference between the first and second rows of table 8.3 relative to table 8.2. The normalization factor has a large influence because the terms of trade effect of the country reallocation substantially increases some of the marginal shadow rents (a rise in trade is associated with an improvement in the terms of trade, raising the shadow price) over the value for the commodity-alone reallocation.[15] The scale in table 8.3 is much more appropriate to comparisons of sources of inefficiency in the quota allocation, since it is a marginal concept.

A careful reader might note that the reallocation in table 8.3 is not strictly comparable to the reallocation in table 8.2 due to the allowance for rent sharing in the latter but not in the former. This plays a minor role in the results, as it turns out. A calculation of the coefficient of trade utilization under the assumption of full rent retention yields gains of .132 under commodity reallocation and 1.35 under commodity-by-country reallocation (see table 8.4 below), so that commodity-alone reallocation gets about 10 percent of the full gain, as opposed to 16 percent under the rent-sharing assumption and less than 2 percent with the old measure.

Since future applications of the coefficient of trade utilization will probably be with less adequate data, sensitivity to bad data is an important issue. There is no substitute for good information on the quota premiums, but the results of this study suggest that the other elements of the shadow price of quotas may not be of critical importance. Table 8.4 shows the coefficient of trade utilization gain from the efficient quota under the two cases of supply reallocation with alternately the assumption of a pure import (full rent retention) quota, the pure quota plus a tariff on other goods, and the main case of a 50 percent rent retention quota plus a tariff on other goods. The two effects go in opposite directions under the separability assumption, hence they tend to cancel, as seen in the first row. In the second row this effect is combined with the effect of a terms of trade improvement from the country reallocation. Since

15. Let p_i^* be the average foreign price of imported cheese in category i. The country reallocation causes a drop in p_i^*. For the purposes of the calculation, this drop is related to the change in Q_i by calculating the "derivative" dp_i^*/dQ_i. The shadow price of the quota includes the component $-(1 - \omega)p_Q^* Q$, from differentiating (1). Under the circumstances of a reallocation toward low-price producers, $p_Q^* Q$ equals $\Sigma Q_i[dp_i^*/dQ_i]$ and is negative. Thus the shadow price of the quota is increased by the inclusion of this term.

half of the terms of trade improvement will accrue to foreigners as rent (based on the rent-sharing data discussed above), and since this is bigger than the reduction in the domestic price as a result of the reform, the result is that the last column of the second row (.891) is less than the second column (1.314).

8.4 Conclusion

This paper has illustrated the use of the coefficient of trade utilization concept for trade reform and for time-series evaluation of fixed trade policy in the U.S. market for imported cheese from 1964 to 1979. The new concept is readily operational and offers distinct advantages over current methods because it solves the comparability problem. The significance of this is illustrated in two ways. In the first, a time-series index allows the intertemporal comparison of the quota policy implied in sixteen annual observations. In the second, two different quota reforms are compared in importance on a consistent basis. In both cases, the coefficient of trade utilization gives quite different implications than the common alternative.

In future work I plan to expand the set of commodities covered and extend the years covered, looking to build a time series capable of assessing the overall trend in U.S. trade policy. I encourage other investigators to begin using this concept for other countries' trade data. Eventually this will lead to a set of measures with which to compare national trade policies, one that is as easy for the public to understand as are productivity measures.

References

Anderson, J. E. 1988. *The Relative Inefficiency of Quotas*. Cambridge, Mass.: MIT Press.
———. 1985. The Relative Inefficiency of Quotas: The Cheese Case. *American Economic Review* 75: 178–90.
———. 1983. An Econometric Model of Imported Cheese Demand. Boston College.
Anderson, J. E., and J. P. Neary. 1992. Trade Reform with Quotas, Partial Rent Retention and Tariffs. *Econometrica,* forthcoming.
———. 1991. A New Approach to Evaluating Trade Reform. Boston College.
———. 1989. The Coefficient of Trade Utilization: Back to the Baldwin Envelope. In *The Political Economy of International Trade: Essays in Honor of Robert Baldwin,* ed. R. Jones and A. Krueger. Oxford: Basil Blackwell.
Boisvert, R. N., E. Hornig, and D. Blandford. 1988. Quota Rents and Subsidies: The Case of U.S. Cheese Import Quotas. Cornell University, manuscript.
Caves, D., L. Christensen, and E. Diewert. 1982. Multilateral Comparisons of Output, Input, and Productivity Using Superlative Index Numbers. *Economic Journal* 92:73–86.
Chipman, J., and J. Moore. 1980. Compensating Variation, Consumer's Surplus, and Welfare. *American Economic Review* 70:933–49.

Deaton, A. S. 1979. The Distance Function and Consumer Behavior, with Applications to Index Numbers and Optimal Taxation. *Review of Economic Studies* 46:391–405.

Deaton, A., and J. Muellbauer. 1980. *Economics and Consumer Behavior.* Cambridge: Cambridge University Press.

Dixit, A., and V. Norman. 1980. *Theory of International Trade.* Cambridge: Cambridge University Press.

Emery, Harlan. 1969. *Dairy Price Supports and Related Programs, 1949–1968.* Agricultural Economic Report no. 165. Washington, D.C.: U.S. Department of Agriculture.

Stern, Nicholas. 1986. A Note on Commodity Taxation: The Choice of Variable and the Slutsky, Hessian and Antonelli Matrices. *Review of Economic Studies* 53:293–99.

Comment   Satya P. Das

The paper has two parts. In the first part, Anderson illustrates and discusses the measure of trade restriction developed earlier by Anderson and Neary,[1] which is named "coefficient of trade utilization" (CTU). In the second part, Anderson attempts to apply this measure to compare the degree of U.S. restrictions on imports of cheese over the sample period 1965–79.

The theory behind the CTU measure is certainly an improvement over the traditional methods in that it is more micro founded. In a nutshell, the theory is as follows. Consider a small open economy. Let there be quantity restrictions on imports of two or more commodities. Let this "quota" vector at time t be denoted by $\bar{Q}_t$. Assuming that these restrictions are binding, the equilibrium domestic prices of these goods are endogenous and are higher than the respective foreign prices, the difference being the "quota rent" per unit. Assuming further that preferences are homothetic and alike across the domestic consuming units so that perfect aggregation holds, let $V(\bar{Q}_t)$ be the indirect utility at the equilibrium. Now consider two periods, 0 and 1, respectively the base and the current period. Let $\bar{Q}_0$ and $\bar{Q}_1$ be the corresponding quota vectors. In general, some elements of $\bar{Q}_1$ will be greater than the corresponding elements in $\bar{Q}_0$ and some will be less. So the problem is: How can we determine whether the current quota systems $\bar{Q}_1$ is more or less restrictive than the original quota system $\bar{Q}_0$? This is an index number problem.

As a solution, CTU is defined by k where

(1) $$V(\bar{Q}_1/k; \ldots) = V(\bar{Q}_0; \ldots)$$

Satya P. Das is professor of economics at Indiana University.

1. J. E. Anderson and J. P. Neary, "The Coefficient of Trade Utilization: Back to the Baldwin Envelope," in *The Political Economy of International Trade: Essays in Honor of Robert Baldwin,* ed. R. Jones and A. Krueger (Oxford: Basil Blackwell, 1989).

There is some intuition in this. If, for example, all quantities in $\bar{Q}_1$ are higher than those in $\bar{Q}_0$, bundle 1 is surely less trade restrictive than bundle 0; k will be clearly greater than unity, so that the CTU associated with bundle 1 is greater than that with bundle 0. The CTU resembles the Hicksian compensating variation in income.

Intuitive as it may seem, there is a tricky problem with the Anderson-Neary formula. It is that by defining a common denominator k for all quantities, some quantities (elements) of $\bar{Q}_1/k$ may exceed the corresponding free trade quantities. If this is so, those (theoretical) quotas are not binding, and hence the corresponding prices will be their foreign prices, implying that the $V(\cdot)$ function is not the same between period 0 and period 1. In other words, the $V(\cdot)$ function in the left-hand and right-hand sides of (1) may not remain invariant. This may invalidate the comparison between $\bar{Q}_0$ and $\bar{Q}_1$. Note that this is true even if both $\bar{Q}_0$ and $\bar{Q}_1$ may be binding.

Assuming that the above problem is somehow solved, more generally, an axiomatic approach may be developed. Let us imagine a scalar k such that

$$(1') \qquad V(\bar{Q}_1,k; \ldots) = V(\bar{Q}_0; \ldots),$$

which defines $k = k(\bar{Q}_0,\bar{Q}_1; \ldots)$. One could begin by specifying some "desired" axioms and then find if there exists a $k(\cdot)$ function which satisfies those axioms. If yes, is it unique? Some of these axioms may be the following:

(a) *Two-way consistency:* If $V(\bar{Q}_1,k_1) = V(\bar{Q}_0)$ and k_1 implies more trade restriction, then k_2 defined by $V(\bar{Q}_0,k_2) = V(\bar{Q}_1)$ should imply less trade restrictions.

(b) *Three-way consistency or transitivity:* If $V(\bar{Q}_1,k_1) = V(\bar{Q}_0)$, $V(\bar{Q}_2,k_2) = V(\bar{Q}_1)$, and both k_1 and k_2 imply more (or less) trade restriction, then k_3 defined by $V(\bar{Q}_2,k_3) = V(\bar{Q}_0)$ should imply more (or less) trade restriction.

(c) *Independence of irrelevant alternatives:* This may perhaps be another desirable axiom, although in some cases it may not be very appropriate. If $V(\bar{Q}_1,Q^*,k^*) = V(\bar{Q}_0,Q^*)$ and $V(\bar{Q}_1,Q^{**},k^{**}) = V(\bar{Q}_0,Q^{**})$, then k^* implies more trade restriction if and only if k^{**} implies more trade restriction.

(d) *Homogeneity:* Let $V(\bar{Q}_1,k; \ldots) = V(\bar{Q}_0; \ldots)$. If $\bar{Q}_1 = \lambda\bar{Q}_0$, then $k = \lambda$.

It is easy to verify that the Anderson-Neary CTU formula does not satisfy axiom (c), because CTU appears as the common denominator of *all* quotas.[2] On the other hand, axiom (c) itself can be argued to be inappropriate if in the quota basket the goods are sufficiently close substitutes of one another. In any event, it will be worthwhile to ask if there is an impossibility or possibility theorem regarding the existence and uniqueness of a k function that satisfies axioms (a)–(d). I am optimistic. My own hunch is that there is a possibility

---

2. If, on the other hand, the CTU is designed to leave out the common quotas in two periods, it would then violate transitivity. This is true whether CTU is defined analogous to the compensating variation or the equivalent variation in income.

theorem. The exact functional form would of course depend upon the form of the indirect utility function.

Coming to the empirical part, one of the major limitations, as the author points out, is the supply side of the model. The firm behavior is mostly assumed away. Doing so, Anderson ends up with a demand system model that is structural, whereas the equations that determine price are in reduced form. This is presumably due to a data problem—lack of firm-level production and other data. However, given that such data are becoming increasingly available, I suppose that these types of problems will be overcome in the near future.

To sum up, this is an interesting and useful paper. Although, as I have illustrated, the CTU measure has its weaknesses as an index of trade restrictions, I think that it is a significant conceptual improvement over the usual indices of trade restriction.

9

The Impact of Permanent and Temporary Import Surcharges on the U.S. Trade Deficit

Barry Eichengreen and Lawrence H. Goulder

9.1 Introduction

External imbalances and protectionist pressures traditionally go hand in hand. The 1980s were a decade of exceptionally pronounced external imbalances for the United States. Predictably, the decade was marked by a steady stream of trade and tax policy proposals intended to reduce the trade deficit, stem foreign capital inflows, and reverse America's loss of net foreign creditor status. Examples range from the 1985 Branson-Pearce proposal for a 20 percent import surcharge to the Gephardt amendment to the recent trade bill, which would apply tariffs on imports from countries running large bilateral trade surpluses with the United States.[1]

The logic for these proposals is straightforward. Tariffs raise the price of importables and shift U.S. expenditure toward domestic goods, thereby closing the trade gap. This is the implication of static analyses of the relationship between tariffs and the trade balance familiar since at least the time of Meade (1951). Several issues must be confronted, however, before leaping from this simple logic to policy recommendations. First, the standard static analysis of the effects of trade policy initiatives ignores intertemporal adjustments that influence the trade balance. Temporary tariffs, for example, tend to raise the

Barry Eichengreen is professor of economics at the University of California, Berkeley, and a research associate of the National Bureau of Economic Research. Lawrence H. Goulder is visiting associate professor of economics at Stanford University and a faculty research fellow of the National Bureau of Economic Research.

The authors wish to thank Robert Baldwin, Drusilla Brown, and David Tarr for helpful comments and suggestions. They also thank David Bowman and Philippe Thalmann for research assistance, and the Stanford University Center for Economic Policy Research and the Pew Charitable Trusts for financial support.

1. See Branson and Pearce (1985). Their proposal coincided with the introduction of no fewer than ten separate bills to impose some form of surcharge in the first half of 1985 (Kaempfer and Willett 1987, 27).

prices of current goods relative to future goods. This increases the consumption rate of interest facing domestic consumers, which encourages consumers to shift absorption toward the future, weakening the capital account and strengthening the trade balance. However, by reducing current absorption, temporary tariffs depress world interest rates, encouraging households to shift absorption back toward the present. The intertemporal substitution to which this gives rise may offset the impact on the trade balance of within-period substitution between importables and exportables. Thus, a temporary tariff, by reducing world interest rates, can induce domestic households to increase current spending to such an extent that the trade balance actually worsens. Because of interest rate effects, a permanent tariff can also worsen the trade balance in the short run.

Second, even if permanent and temporary import surcharges would in fact succeed in reducing the trade deficit, it still is unclear which would do so at lower cost. The answer depends in part on what produced the trade deficit in the first place. The two leading interpretations of U.S. trade deficits in the 1980s are that they were produced by private and public savings shortfalls, respectively. The private saving shortfall is typically ascribed to the combination of an autonomous fall in household savings propensities and investment-friendly tax reforms (Poole 1989; Makin 1990). The public saving shortfall is commonly traced to the tax cuts and public spending increases that produced the exceptionally large federal budget deficits of the 1980s. Which interpretation of the origins of the trade deficit one subscribes to may well have implications for the policy one recommends.

The extant literature is virtually silent on these issues. We address them in this paper by analyzing alternative trade policies designed to close the U.S. current account deficit. We start with an analytical model that can be used to sketch the impact on the trade balance and national welfare of permanent and temporary tariffs. We then incorporate these analytical relationships into a dynamic, disaggregated computable general equilibrium model of the U.S. economy, and simulate the effects of temporary and permanent import surcharges.[2] Simulations are performed under different assumptions about the source of the trade deficit.[3]

Results from the analytical model reveal that, even under restrictive assumptions, the policy initiatives have ambiguous effects on the trade balance and welfare rankings are indeterminate. This makes clear the need to impose realistic parameter values to make headway on the policy issues. The numeri-

2. The case of temporary import surcharges is probably more realistic. But the comparison with permanent surcharges is useful for bringing out some of the distinguishing features of the temporary policy.

3. The analysis of Iishi, McKibbin, and Sachs (1985) is similar to ours in its attention to intertemporal adjustments. Like ours, their analysis explores the effects of a uniform import tax. However, their model does not provide the same degree of sectoral disaggregation. Nor does it consider alternative assumptions regarding the sources of the trade deficit and the timing of the tariff.

cal simulation model employed in this paper does precisely this. The simulation model extends the analytical model by incorporating production and a government sector whose functions extend beyond merely transferring revenues to households in lump-sum fashion. In addition, the simulation model disaggregates U.S. production, permitting an assessment of the intersectoral impact of different policies. In contrast with other simulation models that examine intersectoral effects of trade initiatives, the model employed here is rigorously intertemporal, capturing the dynamic connections between import surcharges, domestic saving and investment, and the trade balance.

Several important findings emerge from our simulation analysis. Under a wide range of parameter values, both temporary and permanent import surcharges succeed initially in improving the trade balance. The temporary surcharge has a larger short-run impact, but the permanent surcharge raises domestic welfare by a greater amount. Although both policies reduce the trade deficit initially, both yield larger deficits subsequently. Under certain assumptions regarding the sources of the trade deficit, both policies delay the date at which the U.S. deficit is converted to a surplus.

The effects of the two policies are sensitive to assumptions about what produced the trade deficit in the first place and to the timing of the policy response. The short-run effects on the trade balance are also sensitive to assumptions about individual portfolio behavior.

In interpreting our results, it is important to bear in mind that we are not primarily concerned in this paper with the questions whether reducing the trade deficit should constitute a policy objective or whether tariff policies are the best means to this end. Our attention to permanent and temporary tariffs is motivated largely by the recognition that policymakers face substantial political pressures to introduce these measures. Under these circumstances, a close examination of their potential effects seems worthwhile.

9.2 A Simple Analytical Model

In this section we sketch the principal channels through which permanent and temporary tariffs influence the trade balance and national welfare. The vehicle is the two-period model of Gardner and Kimbrough (1989), which extends to two countries earlier work by Svensson and Razin (1983).

The attraction of the Gardner-Kimbrough framework is that it can capture the incentives for both intersectoral and intertemporal substitution produced by temporary and permanent tariffs. Because two countries are considered, it is possible to analyze meaningfully the terms-of-trade effects and international repercussions of policy initiatives. Because commodity demands derive from intertemporal optimization by utility-maximizing households, the analytical model captures the intertemporal nature of the trade balance and can be used for welfare analysis.

As always, these advantages are purchased at a cost. Production is ignored.

Consumer demands are specialized to a particular functional form. Because there are only two periods, it is not possible to distinguish meaningfully the period 1 trade balance from the period 2 net foreign asset position. Imperfect substitutability between domestic and foreign financial assets is not considered. Yet even with these restrictive assumptions, indeterminacies arise.

Each economy is represented by a single consumer endowed in each period with fixed quantities of two perishable commodities: m denotes the home importable and x the home exportable. (We follow Gardner and Kimbrough's notation throughout.) It is assumed that a given country exports the same good in both periods.

Commodity and credit markets are competitive and international trade and lending are free. The nominal prices of m and x are p^* and q^* on world markets and p and q gross of domestic tariffs. The nominal discount factor D is defined as one over one plus the nominal interest rate.

The domestic consumer's intertemporal budget constraint is

$$(1) \qquad \begin{aligned} p^1m^1 + q^1x^1 &+ D\,(p^2m^2 + q^2x^2) \\ &= p^1\bar{m}^1 + q^1\bar{x}^1 + T^1 + D(p^2\bar{m}^2 + q^2\bar{x}^2 + T^2), \end{aligned}$$

where the superscripts 1 and 2 denote periods, m and x denote consumption of the two goods, and $\bar{m}$ and $\bar{x}$ denote endowments of the two goods. T denotes net government revenues, which are redistributed to consumers in lump-sum fashion. (The foreign consumer's problem is identical, except that no government revenues are collected or rebated abroad.) The government's budget constraint is

$$(2) \qquad T^1 + DT^2 = \tau^1 p^{*1}\,(m^1 - \bar{m}^1) + D\tau^2 p^{*2}(m^2 - \bar{m}^2),$$

where τ is the ad valorem rate of import taxation. The price index $\Pi(p,q)$ is the unit expenditure function associated with consumption bundle c.

The consumer maximizes lifetime utility:

$$(3) \qquad U[c^1(m^1,x^1),\ c^2(m^2,x^2)].$$

The utility function is assumed to be weakly separable. In both periods, c is assumed to be linearly homogeneous. We further specialize c and U below.

The consumer's problem is solved in two steps. First, the consumer minimizes spending in each period subject to a given level of utility, yielding the expenditure function:

$$(4) \qquad \Pi^t(p^t,q^t)c^t \equiv \min\,\{p^tm^t + q^tx^t : c^t(m^t,x^t) \geq c^t\}, \quad t = 1, 2.$$

The elasticities of the price index with respect to nominal prices are the shares of expenditure falling on importables and exportables α and $(1 - \alpha)$ (see eq. [13] below).

Second, the consumer minimizes lifetime expenditure for a given level of lifetime utility u. This yields the lifetime expenditure function

(5) $$e(1,\delta,u) \equiv \min\{c^1 + \delta c^2 : U(c^1,c^2) \geq u\},$$

where $\delta = \Pi^2(\cdot)D/\Pi^1(\cdot)$ is one over one plus the domestic real interest rate. The budget constraints imply that, in equilibrium:

(6) $$e(1,\delta,u) = \frac{\theta^1\bar{m}^1 + \bar{x}^1 + \tau^1\theta^{*1}(m^1 - \bar{m}^1)}{\Pi^1(\theta^1, 1)}$$
$$+ \delta\frac{\theta^2\bar{m}^2 + \bar{x}^2 + \tau^2\theta^{*2}(m^2 - \bar{m}^2)}{\Pi^2(\theta^2,1)}$$

(7) $$e^*(1,\delta^*,u^*) = \frac{\theta^{*1}\bar{m}^1 + \bar{x}^1}{\Pi^{*1}(\theta^{*1}, 1)} + \delta^*\frac{\theta^{*2}\bar{m}^{*2} + \bar{x}^{*2}}{\Pi^{*2}(\theta^{*2}, 1)},$$

where $\theta = (1 + \tau)\theta^*$ is the within-period domestic price of importables in terms of exportables $(\theta^* = p^*/q^*)$, or the terms of trade. Commodity markets clear

(8) $$m^1(\cdot) + m^{*1}(\cdot) = \bar{m}^1 + \bar{m}^{*1},$$

(9) $$m^2(\cdot) + m^{*2}(\cdot) = \bar{m}^2 + \bar{m}^{*2},$$

(10) $$x^2(\cdot) + x^{*2}(\cdot) = \bar{x}^2 + \bar{x}^{*2}.$$

The assumptions of perfect capital mobility and perfect asset substitutability imply

(11) $$\delta = \left[\frac{\Pi^2(\theta^2,1)}{\Pi^{*2}(\theta^{*2},1)} \cdot \frac{\Pi^{*1}(\theta^{*1},1)}{\Pi^1(\theta^1,1)}\right]\delta^*,$$

The nominal rate of return available to foreigners in their own country must equal the nominal rate of return available to them on loans to the domestic country.

The home country's period 1 real trade balance, at world prices, is

(12) $$b^1 = \frac{\theta^{*1}\bar{m}^1 + \bar{x}^1 - (\theta^{*1}m^1 + x^1)}{\Pi^1(\theta^{*1},1)}.$$

Henceforth b^1 is assumed to be negative.

To keep the results as simple as possible, we follow Gardner and Kimbrough and limit our attention to the case where domestic and foreign consumers have identical tastes of the form

(13) $$U = \frac{(c^1)^{1-(1/\sigma)}}{1 - 1/\sigma} + \rho\frac{(c^2)^{1-(1/\sigma)}}{1 - 1/\sigma}, \quad c^t = (m^t)^\alpha(x^t)^{1-\alpha},$$

where σ is the intertemporal elasticity of substitution in consumption and ρ is the subjective discount factor $(0 < \rho < 1)$. From the assumptions of identical tastes and free trade equilibrium, it follows that each country's consumption of each good in each period equals its share of world wealth. Domestic wealth is defined as

$$(14) \qquad W = \frac{\theta^{*1}\bar{m}^1 + \bar{x}^1}{\Pi^1(\theta^{*1},1)} + \delta^* \frac{\theta^{*2}\bar{m}^2 + \bar{x}^2}{\Pi^2(\theta^{*2},1)}$$

while foreign wealth is defined analogously.

9.2.1 Permanent Tariffs

Here we report Gardner and Kimbrough's results for the effect of a permanent tariff on the terms of trade, the real discount factor, and the trade balance. We start from free trade equilibrium. A permanent tariff ($d\tau^1 = d\tau^2 = d\tau > 0$) alters the terms of trade in both periods but not the real discount factor:

$$(15) \qquad \hat{\theta}^{*1} = \hat{\theta}^{*2} = \frac{-W}{W + W^*}d\tau \text{ and } \hat{\delta}^* = 0,$$

$$\hat{\theta}^1 = \hat{\theta}^2 = \frac{W^*}{W + W^*}d\tau \text{ and } \hat{\delta} = 0,$$

where "$\hat{\ }$" is used to denote a percentage change. A permanent tariff imposed by the home country improves its terms of trade to the same extent in each period. By switching domestic demand away from imports, it drives down the tariff-exclusive price of the good exported by the foreign country. The magnitude of the terms of trade improvement is an increasing function of the share of the home country in world wealth. Since any shift in the intertemporal pattern of spending at home is mirrored by an offsetting shift abroad, there is no change in the intertemporal terms of trade.

The impact of the permanent tariff on the trade balance is given in the first panel of table 9.1. Note that the trade balance may either strengthen or weaken. Insofar as the permanent tariff improves the current terms of trade, higher incomes now are used to support higher spending later. Current absorption falls relative to current income, and the trade balance improves. This effect is captured by the bracketed term preceding the minus sign in the fourth row of table 9.1. Insofar as the permanent tariff improves the future terms of trade, higher incomes later are used to support higher spending now. Period 1 absorption rises relative to period 1 income, and the trade balance worsens. This effect is captured by the bracketed term following the minus sign. Since the terms of trade improve by the same amount in each period, current income rises relative to future income (the trade balance improves) when, under free trade, current imports are large relative to future imports. Hence the two ($m^i - \bar{m}^i$) terms enter with opposite signs.

The impact of the permanent tariff on welfare is also given in the first panel of table 9.1. Assuming that $m^i > \bar{m}^i$ in both periods, this expression is unambiguously positive. The permanent tariff is unambiguously welfare improving since it strengthens the home country's terms of trade in both periods.

9.2.2 Temporary Tariffs

A temporary tariff ($d\tau^1 > 0$, $d\tau^2 = 0$) affects both intersectoral prices (the terms of trade) and intertemporal prices (the real discount factor). It raises the

Table 9.1   **Effects of Alternative Policies in the Analytical Model**

Variable	Effect

1. Effects of Permanent Tariff

$\hat{\theta}^1$

$$\frac{W^*}{W + W^*} d\tau$$

$\hat{\theta}^2$

$$\frac{W^*}{W + W^*} d\tau$$

$\hat{\delta}$ 0

∂b_1

$$\left\{ \left[(1 - \beta) \left[\frac{\theta_1^*(m^1 - \bar{m}^1)}{\Pi(\theta_1^*)} + \alpha b_1 \right] - \beta\delta^* \left[\frac{\theta_2^*(m^2 - \bar{m}^2)}{\Pi(\theta_2^*)} + \alpha b_2 \right] \right] \frac{W}{W + W^*} \right\} d\tau$$

∂U

$$\left\{ \beta^{-1/\sigma} W^{-1/\sigma} \left[\frac{\theta_1^*(m^1 - \bar{m}^1)}{\Pi(\theta_1^*)} + \delta^* \frac{\theta_2^*(m^2 - \bar{m}^2)}{\Pi(\theta_2^*)} \right] \frac{W}{W + W^*} \right\} d\tau$$

$$\frac{\partial U}{\partial b_1} \qquad \frac{c_1^{-1/\sigma}}{[(e_m^1 + \alpha b_1)/(e_m^1 + \delta^* e_m^2)] - \beta}$$

2. Effects of Temporary Tariff

$\hat{\theta}^1$

$$\frac{W^*}{W + W^*} d\tau^1$$

$\hat{\theta}^2$ 0

$\hat{\delta}$

$$\frac{-\alpha W^*}{W + W^*} d\tau^1$$

∂b_1

$$W \left[\beta(1 - \beta)\sigma\alpha \frac{W^*}{W + W^*} + (1 - \beta) \left[\frac{\theta^{*1}(m^1 - \bar{m}^1)}{\Pi^1 W} + \alpha\frac{b^1}{W} \right] \right]$$
$$\frac{W}{W + W^*} + \beta \frac{b^1}{W} \frac{\alpha W}{W + W^*} \right] d\tau^1$$

∂U

$$\left[\frac{1}{e_u} \frac{\theta_1^*(m^1 - \bar{m}^1)}{\Pi(\theta_1^*)} \frac{W}{W + W^*} \right]$$

$$\frac{\partial U}{\partial b_1} \qquad \frac{c_1^{-1/\sigma}}{\alpha[\beta(1 - \beta)\sigma W^* + b_1]/e_m^1 + (1 - \beta)}$$

Notes: $\beta \equiv \dfrac{1}{1 + \delta^*(\rho/\delta^*)^\sigma}$

is the share of wealth devoted to period 1 consumption in free trade equilibrium.

  $e_m^i \equiv \theta_i^*(m^i - \bar{m}^i)/[\Pi(\theta_i^*)]$

is the "real" value of imports.

price of current consumption in terms of future consumption for residents of the home country. Domestic consumers wish to shift consumption from the present to the future. To prevent an excess supply of commodities from emerging in the first period, world real interest rates must fall. Hence $d(\delta)/d(\tau^1) < 0$, as shown in the second panel of table 9.1.

A temporary tariff, like its permanent counterpart, has an ambiguous effect on the trade balance. The rise in the price of current domestic consumption in terms of future domestic consumption shifts absorption toward the future, strengthening the trade balance. The larger the intertemporal elasticity of substitution σ, the larger this effect. But the decline in world real interest rates due to the fall in period 1 consumption shifts absorption back toward the present, weakening the trade balance. Moreover, if the home country is running a trade deficit in period 1, then the decline in world real interest rates reduces the cost of period 1 borrowing, increases domestic wealth, and induces a rise in period 1 consumption of both goods. The larger the period 1 trade deficit, the larger this income effect, which also serves to weaken the period 1 trade balance.

As in the case of a permanent tariff, domestic welfare rises unambiguously because of the improvement in the period 1 terms of trade.

Given the ambiguous effect of each of these policies on the period 1 balance of trade, it is difficult to say anything definitive about which policy is capable of reducing the period 1 deficit at lowest cost. But if we restrict our attention to cases in which the policies each improve the period 1 trade balance, then it is possible to make some headway on these issues.

In this case, the permanent tariff improves the trade deficit at lower cost than the temporary tariff when

$$(17) \quad \frac{e_m^1 c_1^{-1/\sigma}}{\alpha b_1 + (1 - \beta)e_m^1} > \frac{e_m^1 c_1^{-1/\sigma}}{\alpha[\beta(1 - \beta)\sigma W^* + b_1] + (1 - \beta)e_m^1}.$$

Assuming that both the permanent and temporary tariff improve the trade balance, this inequality always holds. The permanent tariff does not distort the intertemporal pattern of consumption, so it improves the period 1 deficit at relatively low cost. The denominator of the right-hand side of equation (17) differs from its counterpart by a term that reflects the additional welfare loss attributable to distorting the intertemporal pattern of consumption.[4]

A main conclusion of this section is that, even in a relatively restrictive analytical framework, the impact of the two policies on the trade balance is ambiguous once the scope of both intersectoral and intertemporal substitution is acknowledged. Given the difficulty of pinning down the direction, much less the magnitude, of the change in the trade balance, it is impossible to unambiguously rank the policies according to the welfare cost of a given change in the trade balance produced by their imposition. Only if it is assumed arbitrarily that within-period substitution effects dominate intertemporal substitution effects so that both the permanent and temporary tariff improve the trade balance is it possible to say anything definitive.[5]

4. The denominator on the right-hand side of eq. (17) differs from its counterpart by the term $\alpha\beta(1 - \beta)\sigma W^*$. This term, which is an increasing function of the intertemporal elasticity of substitution σ, reflects the additional welfare loss alluded to in the text.

5. With the addition of further complications such as commodity production and imperfect substitutability between domestic and foreign assets, it becomes harder still to derive unambiguous closed-form solutions for the effects of temporary and permanent tariffs. An exogenous level

We can reach more definitive conclusions by employing numerical simulation. This is the approach we adopt in the remainder of the paper.

9.3   An Overview of the Simulation Model

Simulation enables us to represent the economy more realistically than in the analytical model, where the goal of obtaining closed-form relationships mandates simplicity. In contrast with the analytical framework, our simulation model incorporates production decisions as well as detail on the functions of the government sector. The model generalizes along the time dimension, incorporating a large number of periods and thereby illuminating real-time aspects of the adjustment process. Since the solution does not involve differentiation or linearization, experiments need not be restricted to marginal policy changes.

In this section we provide a nontechnical overview of the model. Readers requiring more information are referred to our previous papers (Goulder and Eichengreen 1989a, 1989b). The appendix provides detail on the main structural innovation not contained in the version of the model reported in these papers: namely, the extension of the treatment of government financing to allow for deficit as well as tax finance.

Our model has four features that distinguish it from other general equilibrium simulation models and render it particularly suitable for the questions at hand. First, the decisions of forward-looking households and firms are based on intertemporal optimization. This makes the model particularly useful for analyzing the impact of temporary policies and for contrasting their effects with those of permanent initiatives. We derive overall consumption and saving of each household as the solution to its intertemporal optimization problem. Holding other variables constant, increases in current interest rates induce households to save more. Critically, however, current consumption and savings decisions depend not only on current income and interest rates but also on the entire future paths of these and other variables. Once the level of current consumption expenditure is determined, households allocate this expenditure across domestic and foreign goods as a function of relative commodity prices.

Similarly, in making investment decisions, forward-looking managers consider not just current profits but future profitability as well. Their investment

---

of commodity production would have no substantive implications for the results. But if it was assumed, as in the simulation model below, that investment and hence productive capacity were declining functions of the real interest rate, a temporary tariff, by reducing the real interest rate, could stimulate investment and production. Insofar as the sensitivity of investment varied across countries, this could modify the terms-of-trade effects described above. It is even harder to generalize about the likely impact of imperfect asset substitutability, which would hinge on the specification of portfolio behavior. Below we introduce a specification derived from optimizing assumptions and consistent with the literature on mean-variance analysis.

decisions balance the costs of new capital against the higher future revenues made possible by a larger capital stock, as in Summers (1981).[6] Though managers' investment decisions control the evolution of future capital stocks, current capital stocks are not a decision variable. Firms combine the fixed current capital stocks with variable quantities of labor in a CES production function to produce value added.[7] Value added combines with composite intermediate inputs in fixed proportions to produce gross output. Intermediate inputs can be obtained at home and abroad. We adopt the Armington assumption that domestic and foreign intermediates are imperfect substitutes for one another. In each industry, they are combined in a CES function to produce a composite intermediate input. In constructing the composite, firms choose the mix of domestic and foreign intermediates that minimizes costs.

A second distinguishing feature that makes the model particularly well suited to analyze trade deficits and international financial flows is its integrated treatment of the current and capital accounts of the balance of payments. Households select the optimal portfolio shares of domestic and foreign assets as a function of relative rates of return. Changes in asset supplies and demands alter asset prices and rates of return as necessary to equilibrate financial markets. Financial capital is treated as perfectly mobile internationally (there are no impediments to exchanging assets in international markets), but assets denominated in domestic and foreign currencies are assumed to be imperfect substitutes in portfolios. Supplies of foreign (domestic) assets available to domestic (foreign) investors change over time through the capital account of the balance of payments. Exchange rates, interest rates, prices, and quantities adjust to bring about balance-of-payments equilibrium in each period.

The determination of current and capital account balances as a function of household and firm decisions can be understood in the following way. Savings and portfolio decisions of domestic and foreign households determine supplies of loanable funds in each country. Investment decisions of firms at home and abroad determine the demand for loanable funds in each country. Interest rates at home and abroad adjust in each period to clear the market for loanable funds in each country. The excess of saving over investment in a country is the current account surplus (the capital account deficit).

The third distinguishing feature of our model is its detailed treatment of the public sector. The model includes a government at home and abroad. Both governments collect taxes, distribute transfers, and purchase goods and services. The model is flexible regarding the financing opportunities of each government: as described in the appendix, marginal increases in government spending are financed through taxes or bonds, depending on the specification desired.

6. Costs of investment include both the acquisition costs of the new capital (net of investment tax credits) and adjustment costs incurred in the course of installation.

7. Labor is immobile internationally but perfectly mobile across sectors within a country. Aggregate labor supply of each country grows at a constant exogenous rate.

A fourth distinguishing feature, closely related to the previous three, is the model's symmetric treatment of the domestic economy and the foreign economy (rest of the world). The formal specifications for household, producer, and government behavior are the same in both economies. Thus, foreign consumption decisions (including demands for U.S. exports of consumer goods and financial assets) stem from intertemporal utility maximization, and foreign production decisions (including demands for U.S. exports of intermediate inputs) reflect intertemporal profit maximization. Supply prices of imports to the United States are based on foreign factor costs and production technologies. This is in contrast with the approach often adopted in trade models, in which upward-sloping supply functions are simply posited for the foreign country rather than derived from profit-maximizing production decisions.

The model incorporates considerable detail on U.S. individual and business taxes. Source- and residence-based features of the U.S. tax system are recognized, so that tax obligations depend both on the location of factors and the residence of their owners. This tax detail is important for analyzing effects of government policy on saving and investment decisions, both of which critically influence the dynamics of the current account.

The model is benchmarked to 1983. The benchmark data set distinguishes ten U.S. industries. In this paper, we organize these ten industries into three producing sectors: the exportables sector, which includes the export-oriented industries agriculture, machinery, miscellaneous manufacturing, and services (except housing services); the importables sector, containing the import-competing industries oil refining, textiles, metals, and motor vehicles; and the nontradables sector, consisting of the construction and housing services industries.[8] Table 9.2 compares the three sectors in terms of their orientation toward exports and the extent to which they compete with imports for the domestic market.

9.4 Design of the Policy Experiments

9.4.1 The Revised Baseline

In previous applications of the model, we analyzed the impact of policy initiatives by comparing a steady-state baseline simulation with a revised-case simulation generated in response to the policy initiative. Along the steady-state baseline, all quantities grow at the same rate, and relative prices remain unchanged. Critically for present purposes, the U.S. capital account, current account and trade balance are all zero along the steady-state baseline path. The U.S. net foreign asset position is also zero all along this path.

Clearly, a steady state in which trade is balanced is not an appropriate baseline from which to consider the effects of trade policies designed to reduce the

8. In our benchmark data set, the housing services industry does not engage in international trade. The construction industry exports a very small share of its output and does not import.

Table 9.2   Industry Characteristics (in percentage)

Producing Sector	Export Intensity[a]	Import Substitution[b]
Exportables	7.9	0.9
Importables	4.7	15.1
Nontradables	0.0	0.0

[a]Share of exports in total demand for gross output.
[b]Imports as share of total domestic demand for output of corresponding sector.

trade deficit. In this paper we introduce a revised baseline incorporating external imbalances; policy shocks are then superimposed on this revised baseline.

To produce the revised baseline, we take the following approach. We first calibrate the model to generate steady-state growth.[9] We then introduce changes in parameters or data to generate a revised baseline that includes a growing trade deficit and increasing U.S. indebtedness to foreigners. This revised baseline serves as a reference path for measuring the effects of subsequent policy initiatives. In the absence of further shocks, the economy would continue along the revised baseline path and gradually approach a new steady state. However, in our policy experiments, we introduce an unanticipated import surcharge before the economy has reached its new steady state. Thus the import surcharge is imposed in an economy out of long-run equilibrium that is running trade deficits. We specify the policy shocks as unanticipated; hence producers and households revise their plans on imposition of the policy change. Subsequent to the policy change, economic outcomes differ from those along the projected baseline path. A major methodological innovation in this paper is the integration of an intertemporally optimizing baseline (out of long-run equilibrium) with an intertemporally optimizing path under the policy shock.[10]

In generating a revised baseline, one must incorporate assumptions about the sources of the trade deficits and associated net indebtedness to foreigners. At issue, fundamentally, are the causes of the observed shortfall of domestic personal saving relative to domestic private investment and the observed increase (relative to GNP) in public dissaving. There is no consensus on what caused these developments in the 1980s.[11] A complete analysis would first assess the significance of a range of domestic factors—perhaps including an

9. The calibration procedure is described in Goulder and Eichengreen (1989a).

10. The baseline path reflects behavior that is intertemporally optimizing conditional on the assumption of no future policy changes. Decisions of households and producers are guided by expectations that conform to the future economic outcomes that would obtain if no further policy shocks were introduced. The surprise policy shocks superimposed on the baseline path compel agents to revise their optimal plans. These agents display perfect foresight from the moment of the policy shock.

11. Again, for discussion of the alternatives, see Poole (1990) and Makin (1990).

autonomous decline in household savings propensities, the introduction of liberalized investment incentives (notably, acceleration of depreciation allowances), the growth of federal budget deficits, and the exchange rate effects of monetary policy—as well as behavioral and policy changes emanating from abroad. Considering the effects on the trade deficit of each of these factors and the impact of alternative policies adopted in response would yield a proliferation of simulation results. In this paper, we focus our attention on two of the most often cited explanations for the trade deficits of the 1980s: declining household savings propensities and rising government budget deficits. The U.S. personal saving rate declined more or less steadily from 7.5 percent in 1981 to 3.3 percent in 1989.[12] The U.S. public sector budget (all levels of government) moved from balance in the late 1970s to a deficit of approximately 3.8 percent of GNP in 1989.[13] The decision to concentrate on these factors does not reflect a belief on our part that they were necessarily the principal causes of the trade deficit.[14] Rather, we focus on them because of their prominence in the literature and because they are a logical point of departure given that the channels through which they affect the trade deficit are relatively straightforward.

We consider these two sources of the trade deficit sequentially. Our first experiments employ a baseline generated by a shift in domestic household saving propensities. To create this baseline, we increase domestic households' rate of time preference from its original value of .0048 to a new value of .0078. With higher time preference, domestic households increase current consumption and reduce their saving.[15]

Figure 9.1 displays the path of the U.S. trade balance along this revised baseline path. In contrast with the original steady-state baseline, in which domestic saving matched domestic investment, along the revised baseline domestic saving initially falls short of domestic investment. This precipitates a U.S. trade deficit in the short run. The deficit is financed by capital inflows which, over time, increase the nation's net indebtedness to foreigners.

Figure 9.1 shows that, along the revised baseline path, the deficit switches to surplus after about thirteen years. Surpluses are necessary eventually to service debt to foreigners. This can be seen from the relationship between the trade balance, B, the interest rate, i, and the value of net foreign wealth, Z. In any given period s, the current account, $B_s + i_s Z_s$, determines the accumulation of foreign wealth:

(18) $$Z_{s+1} - Z_s = B_s + i_s Z_s.$$

12. Schultze (1990) documents the fall in the private savings rate over the period.
13. Again, Schultze (1990) discusses these trends.
14. Indeed, subsequent simulation analyses provide reason for skepticism on this score.
15. In section 9.5.3 below, we add government budget deficits to the decline in household savings propensities as a second potential source of trade deficits.

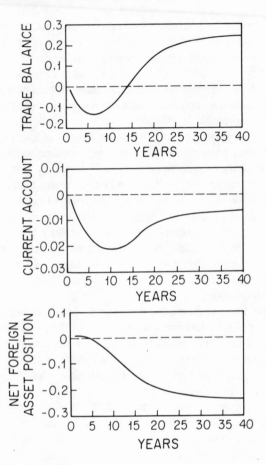

Fig. 9.1   Baseline dynamics
Note: All values are expressed as percentages of baseline GNP.

Solving (18) recursively from period t (the current period) forward under the assumption that Z cannot grow indefinitely at a rate greater than i yields the intertemporal constraint on the accumulation of net foreign wealth:

$$(19) \qquad -Z_t = \sum_{s=t}^{\infty} B_s \prod_{u=t}^{s} \frac{1}{1+i_u}.$$

Equation (19) states that the present value of a nation's current and prospective trade balances must equal its net foreign indebtedness, that is, the negative of its net foreign wealth.

9.4.2   Policy Initiatives

To examine the effects of permanent and temporary import surcharges, we introduce the policy shocks at a point along the revised baseline path. The surcharges considered are across-the-board increases in U.S. tariffs on imported intermediate and consumer goods. In the original data set, tariffs are modeled on an ad valorem basis; the surcharges raise the ad valorem rates by ten percentage points.

We impose the policy shocks in the eighth year of the baseline. The first year of the baseline corresponds to the benchmark year 1983. The policy shocks therefore occur in the period corresponding to 1990. We assume no foreign tariff retaliation at any time. This assumption should be kept in mind when interpreting the effects of these policies on domestic welfare.

In these first experiments, the path of real government expenditure is the same under each policy change as in the baseline.[16] Government revenues are kept in balance with expenditures through lump-sum reductions in personal income taxes that compensate for any revenue effects from the import surcharges.[17] An alternative government financing scheme, which allows us to consider the trade balance effects of budget deficits, is introduced in section 9.5.3 below.

9.5   Simulation Results

9.5.1   Permanent Import Surcharge

Table 9.3 summarizes the aggregate effects of a permanent import surcharge. The surcharge leads to an improvement in the U.S. terms of trade as the nation exploits more fully its monopsony power. (The assumption of no retaliation is crucial here.) The surcharge expands the wedge between the resource cost of imported goods—the world price—and the price to domestic purchasers of imports. Although this has adverse effects on resource allocation, the beneficial terms-of-trade effect more than compensates, and U.S. permanent real income and consumption rise. Correspondingly, U.S. welfare rises, by 0.59 percent.[18] These results indicate that preexisting tariff rates are below optimal tariff levels.[19]

---

16. This facilitates welfare evaluation. Since the contribution to individual utility of government expenditure on public goods is not known, changes in government expenditure on these goods would introduce effects on individual welfare that are not captured in the model's utility calculations. On the assumption that public and private goods are separable in utility, holding government expenditure constant permits a rigorous assessment of welfare effects based on the changes in consumption of private goods.

17. Although the largest revenue effects are experienced by the domestic government, the policy changes also the affect revenues of the foreign government. Lump-sum adjustments to the foreign household's individual income taxes maintain the desired revenue yield for the foreign government.

18. Percentage changes in welfare are the dynamic equivalent variation as a percentage of household wealth in the revised baseline. A welfare change of 0.59 percent therefore means that the policy change raises the household's utility by the same amount as a one-time lump-sum payment equal in value to 0.59 percent of its total (human and financial) wealth.

19. Optimum ad valorem tariffs in our model are about 30 percent.

Table 9.3   Aggregate Effects of Import Surcharges

	Permanent Surcharge —Years after Policy Shock—				Temporary Surcharge —Years after Policy Shock—				
	0 (1990)	4	14	Inf.	0 (1990)	4	5 (Removal)	14	Inf.
Average import price (net of tariff)[a]	−3.778	−3.987	−4.114	−4.093	−3.400	−3.411	−0.578	−0.122	0.000
Terms of trade[b]	3.696	4.035	4.232	4.246	3.436	3.459	0.568	0.165	0.000
Real consumption rate of interest									
Domestic	0.067	0.029	−0.017	0.000	0.026	−0.264	0.735	−0.061	0.000
Foreign	−0.064	−0.061	−0.053	0.000	−0.050	−0.184	0.111	−0.030	0.000
U.S. economy									
Consumption	0.156	0.338	0.638	0.720	−0.062	0.003	0.340	0.222	0.000
Investment[c]	0.357	0.486	0.680	0.480	0.414	0.492	0.553	0.647	0.000
Personal saving	1.811	1.368	0.809	0.661	3.772	4.359	−4.820	0.303	0.000
Household wealth	1.099	1.341	1.681	0.663	0.517	0.593	1.106	0.952	0.000
Foreign economy									
Consumption	−0.269	−0.320	−0.343	−0.466	−0.212	−0.202	−0.198	−0.050	0.000
Investment[c]	0.198	0.201	0.297	−0.421	0.241	0.300	0.271	0.270	0.000
Personal saving	−0.271	−0.028	0.294	−0.634	−0.798	−1.258	0.513	0.461	0.000
Household wealth	0.115	0.066	0.076	−0.468	0.170	0.176	0.181	0.440	0.000

Value of imports (net of tariff)	-10.94	-10.80	-10.57	-10.56	-11.09	-11.04	0.45	0.29	0.00
Value of exports	-10.20	-10.53	-11.11	-11.30	-9.15	-9.15	-1.54	-0.33	0.00
Balance of payments									
Trade balance	0.067	0.011	-0.010	-0.080	0.224	0.212	-0.228	-0.072	0.000
Net interest income	0.018	0.024	0.014	0.124	0.049	0.123	0.242	0.028	0.000
Capital account	-0.073	-0.035	-0.004	-0.040	-0.271	-0.334	-0.015	0.044	0.000
Net foreign asset position	0.237	0.303	0.154	1.310	0.265	0.454	0.323	0.031	0.000
Welfare[d]									
Domestic households		0.587				0.521			
Foreign households		-0.294				-0.246			

Notes: All figures express percentage changes from the baseline path, except for those corresponding to consumption rates of interest (which are in changes from the baseline, in basis points) and balance of payments accounts (which are in changes from the baseline path, divided by baseline GNP).

[a]Weighted-average dollar price of imports divided by U.S. producer price index. Weights are baseline import shares.

[b]Computed as the export-weighted index of domestic prices divided by the import-weighted index of net-of-tariff foreign prices.

[c]Financed in part by retained earnings.

[d]Welfare gain is the dynamic equivalent variation as a percentage of baseline wealth. The dynamic equivalent variation is the level of compensation which, if provided as a lump sum to a household facing baseline prices and policies, would enable the household to enjoy the same level of intertemporal utility as is enjoyed under the policy change. Hence a positive equivalent variation implies that the policy change is welfare-improving. The welfare measure is dynamic in that the uility levels which underlie it reflect consumption during the transition as well as in the study state.

Significant changes occur over time. Following the introduction of the surcharge, the beneficial terms of trade effects grow as the U.S. shifts additional capital and labor into the importables sector. World import prices fall over time, but because of the surcharge, prices to domestic purchasers of imports remain above the levels for corresponding years in the baseline scenario.[20] Consistent with the continued improvement in the terms of trade, U.S. wealth and consumption increase over time (relative to the baseline path), while foreign wealth and consumption decline.

U.S. investment also rises following the imposition of the surcharge. The terms of trade improvement increases the profitability of domestic production (for most industries), thereby raising the shadow value of new capital (tax-adjusted q) and encouraging a higher rate of investment. Domestic saving also increases, reflecting the higher incomes made possible by the terms-of-trade improvement.

The policy change causes the domestic household's consumption rate of interest (and other domestic interest rates) to rise relative to corresponding foreign rates. Higher relative rates are necessary to induce portfolio investors to hold the stock of U.S.-located financial wealth, which increases in value considerably relative to foreign-located financial wealth.[21] The higher rates reinforce the positive effect of higher domestic incomes on domestic saving. As a result, the increase in domestic saving exceeds the increase in domestic investment initially.[22] Thus, in the short run, imports of foreign capital decline, net borrowing falls, and the trade balance improves. This is shown in figure 9.2a, where the solid curve is the trade balance path under the surcharge and the dashed curve is the path under the baseline. (The two curves coincide

---

20. The time profile of the terms of trade depends on supply as well as demand considerations. With different parameters (more elastic investment responses, for example), the terms of trade could worsen, rather than improve, over time. This is the case because the surcharge raises U.S. investment relative to investment by foreign producers and ultimately lowers the foreign capital stock relative to the U.S. stock of capital. This exerts a negative influence on the U.S. terms of trade by reducing the supply of foreign goods relative to U.S. goods. In our simulations, however, this supply-side effect is more than offset by demand-side effects.

21. The revaluation of U.S. assets reflects the increased profitability of producing in the United States as a result of the improvement in the terms of trade. As mentioned in sec. 9.3, the model treats domestic and foreign assets as imperfect substitutes in portfolios. The significant increase in U.S. asset prices occasioned by the permanent surcharge causes the shares of U.S. assets in portfolios to rise. Without adjustment in relative rates of return, domestic and foreign households would not wish to maintain such shares; they would wish to hold less than the total value of U.S.-located assets and more than the total value of foreign-located assets. The required increase in U.S. rates relative to foreign rates is inversely related to the degree of substitutability between U.S. and foreign assets in portfolios.

The reduction in foreign interest rates occasioned by these asset valuation effects explains why the surcharge induces an increase in foreign investment, despite the adverse effects on foreign income and wealth.

22. If costs of adjusting the capital stock were reduced or the intertemporal elasticity of substitution in consumption was raised, the short-run investment response would rise relative to saving, attenuating and conceivably reversing the improvement in the trade balance. See sec. 9.5.5 below.

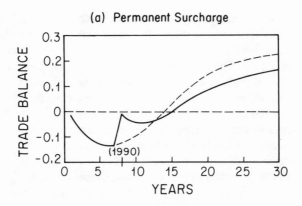

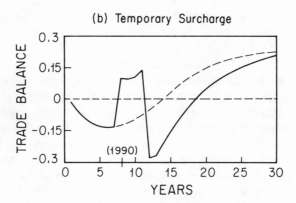

Fig. 9.2 Effects of import surcharges on the trade balance
Note: Trade balance as percentage of baseline GNP.

in the first seven years, since the policy shock, introduced in year 8, is unanticipated.)

Subsequent changes in the trade balance depend on how the surcharge affects the U.S. net foreign asset position. Equation (19) indicates that the change in the present value of prospective trade balances must equal the change in the nation's net foreign indebtedness. Table 9.3 shows that the policy improves slightly the U.S. net foreign asset position on implementation.[23]

23. The U.S. net foreign asset position is the difference in the value of U.S.-owned nonhuman wealth located abroad and foreign-owned nonhuman wealth in the U.S. One might expect the surcharge to raise the value of foreign-owned (as well as domestically owned) nonhuman wealth in the United States and thus to *worsen* the net foreign asset position. However, this does not occur, mainly because of portfolio responses. By reducing U.S. demands for foreign imports, the surcharge strengthens the dollar. This increases the value in foreign currency of foreigners' holdings of U.S. assets. Foreigners prefer not to devote such a large share of their portfolios to U.S. assets and consequently they reduce their holdings of U.S. assets. The reduced holdings of U.S.

Thus, while the surcharge may improve the trade balance initially, these smaller short-run deficits must at least be matched (in present value) by larger long-run deficits (smaller long-run surpluses). The results in figure 9.2 confirm this requirement. The figure shows that the direction of the influence of the surcharge on the trade balance is reversed starting about five years after the policy is introduced, when the trade balance falls below the baseline path.

In light of the budget constraints implicitly faced by each nation, it should not be surprising that the surcharge fails to generate a permanent improvement in the trade balance. The only way policies can permanently improve the trade balance (in the sense of raising the present value of the stream of future trade balances) is to induce an immediate worsening of the current net foreign asset position. When the net foreign asset position falls, higher net exports are required to service indebtedness to foreigners. However, increases in foreign indebtedness, *ceteris paribus,* imply reduced national wealth and welfare. This illustrates the illegitimacy of using changes in the trade balance as indicators of national well-being. In the policy examined here, the welfare gains generated by the surcharge are attributable to an expanded use of monopsony power, not to changes in the trade balance per se.

Our findings that a permanent import surcharge raises domestic welfare and improves the trade balance in the short run parallel the results obtained by Iishi, McKibbin, and Sachs (1985) in the only other intertemporal empirical study of an import surcharge of which we are aware. The model used in their analysis divides the world into five regions but does not contain the sector disaggregation of our model. They consider a 30 percent U.S. tariff on imports from Japan (but not on imports from the rest of the world), finding that the U.S. trade balance improves by (1984) $3.8 billion in the first year, consistent with our results. Other studies of import surcharges have employed static models. In such studies, it is difficult to ascertain the aggregate trade balance effects, since important connections between import surcharges, saving and investment decisions, and the capital account are left out.[24]

9.5.2   Temporary Import Surcharge

In our second experiment, we introduce a temporary 10 percent surcharge. The surcharge is imposed in the eighth period (1990) and removed five peri-

---

assets improve the U.S. net asset position. Despite these responses, the share of the foreigner's portfolio represented by U.S. assets, when expressed in foreign (or any common) currency, is higher after the policy change (in keeping with the increase in U.S. interest rates relative to foreign rates). These results depend on assumptions about the responsiveness of desired portfolio shares to changes in relative rates of return. Alternative assumptions are considered in sec. 9.5.5 below.

24. Many static models assume flexible exchange rates and a capital account balance of zero. Although such models may provide insight into the sectoral effects of import surcharges, they cannot capture aggregate trade balance effects, since the assumptions guarantee a zero trade balance at all times.

Deardoff, Stern, and Abraham (1987) employ a highly disaggregated static general equilibrium ods later (1995). We model the surcharge as unanticipated; upon implementation, however, households are fully aware of the temporary nature of the policy and plan accordingly.

The analytical model of section 9.2 yielded ambiguous results for the effects of a temporary tariff on the trade balance. In that model, the temporary surcharge gives rise to two additional effects beyond those produced by a permanent surcharge: it increases the cost of current imports relative to future imports, shifting expenditure toward the future; at the same time it depresses world interest rates (a consequence of reduced current expenditure), which reduces debt service costs and encourages absorption. Results from the simulation model (fig. 9.2b) indicate that the first effect dominates, since the impact of the temporary surcharge on the trade balance is positive and larger than the impact of its permanent counterpart. Figure 9.2b reveals that, in the short term, the temporary surcharge produces much larger positive effects on the trade balance than does the permanent surcharge. This is an indication that the expenditure effect is substantial, a result that is evidenced by the pronounced decline in domestic consumption following the introduction of the temporary surcharge (table 9.3).

Other aggregate effects are displayed in the right-hand set of columns of table 9.3. The U.S. terms of trade improve with implementation of the surcharge. With its removal, the improvement in the terms of trade nearly vanishes as import prices move back toward baseline levels. However, because of costs of adjustment, the reduced import dependency attained during the imposition of the temporary tariff lingers after its removal. Because of adjustment costs, the capital stock is only gradually redeployed to the exportables sector, and import demands return gradually to baseline levels (for corresponding years). Hence import prices and the terms of trade return to baseline levels only asymptotically.

In table 9.3, the personal saving figures for the period when the temporary surcharge is removed are dramatically different from the figures for prior periods. Savings rates of both domestic and foreign households jump discretely when the surcharge is lifted. These swings in savings rates are necessary to maintain smooth paths of consumption despite the abrupt changes in incomes (reductions for U.S. households, increases for foreign households) that come about at the moment the surcharge is removed.

---

model to investigate the effects of a 20 percent import surcharge. In their model, the capital account balance is usually exogenous. However, in one experiment they fix the exchange rate and assume that the capital account adjusts to bring about balance-of-payments equilibrium. In this simulation the surcharge improves the trade balance and reduces the capital account balance; the magnitude of these effects is not reported.

Rousslang and Suomela (1985) apply a static partial equilibrium model to examine the consequences of a 20 percent import surcharge. To allow for effects on the capital account balance, the authors assume that each dollar of revenue from the surcharge reduces capital inflows and the trade deficit by 40 cents. This investigation indicates that an import surcharge introduced in 1985 would improve the trade balance by $22 billion, or about 0.5 percent of 1985 GNP.

All quantities ultimately approach the baseline levels after the temporary surcharge is withdrawn. Domestic consumption and wealth, in particular, fall back to baseline levels as the United States relinquishes monopsony power gains. U.S. households enjoy smaller welfare gains under the temporary surcharge. This reflects the relatively limited exercise of monopsony power under this policy as well as the intertemporal distortions initiated by the temporary tariff.

For many variables, the return to baseline levels is gradual, however. In the first ten years after the surcharge's removal, the trade balance is considerably weaker than in corresponding periods for the baseline. So long as the temporary surcharge was in effect, it switched expenditure away from imports and shifted the trade balance from deficit to surplus. This moderated the accumulation of foreign debt, reducing the trade surpluses that are required subsequently to service debt to foreigners. Since the need to run trade surpluses to service foreign debt is attenuated, the date at which deficits finally give way to surpluses is considerably delayed.

The policy implication is that a temporary import surcharge, even if it succeeds in reducing the trade deficit in the short run, may have important, and, from the perspective of policymakers, undesirable longer-run effects. In our simulations, the imposition of a temporary import surcharge causes an even larger trade deficit to emerge following the policy's removal. Interposition of the surcharge delays quite significantly the date at which trade deficits are finally eliminated.

9.5.3   Significance of Initial Conditions

Baseline with Historical Public Sector Dissaving

To gauge the robustness of these results, we perform additional experiments, altering either baseline conditions or the timing of the policy shock. We first consider an alternative baseline that incorporates not only the shift in household saving behavior of the previous baseline but also historical changes in public sector saving.

In the baseline considered previously, levels of real government purchases, government transfers, and inframarginal tax collections all increased exogenously at the steady-state rate given by the growth of the labor force. In this alternative baseline, in the first six periods (corresponding to the interval 1983–88) we set government purchases and transfers at levels corresponding to their recent historical values.[25] In these same periods we adjust inframarginal taxes so that total tax revenues correspond to recent experience.

The government budget constraint requires us to specify future financing

---

25. We impose levels that yield ratios of spending to GNP and transfers to GNP that match recent historical ratios. This adjusts for minor differences between levels of GNP in the model and the real world.

rules as well as the historical tax and spending levels. We assume that purchases and transfers as percentages of GNP remain at the same levels as in the
last year for which we have data, namely, 1989. Inframarginal taxes then adjust gradually to return the government debt–capital ratio to the benchmark
ratio in the new steady state.

While this alternative baseline accounts for changes in government saving,
it does not purport to capture the details of fiscal policy changes. Although we
adjust overall government expenditure, we make no changes to government
expenditure shares and thus do not capture historical changes in the composition of government spending across commodities. Similarly, we introduce
changes in overall tax revenues through changes in inframarginal taxes: we do
not endeavor to replicate the numerous specific changes in particular tax rates
that took place in the 1980s.

In figure 9.3a, the dashed curve traces the new baseline path. Combining
the rise in households' time preference with the rise in government budget

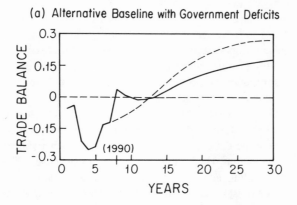

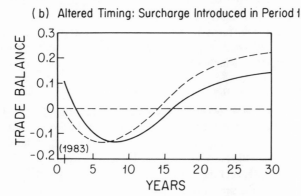

Fig. 9.3   Effects of permanent surcharge on trade balance
Note: Trade balance as percentage of baseline GNP.

deficits nearly doubles the magnitude of the trade deficit. The duration of the baseline trade deficit is essentially unchanged: along the new baseline path the trade deficit converts to surplus in the thirteenth period (1995).

The solid curve in the figure indicates the path generated by the introduction of a permanent import surcharge. As before, the surcharge is imposed in the eighth period (1990).

Although the addition of government budget deficits nearly doubles the magnitude of the trade deficits that emerge in the first few years following the shock, the swing from trade balance to a deficit of 0.25 percent of GNP is only about 15 percent of the swing observed in the data. The implication is that other factors (such as investment-promoting changes in tax policy, as analyzed in Goulder and Eichengreen (1989a), the effects on the exchange rate and international competitiveness of disinflationary U.S. monetary policies at the beginning of the 1980s, complementary changes in monetary and fiscal policies abroad) were responsible for the largest part of the trade deficits of the 1980s.

The effects of the permanent import surcharge on the trade balance are broadly similar to those under the previous baseline. The similarities extend to other variables, as indicated by the results in table 9.4. But where previously the permanent import surcharge reduced the magnitude of the trade deficit on impact without eliminating it entirely, now the trade balance swings from deficit to surplus when the surcharge is imposed. In addition, when the decline in domestic savings propensities was the sole source of the deficit, a permanent surcharge considerably delayed the date at which deficits ultimately give way to surpluses; now, when increased government spending also contributes to the trade deficit, the imposition of the surcharge does not significantly shift the date at which deficits give way to surpluses. The changes in government spending and, consequently, their trade-balance effects are front-loaded; hence most of the additional foreign debt is already accumulated by the date at which the surcharge is imposed. The date of the switch from trade deficit to surplus is largely regulated by the amount of foreign debt that must be serviced; since most of this debt has already accumulated by the time the surcharge is imposed, the switch from trade deficit to surplus occurs at roughly the same time whether or not the surcharge is applied.

Altered Timing of the Permanent Surcharge

We also perform an experiment that employs the original revised baseline but introduces the permanent surcharge earlier—in the first period. This experiment helps reveal the significance of initial conditions at the time of the policy shock. Along the baseline path, the United States runs a capital account surplus. Hence, the earlier the introduction of the surcharge, the lower is U.S. net indebtedness at the time it is imposed.

Figure 9.3b indicates that in this scenario the surcharge generates a similar pattern for the trade balance but initiates it earlier in time. Since the earlier

Table 9.4   Effects under Alternative Baseline and Timing Assumptions (percentage changes from corresponding baseline)

	Initial Baseline—Shock in Period 8 —Years after Policy Shock—			Baseline with Govt. Deficits—Shock in Period 8 —Years after Policy Shock—			Initial Baseline—Shock in Period 1 —Years after Policy Shock—		
	0	4	Inf.	0	4	Inf.	0	4	Inf.
Terms of trade	3.696	4.035	4.246	3.717	3.970	4.248	3.711	4.003	4.246
U.S. economy									
Consumption	0.156	0.338	0.720	0.125	0.298	0.720	0.260	0.366	0.720
Investment	0.357	0.486	0.480	0.346	0.518	0.479	0.013	0.120	0.480
Household wealth	1.099	1.341	0.663	0.785	1.018	0.663	0.391	0.533	0.663
Balance of payments									
Trade balance	0.067	0.011	-0.085	0.133	0.047	-0.085	0.115	0.048	-0.086
Net interest income	0.018	0.024	0.124	0.042	0.078	0.125	0.026	0.058	0.125
Capital account	-0.073	-0.035	-0.040	-0.175	-0.118	-0.040	-0.142	-0.107	-0.040
Net foreign asset position	0.237	0.303	1.310	0.254	0.327	1.311	0.450	0.546	1.310
Domestic welfare			0.587			0.602			0.612

imposition of the surcharge reduces the magnitude of the trade deficits in the first few periods, it slows the accumulation of foreign debt and moderates the trade surpluses required in the long run to finance debt service. For these same reasons it delays the date at which deficits give way permanently to surpluses. Thus, earlier surcharges reduce short-run trade deficits but delay their elimination. Table 9.4 shows that the effects on many other variables of the period 1 surcharge are broadly similar to the effects when the surcharge is introduced in period 8. The improvement in welfare is larger when the surcharge is introduced earlier. In part this reflects the differences in net foreign indebtedness when the shock is initiated. The earlier the introduction of the surcharge, the larger the fraction of U.S.-located capital that is owned by domestic residents. Hence these residents capture a larger share of the gains associated with positive terms-of-trade effects and related increases in the equity values of U.S. firms.

9.5.4   Industry Effects

Table 9.5 contrasts the effects of the surcharges on the exportables, importables, and nontradables sectors. The trade protection afforded by the surcharge raises profits to import-competing industries, stimulating higher investment and increased output. Nontradable-goods industries also benefit,

Table 9.5   **Intersectoral Effects**
(percentage changes from initial baseline path)

Sector	Permanent Surcharge —Years after Policy Shock—			Temporary Surcharge —Years after Policy Shock—		
	0	5	Inf.	0	5	Inf.
					(Removal)	
Exportables						
Gross output	−0.216	−0.210	−0.253	−0.234	0.039	0.000
Profits after tax	−0.934	−0.725	−0.571	−0.825	0.661	0.000
Gross investment	−0.155	−0.028	−0.330	0.266	0.556	0.000
Importables						
Gross output	1.366	1.347	1.374	1.466	−0.098	0.000
Profits after tax	1.756	1.528	1.076	2.001	−0.039	0.000
Gross investment	1.399	1.509	1.238	0.951	0.612	0.000
Nontradables						
Gross output	0.024	0.211	0.723	0.069	0.215	0.000
Profits after tax	0.983	1.263	0.843	0.728	1.357	0.000
Gross investment	0.604	0.822	1.100	0.453	0.538	0.000
Total domestic						
Gross output	0.070	0.103	0.163	0.081	0.047	0.000
Profits after tax	0.242	0.442	0.264	0.191	0.922	0.000
Gross investment	0.334	0.503	0.480	0.411	0.550	0.000

since the improvement in the terms of trade increases domestic incomes and stimulates the demand at home for nontraded as well as traded goods. Expectations of higher incomes and output encourage investment by nontradables industries. The exportables sector does not benefit, since the changes in the terms of trade discourage purchases of U.S. exportable goods.

In the case of the permanent surcharge, the effects are surprisingly uniform over time. This is in contrast to the very uneven pattern of the trade balance. It is consistent, however, with the flat profile of the terms of trade following the policy shock.

Note that the short-run impact on the output of nontraded goods is not a simple increasing function of the duration of the import surcharge. When the import surcharge is known to be temporary, production of nontradables rises by more in the first period following the surcharge—this despite the fact that domestic real incomes rise by more when the surcharge is permanent. Output rises by less initially when the import surcharge is permanent because more of the resources of this sector are devoted to building up the permanent productive capacity of industries producing nontraded goods. (The short-run investment response is 33 percent larger.) When the surcharge is temporary, a greater proportion of the resources of the nontradables sector are devoted to current production rather than investment in future capacity.

9.5.5   Sensitivity Analysis

Table 9.6 summarizes the results under alternative parameter assumptions. The table shows the effects of a permanent surcharge introduced in the eighth period (1990). The baseline employed here is the first revised baseline (incorporating a shift in private savings propensities but not historical public dissaving).

The Armington elasticities are elasticities of substitution between domestic and foreign goods in U.S. production and consumption. Larger Armington elasticities (more price elastic demands) in the United States imply larger terms-of-trade effects and more substantial increases in the real incomes and wealth of domestic residents. This implies larger domestic welfare gains and larger effects on the trade balance. Welfare gains are approximately 40 percent larger when Armington elasticities are doubled than in the central case.

Higher adjustment costs slow the (positive) investment response to the increase in domestic wealth and profitability generated by the surcharge. Hence they make for a longer transition to the steady state. The slower investment response leads to lower domestic absorption in the short run under the high adjustment-cost scenario. The rise in investment is smaller relative to the rise in saving; hence the improvement in the trade balance is greater.

The portfolio substitution elasticity ξ regulates the extent to which households adjust the shares of their portfolios devoted to domestic and foreign assets in response to rate of return differentials. The central case value of ξ is

Table 9.6   Sensitivity Analysis

	Terms of Trade		Trade Balance		U.S. Consumption		U.S. Investment		U.S. Household Welfare	Foreign Household Welfare
	SR	LR	SR	LR	SR	LR	SR	LR		
Central case	3.696	4.246	0.067	−0.080	0.156	0.720	0.357	0.480	0.587	−0.294
Armington elasticities										
U.S. values halved	2.212	4.231	0.066	−0.052	0.008	0.418	0.291	0.161	0.377	−0.161
U.S. values doubled	4.022	4.258	0.494	−0.110	0.104	1.047	0.747	0.822	0.821	−0.393
Adjustment costs										
U.S. values halved	3.594	2.773	0.056	−0.074	0.124	0.696	0.363	0.457	0.589	−0.309
U.S. values doubled	3.601	5.898	0.099	−0.085	0.059	0.741	0.337	0.497	0.581	−0.270
Portfolio substitution										
ξ = 0.5	3.672	4.269	0.135	−0.079	0.144	0.722	0.234	0.482	0.591	−0.296
ξ = 2.0	3.896	4.187	0.026	−0.084	0.193	0.716	0.441	0.473	0.547	−0.275

Notes: All figures express percentage changes from the first revised baseline except for trade balance figures, which are changes as a percentage of baseline GNP. "SR" and "LR" refer to effects in the year of the policy change and in the new steady state. The low and high adjustment cost simulations halve and double the parameter β of the adjustment cost function $\theta(I/K) = [(\beta/2)(I/K - \gamma)^2](I/K)^{-1}$ with compensating changes in γ that leave the value of θ unchanged at the benchmark value for I/K. Central case values for β and γ are 19.607 and 0.076. The central case value for the portfolio substitution elasticity ξ is 1.0 for both domestic and foreign households.

unity for both domestic and foreign households. As discussed in section 9.5.1 and 9.5.2, the import surcharge raises the market value of U.S.-located capital. With a higher value for ξ, the U.S. rate of return does not have to rise as much in the short run to induce households to hold the higher-valued U.S. assets. For this reason, domestic consumption and investment increase by more in the short run than in the central case, and the short-run improvement in the trade balance is smaller. Trade balance effects are fairly sensitive to values of this parameter.

9.6 Conclusions

In this paper we have considered the impact of permanent and temporary import surcharges on the magnitude and time profile of the U.S. trade deficit. To do this we have employed analytical and numerical models which highlight opportunities for intertemporal as well as intersectoral substitution and which trace their implications for the trade balance and other economic variables.

Our simulation experiments indicate that both temporary and permanent import surcharges improve the trade balance in the short run. While static analyses have suggested positive trade balance effects from import surcharges (because of the familiar expenditure-switching effect), our dynamic analysis reveals a number of other, less easily anticipated consequences. For example, a temporary surcharge has a larger short-run impact on the trade balance, but a permanent one has a larger impact on welfare. This points up the danger of drawing inferences about the desirability of alternative policies from the behavior of a few highly visible magnitudes (such as the trade balance) that are linked only indirectly to the ultimate determinants of welfare.

The alternative policies also have very different effects across sectors. Import surcharges naturally benefit domestic import-competing industries. But improvements in the terms of trade lead to higher real incomes and also indirectly stimulate activity in the nontradables sector. The stimulus to the production of nontradables is not, however, a simple increasing function of the duration of the surcharge.

While both policies reduce the trade deficit initially, both produce larger deficits (smaller surpluses) in the longer term. The magnitude of the trade balance effects is fairly sensitive to assumptions about household portfolio behavior. Welfare effects are sensitive to the timing of the policy initiative and the extent of U.S. indebtedness at the time import surcharges are introduced. Under certain assumptions about the source of the deficit, both policies delay the date by which the initial deficits are finally eliminated.

These differing short- and long-run effects underscore the usefulness of analyzing the trade balance effects of commercial policies with a dynamic framework that incorporates intertemporal balance of payments constraints.

Appendix
Modeling of Government Expenditure and Finance

In each period t, the government must satisfy the cash-flow equation

(A1) $$G_t + r_t b_t = T_t + b_{t+1} - b_t,$$

where b_t is the stock of debt outstanding at the beginning of period t, G_t is the value of government expenditure (purchases of goods and services plus transfers) in period t, r_t is the gross rate of interest paid on government debt in period t, and T_t is tax revenue in period t.

Applying (A1) recursively from time periods 1 to T yields

(A2) $$b_{T+1} [\Pi_{s=1}^{T}(1 + r_s)]^{-1} = b_1 + \sum_{t=1}^{T} [\Pi_{s=1}^{T}(1 + r_s)]^{-1}(G_t - T_t).$$

If debt cannot indefinitely increase at a rate greater than the interest rate, then

(A3) $$\lim_{t \to \infty} b_{t+1}[\Pi_{s=1}^{t}(1 + r_s)]^{-1} = 0.$$

Applying (A3) to (A2) yields

(A4) $$b_1 = \sum_{t=1}^{\infty}[\Pi_{s=1}^{t}(1 + r_s)]^{-1}(T_t - G_t).$$

Equation (A4) is the government's intertemporal budget constraint. It states that the present value of future tax revenues must exceed the present value of government expenditure (net of interest payments) by an amount equal to the level of government debt outstanding at the beginning of the current period.

The Base Case Path

The model exhibits steady-state growth along the equilibrium path of the base case, or original baseline. Thus r is constant, and G, T, and b all grow at the steady-state nominal growth rate, n. The rate n is equal to $(1 + g)(1 + \pi_0) - 1$, where g is the exogenous growth rate of effective labor services and π_0 is the exogenous growth rate of nominal wages (equal to the inflation rate in the steady state). The deficit, $G_t + r_t b_t - T_t$ (or $b_{t+1} - b_t$), also grows at the rate n, and the deficit-GNP ratio remains constant.

Specifications for Alternative Baseline or for Policy Changes

In simulating a new baseline or a policy change, it is necessary to specify certain terminal conditions as well as the marginal source of government revenue during the transition.

Steady-State Requirements

In the model, agents face infinite horizons. Yet it is only possible to perform actual simulations over a finite number of periods. To be able to account for the performance of the economy after the last simulation period, the economy must achieve some regularity—steady-state growth—by the final simulation period. In particular, b, T, and G must ultimately grow at the steady-state nominal growth rate, n, although they may temporarily grow at other rates during the transition. Rewriting equation (A1) under steady-state conditions yields

(A5) $$\tilde{T} - \tilde{G} = (r_{ss} - n)\tilde{b},$$

where $\tilde{T}$, $\tilde{G}$, and $\tilde{b}$ denote tax revenues, government expenditure, and debt relative to GNP, and r_{ss} is the steady-state rate of interest on government debt. Equation (A5) shows that alternative debt-GNP ratios are consistent with steady-state growth; for a given r_{ss}, a higher $\tilde{b}$ in the steady state requires that $\tilde{T}$ exceed $\tilde{G}$ by a greater amount.

In simulating the effects of parameter or policy changes, we specify a long-run value for $\tilde{b}$; in most cases we select the benchmark debt-GNP ratio.

Debt and Taxes during the Transition

In all simulations, real government expenditure is exogenous, as discussed below. The particular way the government's cash-flow constraint (eq. [A1]) is satisfied during the transition depends on the specification for the marginal source of government revenue.

Marginal Finance with Taxes

This is the specification employed in all simulations in the paper except for those in the historical deficits experiment in section 9.5.3. With marginal financing through taxes, the path of b is exogenous: in each year, b is set at the level that maintains $\tilde{b}$ at the benchmark debt-GNP ratio. The government's cash-flow constraint is satisfied through adjustments in taxes. The model allows the necessary tax revenues to be obtained either through lump-sum adjustments in personal taxes or through changes in marginal income tax rates. In this paper, only lump-sum tax adjustments were employed.

Marginal Finance with Debt Issue

An alternative specification employs new debt issue as the marginal source of government revenue during a specified finite interval, $[t_a,t_b]$, with $t_a \geq 1$ and $t_b < t_n$, where t_n is the last period for which simulations are actually carried out.[26] During the interval $[t_a,t_b]$, there are no revenue-maintaining tax adjustments. Instead, b adjusts in each period to ensure that the cash-flow equation is satisfied. Hence the debt-GNP ratio can depart from the benchmark value and from whatever value is imposed for the steady state.[27] How-

26. We generally employ $t_n = 75$. Under usual parameters the economy is very close to the new steady state by the 75th period.

27. This specification applied in the revised baseline described in section 9.5.3, where the exogenously imposed historical values for taxes and government spending give rise to debt-GNP ratios above the benchmark value.

ever, it is ultimately necessary that the debt-GNP ratio approach the specified steady-state value. Hence, subsequent to period t_b, the debt-GNP ratio $\bar{b}$ is exogenous. Taxes then become the marginal source of revenue and adjust in each period to assure that the government satisfies equation (A1). During the interval $[t_b, t_n]$, we require that $\bar{b}$ approach its specified long-run value in a smooth fashion, according to the relationship

(A6) $$\bar{b}_t = \bar{b}_{ss} + (\bar{b}_{ta} - \bar{b}_{ss})(1 + v)^{ta-t},$$

where v is a positive constant chosen such that equation (A6) yields $\bar{b}_t = \bar{b}_{ss}$ for $t = t_n$.

The Components of G

Government expenditure, G, divides into nominal purchases of nondurable goods and services (GP), nominal government investment (GI), and nominal transfers (GT):

(A7) $$G_t = GP_t + GI_t + GT_t$$

Baseline Values

In the base case (original baseline) and in the first revised baseline, the paths of *real* government purchases and transfers grow at the steady-state real growth rate, g.

In the baseline discussed in section 9.5.3, values for GP and GT for the first eight periods are based on historical values for 1983–89; for subsequent periods, the values of GP and GT are set so that their ratios to GNP gradually converge to the benchmark ratios by the 25th period.

In all baseline simulations, the path of *real* GI grows at the steady-state real growth rate, g.[28]

Values under Policy Changes

In simulating policy changes we fix the paths of GP, GI, and GT so that *real* government purchases, investment, and transfers are the same as in corresponding years of the baseline scenario.[29] This procedure is expressed by

(A8a) $$\frac{GP_t^R}{p_{GP,t}^R} = \frac{GP_t^B}{p_{GP,t}^B} = \qquad t = 1, t_n,$$

(A8b) $$\frac{GI_t^R}{p_{GI,t}^R} = \frac{GI_t^B}{p_{GI,t}^B} = \qquad t = 1, t_n,$$

28. Thus, in contrast with investment by private firms, government investment does not stem from optimizing considerations.
29. Maintaining the same real government purchases between the baseline and policy change simulations facilitates welfare assessments. Since the contribution to individual utility of changes in real government purchases is difficult to establish, welfare evaluations would be problematic if policy changes involved changes in government purchases.

(A8c) $$\frac{GT_t^R}{p_{GT,t}^R} = \frac{GT_t^B}{p_{GT,t}^B} = \qquad t = 1, t_n,$$

The superscripts R and B denote revised case (policy change) and baseline magnitudes, while P_{GP}, P_{GI}, and P_{GT} are price indices for GP, GI, and GT. The price index for government investment, P_{GI}, is the purchase price of the representative capital good. The price index for transfers, P_{GT}, is the consumer price index. The index for government purchases, P_{GP}, is defined below.

Elements of GP

GP divides into purchases of particular outputs of the ns domestic sectors according to fixed expenditure shares:

(A9) $$\alpha_i GP = GPX_i p_i \qquad i = 1, ns.$$

GPX_i and p_i are the quantity demanded and price of output from domestic sector i, and α_i is the corresponding expenditure share. In this paper, $ns = 3$. The ideal price index for government purchases, p_{GP}, is given by

(A10) $$p_{GP} = \Pi_{i=1}^{ns} p_i^{\alpha_i}.$$

Benchmark Values

Table 9A.1 provides benchmark values for the components of government expenditure and revenue. Calibrating the model requires that the benchmark equilibrium result from optimizing behavior and lie on a steady-state growth path. These requirements force some adjustments to actual historical (1983) values; hence it is not possible to generate a benchmark that perfectly coincides with history. However, we consider the benchmark values to be a reasonably close approximation to the actual 1983 figures.

Table 9A.1   Benchmark Values for Government Expenditure and Revenue

	Level	% of Benchmark GNP
Expenditure	910.43	30.5
G		
GP	455.48	15.3
GI	160.36	5.3
GT	294.59	9.9
rb_t	84.28	2.8
Total	994.71	33.4
Revenue		
T	915.50	30.7
$b_{t+1} - b_t$	79.21	2.7
Total	994.71	33.4
Debt, interest rate		
r	.0977	
b_t	862.63	28.9

References

Branson, William, and Joan Pearce. 1985. The Case for an Import Surcharge. Manuscript.

Brown, Drusilla. 1987. Tariffs, the Terms of Trade and National Product Differentiation. *Journal of Policy Modeling* 9:503–26.

Deardorff, Alan, Robert Stern, and Filip Abraham. 1987. The Effects of an Import Surcharge on the U.S. Economy. *Journal of Policy Modeling* 9:285–310.

Gardner, Grant W., and Kent P. Kimbrough. 1989. Tariffs, Interest Rates, and the Trade Balance in the World Economy. *Journal of International Economics* 27:91–110.

Goulder, Lawrence, and Barry Eichengreen. 1989a. Savings Promotion, Investment Promotion and International Competitiveness. In *Trade Policies for International Competitiveness,* ed. Robert C. Feenstra. Chicago: University of Chicago Press.

———. 1989b. Trade Liberalization in General Equilibrium: Intertemporal and Inter-Industry Effects. NBER Working Paper no. 2965.

Iishi, Naoko, Warwick McKibbin, and Jeffrey Sachs. 1985. The Economic Policy Mix, Policy Cooperation, and Protectionism: Some Aspects of Macroeconomic Interdependence among the United States, Japan, and Other Industrial Countries. *Journal of Policy Modeling,* 7:533–72.

Kaempfer, William H., and Thomas D. Willett. 1987. An Import Surcharge Wouldn't Help America's Trade Deficit. *The World Economy* (March): 27–37.

Makin, John. 1990. The Impact of Fiscal Policy on the Balance of Payments: Recent Experience in the United States. In *Fiscal Policy, Economic Adjustment and Financial Markets,* ed. Mario Monti. Washington D.C.: IMF.

Melo, Jaime de, and David Tarr. Forthcoming. *A General Equilibrium Analysis of U.S. Foreign Trade Policy.* Cambridge, Mass.: MIT Press.

Meade, James. 1951. *The Balance of Payments.* London: Oxford University Press.

Poole, William. 1989. Comment on "An Evaluation of Policies to Resolve the Trade Deficit." In *U.S. Trade Deficit: Causes, Consequences and Cures,* ed. Albert E. Berger. Boston: Kluwer Academic Publishers.

Rousslang, Donald, and John Suomela. 1985. The Trade Effects of a U.S. Import Surcharge. *Journal of World Trade Law* 19(5):441–50 .

Schultze, Charles L. 1990. Use the Peace Dividend to Increase Saving. *Challenge* 33 (March/April): 11–26.

Summers, Lawrence. 1981. Taxation and Corporate Investment: A q-Theory Approach. *Brookings Papers on Economic Activity* (January): 67–127.

Svensson, Lars, and Assaf Razin. 1983. The Terms of Trade and the Current Account: The Harberger-Laursen-Metzler Effect. *Journal of Political Economy* 91:97–125.

Comment   David G. Tarr

This is a very innovative model in its dynamic characteristics with a great deal of potential for interesting policy conclusions. In general it is a well written paper that takes pains to provide intuition for the results it finds. I'll return to the additional interesting applications for this model in my conclusion; I turn now to the results.

David G. Tarr is a senior economist at the World Bank in Washington, D.C.

The paper's results regarding the impact on the deficit on the temporary and permanent tariff surcharge make a great deal of sense. I believe there is a problem, however, regarding the result in the paper that the tariff surcharge results in an improvement in welfare. First consider the trade deficit results.

The authors postulate a very sensible balance of trade constraint. Without initial foreign asset holdings, it would reduce in a two-period model to a situation where any first-period trade deficit requires a surplus in the second period, exactly offsetting in present value. The rest of the world doesn't provide a free lunch, nor can it receive one. Any foreign assets held initially will allow the present value of imports to exceed the present value of exports by the amount of these assets. Or any debt initially allows a claim by foreigners on domestic output. The many-period generalization is that the present value of the trade deficit over the infinite horizon is zero (differing only by the initial holdings of foreign assets), that is, no permanent free lunch, deficits must be repaid, and surpluses are reclaimed later. This is clear and intuitive.

What does it mean in this model to "improve the trade deficit," since its present value cannot change. This is interpreted in the paper as twisting the path of the balance of trade toward more net exports (exports minus imports) in the early years. Given any policy change, agents reoptimize subject to the constraint that the present value of the balance of trade cannot change. A new optimal path of the balance of trade is traced out, where if the policy is successful, there is an increase in net exports in the early years that must be exactly offset in present value by a decrease in net exports in later years.

The numerical model finds that an unanticipated temporary tariff surcharge of 10 percent on all imports for five years increases net exports for five years. After five years, the tariff is eliminated and next exports fall over time to make up (in present value) for the trade surplus during the high-tariff years. The tariff increases the price of current imports relative to the price of future imports, and the results are dominated by this substitution effect. We are told that from theory there is also an income effect that could reverse this substitution effect, but the substitution effect is overwhelming in the numerical results. This is a very intuitive result.

The paper also simulates a permanent tariff surcharge of 10 percent. In this scenario, there is no change in the relative price of imports between periods, and no theoretical prediction of the effect of the surcharge on the trade deficit in any year. The numerical model, however, finds a reduction in the trade deficit in the early years but a much smaller effect than the impact of the temporary surcharge. Given the absence of any significant theory predicting this result, I would like to see whether there are parameters that would affect the result. Overall, however, the results on the twisting of the trade deficits make sense.

I now turn to the estimates of how welfare changes as a result of the tariff. For the permanent tariff, welfare is estimated to increase by 0.73 percent of initial wealth. As I recall, in 1984, the value of the capital stock was about $9 trillion including private housing. This means that, in present value, the

United States gains $66 billion from the 10 percent tariff. This suggests extremely strong terms-of-trade effects. The temporary tariff results in less welfare gain because the United States doesn't get the "benefits" of the tariff for as long a period of time.

The authors are very careful to impose caveats regarding this result, most notably regarding the fact that retaliation would negate these results. Nonetheless, the paper provides the result that unilateral tariff increases are substantially welfare augmenting. I believe that one should consider quite seriously the results of models such as this that may provide policymakers with advice that protection is beneficial. This issue needs to be addressed directly because Eichengreen and Goulder are certainly not alone in producing such results.[1]

One possibility is that monopoly and monopsony power in international trade is much stronger than we may have previously believed, and we must adapt our thinking to the fact that terms-of-trade effects dominate unilateral tariff reductions. Another possibility is that there is something about the structure of these models that builds in terms-of-trade effects that are stronger than anyone believes. Strong evidence for the latter hypothesis comes from the fact that analogous models have found welfare losses from tariff reductions due to terms-of-trade effects for very small countries (e.g., Israel) that could not possibly possess monopoly power in trade.[2] Moreover, we are told that the optimal tariff in this model is 35 percent. This is more than 10 percent above the Smoot-Hawley level tariff, and must cast serious doubts on the optimal tariff of this model. Thus, it is necessary to discuss the structure of this model regarding the terms-of-trade effect.

Terms-of-trade benefits from import protection derive from monopsony power in importing or monopoly power in exporting.[3] Let us focus on monopsony power in importing. By monopsony power in importing we mean that the importing country is large in relation to world markets, and a reduction in its quantity of imports will reduce the price at which foreigners supply the product to the importing country.

Conceptually, there is a supply function of imports from the rest of the world in each sector. For a "small" country, it would be of infinite elasticity at the world price. Trade policy couldn't affect the price of imports or terms-of-trade. If the country is a large buyer on world markets, we could postulate a

1. For example, see John Whalley, *Trade Liberalization among Major World Trading Areas* (Cambridge, Mass.: MIT Press, 1985), table 10.2, and Alan Deardorff and Robert Stern, *The Michigan Model of World Production and Trade* (Cambridge, Mass.: MIT Press, 1986), table 4.6, where the terms-of-trade effects are not as strong. These authors have expressed their concern regarding excessive terms-of-trade effects.

2. Drusilla Brown, "Tariffs, the Terms of Trade, and National Product Differentiation," *Journal of Policy Modelling* (1988).

3. Due to the Lerner symmetry theorem, a tax on imports is equivalent to a tax on exports. Thus, an import tariff can be utilized to exploit monopoly power in exporting, albeit inefficiently compared to an export tax. See Jaime de Melo and David Tarr, *A General Equilibrium Analysis of U.S. Foreign Trade Policy* (Cambridge, Mass.: MIT Press, forthcoming).

constant elasticity of supply of imports, that is, $M = Ap^\pi$, with elasticity π, where M is imports in a sector and p is the price of imports. A π percent reduction in quantity will reduce the world price by 1 percent.

Our empirical task would be to obtain information by sector on the extent of monopsony power—on π by sector. For example, in the United States, from a study by Dinopoulos and Kreinin,[4] there is a suggestion of monopsony power in autos, say, $\pi = 5$. For steel with large world excess capacity, or textiles and apparel with suppliers in all the developing world, π would be more closely approximated as infinite. There is an analogue, which I don't discuss, for simulating monopoly power in exports. The key point is that what is desired is to incorporate monopoly or monopsony power by sector according to econometric evidence. The interaction of the rest of the world's supply function of imports, with the demand function of the home country for imports, will determine the extent of the benefits from an optimal tariff to reduce imports.[5]

In single-country computable general equilibrium models for trade policy, the rest of the world is treated parametrically. This means that π may simply be selected parametrically by sector to simulate the extent of monopsony power that is obtained from econometric or other evidence.[6] In the Eichengreen-Goulder model, however, the rest of the world is treated as an agent with all the same optimization procedures that exist in the home country. In particular, the rest of the world's supply of exports in each sector is determined through optimization and cannot be selected parametrically. This provides a certain theoretical elegance over single-country models. The problem with this approach is that the supply function is not derived explicitly. More problematical, we are not told the elasticity of that supply function or how we can change parameters in the model to simulate an elasticity of supply consistent with evidence for each sector. The implication of all this lack of information on the supply elasticity is that even if we have precise information on monopoly power in, say, eight of the ten sectors in the Eichengreen-Goulder model, we do not know how to choose parameters in the model to simulate this.

Conventional wisdom has been that increasing the Armington elasticity will reduce the terms-of-trade effects; Goulder and Eichengreen, however, obtain opposite results in their sensitivity analysis: the United States gains even more from the tariff if the Armingtom elasticities are increased. The problem can be understood from Drusilla Brown's (1988) paper. She explains that in-

4. Elias Dinopoulos and Mordechai Kreinin, "Effects of the U.S.-Japan Auto VER on European Prices and U.S. Welfare," *Review of Economics and Statistics*, pp. 484–91.

5. This model imposes the usual Armington assumption that imports and domestic commodities in all sectors combine in a CES composite commodity, with composite price. There is an implied derived demand for imports, which could be graphed as a function of the import price, with the composite quantity and price as parameters.

6. de Melo and Tarr, *A General Equilibrium Analysis*.

creasing the Armington elasticity reduces monopsony power but simultaneously increases monopoly power.[7] She argues that simply changing the Armington elasticity cannot expunge the terms-of-trade effects. The combined modeling features of national product differentiation (the Armington assumption) and a single rest of the world as an optimizing agent has entraped the authors into very strong terms-of-trade effects.

I conclude on an optimistic note for this model and work. Clearly one of the most, if not the most interesting and exciting areas of research in trade policy in the 1990s will be the dynamic gains from trade liberalization. Although economists have often claimed that the dynamic gains from trade liberalization may exceed the static gains, there has been, until recently, no quantification of these effects. The new work by Romer, Krugman, Richard Baldwin, Grossman and Helpman and Dinopoulous and Segerstrom is establishing the theoretical relationship between trade liberalization and growth. This work will need to be implemented in a dynamic multisector model for effective quantification. By developing a dynamic multicountry model, Eichengreen and Goulder are well ahead in the game of being equipped to handle these exciting issues.

Comment   Drusilla K. Brown

Those who work with CGE models often begin with an analytical model that generates ambiguous conclusions. The computer work is then represented as an attempt to resolve the competing influences of two or more economic forces on the variables in question. More often than not, however, we see something completely unexpected. The empirical results reveal heretofore unknown or underappreciated economic mechanics that strongly alter our view of the world. While theoretical ambiguity may remain, it pales in comparison to other powerful economic forces at work determining the outcome.

Such is the case with Eichengreen and Goulder's study of the impact of an import surcharge on the trade balance. Their model is quite an elegant piece of work and nicely illustrates the power of CGE models to contribute to our understanding of economic theory and its application to real world problems. Eichengreen and Goulder bring together two distinct paradigms: the Heckscher-Ohlin model of international trade and the intertemporal optimization model. The international allocation of capital is central to the predictions of the H-O model, but we have little intuition concerning the interaction

7. She offers some solutions to reducing excessive terms-of-trade effects. One solution is to nest imports into imports from different countries, providing another parameter. The additional parameter will allow the reduction of terms-of-trade effects to be consistent with econometric estimates.

Drusilla K. Brown is assistant professor of economics at Tufts University.

between trade policy and the savings-investment behavior that ultimately determines capital formation. The computer results presented here advance our understanding considerably.

Let us look first at the permanent import surcharge. Trade economists, thinking in a Heckscher-Ohlin framework, would normally be skeptical of the notion that import protection could improve the current account. Yet contrary evidence from the Eichengreen-Goulder model is quite compelling. A 10 percent import surcharge practically eliminates the U.S. current account deficit within one year.

We can determine the impact of a surcharge on the current account by analyzing the capital account. Consider savings behavior first. The tariff has the expected effect of improving the U.S. terms of trade and raising permanent income in the United States. As long as household savings is positive in the current period, the volume of savings will rise. The opposite occurs in the rest of the world. Terms of trade deteriorate, permanent income falls, and the volume of savings declines.

The key question is, Will investment in the United States rise by more or less than U.S. savings? Two sources of capital misallocation drive investment. First, the country that has relatively capital-intensive imports must ultimately attract capital. That is, the tariff will narrow the difference in relative factor abundance between the two countries. It appears from table 9.3 as if the capital stock in the United States grows relative to the rest of the world in the long run. Thus, during some period of the adjustment, the tariff must contribute to a capital account surplus as capital is effectively transferred to the United States from the foreign economy.

However, immediately following the imposition of the tariff and for at least fourteen years thereafter, investment in *both* countries rises above the baseline. The reason is that there is also intersectoral capital misallocation. Both countries must reallocate capital from their respective export sector to the import-competing sector. Capital leaves the export sector through depreciation and enters the import-competing sector through investment. Firms in the expanding sector find it profitable to raise their capital stock at a rate that exceeds the rate of capital depreciation. Consequently, the total capital stock in each country rises in the initial transition to the long run.

We thus have a situation in which both countries require considerable new investment but foreign savings has declined relative to U.S. savings. The end result is that U.S. savings partially finances intersectoral capital reallocation in the rest of the world. Immediately following the import surcharge, the U.S. current account improves as a result of increased capital exports. This is the case even though the United States must eventually become a capital importer.

The fundamental lesson here is that due to the process by which capital moves from one sector to another, the rate of depreciation in the contracting sector can easily (and is, indeed, likely to) be slower than the investment in the expanding sector. Consequently, the capital stock rises in both countries during the medium run, even though in the long run the foreign economy will lose capital.

Similar forces are at work in the case of the temporary import surcharge. The impact on savings is enhanced because, unlike the permanent tax, the temporary import surcharge alters the relationship between current and future income.

Interestingly, the temporary surcharge also causes a greater disturbance in the optimal capital stock path, particularly in the case of the foreign economy. Apparently, the "temporary" surcharge remains in place long enough to alter the profit-maximizing intersectoral capital allocation. In both countries, capital appears to migrate from the export sector to the import-competing sector while the surcharge is in place. Then, in the years following removal, investment remains elevated in the foreign country as capital is returned to the export sector.

There are a couple of lessons that we can draw from this work. From a theoretical perspective, the Eichengreen-Goulder results ought to leave us somewhat dissatisfied with traditional tariff analysis. Both our textbook models and empirical models typically treat factors of production as facing severe barriers to international mobility. This would be a reasonable assumption if the time horizon for intersectoral capital flows were shorter than that for international flows. However, this is clearly not a reasonable assumption particularly when analyzing trade among industrialized countries. In most cases, the process by which capital moves intersectorally is basically the same as that for international capital mobility. Our reference model for trade policy analysis should be adjusted accordingly.

I would like to turn now to a an alternative policy application of the Eichengreen-Goulder results. Their theoretical insights can provide us with a sensible reinterpretation of recent events surrounding the implementation of the Canada-U.S. free trade agreement. During the negotiation there was considerable concern in Canada that U.S. firms would repatriate capital that had previously been installed in Canada for the purpose of jumping Canada's tariff wall. However, shortly after the 1987 parliamentary elections which ensured approval of the agreement in Canada, Canada began experiencing a considerable capital *inflow* and an appreciating Canadian dollar. A popular explanation for this phenomenon was that Japanese firms were entering Canada in order to take advantage of new access to the large U.S. markets. While this argument seemed intuitively appealing, it did not explain why Japanese firms did not install their capital in the United States directly. To further confuse the issue, around the middle of 1989, we increasingly heard stories of plant closings as production moved south of the border. The Canadian dollar has since began to slide and a recession is impending.

These curious events conform well to the predictions that we might expect from the Eichengreen-Goulder model. We can understand the initial capital inflow and currency appreciation as part of the intersectoral reallocation that is expected to be considerable in Canada (but not in the United States). However, the initial capital inflow does not give us any information concerning the long-run equilibrium Canada-U.S. capital allocation. Indeed, it appears likely that we will observe considerable repatriation of U.S. capital in the long run, despite the initial investment surge in Canada.

There is a wealth of other important trade issues which can be usefully analyzed by combining the H-O and intertemporal maximization models. Some obvious examples are the determination of foreign direct investment and the long-run effectiveness and efficiency consequence of international trade barriers. Initially, the Eichengreen-Goulder model may seem unnecessarily complex and forbidding, but their work is readily accessible and provides us with a rich understanding of current trade policy problems.

10 Industrial Organization and Trade Liberalization: Evidence from Korea

Jaime de Melo and David Roland-Holst

10.1 Introduction

The theory of industrial organization has exerted a strong influence on trade theory and commercial policy in recent years. At a theoretical level, the welfare implications of trade policy in the presence of unexploited economies of scale, exit and entry barriers, and oligopolistic markets are now better understood. Concurrent with the flow of new theoretical contributions,[1] a number of case studies, mostly partial equilibrium, have sought to evaluate the welfare and resource allocation effects of trade liberalization in sectors like autos where the above characteristics are an important feature of industrial organization.[2] Most case studies have been for developed countries, yet it is in developing countries, particularly the emerging so-called semi-industrial countries, that the interaction of unexploited economies of scale and oligopolistic market structures is likely to be greatest.[3]

A case in point is the Republic of Korea. Following a drive to develop heavy and chemical industries in the mid-1970s, Korea found itself with an

Jaime de Melo is an economist at the World Bank, teaches at the University of Geneva, and is a fellow of the CEPR. David Roland-Holst teaches at Mills College and was visiting at the U.S. International Trade Commission when this paper was written.

This paper draws on joint work with David Tarr. We thank Robert Baldwin, Drusilla Brown, Dani Rodrik, and Marie Thursby for comments on an earlier draft, and Maria Ameal for logistic support. This paper is part of a research project, "Industrial Competition, Productive Efficiency, and Their Relation to Trade Regimes," funded by the World Bank (RPO 674-46). The views expressed here are those of the authors, not their affiliated institutions.

1. Early contributions include Corden (1967) and Snape (1977). Major contributions in the new literature are surveyed in Helpman and Krugman (1985, 1989), and in the edited volumes by Kierkowski (1984) and Krugman (1988). For a recent survey, see Harris (1989).

2. See, for example, Dixit (1988) and Smith and Venables (1988).

3. Developing country case studies include Bergsman (1974), Rodrik (1988), Gunasekera and Tyers (1988), Devarajan and Rodrik (1989a, 1989b), and Condon and de Melo (1991).

extremely concentrated domestic industrial structure in the early 1980s, when it embarked on cautious trade liberalization. Government policies had not only erected entry barriers into those sectors in the hands of conglomerates but also conferred a high level of protection from import competition. In many ways Korea resembles the ideal case so often referred to in the recent research on trade policy in imperfectly competitive environments. Indeed the evidence we review in this paper indicates that protection in sectors with unexploited economies of scale erected entry barriers, which in turn allowed firms to exploit market power. What then would be the effects of an across-the-board trade liberalization in this environment?

In this paper, we apply a computable general equilibrium (CGE) model developed in de Melo and Tarr (forthcoming) to assess the welfare and resource allocation effects of trade liberalization in Korea. A CGE model is particularly relevant for such an exercise because of the relatively high and dispersed protection in the Korean economy and because of the importance of economies of scale in several sectors. Our calculations are derived from a seven-sector model calibrated to 1982, a year that has especially good protection estimates. Three sectors—consumer goods, producer goods, and heavy industry—are calibrated to increasing returns to scale (IRTS). In some simulations, in line with the empirical evidence, we allow these sectors to earn supernormal profits when protected. To anticipate our results, the welfare gains from a move to free trade reach up to 10 percent of GDP, an estimate tenfold larger than the corresponding gains under constant returns to scale (CRTS). Even if, when protected, these sectors cannot earn above normal profits, our estimates of the welfare gains reach up to 5 percent of GDP.

Our results stand in sharp contrast to other estimates of the costs of protection, one exception being the work of Harris (1984) on Canada. To judge the plausibility of these results, one must question whether our model of the Korean industrial organization structure is a reasonable one. Therefore, in section 10.2 we go into some detail on recent Korean industrial organization and industrial policies, as we believe they provide good support for our modeling of trade policy in the Korean environment. Section 10.3 discusses our modeling of imperfectly competitive markets and how we calibrated the model to 1982 data. Results are in section 10.4 and conclusions follow in section 10.5.

10.2   Trade Policies, Industrial Structure, and Industrial Organization Policies in Korea

Until the move to a sectoral development strategy focusing on heavy and chemical industries (HCIs) between 1973 and 1979, Korea's outward-oriented strategy was predicated on superior organizational ability and emphasis in development of labor-intensive activities. During this early phase (prior to 1973), Korea's innovative policies included a rationalized exchange rate regime, strong export incentives, selective import liberalization, directed credit, and a host of finely tuned export promotion instruments. A key feature of that phase was high protection of the domestic market in industries in which Korea did not face favorable international prospects, combined with low protection in industries where Korean products were competitive. As a result, unlike many other countries following an active industrialization strategy, Korea offered little incentive for industries producing exportables to keep them at home. Examples of heavily protected sectors (effective protection rates for 1968 in parenthesis) were transport equipment (163 percent), durable construction (64 percent), and machinery (44 percent).

The shift toward HCIs was achieved by directing to these sectors up to four-fifths of manufacturing investment credit, usually at preferential rates, by providing protection, and by encouraging the development of conglomerates ("Jaebol"). These policies recognized that most industries favored by the HCI drive have large economies of scale and hence that efficient production implied capacities well beyond the scale of the domestic market. However, this shift from a broad, export-led strategy toward a more typical sector orientation had some undesirable side effects, including underutilized capacity and a sharp decline in the incremental output-capital ratio, effects that eventually led to a return toward greater industrial neutrality and cautious import liberalization starting in 1979. Nonetheless, it should be recognized that the HCI drive achieved many objectives, including the target of 50 percent of export sales for the HCIs and the successful transition to an economy fully based on modern technology by a leapfrog strategy with respect to technological requirements during the HCI drive.[4]

A legacy of the HCI drive, however, has been an extremely concentrated industrial structure by international standards (see table 10.1, panel A). For example, in 1982, the top fifty Korean firms accounted for 37 percent of total sales, while the corresponding figure for Japan is 27 percent for the top one hundred firms and for Taiwan 16 percent for the top fifty firms. Furthermore, the percentage of sales classified as "competitive" (three-firm concentration ratio less than 60 percent), which has been relatively low since 1970, declined as a result of the HCI drive.[5]

Various factors led to accelerated economic concentration. The introduction of mass production techniques into a small domestic market at a relatively early stage of development allowed conglomerates to accumulate stocks of superior human and physical capital while they were protected from domestic and international competition by various institutional barriers erected to limit new entry into the market. In addition, sometimes the government's economic policy intensified concentration. During the HCI drive, overlapping investment was prevented in the most important industrial branches. Furthermore, Lee, Urata, and Choi (1988) conclude that the protection and incentive poli-

---

4. For further discussion of the HCI drive see World Bank (1987).
5. The market share of the twenty leading Jaebol continued to rise until the early 1980s.

Table 10.1   Commodity Market Structure and Performance in Korean
                  Manufacturing

A. Commodity Market Structure, 1982[a]

	Monopoly	Duopoly	Oligopoly	Competitive	Total
Number of	533	251	1,071	405	2260
commodities	(23.6)	(11.1)	(47.4)	(17.9)	(100)
Sales	5,649	3,275	24,967	15,481	49,372
(billion won)	(11.4)	(6.6)	(50.6)	(31.4)	(100)

B. Performance of Different Market Structures (average of 1978 and 1983)

	Monopoly/ Oligopoly	Competitive	Protected	Less Protected	High Export Share	Low Export Share
Price cost margin[b] (mean)	29.0	26.0	34.0	24.0	25.0	29.0

Note: Monopoly if $CR1 > 80$ percent, $S1/S2 < 10$; duopoly if $CR2 > 80$ percent, $S1/S2 < 5$, $S3 < 5$ percent; oligopoly if $CR3 > 60$ percent (monopoly and duopoly excluded); competitive if $CR3 > 60$ percent, where CRi inicates i-firm concentration ratio, and Si indicates area of largest ith firm.
Source: K. Lee, S. Urata, and I. Choi, "Recent Developments in industrial organization in Korea," World Bank Working Paper (Washington, D.C., 1988), tables 3 and 8.
[a]Numbers in parentheses are percentages; totals sum to 100.
[b]Percent; PCM is calculated as value of sales less labor costs divided by value of sales ($\times$ 100).

cies, including taxation, banking, and commercial policy measures, operated almost exclusively to the advantage of the conglomerates.

Many observers of Korea agree that conglomerates exercise market power on domestic sales. However, the data in table 10.1, panel B, suggest that sectors competing in international markets (i.e., sectors with high export shares and/or low rates of protection) price more competitively.[6] One way of finding out if this is so is by cross-section regressions linking performance with structure. Such regressions, traditionally carried out by industrial organization economists, attempt to isolate the effects of industry structure on sectoral average price-cost margin (PCMs) after controlling for other factors affecting the PCM, such as differences in technology across sectors. In the Korean case, estimates by Lee, Urata, and Choi (1988) for sixty-five manufacturing sectors for 1983 show that, after controlling for capital intensity, R&D expenditures (and other factors), the PCM is positively (and significantly) related to concentration.[7] More interestingly, they also find a statisti-

6. Mean price-cost margins (PCMs) for protected sectors were a third higher than for less protected sectors in 1982.
7. The positive correlation between PCM and concentration does not necessarily support the "structuralist view" that sees in this relationship rent-seeking behavior by oligopolistic firms. It

cally significant negative correlation between PCMs and import shares in domestic sales, suggesting that imports exert a discipline on the pricing of domestic firms.[8] These authors also note that the pace of import liberalization was accelerated in markets dominated by a few firms.

Perhaps the most telling indication that regulation of market structure became a major concern for Korean industrial policy comes from the vigorous enforcement of the Monopoly Regulation Act of 1981. About 10 percent of firms designated by the government as dominating their respective markets were accused of having their market position. Administrative recommendations and orders were issued to trade associations that had clauses permitting undue concerting activities in their articles of incorporation. Over two hundred cases in violation of the provisions against unfair trade practices were leveled between 1981 and 1985. Moreover, 35 percent of the 2,600 applications for international agreements during this period were judged to contain provisions restricting competition or involving unfair trade practices and had to be revised.

Two stylized facts emerge from this discussion and from the data in table 10.1. First, Korea appears to have achieved a very concentrated industrial structure by the early 1980s, as a legacy of the HCI drive when industrial policy discouraged firm entry. Second, the evidence suggests that, after controlling for other factors, highly protected sectors were earning above normal profits. By creating barriers to entry, protection allowed conglomerates to exercise market power. These stylized facts are incorporated in the model outlined below.

10.3. Modeling Imperfectly Competitive Domestic Markets[9]

On the basis of the evidence discussed above, we concentrate on modeling the implications of imperfectly competitive behavior in domestic markets in sectors with IRTS. At the same time, in the absence of evidence to the contrary, we assume that Korean exports are sold in competitive world markets. We also assume that Korea is a small economy in the markets in which it trades. This implies that there are no induced terms-of-trade effects from changes in trade policy. While this small-country assumption may be debatable for a few export markets in which Korea competes, it has the great advantage of simplifying the interpretation of welfare calculations and, in any case, could be relaxed without difficulty as in de Melo and Tarr (forthcoming).

---

could also reflect the superior performance of large firms according to the "efficiency-based view." However, in the case of Korea, evidence indicates that the efficiency of small and medium-sized firms had caught up with that of large firms by the end of the 1970s. See Kim (1985).

8. This result is known in the industrial organization literature as the "import discipline" hypothesis. See the symposia led by Caves (1980) and Geroski and Jacquemin (1981).

9. For a fuller description of the model, see de Melo and Tarr (forthcoming).

Apart from the treatment of imperfect competition discussed below, the CGE model is quite standard. In this application two primary factors, labor and capital, are in fixed supply but mobile between sectors. Intersectoral mobility leads to equal rewards across sectors for each type of factor. Domestic demand includes two components, final and intermediate. The government collects (and distributes in lump sum) revenues from tariff collection.

Substitution possibilities in production and demand are summarized in figure 10.1. Production possibilities are parametrized by assuming CES functions for value-added and Leontief functions between intermediates (as a whole) and value added, as well as within intermediates. However, within each sector, intermediate demand is a CES function between the domestically produced intermediate and the competing foreign intermediate. To give an example, no substitution in purchases is allowed between consumer goods and producer goods, but substitution in purchases is allowed between domestically produced consumer goods and foreign-produced consumer goods when their relative prices change as a result of a change in trade policy. Likewise in consumption demand, the demand system derived from the Stone-Geary utility indicator allows for nonunitary income elasticities of demand and nonzero cross-price elasticities of demand between domestically produced and foreign-produced consumption good.

Traded goods are imperfect substitutes by country of origin (CES assumption). In each sector, goods produced domestically are imperfect substitutes for imports. As in the case analyzed by Snape (1977), changes in trade policy will shift the demand curve of domestic firms. Likewise, goods supplied on the domestic market are imperfect substitutes for goods supplied for export (CET assumption). The implications of this treatment of foreign trade with production differentiation on the import and export sides is analyzed in greater detail in de Melo and Robinson (1989), where it is shown that the domestic country's foreign offer curve has the usual shape.

For sectors with IRTS, goods are produced by N_i identical firms. All goods produced for domestic sales in the same sector are perfect substitutes, allowing us to aggregate sectoral demand and supplies. The assumption that product differentiation is modeled at the national level rather than at the firm level has three implications for the welfare estimates reported below. First, because all domestic firms are identical and supply a homogeneous product, one cannot capture product variety and hence we may underestimate the benefits of trade liberalization as additional product variety occurs. Second, the assumption of national product differentiation implies that the domestic firms' perceived elasticity of demand (defined below in eq. [3]) only depends on the number of competing domestic firms rather than on the total number of competing firms in the world. Our numerical results, however, show that the value of the perceived elasticity of demand is quite insensitive to firm entry/exit. Third, the assumption of national product differentiation implies that adjustment to achieve zero profits occurs by firm entry/exit. In the case of firm entry,

A. SUBSTITUTION IN PRODUCTION

PRODUCTION AND ITS ALLOCATION

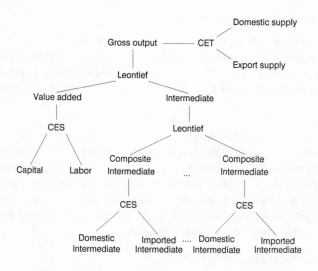

B. SUBSTITUTION IN FINAL DEMAND

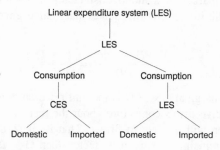

Fig. 10.1   Model structure

one gets market fragmentation that may overstate scale inefficiency.[10] If Korean firms are indeed "small" in the market in which they compete, an increase in the number of Korean firms would have little effect on their demand. Hence adjustment to zero profits would occur by an alternative mechanism. One possible adjustment is that which occurs when incumbent firms price competitively, just covering average costs.

In view of these implications of the national product differentiation assumption, we shall contrast two pricing hypotheses in IRTS sectors against the alternative of CRTS where marginal cost pricing prevails. Furthermore, we

10. For an approach that relies on product differentiation at the firm level see Brown and Stern (1989).

shall consider for each pricing hypothesis the possibility that protection, by creating barriers to entry, allows for supernormal profits.

10.3.1   Contestable Market Pricing

In the first alternative, we specify an analogue to the case of perfect competition under CRTS. We assume costless entry/exit, so that the threat of entry forces incumbent firms to price at average cost. We shall refer to this hypothesis as the *contestable market* pricing rule. Omitting sectoral subscripts:

$$(1) \qquad\qquad PX = AC$$

for each sector with IRTS, where *PX* is the weighted sum of the unit sales prices on the domestic *(PD)* and export *(PE)* markets (recall that in the export market the unit sales price in domestic currency is determined by the exogenously given price in foreign currency times the exchange rate) and *AC* is average costs. As shown below, this pricing rule represents only a small departure from competitive pricing and has the advantage of isolating the role of market structure from that of market conduct.

10.3.2   Monopolistic Competition

In the second alternative, we assume that each identical firm behaves in the domestic market as a monopolist facing a downward-sloping demand curve. In equilibrium, each firm equates marginal revenue with marginal costs, that is,

$$(2) \qquad\qquad \frac{PD - MC}{PD} = \frac{1 + \Omega}{N \epsilon},$$

where *MC* is marginal cost, *PD* is the unit price on domestic sales, and ϵ is the representative firm's conjecture about the response of competitors to its output decision with respect to firm j. That is, if Q_{-j} denotes the aggregate output of the remaining firms in its sector, then $\Omega \equiv \Delta Q_{-j}/\Delta Q_j$. We refer to this specification as the *monopolistic competition* or *exogenous conjectures* case (to distinguish it from the variant below where conjectures are endogenous).

For the functional forms selected to represent import demand and export supply, de Melo and Tarr (forthcoming) show that the perceived elasticity of demand facing each firm is given by

$$(3) \qquad\qquad \epsilon = \epsilon^F S^F + \epsilon^V S^V,$$

where S^F and S^V denote the shares of final and intermediate goods in total demand, respectively, and ϵ^F and ϵ^V are functions of the parameters describing substitution effects in intermediate and final demand.

Expression (3), which is obtained by differentiating the first-order conditions describing demand for domestic and imported goods, indicates that the perceived elasticity of demand is a share-weighted average of the price elasticities of demand for final (ϵ^F) and intermediate (ϵ^V) goods. Because the shares depend on quantities demanded that are themselves price-responsive, the perceived elasticity of demand is itself endogenous and will increase in response to trade liberalization. This implies that there is a "pro-competitive" effect of trade liberalization in the monopolistic competition model.

Whereas the threat of entry insures zero profits in the contestable market alternative, in the conjectural variation case we have to make assumptions about entry and exit. In one closure, we assume no entry/exit. One can think of this alternative as the *short-run monopolistic competition* case. In the other, which is more representative of a long-run equilibrium, entry/exit ensures zero profits. Then the model also includes explicitly the zero profit condition

$$(4) \qquad\qquad \pi = 0,$$

where π is the profit rate.

One might expect the degree of firm collusion to vary with the number of firms. The fewer the number of firms, the more collusive behavior is likely to be. Indeed, if N represents the number of firms, one would expect that $\Omega \to 0$ as $N \to \infty$ so that firms behave competitively as N becomes large. In our case, N is an arbitrary number normalized to unity in the calibration. To capture the idea that firms' conjectures depend on the number of firms, and, more important, to account for the fact that firm entry implies the availability of a larger number of varieties, we add the following equation to determine conjectures:

$$(5) \qquad\qquad \Omega = \Delta Q_{-j}/\Delta Q_j = N^{-1}.$$

We refer to this variant as the *endogenous conjectures* case. This means that, as firms enter (exit), incumbents adapt their conjectures and price more (less) competitively. Equation (5) can be viewed as a shortcut to account for product variety and the influence of the number of firms on behavior.[11]

10.3.3   Supernormal Profits

In light of the evidence in section 10.2, we present a variant of the model in which protection allows for supernormal profit because of barriers to entry. Supernormal profits exist because of protection. This variant is applied to both pricing rules described above. In the presence of supernormal profits, firms sell in the domestic market at a price $\tilde{P}D > PD$. The rate of supernormal profit, ψ, per unit of domestic sales, is an exogenous parameter. Then, in the contestable market case, equation (1) is replaced by

$$(1') \qquad\qquad PX\,(\tilde{P}D, PE) = AC\,(1 + \psi),$$

which is contestable for $\psi = 0$. In the conjectural variation case, equation (4) is replaced by

---

11. While the conjectural variation approach is a convenient way of parametrizing oligopolistic behavior and suitable for a static simulation exercise, it is inadequate to study detailed interactions under dynamic oligopoly. For a critique of the conjectural variation approach see Shapiro (1989).

(4') $\pi = \psi,$

which sets the profit rate to its exogenously determined value. In the experiments reported below, we assume that liberalization eliminates the market power of domestic firms in the domestic market. Therefore removing protection entails concurrently setting $\psi = 0$ in equation (1') or (4'). To control for the effect of entry/exit in the monopolistic competition case, we also run this specification with no entry/exit under both profitability scenarios.

10.3.4 Data and Calibration

In the application, we remove protection in a model where the economy is disaggregated into seven sectors. Table 10.2 gives the aggregation and structure of production and final demand. The base case against which we contrast our various pricing rules assumes constant returns to scale (CRTS) for all sectors. When we assume IRTS, three sectors have increasing returns: consumer goods, producer goods, and heavy industry. Together, these three sectors account for 42 percent of value added. Each of the three pricing hypotheses requires a different calibration so as to replicate quantities and values contained in base data.

In the case of normal initial profits ($\psi = 0$), to incorporate fixed costs while replicating observed prices and quantities in the CRTS case, we reduce the primary variable cost component to total costs by the amount of fixed costs. In the case of monopolistic competition, equation (2) is also solved to yield the value of the conjecture Ω. This implies that the conjecture is in fact calibrated.[12] Hence we denote the calibrated conjecture by $\tilde{\Omega}$. The calibrated values of $\tilde{\Omega}$ appear in table 10.4 below.

In the presence of supernormal profits, we allocate fixed costs as before and then, given the profit rate ψ and all quantities and foreign prices, we solve for the domestic price vector $\bar{P}D$ which satisfies the firm's profitability constraint.[13] As before, the value of $\tilde{\Omega}$ is obtained from equation (2) but with the new set of domestic prices.

For the seven sectors in the present aggregation, table 10.2 gives the composition of sectoral output, exports and imports. Also included are estimates for (1) elasticity of capital/labor substitution; (2) import price elasticities of demand; (3) export supply price elasticities. The last column of table 10.2 gives the value of the calibrated price elasticity of demand, ϵ.

---

12. An equivalent approach is to read in Cournot conjectures and calibrate for N_i, the Cournot-equivalent number of firms. An alternative (but in our view less appealing) approach is to solve for marginal costs or demand elasticities, both of which are likely to be more reliable information than conjectures. In any case, the system of eqs. (2) and (3) can only deliver two of the three variables Ω, N, and ϵ.

13. Because of interindustry relationships, this calibration involves solving simultaneously for the vector of domestic prices, $\bar{P}D$.

Table 10.2   Structure of Production, Trade, and Elasticity Values

	Share in Gross Output (X) (1)	Exports/ Output (E/X) (2)	Imports/ Domestic Sales (M/D) (3)	Elasticity of Substitution in Production (σp) (4)	Export Supply Elasticity[a] (σr) (5)	Import Elasticity of Demand[a] (σv) (6)	Nominal Tariff Rate[b] (tm) (7)	Price Elasticity of Demand for Domestic Sales (ε) (8)
Primary	8.9%	4.9%	64.4%	2.5	0.75	1.8	59.7	—
Food processing	9.6	2.5	6.7	1.5	1.5	2.5	18.4	—
Consumer goods	14.4	32.5	11.2	1.0	1.5	2.4	15.7	1.49
Producer goods	20.1	16.6	19.7	0.9	1.5	2.2	17.6	1.30
Heavy industry	7.7	31.9	47.3	0.9	1.5	1.9	28.3	1.31
Traded services	13.2	24.4	6.1	1.5	1.5	2.0	0.0	—
Nontraded services	26.1	—	—	0.9	—	0.4	—	—

[a]Income compensated price elasticity of export supply (import demand).
[b]Nominal tariff rate includes an estimate of tariff equivalent protection conferred by existing nontariff barriers.

10.4   Simulation Results

The simulations consist of the abolition of the import protection Korea had in 1982, the year for the most recent input-output table. Column (7) in table 10.2 gives the nominal tariff structure of Korea in that year. The protection rates reported here are based on direct comparisons of domestic and international prices. Hence they include tariff equivalent protection by existing non-tariff measures, and are as reliable an estimate of protection as one is likely to obtain. The most notable feature of the tariff structure displayed in column (4) is the high protection conferred on the primary sector. This reflects Korea's tradition of protecting its agricultural sector.

Tables 10.3 and 10.4 report the welfare and sectoral resource pull effects of removing protection under the pricing alternatives described above. To facilitate interpretation of results, we compare them with those obtained under CRTS. Recall that for the cases with IRTS, the three sectors with increasing returns are consumer goods, producer goods, and heavy industry. Simulations are for two sets of parameter values describing unexploited economies of scale in the base solution. For the case of low economies of scale, we assume for all three sectors a cost-disadvantage ratio (CDR) of 0.10, which is thought to be a conservative value for Korean manufacturing. For the case of medium/high economies of scale, a cost-disadvantage ratio of 0.20 is assumed. Each set of CDRs is applied to the three pricing rules described earlier. For profits, we also assume two alternatives. In the first, normal profits ($\pi = 0$) are as-

Table 10.3   **Aggregate Welfare Effects of Trade Liberalization**

	CRTS	Contestable Market		Monopolistic Competition			
				No Entry/Exit		Entry/Exit	
	(1)	(2)	(3)	(4)	(5)	(6)	(7)
Cost Disadvantage Ratio[a]	0.0	0.10	0.20	0.10	0.20	0.10	0.20
		% of Base-Year National Income					
Equivalent variation (EV)[b]	1.1						
$\pi = 0$		2.6	5.3	2.1	4.7	−0.6	2.8
$\pi = 10\%$		4.9	10.2	2.5	5.2	1.6	6.0
Scale efficiency gain (SE)[c]	0.0						
$\pi = 0$		1.3	3.4	0.8	3.0	−1.4	1.5
$\pi = 10\%$		2.0	5.8	0.7	2.5	−0.4	2.9

[a]CDR = $1 - MC/AC$.

[b]EV = C [IU $(P_1, Y_1,)P_1$] − C[IU $(P_0,Y_0]$, where C is the cost function associated with the indirect utility function (IU) corresponding to the LES utility function describing consumer choice.

[c]SE = $[TC (P_0, X_0) - TC (P_0, X_1)]/\text{GDP}_0$ is a vector of product and factor prices, and GDP_0 is real GDP prior to the removal of protection.

Table 10.4   **Sectoral Results (CDR = 0.1)**
                       (percentage changes)

| | | Contestable Market | | Monopolistic Competition | | | |
| | | | | No Entry/Exit | | Entry/Exit | |
	CRTS (1)	$\pi=0$ (2)	$\pi=10$ (3)	$\pi=0$ (4)	$\pi=10$ (5)	$\pi=0$ (6)	$\pi=10$ (7)
Consumer goods:							
X	12.4	19.0	31.7	10.0	9.4	6.9	22.7
E	25.1	34.9	57.9	20.7	21.3	17.4	45.3
SE		1.6	1.9	0.3	0.3	−1.8	−0.1
ε				0.9	0.9	0.8	1.4
Ω						0.2	0.4
N						25.8	23.8
Producer goods:							
X	12.9	17.2	26.5	12.9	10.9	10.1	18.8
E	40.1	48.2	69.9	39.9	37.8	36.6	55.8
SE		1.6	2.0	0.6	0.4	−1.1	−0.4
ε				0.2	0.3	0.2	0.2
Ω						0.2	0.3
N						21.6	24.1
Heavy industry:							
X	−1.7	−5.1	8.4	−3.3	−1.7	−5.5	4.3
E	9.7	2.8	23.8	6.9	10.3	4.6	19.5
SE		−0.6	0.7	−0.1	0.0	−1.8	−1.0
ε				2.6	2.6	2.5	3.1
Ω						0.2	0.3
N						10.7	17.0

Note: X = gross output; E = exports; SE = scale efficiency measure (see table 10.3) expressed as a percentage of sectoral sales at current prices; ε = elasticity of demand (defined in eq. [3]); Ω = calibrated conjecture; N = number of firms (initially set equal to 1).

sumed, regardless of whether there is protection. In the second case, in line with the pattern of PCM values described in section 10.2, we assume that a supernormal profit rate of 10 percent ($\pi = 10$) is achievable under protection because of the barriers to entry from restricted foreign competition.

Two measures of the gains/losses from removing protection are reported in table 10.3. The equivalent variation (EV) measure is derived from the indirect utility (IU) function associated with the Stone-Geary utility function assumed for final demand. EV is an aggregate measure of both efficiency gains in production and in consumption. It measures how much the representative consumer would have to be compensated, at the new set of prices, to be indifferent to the bundle of goods now available at the initial set of prices. The second measure is the scale efficiency gain/loss (SE) from moving along the average cost curve. Like EV, SE evaluates the new output level at old prices, so that the measure controls for shifts in the average cost curve induced by changes in factor and product prices.

Figure 10.2 illustrates the measure of scale efficiency change used in table 10.3. Prior to removing protection, the observed cost output combination is (C_0, X_0). As a result of the removal of protection, relative product and factor prices change, leading to a shift in the cost curve. Consider two cases. In figure 10.2, panel A, there is output expansion, leading to an estimated scale efficiency gain indicated by the shaded area. In contrast, in panel B there is output contraction and, therefore, a scale efficiency loss, again indicated by the shaded area. In both cases, the scale efficiency change is measured by evaluating the cost function at the initial vector of product and factor prices. The measure (SE) reported in table 10.3 is the sum of the sectoral gains and losses.

Table 10.3 expresses both EV and SE as a percentage of initial national income (GDP). In the reference case of CRTS, liberalization yields a 1.1 percent increase in welfare (col. 1). Because there are no scale efficiency effects, the welfare gain under CRTS is the sum of the traditional producer and consumer surplus gains from removing distortions.

Now compare this result with the corresponding estimate under contestable market pricing. In this specification there is no firm entry, so scale efficiency gains/losses vary directly with sectoral output. Sectors that expand (contract) will achieve scale economy gains (losses). In the case of no initial supernormal profits, welfare gains are higher than under CRTS because, on average, sectors with IRTS expand as a result of removing protection. This is so because resources are pulled out of the heavily protected primary sector into industry, where three out of the five sectors have IRTS.

As expected, welfare gains are greater the greater the degree of unrealized scale economies. Doubling the value of CDR approximately doubles the overall welfare gain, although it almost triples the associated scale efficiency gains. Note also that the EV measure under IRTS is greater than the sum of the EV measure under CRTS and the corresponding SE measure. This is so because there is a further gain as average cost pricing comes closer to marginal cost pricing.

When trade liberalization eliminates supernormal profits ($\pi = 10$ percent), welfare and scale efficiency gains increase substantially. This is one aspect of the pro-competitive effect of trade liberalization (the other appears in the form of a higher elasticity of demand in the monopolistic competition model; see table 10.4). For example, with the combination (CDR = 10 percent, $\pi = 10$ percent), EV = 4.9 percent of GDP. Compared with the case of no initial profits (EV = 2.6 percent of GDP), the greater welfare gain can be decomposed into two components: the first is the scale efficiency gain (2.0 percent versus 1.1 percent) as firms expand more because they can no longer price restrictively. The second component is again due to the welfare gains of pricing closer to marginal costs. This effect is about $1.8 = 4.9 - (1.1 + 2.0)$ percent of initial GDP. In the not implausible combination

A: SCALE EFFICIENCY GAIN

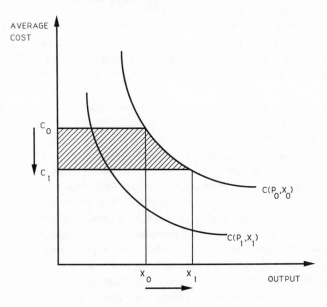

B: SCALE EFFICIENCY LOSS

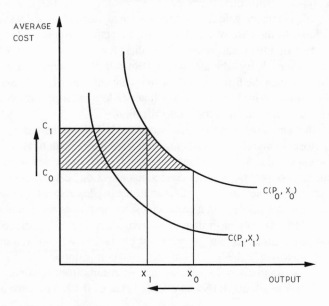

Fig. 10.2 Efficiency effects on aggregate welfare

(CDR = 20 percent, π = 10 percent), welfare gains from trade liberalization are estimated at 10.2 percent of GDP.

The monopolistic competition case is more complicated, since there are three additional adjustment mechanisms that affect the calculated welfare gain measure. First, there may be firm entry/exit to attain exogenously specified profit rates. A second factor is the endogeneity of oligopoly behavior, an effect we consider later. As firms enter (exit), incumbents adapt their conjectures and price less (more) competitively. Third, but apparently less significant, is the pro-competitive effect that is due to trade liberalization raising the elasticity of sectoral domestic demand, ε (see table 10.4).[14]

Compare contestable market pricing and monopolistic competition with no entry/exit (cols. 4 and 5). In the contestable market case, scale efficiency gains are higher because firms expand output to maintain or to achieve zero profits. On the other hand, in the monopolistic competition case, with no entry/exit, firms may make profits, realizing lower scale efficiency gains. At the same time, profits reduce welfare gains as prices diverge further from marginal costs. These two factors explain why welfare gains are larger under contestable market pricing. The larger difference in welfare gains for the specification with positive profits in the base results from substantially greater output expansion to achieve the necessary price reductions after the removal of protection.

Now consider firm entry, which exerts a crowding effect that diminishes the overall scale efficiency gain (this is the effect analyzed in Horstmann and Markusen 1986). In the case of CDR = 0.10, this effect dominates the positive output effect of liberalization on scale efficiency, so that overall scale efficiency is reduced.[15] By contrast, with CDR = 0.20, average sectoral output expands more than the firm population and scale efficiency is increased. In the case of zero initial profits, the scale efficiency loss is large enough to offset the other welfare gains from trade liberalization.

When there are profits in the initial situation, as before, there is a gain from moving closer to marginal cost pricing with trade liberalization. However, two other effects are also at work. On the one hand, more firm entry is required to eliminate excess profits, with its deleterious effect on scale efficiency. However, there is a counterbalancing effect as firm entry leads to more competitive behavior. The net result is that scale efficiency improves more and that the overall welfare gain is greater than in the zero initial profit scenario. Since we have not taken direct account of increased product variety on welfare, these results may understate the benefits of increased competition.

Table 10.4 summarizes the microeconomic results from removing protection for the sectors with IRTS and a CDR value of 0.10. The table also dis-

---

14. This effect is also discussed by Devarajan and Rodrik (1989b).

15. The reduction in scale efficiency obtained here also occurs for certain parameter configurations in the theoretical models of Krugman (1984), Snape (1977), and Venables (1985).

plays the value of $\bar{\Omega}$, which suggests that all three sectors are more competitive than Cournot. For each of the three sectors with IRTS, exports expand, even though under most scenarios output contracts for heavy industry (the most protected sector after agriculture). The reasons for export expansion despite output contraction is that removing protection leads to a real exchange rate depreciation, a general equilibrium effect.

Consumer and producer goods follow similar patterns: with $\pi = 0$, expansion is greatest under contestable mark-up pricing and least under monopolistic competition with CRTS in the middle. The reason for a stronger expansion under contestable market pricing is the absence of firm entry that impedes the realization of economies of scale. Interestingly, the scale efficiency loss caused by firm entry (the number of firms increases by between 21 and 25 percent) can dampen output expansion below that achieved under CRTS when $\pi = 0$. Compare columns (6) and (1) in the case of consumer goods, where firm entry is greatest and scale efficiency loss greatest. Output expansion under monopolistic competition is only half that achieved under CRTS. There are two reasons for this smaller output expansion. First, the higher price for domestic sales resulting from less efficient scale means less demand for domestic consumer goods (and greater demand for imported consumer goods). Second, because of interindustry linkages, under monopolistic competition production costs go up in sectors that are intensive purchasers of producer goods and heavy industry.

When protection alters market structure by allowing for supernormal profits (cols. 3 and 5), removing protection leads to a magnification effect on resource pulls. The magnification effect is stronger under monopolistic competition for consumer and producer goods than under contestable market pricing. For heavy industry, the (exogenous) pro-competitive effect of eliminating profits is sufficient to compensate for the negative resource pull effect of eliminating protection. This example illustrates the possibility that sectors that would be predicted to contract because of liberalization expand instead because they become more competitive. Even in this highly aggregated model, a ranking of sectors in ascending order of effective protection would thus not be an accurate ranking of comparative advantage.

The other pro-competitive effect of trade liberalization comes from the greater elasticity of demand facing firms after protection is eliminated. For the functional forms specified here, the results in table 10.4 indicate that this effect is small. However, one cannot judge the likely importance of this effect from the simulations reported here, since constant substitution elasticities are maintained throughout. Changes in the values of ϵ are entirely accounted for by changes in import (and domestic) shares in final and intermediate demand.

So far, all the results for the monopolistic competition case are with exogenous conjecture. We have seen that firm entry to eliminate profits reduces the welfare gains of trade liberalization because of less scale efficiency gain. Moving to the assumption of endogenous conjecture (eq. [5]) increases scale efficiency because incumbent firms price more competitively as new firms enter. As a result, welfare gains under the monopolistic competition scenario with endogenous conjectures (not reported here) are between those obtained under contestable market pricing and those obtained under monopolistic competition with exogenous conjectures.

10.5   Conclusions

This paper has developed a simulation model to evaluate the welfare effects of trade liberalization. In contrast with previous general equilibrium simulation exercises, this paper decomposes the welfare effects of trade policy changes into its various components. Although the calibrated simulation exercise for Korea relies on judgmental parameter values to represent demand and supply elasticities, evidence on the links between trade policies, industrial structure, and industrial organization policies in Korea provides good support for the alternative modeling approaches adopted here. The estimated gains from trade liberalization were found to be quite sensitive to the specification of firm pricing behavior in the three manufacturing sectors with IRTS.

In the benchmark case of across-the-board CRTS, elimination of protection yields a welfare gain of 1.1 percent of GDP. This gain represents the traditional production and consumption costs of protection. Under IRTS and no firm entry, net scale efficiency gains (scale efficiency gains in consumer goods and producer goods coupled with scale efficiency losses in heavy industry) give an additional gain between 1.3 and 3.4 percent of GDP, depending on the extent of unrealized economies of scale. If it is recognized, as the evidence suggests, that protection allowed Korean conglomerates to act collusively in their sales on the domestic market, one would obtain an additional welfare gain of between 1.3 and 4.9 percent of GDP, thereby yielding a total gain of between 5 percent of GDP if unexploited economies of scale are small and 10 percent of GDP if they are in a range commonly attributed to them in this country (a cost disadvantage ratio of 20 percent).

Welfare gain estimates are, however, much lower if the contestable market scenario is replaced by one with the assumption of monopolistic competition, even if one recognizes that firm entry/exit may occur. Under the monopolistic competition scenario where liberalization is accompanied by firm entry, the number of firms increases by between 10 and 25 percent in sectors with IRTS. Trade liberalization results in scale efficiency losses. In some cases there is sufficient entry to yield a net aggregate welfare loss if firms are not allowed to make excess profits under protection. If firms are allowed to earn supernormal profits under protection, aggregate welfare gains are between 1.6 and 6.0 percent of GDP.

In the Korean example, trade liberalization would favor industry since agriculture is the most heavily protected sector. In many other semi-industrial countries, elimination of protection would involve a resource shift out of manufacturing. A case in point is Chile, where trade liberalization involved a relative expansion of agriculture. In this case, scale efficiency gains would only be achieved if the elimination of protection were accompanied by firm exit, and the scale efficiency gains of trade liberalization would be greater in a world of monopolistic competition than in one of contestable market pricing. However, the competitive effects of trade liberalization could be even greater than those estimated here.

It should be apparent from this summary description of the results that the welfare cost estimates of protection are quite sensitive to the specification of market structure and conduct and, in particular, to the firm entry/exit patterns accompanying trade liberalization. In the Korean case, estimates of the gains from trade liberalization are much larger under IRTS than under CRTS, if inefficient firm entry is forestalled while the competitive discipline imposed by greater import competition is maintained on the domestic market.

References

Bergsman, J. 1974. Commercial policy, allocative efficiency and X-efficiency. *Quarterly Journal of Economics* 88: 409–33.

Brown, D., and R. M. Stern. 1989. US-Canada bilateral tariff elimination: The role of product differentiation and market structure. In *Trade Policies for International Competitiveness,* ed. R. Feenstra. Chicago: University of Chicago Press.

Caves, R. 1980. Introduction to the symposium on trade and industrial organization. *Journal of Industrial Economics* 29(2): 11–28.

Condon, T., and J. de Melo. 1991. Industrial organization implications of QR trade regimes: Evidence and welfare costs. *Empirical Economics* 16:139–53.

Corden, M. 1967. Monopoly, tariffs, and subsidies. *Economica* 34: 50–58.

Devarajan, S., and D. Rodrik. 1989a. Trade liberalization in developing countries: Do imperfect competition and economies of scale matter? *American Economic Review* 79, no. 2 (May):283–87.

———. 1989b. Pro-competitive effects of trade reform: Results from a CGE model for Cameroon. Working Paper, J. F. Kennedy School of Government, Harvard University.

Dixit, A. 1989. Comparative statics for oligopoly. *International Economic Review* 27: 107–22.

———. 1988. Optimal trade and industrial policies for the US automobile industry. In *Empirical Methods for International Trade,* ed. R. Feenstra. Cambridge: MIT Press.

Geroski, P., and A. Jacquemin. 1981. Imports as competitive discipline. In Symposium on industrial organization and international trade, ed. P. Geroski and A. Jacquemin. *Recherches economiques de Louvain* 47: 197–208.

Gunasekera, D. B. H., and R. Tyers. 1988. Imperfect competition and returns to scale in a newly industrializing economy: A general equilibrium analysis of Korean trade policy. National Centre for Development Studies, Australian National University, Canberra. Manuscript.

Harris, R. G. 1984. Applied general equilibrium analysis of small open economies with scale economies and imperfect competition. *American Economic Review* 74(5): 1017–32.

———. 1989. The new protection revisited. *Canadian Journal of Economics* 24(4): 751–78.

Helpman, E., and P. Krugman. 1985. *Market Structure and Foreign Trade.* Cambridge, Mass.: MIT Press.

———. 1989. *Trade Policy and Market Structure.* Cambridge, Mass.: MIT Press.

Horstmann, I., and J. Markusen. 1986. Up your average cost curve: Inefficient entry and the new protectionism. *Journal of International Economics* 20: 225–48.

Kierkowski, H. (ed.). 1984. *Monopolistic Competition and International Trade.* Oxford: Oxford University Press.

Kim, J. W. 1985. The rate of TFP changes in small and medium industries and economic development: The case of Korea's manufacturing. Working Paper No. 85-01. Seoul: Korean Development Institute.

Krugman, P. 1984. Import protection as export promotion: International competition in the presence of oligopoly and economies of scale. In *Monopolistic Competition and International Trade,* ed. H. Kierzkowski. Oxford: Oxford University Press.

———. (ed.). 1988. *Strategic Trade Policy and the New International Economics.* Cambridge, Mass.: MIT Press.

Lee, K., S. Urata, and I. Choi. 1988. Recent developments in industrial organization in Korea. World Bank Working Paper, Washington, D.C.

Melo, J. de, and S. Robinson. 1989. Product differentiation and the treatment of foreign trade in computable general equilibrium models. *Journal of International Economics* 27: 47–67.

Melo, J. de, and D. Tarr. Forthcoming. *A General Equilibrium Analysis of U.S. Trade Policy.* Cambridge, Mass.: MIT Press.

Rodrik, D. 1988. Imperfect competition, scale economies, and trade policy in developing countries. In *Trade Policy Issues and Empirical Analysis,* ed. R. E. Baldwin. Chicago: University of Chicago Press.

Shapiro, C. 1989. Theories of oligopoly behavior. In *Handbook of Industrial Organization,* ed. R. Schmalensee and R. Willig. Amsterdam: North-Holland.

Smith, A., and A. Venables. 1988. Completing the internal market in European community: Some industry simulations. *European Economic Review* 32(7): 1501–25.

Snape, R. 1977. Trade policy in the presence of economics of scale and product variety. *Economic Record* 53(144): 525–33.

Venables, A. 1985. Trade and trade policy with imperfect competition: The case of identical products and free entry. *Journal of International Economics* 19: 1–19.

World Bank. 1987. *Korea: Managing the Industrial Transition.* Washington, D.C.: World Bank.

Comment   Dani Rodrik

It has now become commmonplace to point out that the markets of developing countries are rife with imperfect competition and unexploited scale economies, on account of which trade liberalization can either go horribly wrong or magnify the conventional gains from trade. Since sensible theoretical models

Dani Rodrik is an associate professor of public policy at Harvard University and a faculty research fellow at the National Bureau of Economic Research.

can be constructed to demonstrate the possibility of either outcome, we must rely on empirical evidence to fortify our intuition regarding likely scenarios. The problem is that empirical evidence is hard to come by and even harder to interpret. Very few developing countries have undertaken genuine and substantial import liberalization prior to the 1980s; and the more recent cases are too fresh to yield much evidence. With regard to the few cases of genuine liberalization there is the thorny issue of how to disentangle the effects of the macroeconomic context from trade policy proper.

While numerical simulation exercises perhaps ought not count as empirical evidence, they are nonetheless useful in sharpening our intuition about the range of possible outcomes. General equilibrium models of developing countries that are sensitive to market structure issues can be counted with the fingers of one hand. Therefore, the marginal value of the type of exercise carried out by de Melo and Roland-Holst is quite high. In this case, unlike with partial-equilibrium simulation exercises applied to the trade problems of advanced industrial countries, we have not yet reached a point of sharply diminishing returns.

The basic story told in the paper is sensible and, in its broad outlines, would appear to be robust to minor changes in calibration and specification. In Korea, trade protection in the early 1980s favored the primary sector (agriculture) over industry. Consequently, we expect trade liberalization to direct resources toward industry. Now, since it is industry where excess profits and unexploited scale economies reside, such resource pulls would tend to magnify the conventional gains from liberalization. And this is generally the outcome in the scenarios labeled "contestable markets." The fly in the ointment comes with the conjectural variations model under free entry. The increased profitability of the manufacturing sectors attracts entry, which is disadvantageous in view of the duplication of fixed costs. With such entry, the scale diseconomies can be large enough to outweigh the conventional gains from liberalization.

Fortunately, the actual behavior of the South Korean economy tends to rule out the second scenario. In a comparison of the Korean economy with Taiwan's, Tibor Scitovsky presents the following striking facts: between 1966 and 1976, the number of manufacturing firms in Taiwan increased by 150 percent while the number of employees per firm increased by 29 percent; in Korea, the number of firms increased only by 10 percent, while average firm size increased by 176 percent.[1] It would appear that the last thing one needs to worry about in Korea is the threat of excessive entry. Hence, I would have preferred to see the model run under the assumption of no entry/exit, especially since the authors spend considerable effort to motivate the presence of excess profits in Korean industry.

1. Tibor Scitovsky, "Economic Development in Taiwan and Korea, 1965–81," in *Models of Development: A Comparative Study of Economic Growth in South Korea and Taiwan*, ed. Lawrence J. Lau (San Francisco: ICS Press, 1986), 146.

Related to this last point, the authors' liberalization experiments in fact combine two conceptually separate shocks: one, the conventional shock, is the elimination of all tariffs; the other, the unconventional one, is the reduction of all excess profits to zero. Now, the whole point of having a structural model of imperfect competition is to determine the level of profits (i.e., price-cost margins) endogenously. Within the context of the authors' model, there is no reason why trade liberalization on its own should drive excess profits to zero, since domestic and foreign goods are imperfect substitutes for each other. Imposing a zero-profit condition under liberalization amounts to comparing a short-run equilibrium under protection (with excess profits) to a long-run equilibrium under free trade (with zero profits). This may not be quite the right comparison. If, contrary to the evidence, one is willing to believe in free entry, one may still want to compare the *long-run* equilibria under the two policy regimes.

There are also difficulties in interpreting the contestable-markets scenario. First, the assumption of increasing returns to scale has the implication under this scenario that the entire manufacturing sector in Korea contains only three firms, one each in producer goods, consumer goods, and heavy industry. Korean industry may be highly concentrated, but perhaps not to that extent. Second, the assumption of excess profits sits ill at ease with the assumption of contestability. Perhaps the incumbents have a cost advantage that accounts for these profits; but then why would these profits necessarily go to zero as a result of trade liberalization?

Another unconventional feature of the model is that the conjectural variation parameter is endogenized by making it proportional to the inverse of the number of firms. Given the inherent difficulties with conjectural-variations models, this compounds interpretational problems. And it does not appear to be necessary. Even if the cleaner Cournot assumption is made, the fact that the price-cost margin of the representative firm is decreasing in the number of firms ensures the result that the authors are most interested in obtaining: the reduction in profits with entry.

In conclusion, this is an instructive paper from which we learn that the structure of protection in Korea has probably pulled resources away from manufacturing industries where they could have contributed to the further realization of scale economies. Some of the unconventional features of the model notwithstanding, this is a useful lesson. But as de Melo and Roland-Holst also stress, its relevance to other developing countries may be limited as the typical pattern of protection in these countries is biased in favor of, and not against, industry.

Comment   Marie Thursby

de Melo and Roland-Holst use a seven-sector CGE model to examine the effects of trade liberalization in South Korea. Four sectors exhibit perfect competition with constant returns to scale, and three (consumer goods, producer goods, and heavy industries) are imperfectly competitive with increasing returns to scale (IRTS). The question addressed is whether liberalization rationalizes production in the IRTS sectors. With protectionist policies, such sectors may be characterized by too many firms producing at a relatively high average cost. If liberalization leads to an increase in firm size (hence, a lower average total cost), then production is rationalized, but if equilibrium firm size is smaller after liberalization, derationalization occurs.

The authors argue effectively that Korea is an ideal case to study since government policies in the 1970s led to an oligopolistic industry structure with unexploited scale economies. The Korean case is an interesting one, and a general equilibrium approach is clearly the appropriate one for this case. With the high degree of Korean agricultural protection, one would expect the major impacts of trade liberalization on the IRTS sectors to be general equilibrium effects. Because of this, it would be nice if the authors were to give us more information related to these effects. In particular (and, as the authors state), rationalization is a function of factor price changes and, hence, resource pulls across sectors. It would be easier to interpret the rationalization effects if we knew the factor price changes implied by each of the simulations. For example, a change in factor prices will shift the average cost curves of firms, while liberalization per se will have a pro-competitive effect on the perceived elasticity of demand. Each of these will affect rationalization, so that information about factor price changes can be useful in sorting out the two effects.

It would also be nice to see some sensitivity analysis other than that done for scale economies. Besides sensitivity to the elasticities of substitution in production, sensitivity to the elasticity of substitution in consumption (and hence, demand elasticities) is of interest. Sensitivity analyses in other CGE studies of trade liberalization with imperfect competition have shown the results can be quite sensitive to the elasticity of substitution in consumption.[1]

The most interesting aspect of the paper, but the most disappointing in some respects, concerns the effects of market structure on rationalization. The authors do a good job of relating rationalization to the degree of unexploited scale economies and to entry and exit. They also show that assumptions about profit margins and firm behavior are important in determining welfare effects.

Marie Thursby is professor of economics at Purdue University and a research associate of the National Bureau of Economic Research.

1. D. K. Brown and R. M. Stern, "U.S.-Canada Bilateral Tariff Elimination: The Role of Product Differentiation and Market Structure," in *Trade Policies for International Competitiveness*, ed. R. C. Feenstra (Chicago: University of Chicago Press, 1989), 233.

Unfortunately, the market assumptions used are a bit ad hoc. In these models N identical firms are assumed to produce a homogeneous commodity, and a conjectural variation model is used to proxy effects of product differentiation among firms within the country. The only product differentiation allowed is at the national level by employing the Armington assumption (both on the import and export side). Since firm product differentiation would imply intra-industry trade, it would yield different results in terms of intersectoral resource pulls with trade liberalization. In the case of Canada-U.S. trade liberalization, Brown and Stern show that the two types of differentiation have dramatically different effects.[2] In all fairness, de Melo and Roland-Holst do note the limitations of the Armington assumption. Since market structure appears to be an important feature of the analysis, a more explicit approach to modeling behavior would have been preferable.

2. Ibid.

Contributors

James E. Anderson
Department of Economics
Boston College
Chestnut Hill, MA 02167

Bee-Yan Aw
Department of Economics
The Pennsylvania State University
University Park, PA 16802

Robert E. Baldwin
Department of Economics
Social Science Building 6462
University of Wisconsin
1180 Observatory Drive
Madison, WI 53706

Thomas O. Bayard
Institute for International Economics
11 DuPont Circle, NW
Washington, DC 20036

Drusilla K. Brown
Department of Economics
Tufts University
Medford, MA 02155

Richard H. Clarida
Department of Economics
International Affairs Building,
    Room 1020
Columbia University
420 West 118th Street
New York, NY 10027

Satya P. Das
Department of Economics
Indiana University
Bloomington, IN 47405

Elias Dinopoulos
Department of Economics
331 Matherly Hall
University of Florida
Gainesville, FL 32611

Barry Eichengreen
Department of Economics
787 Evans Hall
University of California
Berkeley, CA 94720

K. C. Fung
Board of Studies in Economics
Crown College
University of California
Santa Cruz, CA 95064

Lawrence H. Goulder
Department of Economics
452 Encina Hall
Stanford University
Stanford, CA 94305–6072

Mordechai E. Kreinin
Department of Economics
Marshall Hall
Michigan State University
East Lansing, MI 48824

Kala Krishna
Department of Economics
Littauer 215
Harvard University
Cambridge, MA 02138

Robert Z. Lawrence
The Brookings Institution
1775 Massachusetts Avenue, NW
Washington D.C. 20036

Stefanie Ann Lenway
Carlson School of Management
University of Minnesota
271 19th Avenue South, Room 835
Minneapolis, MN 55455

Robert E. Lipsey
National Bureau of Economic Research
269 Mercer Street, 8th Floor
New York, NY 10003

Timothy J. McKeown
Department of Political Science
University of North Carolina
Chapel Hill, NC 27599

Keith E. Maskus
Department of Economics
Campus Box 256
University of Colorado
Boulder, CO 80309–0256

Jaime de Melo
The World Bank
1818 H Street, NW
Washington, DC 20433

Michael O. Moore
Department of Economics
George Washington University
2201 G Street, NW
Washington, D.C. 20052

Peter A. Petri
Department of Economics
Brandeis University
Waltham, MA 02254

Thomas J. Prusa
Department of Economics
State University of New York
Stony Brook, NY 11794–4384

J. David Richardson
Department of Economics
Maxwell School of Citizenship and
    Public Affairs
Syracuse University
Syracuse, NY 13244

Mark J. Roberts
Department of Economics
The Pennsylvania State University
608 Kern Graduate Building
University Park, PA 16802

Dani Rodrik
John F. Kennedy School of Government
Harvard University
79 John F. Kennedy Street
Cambridge, MA 02138

David Roland-Holst
Department of Economics
Mills College
5000 MacArthur Boulevard
Oakland, CA 94613

Douglas A. Schuler
Carlson School of Management
University of Minnesota
271 19th Avenue South, Room 835
Minneapolis, MN 55455

Robert W. Staiger
Department of Economics
Encina Hall
Stanford University
Stanford, CA 94305–6072

Robert M. Stern
Department of Economics
University of Michigan
Ann Arbor, MI 48109–1220

Guido Tabellini
Institute for Economic Research
Innocenzo Gasparini
20090 Opera (Milano), Italy

Wendy E. Takacs
Department of Economics
University of Maryland, Baltimore
    County
Baltimore, MD 21228

David G. Tarr
The World Bank
1818 H Street, NW
Washington, DC 20433

Marie Thursby
Department of Economics
Krannert Graduate School of
    Management
Purdue University
West Lafayette, IN 47907

James R. Tybout
Department of Economics
Georgetown University
Washington, DC 20057

Author Index

315

Subject Index